MANCHESTER CITY Player by Player

TONY MATTHEWS

FOREWORD BY ASA HARTFORD

AMBERLEY

Acknowledgements

I would like to thank the following for their input and support in respect of this, book number 120 that I have written/co-compiled on football since 1975. First and foremost, and significantly so, to Pat Bristoe (doingthe92.co.uk); Phil Goldstone (City supporter); Mark Metcalf (Halifax Town/Sunderland); Simon Marland (Bolton Wanderers); Paul Days (Sunderland); West Bromwich Albion photographer Laurie Rampling (Essex); Paul Joannou (Newcastle United); Rob Budd and Nick Oldham (Football Trader); Peter Hurt (Crystal Palace FC); David Wallis (ex-Setanta Sport); Phil Goldstone (MG Solutions, Leeds, a City fan); Tom Furby and Amberley Publishing for their dedicated support and expertise in the production and publication of the finished work; and finally my darling wife, Margaret, who once again has backed me to the hilt, despite my dominance of the computer keyboard!

First published 2013

Amberley Publishing
The Hill, Stroud
Gloucestershire, GL5 4EP

www.amberley-books.com

British Library Cataloguing in Publication Data.
A catalogue record for this book is available from the British Library.

ISBN 978 1 4456 1725 1 (print)
ISBN 978 1 4456 1737 4 (ebook)

Typesetting and Origination by Amberley Publishing.
Printed in the UK.

Contents

Foreword by Asa Hartford

Having been associated with Manchester City for eighteen years as a player, coach and manager, I was both flattered and delighted when Tony asked me to write the foreword to this first major survey on the players who have represented the club over the last 125 seasons.

As the first of its kind on the Blues, this superb Who's Who is a welcome and long-overdue addition to the many written histories already published about the club, and will prove a great help to hundreds of people; not only supporters, but ex-players and even journalists. There's no doubt that a few arguments will be settled in pubs and clubs when these obvious questions are asked: Where did he move to? How many goals did he score? How many appearances did he make? And did he win international honours?

Tony, who I have known since my days with West Bromwich Albion, has worked overtime compiling the 130,000-word manuscript for this encyclopedia that features details of the 850 or so players who have donned the famous sky blue strip at competitive level. Apart from all the well-known household names, the multimillion-pound superstars, who, over the years, have given the club great service, making 200, or 300, or even 400 or more appearances and scoring a hatful of goals, this book also includes the reliable reserves; the unsung heroes, the loanees who figured in one senior match for just a few minutes, perhaps as a late substitute, yet played influential, if largely unforgotten roles in the making of Manchester City football club.

I am always interested in what happened to my colleagues after they left City, and I often reflect on the glory days of a Wembley Cup final, my international career, what I achieved as a manager and coach. All this information – and more – is packed efficiently into this book.

Finally, before you start checking out the careers and stats of the players listed, I will say that everyone who spent time with the club, will, deep down, always have a soft spot for City. I will.

Asa Hartford

Introduction

Having never written anything major before on Manchester City football club (other than compiling the 'visitors' pages in various club programmes), I had to start my research from scratch.

It's been a challenge – I can tell you that for nothing – having initially commenced work on it over a year ago.

On the following pages you will find multitudinous, authentic personal details of every player who has appeared, and scored, at senior level for the club that was known as Ardwick for seven years (1887–94) and Manchester City (from 1894).

From those footballers who joined the club at the outset, to the eleven who appeared in the club's first ever competitive match – an FA Cup tie against Liverpool in October 1890 – through to the team that played in the last Premiership game of the 2012/13 season; all the one-match wonders; and yes, those who came off the substitute's bench to take part in a game for just a few minutes. They all get a mention.

With the help of the Internet, Genes United and many other sources, quite a lot of extra information regarding the careers of certain older players (pre-1900) has been discovered, including places and dates of births and deaths and other clubs served. However, I have to confess that it has been impossible to ascertain every player's exact date of birth or death (both in some cases). Details of births between 1850 and 1880 are rather sketchy; deaths even more so. Therefore I have chosen to use the words *c.*, after or before, when I am not sure of a date or death, while in some cases no dates are given at all.

The appearance and goalscoring records for each player cover the Premiership (from 1992), Football League Divisions One and Two (from 1892), FA Cup (from 1890), League Cup (all guises from 1960), European Cup/Champions League, Inter Cities Fairs Cup/European Fairs Cup, UEFA Cup, European Cup Winner's Cup, Football Alliance (1891/92), FA Charity/Community Shield, Anglo-Scottish Cup, Tennent-Caledonian Cup, Anglo-Italian Cup, Texaco Cup and Full Members' Cup.

Records for the First World War and Second World War seasons (including the three void FL games, played at the start of 1939/40) have been listed separately. All substitute appearances are included in the player's overall total, and the statistics are believed to be correct up to the end of the 2012/13 season.

Throughout the book, the name of the club, in most cases, has been referred to as City or the Blues. Ardwick appears only occasionally.

Many abbreviations have also been used, the common ones being: AGT (Autoglass Trophy), AWS (Auto Windscreen Shield), apps/goals (appearances), *c.* (around), CC (cricket club), CoMS (City of Manchester Stadium), cs (close season), FA (Football Association), FAC (FA Cup), FACS (FA Charity/Community Shield), FC (Football Club), FL (Football League), LC (League Cup), FMC (Full Members' Cup), FWA (Football Writers' Association), 'N' (North), NASL (North American Soccer League), PFA (Professional Footballers' Association), PL (Premier League), q.v (quod vide: which see), SFWA (Scottish Football Writers Association), SPFA (Scottish Professional Footballers Association), 'S' (South), sub (substitute), *v.* (versus), YTS (Youth Training Scheme), etc.

Where a single year appears in the text (when I refer to an individual player's career) this indicates, in most cases, the second half of a season: for example 1975 is 1974/75. However, when the figures (dates) appear 1975–80, this means seasons 1975/76 to 1979/80 inclusive and not 1974/75 to 1980/81. The starting date of a player's time with City is from when he first joined the club, whether it was as a schoolboy, an apprentice, an amateur, on the YTS, as a professional or a loanee.

Some transfer fees will differ from previous references as new information has come to light, and therefore if you can add anything further to what I have produced here, or indeed spot any discrepancies, errors, even omissions, I would appreciate it very much if you could contact me (via the publishers) so that all can be amended/added in respect of any future publications. People often reveal unknown facts and stats from all sources when football is the topic of conversation.

My football collection, at the minute, comprises 1,100 books (121 written/compiled by myself), approximately 2,000 photographs/cards/images/caricatures, several scrapbooks (some dating back to the early 1900s), old newspapers and magazines, and a full set of West Bromwich Albion programmes (1905 to 2013) that are safe and sound in the club's museum. So there's no shortage of information at hand!

Tony Matthews

A

ABBOTT, James (Forward)
*Apps/goals: 3/2 Born: Patricroft, Eccles,
Manchester, 1891 Died: c. 1960*
Career: Barton Albion, Eccles Borough, CITY
(April 1913–April 1915), Portsmouth, retired 1919.
Details: Reserve to Harry Taylor, Jim Abbott's
three League appearances for City came in
September 1913 when he partnered Sid Hoad on
the right-wing. He scored on his debut in a 3-1 win
at Sheffield United and also netted against Derby.

ABDOUN, Djamel (Midfield)
*Apps: 1 Born: Montreuil, Seine-Saint-Denis,
France, 14/2/1986*
Career: Paris St Germain, Al Ajaccio, CITY
(loan, January 2007), Sedan (loan), Nantes,
Kavala/Greece, Olympiacos.
Details: Djamel Abdoun, born to Algerian parents,
came off the bench to help City beat Southampton
3-1 in a fourth-round FA Cup tie – his only outing for
the club. He represented France at U17, U18 and U20
levels before gaining eleven full caps for Algeria.

ADCOCK, Anthony Charles (Forward)
*Apps/goals: 22/9 Born: Bethnal Green, London,
27/2/1963*
Career: Colchester United, CITY (£85,000, June
1987/January 1988), Northampton Town (£85,000
plus Trevor Morley, valued at £90,000), Bradford
City (£190,000), Northampton Town, Peterborough
United, Luton Town, Colchester United, Heybridge
Swifts (loan/signed); retired 2000.
Details: Tony Adcock's career was spent mainly
in the lower Divisions, and over a period of
eighteen years he scored 249 goals in 704 senior
appearances. Manager Mel Machin's first signing,
the highlight of his short yet sweet six-month spell
at Maine Road came in November 1987 when,
along with David White and Paul Stewart, he
netted a hat-trick in a 10–1 League victory over
Huddersfield. Four days later he bagged another
treble in a 6-2 FMC win over Plymouth. Adcock
helped both Colchester and Peterborough win
play-off finals.

ADEBAYOR, Sheyi Emmanuel (Striker)
Apps/goals: 45/19 Born: Lomé, Togo, 26/2/1984
Career: OC Agaza, Metz, AS Monaco, Arsenal,
CITY (£25m, July 2009–August 2012), Real
Madrid (loan), Tottenham Hotspur (loan/signed,
£5 million).
Details: 'Manny' Adebayor became only the
sixth player ever to score in his first four games
for City – netting after just three minutes on
his debut at Blackburn, bagging the winners in
his first home game versus Wolves and then at
Portsmouth, and finding the target in a 4-2 win
over his former employers Arsenal. In the latter
fixture, his ex-teammate Robin van Persie accused
him of deliberately kicking him in the face. He was
found guilty of violent conduct and banned for
three matches.
Sent off for having a swipe at Ryan Shawcross
in a 3-1 FA Cup defeat at Stoke in February 2010,
eight months later Adebayor became the first City
player to score a hat-trick in a major European
competition – in the Europa League game against
Lech Poznan.
After slipping down the pecking order at The
Etihad Stadium, following the arrival of Dzeko,
Tévez and Balotelli, Adebayor was loaned out to
Real Madrid in January 2011, and after helping the
Spanish giants win the Copa del Rey, he returned to
City, only to be told by manager Roberto Mancini
he was no longer part of his plans. Subsequently
joining Spurs on loan, he signed for the London
club permanently twelve months later. At the end
of the 2012/13 season, his club record stood at 447
appearances and sixty goals, plus twenty-seven
goals in fifty-seven internationals for Togo.
In January 2010, Adebayor was on board the
Togo national team bus when it was attacked by
gunfire on the way to the African World Cup. All the
players survived but three other people were killed
and as a result Togo withdrew from the tournament.
Adebayor also quit international football.

AGÜERO, Sergio Leonel del Castillo (Striker)
*Apps/goals: 88/47 Born: Quilmes, Argentina,
2/6/1988*
Career: Independiente, Atlético Madrid, CITY
(record £38.5 million, July 2011)
Details: Agüero's ninety-fourth-minute winner
against QPR on the final day of the 2011/12 season
clinched the Premiership title for City – and no one
will ever forget the celebrations that followed! His
breathtaking goal sent the Etihad Stadium crowd
into frenzy, along with his teammates.

A short, snappy, clever and purposeful striker, Sergio Agüero joined City after scoring over a hundred goals in Spain, and in his first season in English football netted thirty goals, following up with another seventeen in 2012/13, when he was City's joint top scorer with Carlos Tévez.

Having represented his country at U17, U18 and U20 levels, and starred in the 2008 Beijing Olympics, he has now taken his number of senior caps to forty-five with eighteen goals scored.

Agüero, nicknamed 'Kun', is married to Giannina, daughter of football legend Diego Maradona.

AIMSON, Paul Edward (Forward)
Apps/goals: 19/6 Born: Prestbury, Cheshire, 3/8/1943 Died: Christchurch, Dorset, 9/1/2008
Career: Stafford Boys, CITY (January 1958–July 1964), York City (£1,000), Bury (£10,000), Bradford City (£5,000), Huddersfield Town (£12,000), York City (£8,000), Bournemouth (£12,000), Colchester United (record £11,000); retired 1974.
Details: Paul Aimson made his City debut in a 4-1 League defeat at Blackburn in December 1961, and thereafter became a very efficient marksman; alas, not at Maine Road, although he did top the second XI's scoring charts in successive seasons 1961–63. He netted over 150 goals in senior football, helping York gain promotion in 1964/65 and 1970/71, scoring what is believed to be the fastest-ever goal by a 'Minsterman' in senior football, after just 9.5 seconds *v.* Torquay in October 1971. Aimson died from a heart attack at his home in Dorset.

ALBINSON, George (Half-back)
Apps: 3 Born: Prestwich, 14/2/1897 Died: Rochdale, 12/4/1975
Career: Manchester United, CITY (May 1921–May 1922), Accrington Stanley, Crewe Alexandra, Witton Albion; retired 1934; worked for *The Daily Herald* (Manchester) from 1935.
Details: Originally an inside-forward before switching to half-back, George Albinson was a reserve with City who later did well with Crewe, gaining a Cheshire County League Championship medal.

ALISON, James (Forward)
Apps: 20 Born: Peebles, Scotland, 11/10/1923 Died: c. 1993.
Career: Falkirk, CITY (December 1949–July 1952), Aldershot; returned to Scotland in 1957.
Details: Able to play in any forward position, reserve Jimmy Alison made eleven appearances for City in 1949/50 and nine the following season. He later scored eight goals in 171 League games for Aldershot.

ALLAN, John (Inside-forward)
Apps/goals: 9/1 Born: Glasgow, 1903 Died: Scotland, c. 1987
Career: Glasgow Royal, Leicester City, CITY (March 1927/May 1928), Scottish Interim League.
Details: 'Watty' Allan failed to make the first team at Leicester and only managed nine appearances during his time with City, scoring his only goal in a 4-0 home win over Stoke in November 1927.

ALLEN, Albert John (Full-back)
Apps: 56 Born: Moston, Manchester, 16/10/1891 Died: Higher Blackley, 23/10/1971
Career: Higher Blackley, Barrowfields, Glossop, CITY (July 1915–June 1924), Southport, Crewe Alexandra, Southport, Lancaster Town; retired c. 1929.
Details: After a handful of First World War outings for City, Jack Allen acted as reserve to left-back Eli Fletcher during the early 1920s before having his best season with the club in 1922/23 when he lined up in twenty-seven Division One matches. After leaving City, he added another 101 League appearances to his tally.

ALLEN, Clive Darren (Striker)
Apps/goals: 68/21 Born: Stepney, East London, 20/5/1961
Career: Havering Schools, Essex Schools, London Schools, Queen's Park Rangers, Arsenal, Crystal Palace, Queen's Park Rangers, Tottenham Hotspur, Bordeaux/France, CITY (£1.1 million, July 1989–December 1991), Chelsea (for £250,00), West Ham United, Carlisle United; retired 1995; Tottenham Hotspur (Youth Development coach, assistant-manager, caretaker-manager and senior coach); engaged as a Sky TV football analyst; played American football for London Monarchs (NFL/Europe).
Details: Clive Allen joined City just after promotion had been gained. He scored ten League goals in his first season at Maine Road, four in 1990/91 when out of favour with new player-manager Peter Reid, and two in the first four half of 1991/92 before moving to Chelsea. An exceptional striker, Allen netted 232 goals in 485 career appearances, including a record forty-nine for Spurs in 1986/87 when he was voted 'Footballer of the Year', despite finishing on the losing side in the FA Cup final. He also has the distinction of being registered with more London clubs than any other player, and when he left QPR for Arsenal in 1980, the fee of £1,232 million was a British club record for a teenager. Allen appeared in only three friendly matches for the Gunners, leaving Highbury within a fortnight!

He played for England in four schoolboy, four youth, three U21 and five full internationals and also represented the Football League. His father, Les, was a member of Tottenham's double-winning team of 1960/61. His brother Bradley and cousins Martin Allen and Paul Allen also played professional football, while his son Oliver, assisted Stevenage.

ALLMARK, John Joseph (Centre-forward)
Apps: 1 Born: Liverpool, 26/5/1912 Died: 1981
Career: Colwyn Bay, CITY (January 1937/May 1938), New Brighton; did not play after Second World War.
Details: Reserve to Fred Tilson, Joe Allmark's only League appearance for City came in a 4-1 defeat at Everton in September 1937.

ALLSOPP, Daniel Lee (Forward)
Apps/goals: 38/6 Born: Melbourne, Australia, 10/8/1978
Career: Victoria Institute for Sport, Knox City, Monbulk, Croydon City Arrows, South Melbourne Lakers, Carlton SC, Port Melbourne Sharks, CITY (trial/£10,000, August 1998–November 2000), Notts County loan), Wrexham (loan), Bristol Rovers (loan), Notts County (£300,000), Hull City, Melbourne Victory, D.C. United, Melbourne Victory; retired October 2012.
Details: On trial from Australia, Danny Allsopp scored in City's friendly against Newquay and in a handful of reserve team matches before manager Joe Royle signed him for £10,000. The striker's four goals then helped City gain promotion to the First Division. Well-built and aggressive, he made the majority of his first-team appearances for City as a second-half substitute, coming off the bench no less than thirty-four times overall. He retired with 165 goals in 438 club appearances behind him. He was capped by his country at U17, U20, U2 and senior levels.

ANDERS, Harold (Winger)
Apps/goals: 33/4 Born: St Helens, 28/11/1926 Died: Runcorn, Cheshire, 3/10/1994
Career: St Helens Town, Preston North End, CITY (March 1953–July 1956), Port Vale, Accrington Stanley, Workington, Runcorn; retired 1963.
Details: A diminutive winger and a good player in his own right, Harry Anders was reserve to Tom Finney at Preston and contested the number seven shirt with Fionan Fagan and then Bill Spurdle at Maine Road.
One of the smallest ever players to appear for City, at 5 foot 2 inches, he made his debut in a 1-0 defeat at Bolton shortly after joining. His brother, Jimmy, also played for Preston and Accrington.

ANELKA, Nicolas Sebastien (Striker)
Apps/goals: 103/45 Born: Les Chesnay, Yvelines, France, 14/3/1979
Career: Trappes Saint-Quentin, Clairefontaine, Paris St Germain (£5,000), Arsenal (£500,000), Real Madrid (£22.9 million), Paris St Germain (£20 million), Liverpool (loan), CITY (£13 million, May 2002–January 2005), Fenerbahçe (£7 million), Bolton Wanderers (£8 million), Chelsea (£15 million), Shanghai Shenhua (player-coach), Juventus (loan), West Bromwich Albion.

Details: Nicolas Anelka, signed by Kevin Keegan for a club record fee, top-scored in his first season at Maine Road with fourteen goals, including a hat-trick in a 3-1 win over Everton and one in the last ever Manchester derby staged at the ground. He also netted against two of his former clubs, Arsenal and Liverpool, striking a last-minute winner at Anfield, having struck home a penalty just moments earlier. In his second season with City, the French international again topped the club's scoring charts with twenty-five goals, before starting the 2004/05 campaign in clinical form with a superb winner to inflict a first-ever defeat on Jose Mourinho as manager of his future club Chelsea.
Anelka won the Premiership with both Arsenal and Chelsea, the Champions League with Real Madrid and other titles with PSG and Fenerbahçe. Capped three times at U20 level, he scored fourteen times in sixty-nine full internationals, helping France win the European Championship and Federations Cup in 2000 and 2001.
At May 2013, his club record stood at 643 appearances and 204 goals. His total transfer fees have amounted to over £86.4 million.

ANGUS, Herbert (Inside/outside-left)
Apps/goals: 3/1 Born: Manchester, 1870 Died: c. 1935
Career: West Manchester, CITY (March 1892/May 1893), Moss Side FC.
Details: A competent reserve, Bert Angus scored on his City debut in a 2-2 Alliance draw at Crewe two weeks after joining the club. He was also on target in City's first-ever League win, 7-0 v. Bootle in September 1892.

ANGUS, William John Alexander (Forward)
Apps/goals: 8/3 Born: Blythswood, Glasgow, 1/12/1868
Career: Third Lanark, CITY (August/December 1892), Southampton St Mary's; returned to play in Scotland, November 1895.
Details: Jack Angus was a deft and aggressive utility forward who scored on his City debut in a 7-0 League win over Bootle in September 1892. He never fitted in at Hyde Road and left the club after four months. He was the first Saints player to be sent off – in a Hampshire Cup tie v. Freemantle in February 1894.

APPLETON, Frederick (Full-back)
Apps: 3 Born: Hyde, 1902 Died: Manchester, c. 1971
Career: Marple FC, CITY (June 1924–May 1929), Chorley.
Details: A City reserve for five years, mainly to Philip McCloy, Fred Appleton made his debut against Clapton Orient in an FA Cup tie in March 1926; his League baptism followed a week later v.

West Ham and his final outing came in October 1927 *v.* Reading.

ARASON, Arni Gautur (Goalkeeper)
Apps: 2 Born: Reykjavik, Iceland, 7/5/1975
    Career: A1 Akranes, Stjarnan, Rosenborg/Norway, CITY (January/May 2004), Valerengen/Norway.
    Details: Signed as cover for David James, 6-foot 2-inch shot-stopper Ami Arason made just two FA Cup appearances for City during his five months with the club. He won four youth, twelve U21 and thirty-three senior caps for Iceland.

ARMITT, George Godfrey Harold (Outside-left)
Apps: 1 Born: Blackburn, c. 1870 Died: 1946
    Career: Blackburn Rovers, CITY (February/ May 1893), Hyde.
    Details: A one-match wonder, George Armitt's only League appearance for City came in a 3-2 home defeat by Sheffield United in March 1893 when he deputised for Bob Milarvie.

ASHWORTH, Samuel Bolton (Left-half)
Apps: 22 Born: Fenton, Stoke-on-Trent, 11/3/1877 Died: Stoke-on-Trent, 30/12/1925
    Career: Stoke Alliance, Fenton Town, Stafford Wednesday, Stafford Rangers, Stoke Nomads, Stoke, Oxford City, Reading, CITY (July 1903/ September 1904), Reading, Everton, Burslem Port Vale, North Staffs Nomads, Northern Nomads, Sheffield, Richmond Association; retired 1911.
    Details: An amateur for twenty years, Sam Ashworth made only sixty-seven League appearances in that time. He played well alongside Tom Hynds in his only season at Hyde Road, helping City finish runners-up in Division One.

ATKINSON, Dalian Robert (Striker)
Apps/goals: 8/2 Born: Shrewsbury, Shropshire, 21/3/1968
    Career: Ipswich Town, Sheffield Wednesday (£450,000), Real Sociedad (£1.75 million), Aston Villa (£1.6 million), Fenerbahçe (£500,000), CITY (seven-day trial, August 1996), Metz (trial), CITY (loan, January 1997, signed, free, March 1997), Everton (trial), Sheffield United (trial), Barnsley (trial), Al-Ittihad, Taejon Citizen (loan), Chonbuk Hyundai Motors/South Korea; retired 2002.
    Details: Dalian Atkinson, a stocky, bustling, quick-fire striker, scored over eighty goals (some of them quite superb) in more than 250 League games in a varied career. Recruited by Blues' manager Frank Clark due to injury problems, his two strikes for City helped beat Stoke on his debut and Grimsby in home League games.
    A League Cup winner with Aston Villa in 1994, he helped Al-Ittihad win the Asian/Saudi Cup in 1999 and gained one England 'B' cap (*v.* Eire, 1990).

AUSTIN, Sydney William (Outside-right)
Apps/goals: 172/47 Born: Arnold, Nottinghamshire, 29/4/1900 Died: Kidderminster, 2/4/1979
    Career: Arnold United, Sheffield United, Arnold St Mary's, Norwich City, CITY (£2,000 plus a game *v.* Norwich, May 1924–December 1931), Worcester City, Chesterfield, Kidderminster Harriers; retired May 1936.
    Details: 'Sam' Austin, a fast-raiding right-winger with a 'clinking shot', scored regularly throughout his career, retiring with almost 100 goals to his credit in more than 370 appearances. He netted twice and hit the woodwork three times in City's 6-1 demolition of rivals United in January 1926, and four months later played in the 1926 FA Cup final. However, during the course of that season he missed a vital penalty that, if he had scored, may well have saved City from relegation. Two years later he netted nine goals in eighteen League games when the Second Division championship was won. Also an adequate goalkeeper, he deputised on three occasions for injured 'keepers during his time with City. Austin gained his only England cap against Ireland in Belfast in October 1925, at a time when the outside-right position was causing some concern, six different players having been used in the previous nine internationals. He also scored thirty-five goals in 152 League appearances for Norwich.

B

BACON, Arthur (Forward)
Apps/goals: 5/1 Born: Birdholme, Derbyshire, 1905 Died: Derby, 27/7/1942
    Career: New Tupton Ivanhoe, Tupton FC, Chesterfield, Derby County, CITY (December 1928/June 1929), Reading, Chesterfield, Coventry City, Burton Town; retired 1939.
    Details: Arthur Bacon, said to be a 'roamer', was a reserve with City for six months, scoring on his home debut *v.* Liverpool. Previously he netted forty-four goals in sixty-nine League games for Reading (bagging a six-timer *v.* Stoke in April 1931) and later hit seventeen in sixteen outings for Coventry.

BACUZZI, Reno David (Full-back)
Apps: 60 Born: Islington, London, 12/10/1940
    Career: Eastbourne, Arsenal, CITY (£20,000, April 1964–September 1966), Reading; a qualified printer who became an estate agent in Dublin.
    Details: Dave Bacuzzi, a clean kicking right-back, missed only one League game in his first season with City, forming an excellent partnership with Vic Gomersall. After losing his place to Bobby Kennedy, he left for Reading, where he took his career League appearance total past the 200 mark.

BAILEY, Alan (Striker)
Apps: 1 Born: Macclesfield, 1/11/1978
Career: CITY (April 1996–August 1999), Macclesfield Town (loan), Stockport County, Burton Albion.

Details: After failing to make the grade with City – his only outing was against Mansfield Town in the AWS in December 1998 – Alan Bailey moved on a free transfer to Stockport where he suffered several injuries.

BAKER, Gerard Austin (Forward)
Apps/goals: 39/14 Born: New Rochelle, New York, 11/4/1938
Career: Carigneuk BC, Larkhall Thistle, Chelsea, Motherwell, St Mirren, CITY (£17,000, November 1960/November 1961), Hibernian (£18,000), Ipswich Town, Coventry City, Brentford (loan), Margate (player-manager), Nuneaton Borough, Bedworth United, Worcester City, Coventry Collier FC (manager); later worked at the Jaguar car factory, Coventry and ran a driving school in Surrey.

Details: After scoring ten goals for St Mirren in a 15–0 Scottish Cup win over Glasgow University and being the Paisley club's top marksman in successive seasons, Gerry Baker was lured to Maine Road by manager Les McDowall. There's no doubt he did well with City, linking up splendidly at times with Denis Law, Peter Dobing, Joe Hayes and Colin Barlow, but within twelve months was back in Scotland. He continued in playing until 1975, retiring with almost 200 goals to his name in 477 club appearances. He also scored twice in seven internationals for the USA in 1968/69. His brother, Joe, played for England while his daughter, Lorraine, came fifth in the 1984 Olympic Games 800m final.

BAKER, Graham Edgar (Midfield)
Apps/goals: 138/21 Born: Southampton, 3/12/1958
Career: Merry Oak School, Southampton Boys, Southampton, CITY (£350,000, August 1982–June 1987), Southampton, Aldershot (loan), Fulham; retired 1992, Petersfield Town (manager), Woking (manager).

Details: Efficient and hard-working, Graham Baker was a regular in City's midfield for three seasons, linking up superbly with Asa Hartford and Paul Power initially and thereafter with Peter Reid, Clive Wilson and others, helping the Blues gain promotion from Division Two in 1985.

A scorer after just fifty-eight seconds of his Southampton debut *v.* Blackpool in 1977, Baker's career realised over 350 club appearances (198 for Saints), and he was capped twice by England at U21 level.

BAKER, James (Half-back)
*Apps/goals: 3/1 Born: Manchester, 1870
Died: c. 1940*
Career: CITY (March 1893–May 1895), Gainsborough Trinity.

Details: Relatively unknown, Jim Baker's three appearances for City were made in March/April 1894; he scored on his debut in a 3-1 win at Rotherham.

BALDWIN, Walter (Forward)
Apps: 2 Born: Sale, Cheshire, 1881 Died: c. 1944
Career: Sale Holmfield, CITY (March 1904–May 1908), Reading; retired during First World War.

Details: A reserve with City for four years, top-scoring three seasons running (1905–08) Walter Baldwin's two League outings came eighteen months apart, against Sheffield Wednesday in September 1906 and Bury in February 1908, both away.

BALL, Michael John (Full-back)
Apps/goals: 63/1 Born: Crosby, Liverpool, 2/10/1979
Career: Liverpool, FA School of Excellence, Everton, Glasgow Rangers (£6.5 million), PSV Eindhoven, CITY (January 2007–July 2009), Wigan Athletic (trial), Blackpool (trial), Leicester City; retired 2012.

Details: A highly competitive full-back who struggled with injuries from January 2009 onwards, Michael Ball's best spell with City came during his first full season when he made thirty-five appearances. He lost his place to Wayne Bridge. Ball unwittingly helped knock City out of the FA Cup in January 2008 when he chose to kick a balloon away instead of clearing his lines, allowing Luton Skelton to nip in to score for Sheffield United who went on to win the tie 2-1!

He won the League Cup twice and the SPL with Rangers, the Dutch Eredivisi title with PSV and was capped once by England *v.* Spain in 2001 – one of eighteen players used by boss Sven-Göran Eriksson during that game. He also represented his country at schoolboy, youth and U21 levels (gaining seven caps in the latter category) and played with Michael Owen and Steven Gerrard in Liverpool's 'A' team.

On 23 January 2012, Ball was fined £6,000 by the FA for homophobic comments made on Twitter about actor and *I'm A Celebrity Get Me Out Of Here* contestant Antony Cotton. The next day, Leicester City sacked him.

BALOTELLI, Mario Barwuah (Striker)
Apps/goals: 80/30 Born: Palermo, Italy 12/8/1990
Career: Lumezzane, Barcelona (trial), Inter Milan, CITY (£24.5 million, August 2010–January 2013), AC Milan (£19 million).

Details: A colleague once said, 'Mario is his own man. If he wants to play he will, if he doesn't he won't!' And that summed up the Italian striker a treat. He could be brilliant one minute, awful the next. Sometimes he was arrogant, grumpy, sarcastic and unwilling to get involved, but all of a sudden step up to score a dramatic goal, while also having the style to tuck away the coolest of penalties.

Roberto Mancini was Balotelli's boss at Inter Milan, but when he left, the striker's disciplinary record fell away. Balotelli then had a strained relationship with new head coach Jose Mourinho and was suspended from Inter's first team in January 2009 after a number of disciplinary problems. In March 2010, he came under criticism by Inter fans after he appeared on the Italian TV show *Striscia la notizia* wearing an AC Milan jersey. This damaged the prospect of him having a long career at the San Siro, but he did make several appearances after that. With doubts over his Inter career, Mancini, who by now was manager of City, decided to give Mario a fresh chance at a new club: but annoyingly his performances and off-field activities continued to be enigmatic and unpredictable. And inevitably this led to him returning to Italy – soon after a dust up with his manager on the training ground.

The tall Italian, nicknamed 'Super Mario', helped City win the FA Cup in 2011 and the Premiership twelve months later, when he netted thirteen goals in the top flight, three of them penalties. Having appeared in sixteen U21 internationals and starred in the 2012 European Championship final, he has steadily increased his tally of full caps which at May 2013 stood at nineteen (eight goals).

Balotelli won four Series 'A' titles, the Coppa Italia and the Italian Super Cup with Inter and following his departure from City, he now hopes to add to his prizes with AC Milan.

BANKS, William (Left-half)
Apps/goals: 26/1 Born: Riccarton, Kilmarnock, Scotland, 2/11/1880 Died: c. 1943
Career: Glenbuck Athletic (football & rugby), Kilmarnock, CITY (December 1905–June 1908), Atherton Combe, Hurlford, Portsmouth, Alberta FC/Canada, CITY (August 1911/January 1912), Kilmarnock, Nithsdale Warriors; retired May 1913.
Details: Billy Banks was a strong-tackling wing-half who made all of his senior appearances during his first spell at Hyde Road, scoring his only goal in a 2-1 home League win over Sheffield Wednesday in December 1905.

BANNISTER, Charles (Centre-half)
Apps/goals: 18/2 Born: Burton-on-Trent, 4/6/1879 Died: Australia, 12/8/1952
Career: Old Stanley FC/Liverpool, Old Town FC, Everton (amateur), CITY (July 1896/March 1897), Oldham County, Lincoln City, Swindon Town, Reading, Swindon Town; emigrated to Australia in 1912, played for Perth YMCA/Australia; retired May 1914.
Details: Charlie Bannister himself once said, 'I may not be able to play football myself but I can stop those who can'. He was not that sort of player, however, being rather modest, yet a tireless worker. Unfortunately, he never really got going with City, scoring his two goals in home League wins over Blackpool and Small Heath. He later made 256 appearances for Swindon and 106 for Lincoln.

BANNISTER, Ernest (Left-back)
Apps: 1 Born: Derby, c. 1885 Died: 1947
Career: Buxton, CITY (May 1907–June 1910), Preston North End; did not play after First World War.
Details: A City reserve, Ernie Bannister made only one League appearance in his three years with the club – against Bury in February 1908 when he deputised for Jimmy Blair in a 0-0 draw.

BANNISTER, James (Inside-forward)
Apps/goals: 47/21 Born: Leyland, 20/9/1881 Died: Leyland, 1950
Career: Leyland, Chorley, CITY (July 1902–December 1906), Manchester United, Preston North End; retired 1912; was landlord of the Ship Inn, Leyland for many years.
Details: Always impressive in his play, clever with the ball, Jimmy Bannister was a regular in City's first team for three seasons, averaging virtually a goal every two games. After leaving Hyde Road, he helped United win the First Division title and scored forty goals in 167 League games for his three major clubs. He was one of seventeen City players suspended in 1906.

BARBER, Lewis Frederick (Goalkeeper)
Apps: 99 Born: Wombwell, 11/4/1906 Died: 1983
Career: Broomhill WMC, Halifax Town, CITY (June 1927, retired injured, May 1932).
Details: Lewis Barber was described as being a 'safe and reliable' goalkeeper whose career was cut short through injury, initially suffered in a 2-0 defeat at Chelsea in November 1930, which subsequently ended a run of eighty-six consecutive appearances that began when he replaced Bert Gray. He made his City debut *v.* Reading in October 1927 – when Gray was on international duty for Wales – and was an ever-present in 1929/30.

BARKAS, Samuel (Full-back)
Apps/goals: 196/1 Born: Tyne Dock, South Shields, 29/12/1909 Died: Bradford, 10/12/1989
Career: Middle Dock FC, Bradford City, CITY (£5,000, April 1934, retired May 1947); Workington (manager), Wigan Athletic (manager); CITY (scout, seasons 1957–59), Leeds United

(scout); later worked in Bradford City's pools and lottery department.

Details: An ex-miner, Sam Barkas was a stylish left-back who always tried to use the ball constructively, rather than booting aimlessly downfield. Teammate Jackie Bray said 'he never made a wild clearance'. He gave City excellent service for thirteen years, accumulating a fine record of 271 senior appearances, which included seventy-five during Second World War – this after he had scored eight goals in 202 FL games for Bradford City.

An international trialist on four occasions, he helped City win the First and Second Division titles in 1937 and 1947 respectively, the latter as captain, and would have gained more than his five England caps but for the presence of Arsenal's Eddie Hapgood. He also represented the Football League on three occasions.

In 1939, Barkas and his City teammate Eric Brook were injured in a three-car pile-up at Wath-on-Dearne, Yorkshire, on their way to play in the Wartime international against Scotland at Newcastle. A soldier during the hostilities, his brothers Tom (Bradford City) and Ted (Birmingham) were also professional footballers.

BARLOW, Colin (Forward)
Apps/goals: 189/80 Born: Manchester, 14/11/1935
   Career: Collyhurst School, Tarporley Boys, CITY (March 1956–August 1963), Oldham Athletic, Doncaster Rovers; retired 1965; went into business; returned to Maine Road in 1994 as the club's first Chief Executive under the Francis Lee regime; resigned as a director in 1997 but still retains a shareholding.
   Details: When he left City, Colin Barlow stood twelfth in the club's list of all-time goalscorers. Taking over from Fionan Fagan, he was a smart, competent right-winger who also played through the middle. Blessed with good pace, he could shoot with both feet and was outstanding between 1957–61, during which time he formed an excellent understanding with right-halves Ken Barnes and Roy Cheetham and up-front partners Joe Hayes, George Hannah and Denis Law. City's top marksman in 1958/59 with eighteen goals, Barlow eventually lost his place to Neil Young. He attended the same school as Brian Kidd and Nobby Stiles.

BARNES, Horace (Forward)
Apps/goals: 235/125 Born: Wadsley Bridge, 3/1/1891 Died: Clayton, Manchester, 12/9/1961
   Career: Wadsley Bridge, Derby County, CITY (record £2,500, May 1914–November 1924), Preston North End, Oldham Athletic, Ashton National; retired 1928; worked in an east Manchester engineering firm until he was seventy.

Details: A crowd of 58,159 saw Horace Barnes score the first-ever goal at Maine Road, in the sixty-eighth minute of a 2-1 win over Sheffield United on 25 August 1923. Two years earlier, in March 1921, his brace helped City end Burnley's record run of thirty League games without defeat.

Clever and willing, with a powerful left-foot shot, Barnes formed a fine partnership with Tommy Browell at City, and during his career amassed over 500 appearances, 450 in the League. And, in fact, he had the pleasure of scoring the last hat-trick at Hyde Road (for City v. Cardiff in December 1922) and also the League goal that secured victory over Sunderland in April 1923. He shares the City record with Fred Tilson for bagging most hat-tricks (eleven).

In September–November of 1915, Barnes scored in eight successive First World War games – a club record. Four years later he played for England against Wales in a Victory international and later twice represented the Football League.

Just before First World War, he scored six goals in the first half-hour playing for The Rest of Cheshire in a challenge match against Port Vale. In 1915, Barnes incurred a fine from the local Magistrate Court for absenting himself from working in a munitions factory so that he could play for City against Stockport. There's a road in Manchester called Horace Barnes Close.

BARNES, Kenneth (Wing-half)
Apps/goals: 283/19 Born: Small Heath, Birmingham, 16/3/1919 Died: 13/7/2010
   Career: Moor Green, Birmingham City (youth), Bolton Wanderers (youth), Stafford Rangers, CITY (£900, May 1950–May 1961), Wrexham (player-manager), Witton Albion (player-manager), Bangor City (manager); CITY (reserve team manager, June 1970, senior coach/assistant-manager, 1973; scout 1974–96).
   Details: Ken Barnes made his League debut for City in January 1952 against Derby County – the only senior appearance he made in his first four years at Maine Road. He eventually gained a regular place in the team at the start of the 1954/55 season and as attacking wing-half became a key member of manager Les McDowall's 'Revie Plan', whereby centre-forward Don Revie was used in a deep lying position. Barnes was a City first-team regular for seven seasons, up to April 1961. He played in the losing FA Cup final of 1955, before gaining a winner's medal twelve months later, having a hand in his team's second goal in a 3-1 win over Birmingham. In December 1957, Barnes became only the third player (at that time) to score a hat-trick of penalties in a top-flight match, obliging in a 6-2 victory over Everton. In fact, he took fifteen spot-kicks for City and missed only two. Later captain of City, Barnes had a strong influence on younger players,

particularly Denis Law who described him as being 'the best uncapped wing-half ever to have played in English football'. The closest Barnes came to winning an international cap was being named as a reserve for a match against Wales in October 1957, although he played three times for the FA. As a manager, he guided Wrexham to promotion in his first season in charge. The dressing room comedian – known as 'Beaky' – Barnes had a reputation as a practical joker, with Bert Trautmann often his target. Awarded a testimonial by the club in April 1975, Barnes was associated with City for a total of forty-six years. The father of Peter Barnes (below) his other son, Keith, played for City's youth team.

BARNES, Peter Simon (Outside-right/left)
Apps/goals: 159/22 Born: Chorlton, Manchester, 10/6/1957

Career: Chorlton High Grammar School, Manchester Boys, Gatley Rangers, CITY (June 1971–August 1979), West Bromwich Albion (record £748,000), Leeds United (record £930,000), Real Betis/Spain, West Ham United, Melbourne JUST/Australia, Manchester United, Coventry City, Manchester United, CITY (January 1987–March 1988), Bolton Wanderers (loan), Port Vale (loan), Hull City, Drogheda United, Sporting Farense/Portugal, Bolton Wanderers, Sunderland, Tampa Bay Rowdies/USA, Northwich Victoria, Wrexham, Radcliffe Borough, Mossley FC, Cliftonville/Ireland, Stockport County, Hamrun Sports/Malta; retired 1994; CITY (part-time coach/Youth Development officer, from August 1994), Runcorn (manager); later Gibralter (coaching), CITY (Academy/junior coach, at Platt Lane training complex, late 1990s), Norway (coaching); also worked as a broadcaster for Piccadilly Radio/Manchester.

Details: Peter Barnes had pace, good ball control and a powerful shot, often passing his full-back on the outside before getting in an accurate cross. Unfortunately, at times he was far too elaborate with his footwork.

A regular for City from October 1975, he scored the opening goal of that season's League Cup final win over Newcastle and the following year gained the first of his twenty-two England caps *v.* Italy; his last followed in 1982 *v.* Holland. He netted three international goals and was a key member of Ron Greenwood's squad, but fell from favour once Bobby Robson had taken over.

Barnes, who scored in four different competitions for City in 1977/78, was voted PFA 'Young Footballer of the Year' in 1976. He also represented his country at youth and U21 levels, gaining nine caps in the latter category, and represented the Football League. Barnes' youngest brother, Mike, was a junior with City (1977–79).

BARNETT, Laurence Hector (Full-back)
Apps: 93 Born: Bramley, Rotherham, 8/5/1903 Died: Yorkshire, 1982

Career: Bradford Park Avenue, Gainsborough Trinity, Barnsley, Blackpool, CITY (May 1930, retired April 1936).

Details: Laurie Barnett, who also played as a half-back, made 107 League appearances before moving to City. An FA Cup winner in 1934, he was described as being 'cool, and kicked a good length' and was rarely given the runaround by an opposing winger. His best season was in 1933/34 when, as Billy Dale's partner, he missed only four League games.

BARR, Albert McDonald (Forward)
Apps/goals: 4/2 Born: Ballymena, 1914 Died: Ireland, c. 1980

Career: Ballymena BC, Glentoran, CITY (May 1936–May 1940); did not play after the Second World War.

Details: Signed as forward cover, Bert Barr scored on his City debut in a 2-2 draw at Portsmouth in September 1937, but made only three more appearances before the outbreak of the Second World War.

BARRASS, Matthew Williamson (Half-back)
Apps/goals: 172/15 Born: Preston Colliery, North Shields, 14/2/1899 Died: Manchester, 24/6/1953

Career: Seaham Harbour Bible Class, Dawdon Colliery, Seaham Harbour, Sunderland (trial), Blackpool, Sheffield Wednesday, CITY (£1,750, July 1926–May 1933), Ashton National; retired 1935; ran a fish and chip shop in Chorlton-cum-Hardy; later a licensee of two Manchester pubs and storekeeper of a Trafford Park factory, Manchester, also a government inspector.

Details: Matt Barrass, who scored fifty-three goals in 168 League games for Blackpool and fourteen in forty-eight for Wednesday, spent seven excellent years at Maine Road. Mercurial but not dominant, he often forced the tempo of the game, with the reverse pass his speciality. Capable in any half-back position and also as a forward, he helped City win the Second Division title in 1928, playing in twenty-eight games and scoring twice in a 2-1 home win over Hull. He missed only two matches the following season and one in 1929/30, but was basically a reserve from November 1930 until his departure.

His son Malcolm played for Bolton in the 1953 FA Cup final and won three England caps while his grandson, Matt, assisted Bury.

BARRETT, Colin (Defender)
Apps/goals: 69/1 Born: Cheadle Hulme near Stockport, 3/8/1952

Career: Cheadle Heath Nomads, Cheadle Town, CITY (January 1970–April 1976), Nottingham Forest, Swindon Town, Andover; retired 1985.

Details: A versatile performer, Colin Barrett won the First Division title and the League Cup with Forest in 1977 and 1979 respectively. Self-assured, totally committed and ever-reliable, he occupied four different positions in City's defence during his six years with the club, with right-back certainly his best! His only City goal came in a 6-0 League Cup win over Scunthorpe in September 1974.

BARRETT, Earl Delisser (Full-back)
Apps: 4 Born: Rochdale, 28/4/1967
Career: CITY (May 1983–November 1987), Chester City (loan), Oldham Athletic, Aston Villa (£1.7 million), Everton (£1.7 million), Sheffield United (loan), Sheffield Wednesday; retired injured, July 1999; subsequently obtained a degree in sports science; CITY (events organiser); part of a consortium considering investing in Port Vale (2008); Oldham Athletic (coach), Stoke City (Academy coach).
Details: Unable to make headway with City, due to the presence of some fine backs, Earl Barrett, pacy, enthusiastic and versatile, went on to have a fine career, amassing over 400 club appearances and gaining three England caps under manager Graham Taylor. Barrett won the Second Division championship with Oldham in 1991, the League Cup with Aston Villa in 1994 and also represented his country in four 'B' and four U21 internationals.

BARRETT, Francis (Goalkeeper)
Apps: 9 Born: Dundee, 2/8/1872 Died: Dundee, 13/8/1907
Career: Dundee Harp, Dundee, Newton Heath, New Brighton Tower, Arbroath, CITY (September 1901/November 1902), Dundee, Aberdeen; retired 1906.
Details: Joining City at the age of twenty-nine, initially as cover for Charlie Williams, Frank Barrett was a shade on the small side and was not on the winning side in any of his five League games for City, conceding nine goals.
A Scottish international, gaining two caps *v.* Ireland and Wales in 1894/95, he made 136 appearances for Newton Heath (1896–1900), and once saved two penalties against Grimsby in 1898. He kept goal for Aberdeen in their first-ever League game in 1903.

BARRY, Gareth (Midfield)
Apps/goals: 174/8 Born: Hastings, 23/2/1981
Career: William Parker Sports College, Brighton & Hove Albion, Aston Villa, CITY (£12 million, June 2009)
Details: Predominantly left-footed, Gareth Barry scored fifty-two goals in 440 appearances for Aston Villa before Mark Hughes stole a march on Liverpool to bring him to City. He netted his first

goal for the Blues in the Manchester derby and ended the 2009/10 season with forty-three outings under his belt, amassing a further 141 appearances over the next three campaigns, while helping City win the FA Cup in 2011 and the Premiership in 2012. In 2013, Barry reached two major appearance milestones: 500 in the PL and 600 at club level. He also upped his tally of England caps to a healthy fifty-three (three goals scored).

BARTON, Joseph Anthony (Midfield)
Apps/goals: 153/17 Born: Huyton, Merseyside, 2/9/1982
Career: St Thomas Becket School, Everton (junior), Liverpool (junior), CITY (September 1997-July 2007), Newcastle United (£5.8 million), Queen's Park Rangers, Olympique Marseille (loan).
Details: After being a junior with both Liverpool clubs, Joey Barton eventually joined City and slowly worked his way through the youth system before making his League debut against Bolton in April 2003. His first-team appearances gradually increased over the following five years, and his midfield performances earned him his first England cap in February 2007 – despite his criticism of some of the team's players! He had earlier played in two U21 internationals. Controversial to the last, both on and off the pitch, Barton went on to make over 150 appearances for City before moving to Newcastle, where he stayed for four years. After a fall-out with QPR, he was loaned to Marseille. Barton's football career and his life have been scarred by numerous controversial incidents and disciplinary problems. In February 2004, with City three-down at Tottenham, he was sent off, but without him, the team responded magnificently, completing one of the greatest comebacks in the club's history by winning 4-3.
He has also been charged, and subsequently convicted, for two violent offences. He was sentenced to six months imprisonment in May 2008 for common assault and affray in Liverpool city centre, and eight weeks later was handed a four month suspended sentence after admitting assault occasioning actual bodily harm on former City teammate Ousmane Dabo at the club's training ground in May 2007. This incident effectively ended his career with City. Barton has also been charged with violent conduct three times by the FA. Some say he's a nice guy... and if he puts his mind to it, he's also a pretty good footballer!

BATTY, Michael (Centre-half)
Apps: 13 Born: Manchester, 10/7/1944
Career: Schoolboy football, CITY (May 1960–February 1966), Rhyl Athletic.
Details: A professional from the age of eighteen, Mike Batty acted as reserve to Bill Leivers, Roy

Cheetham and Roy Gratrix at Maine Road, before dropping out of League football when still only twenty-one. He made his League debut *v.* Bolton in April 1963.

BEAGRIE, Peter Sydney (Forward)
Apps/goals: 65/5 Born: Middlesbrough, 28/11/1965
Career: Middlesbrough, Sheffield United, Stoke City (£210,000), Everton (£750,000), Sunderland (loan), CITY (£1.1 million, March 1994–July 1997), Bradford City, Everton (loan), Wigan Athletic, Scunthorpe United, Grimsby Town; retired 2007; became a TV soccer pundit and co-commentator.
Details: Peter Beagrie – known as the 'Artful Dodger' – had a magical left foot, and in his day was one of the best crossers of a ball in League football. In twenty-four years as a player, he scored 103 goals (and made another 150) in 777 club appearances, having his best spell with Scunthorpe (199 outings). After an excellent first full season with City – four goals in forty-seven matches – he struggled with his form, playing only ten more games in two years. Beagrie was capped twice by England at both 'B' and U21 levels.

BEARDSLEY, Peter Andrew, MBE (Forward)
Apps: 6 Born: Longbenton, Newcastle-upon-Tyne, 18/1/1961
Career: Wallsend Boys' Club, Newcastle United (trial), Carlisle United, Vancouver Whitecaps, Manchester United (£300,000), Vancouver Whitecaps, Newcastle United (£120,000), Liverpool (£1.9 million), Everton (£1 million), Newcastle United (£1.4 million), Bolton Wanderers (£450,000), CITY (loan, February–March 1998), Fulham (loan), Hartlepool United, Melbourne Knights/Australia; retired 1998; England (assistant-manager/coach), Newcastle United (Academy coach, caretaker-manager before appointment of Alan Pardew).
Details: Peter Beardsley was an exceptionally fine footballer, quick-witted, sharp, with a wonderful technique. He amassed a terrific record of almost 1,000 appearances (club/country) and netted over 275 goals. Strike-partner to some of the game's greatest marksmen, namely Ian Rush, Kevin Keegan, Tony Cottee, Gary Lineker and Alan Shearer, he partnered the latter two several times for England for whom he scored nine times in fifty-nine full internationals.
Beardsley also played in two 'B' internationals, won two League championships and the FA Cup with Liverpool and helped Fulham claim the Second Division title. He is one of only a handful of players to have served with both Liverpool clubs and both City and United.

BEASLEY, DaMarcus Lamont (Winger)
Apps/goals: 22/4 Born: Fort Wayne, Indiana, USA, 24/5/1982
Career: LA Galaxy, Chicago Fire (loan), PSV Eindhoven, CITY (loan, August 2006/May 2007), Rangers, Hannover 96, Pueblo FC.
Details: Speedy American DaMarcus Beasley, who scored seventeen goals in ninety-seven internationals for his country and played in the 2002 and 2006 World Cups, was plagued by injury early in his spell with City. However, his goals in the away games at West Ham and Fulham proved crucial in the team's fight against relegation.
He won three trophies in the States, three with PSV, four with Rangers and the CONCACAF Gold Cup three times with the USA, collecting the Golden Boot award in 2005.

BECKFORD, Darren Richmond Lorenzo (Forward)
Apps: 12 Born: Longsight, Manchester, 12/5/1967
Career: CITY (April 1984–June 1987), Bury (loan), Port Vale, Norwich City (record £925,000), Oldham Athletic, Hearts, Preston North End, Walsall, Fulham, Rushden & Diamonds, Southport, Total Network Solutions FC, Bury, Bacup Borough; retired 1999; worked for The Prince's Trust (Manchester); now an attendance officer at Claremont Primary School, Moss Side, Manchester.
Details: In his first full season with City, former England schoolboy and U18 international Darren Beckford scored three hat-tricks in the FA Youth Cup competition *v.* Preston, Billingham and Nottingham Forest. His first-team opportunities were rare but when chosen, he always gave 100 per cent. Beckford went on to score over 100 goals in more than 300 League games during his career. Brother of Jason (below).

BECKFORD, Jason Neil (Winger)
Apps/goals: 25/2 Born: Manchester, 14/2/1970
Career: Manchester Boys, CITY (May 1986–January 1992), Blackburn Rovers (loan), Port Vale (loan), Birmingham City (loan), Stoke City, Millwall, Northampton Town; retired 1996; Bolton Wanderers (coach), Mossley (manager), Bolton Wanderers (coach), Oldham Athletic (coach).
Details: Also an England youth international, Jason Beckford junior did better than his brother with City, but sadly his career ended prematurely through injury at the age of twenty-six, with only fifty-three League games under his belt. He joined Port Vale a month after Darren had left!

BEEBY, Augustus Richard (Goalkeeper)
Apps: 11 Born: Ashbourne, Derbyshire, 1889 Died: Derby, 1950
Career: Osmaston FC, Liverpool, CITY (May 1911/June 1912); did not play after First World War.

Details: Recruited as cover for Walter Smith, Dick Beeby had a run of nine consecutive appearances for City covering a seven-week period between September and November 1911, conceding eighteen goals and being on the winning side just once.

BEESLEY, Paul (Defender)
Apps: 13 Born: Liverpool, 21/7/1965

Career: Marine FC/Liverpool, Wigan Athletic, Leyton Orient, Sheffield United, Leeds United, CITY (£500,000, February–December 1997), Port Vale (loan), West Bromwich Albion (loan), Port Vale, Blackpool, Chester City, Stalybridge Celtic, Ballymena United; retired 2002, Notts County (coach), Leeds United (coach).

Details: A rugged, quick-tackling defender, Paul Beesley had a fine career, amassing almost 550 appearances in eighteen years. A stop-gap signing by City boss Frank Clark, he quickly fell out of favour under new boss Joe Royle.

BELL, Colin, MBE (Midfield)
Apps/goals: 501/153 Born: Heselden, County Durham, 26/2/1946

Career: Horden Schools, Horden Colliery, Sunderland (trial), Newcastle United (trial), Bury, CITY (£47,500, March 1966–August 1979)), San Jose Earthquakes/USA; retired November 1979; later returned to CITY as a part-time coach/youth development officer (1990–95); became a Manchester-based restaurateur in partnership with former Burnley defender Colin Waldron.

Details: Dubbed 'Nijinsky' by the fans, Colin Bell, always full of running, was a great all-round athlete, a forager who scored some great goals in his City tally of 153, including one on his debut at Derby, followed by another two weeks later (the winner at Rotherham) which effectively clinched the Second Division title. He helped the Blues win the First Division championship in 1968, the FA Cup in 1969, the ECWC in 1970 and the League Cup in 1976, finishing as the team's top scorer in 1966/67, 1970/71 and 1974/75.

In 1970, along with his teammate Francis Lee, he earned a place in the England squad for the World Cup finals in Mexico. To help the players acclimatise to the heat, an inter-squad mini-Olympics was organised and Bell won every event!

City's most capped player, with forty-eight games for England (nine goals scored), Bell made his debut against Germany in June 1968 (lost 1-0) and was a regular in the squad for six years, captaining the side against Northern Ireland in 1972. Two years later he played under his former manager, Joe Mercer and also starred in two 'B' and two U23 internationals, represented the Football League on four occasions, the FA twice, an England XI once, and played for the 'The Three' against 'The Six' in the Common Market celebration match in 1973.

Rated as one of England's and indeed City's, finest post-Second World War midfield players, one commentator described Bell as 'the most finished article in the modern game'. His testimonial in 1978 attracted a crowd of 23,936.

His autobiography, *Colin Bell: Reluctant Hero*, was published in 2005.

BELL, Peter Norton (Inside-forward)
Apps/goals: 42/7 Born: Ferryhill, 3/3/1897 Died: Durham, c. 1965

Career: Chilton BC, Durham City, Willington Athletic, Oldham Athletic, Darlington, Raith Rovers, CITY (September 1926–July 1928), Falkirk, Burton Town, Darlington; retired 1932.

Details: Peter Bell helped City win the Second Division title in 1928, scoring three goals in sixteen appearances, having an especially good game in the 7-4 win over Swansea. He played his best football in Scotland.

BELLAMY, Craig Douglas (Striker)
Apps/goals: 51/16 Born: Trowbridge, Cardiff, 13/7/1979

Career: Baden Powell Primary, Trowbridge Junior & Rumney High Schools, Caer Castell FC, Norwich City, Coventry City (£6.5 million), Newcastle United (£6 million), Celtic (loan), Blackburn Rovers (£5 million), Liverpool (£6 million), West Ham United (£7.5 million), CITY (£14 million, January 2009/August 2010), Cardiff City (loan), Liverpool, Cardiff City.

Details: One of the quickest forwards in the game, Craig Bellamy played extremely well during his eighteen months with City, although his two goals in the Manchester derby counted for nothing as United won 4-3! Used on the left by manager Mark Hughes most of the time, the willing workhorse always caused defenders problems, but when Hughes was dismissed, his form dipped, although a knee problem didn't help matters late on.

Capped by his country eight times at U21 level, Bellamy has scored nineteen goals in seventy full internationals and he also represented Team GB in the London 2012 Olympics. He won the Scottish Cup with Celtic and the League Cup with Liverpool, reached the milestone of 500 club appearances with Cardiff in 2012 and helped the Welsh club win the League championship and promotion to the Premiership a year later.

In 2008, the Craig Bellamy Foundation for disadvantaged children was opened in Freetown, Sierra Leone.

BELMADI, Djamel (Midfield)
Apps: 8 Born: Champaigny-sur-Marne, France, 27/3/1976

Career: Paris St Germain, Martigues, Olympic Marseille, Cannes Celta Vigo (loan), Olympic

Marseille, CITY (trial/loan, January/May 2003), Al-Ittihad, Al-Kharitiyath, Southampton, Valenciennes; retired 2010; Lekhwiya/Qatar (manager).

Details: With twenty caps and five goals to his credit for Algeria, Djamel Belmadi teamed up with international colleague Ali Benarbia at City and made his debut in a 4–1 victory over Fulham, alongside another recruit from the French League, David Sommeil. In his brief time with City, Belamdi only made two starts, his eighth appearance coming as a substitute in the final game at Maine Road on 11 May 2003 *v.* Southampton.

While with City, Belmadi and two other players, Daniel Van Buyten and £3.5 million signing Matias Vuoso, were the victims of a £350,000 theft by two employees of the Co-operative Bank, Paul Sherwood and Paul Hanley, who were both later jailed. Belmadi had £230,000 in his account.

BEN HAIM, Tal (Defender)

Apps: 15 Born: Rishon Le Zion, Israel, 31/3/1982

Career: Maccabi Tel Aviv, Bolton Wanderers, Chelsea, CITY (£4.6 million, August 2008/September 2009), Sunderland (loan), Portsmouth, West Ham United (loan), Guangzhou R&F.

Details: An Israeli international with five youth, six U21 and sixty-three senior caps to his name, Tal Ben Haim made his City debut in the UEFA Cup qualifier against EB/Streymour at Barnsley. A steady and consistent defender, he was unable to hold down a regular first-team place and was loaned out to Sunderland before joining hard-up Portsmouth at the other end of the country. He reached the personal milestone of 350 club appearances in 2013.

BENARBIA, Ali (Midfield)

Apps/goals: 78/11 Born: Sidi Bel Abbès, Oran, Algeria, 8/10/1968

Career: Martigues, AS Monaco, Bordeaux, Paris St Germain, CITY (September 2001–July 2003), Al-Rayyan/Qatar, Nadi Qatar; retired 2006.

Details: The little magician had a wonderful first season at Maine Road, missing only four League games as City regained Premiership status as champions. With the vision to deliver a defence-splitting pass, Ali Benarbia had a hand in thirty-five of City's goals in 2001/02 and was deservedly voted into the PFA First Division team of the season. Appointed team captain, unfortunately this seemed to affect his performances in the top flight and he was relegated to the subs' bench. However, he bounced back with confidence and ended the campaign in tip-top form. A firm favourite with the supporters, he played his final game in a City shirt against Barcelona to mark the opening of The City of Manchester Stadium. He won three League titles in France and was capped nine times by Algeria.

BENNETT, Arnold Alfred (Forward)

Apps/goals: 12/6 Born: Eccles, c. 1871 Died: Manchester 1945

Career: local football, CITY (October 1893–May 1896), Eccles Town.

Details: Despite being a permanent reserve for the last two seasons of his career with City (mainly to Billy Meredith), Alf Bennett had an excellent record in 1893/94, scoring a goal every two games, including two fine efforts in a 4-2 win over Northwich Victoria.

BENNETT, David Anthony (Winger/forward)

Apps/goals: 65/15 Born: Moss Side, Manchester, 11/7/1959

Career: Schoolboy football, Ashford Celtic, CITY (August 1976–September 1981), Cardiff City, Coventry City, Sheffield Wednesday, Swindon Town, Shrewsbury Town (loan), Nuneaton Borough; retired 1995; now works as a pundit and co-commentator for Free Radio 80s Coventry and Warwickshire.

Details: Introduced to League football by manager Tony Book as a second-half substitute against Everton in front of almost 40,000 fans at Maine Road in April 1979, Dave Bennett served the club very well over the next two seasons, wearing six different 'shirts', with number '7' being his best! Four of his City goals came just prior to the 1981 FA Cup final defeat by Tottenham Hotspur in which he played. Six years later he returned to Wembley and gained a winner's medal with Coventry, scoring once and making his side's two other goals in a 3-2 win over Spurs! Bennett made over 350 League appearances during his career and represented the Football League. He broke his right leg twice playing for Swindon and Shrewsbury.

He became a role model for aspiring black footballers from the Manchester area. His brother, Gary, was with City 1979–81.

BENNETT, Edward Thomas (Full-back)

Apps: 20 Born: Barton Regis, 10/8/1904; Died: 1957

Career: Swansea Town, Wrexham, CITY (May 1926–May 1929), Norwich City; retired 1931.

Details: Able to play in both full-back position, Ted Bennett was strong and mobile but his League appearances throughout his career were restricted to just seventy-eight, mainly due to knee and ankle injuries. He became 'disenchanted' at City due to limited opportunities.

BENSON, John Harvey (Full-back)

Apps: 52 Born: Arbroath, 23/12/1942 Died: 30/10/2010

Career: Stockport Boys, CITY (July 1978–June 1964), Torquay United (record £6,000), Bournemouth (£12,000), Exeter City (loan),

Norwich City, Bournemouth (player-manager), CITY (coach, October 1980, then caretaker-manager to May 1983), Burnley (manager); coached in Dubai & Kuwait; Barnsley (scout), Norwich City (assistant-manager/coach), Wigan Athletic (coach/caretaker-manager/youth development officer), Birmingham City (coach/assistant-manager/general manager), Sunderland (coach).

Details: John Benson, a very competent defender, made his City debut against WBA in 1962. He amassed over 500 appearances during his playing career, which ended in 1984. He was with Kevin Bond at City, Bournemouth and Burnley.

BENTLEY, James Henry (Left-half)
Apps: 1 Born: Knutsford, c. 1886 Died: 1950
Career: Knutsford, Chester, CITY (May 1910–May 1912), Macclesfield; retired 1915.

Details: Reserve to Tom Holford, Jim Bentley didn't have the greatest of debuts as City lost 6-2 at Sheffield United in February 1912. He was the club's top scorer in second XI football in 1910/11.

BENZIE, Robert (Left-half)
Apps/goals: 13 Born: Greenock, Scotland, 19/9/1903 Died: c. 1970.
Career: Greenock HS, Doncaster Rovers, CITY (April 1925–June 1928); Welsh League football (1928–34).

Details: Bob Benzie made sixty appearances for Doncaster before moving to City, where he acted as reserve to two Scottish internationals, first Charlie Pringle and then Jimmy McMullan.

BERKOVIC, Eyal (Midfield)
Apps/goals: 67/9 Born: Regba, Israel, 2/4/1972
Career: Maccabi Haifa, Southampton (loan), West Ham United (£1.7 million), Celtic (£5.5 million), Blackburn Rovers (loan), CITY (£1.5 illionm, August 2001–January 2004), Portsmouth, Maccabi Tel Aviv; retired May 2006; Maccabi Netanya (manager).

Details: Playmaker Eyal Berkovic produced some brilliant performances during his first two seasons with City before injuries disrupted his rhythm. Superb in the derby games against United, most of his goals were class finishes. His last game for the club was against Newcastle in December 2003; he left a soon afterwards following a public fall-out with manager Keegan.

He retired with an impressive League record of sixty-one goals in 367 appearances. He gained one U18, eleven U21 and eighty-two full caps for Israel, scoring fourteen goals, and helped Maccabi Tel win six trophies in the 1990s.

BETTS, James Barrie (Full-back)
Apps/goals: 117/6 Born: Barnsley, 18/9/1932

Career: Barnsley, Stockport County, CITY (£8,000, June 1960-August 1964), Scunthorpe United; retired injured, 1965; later Lancaster City (manager).

Details: Barrie Betts, solid and well balanced, had over 150 appearances under his belt when he joined City and he continued to perform with confidence during his four years at Maine Road, having his best seasons as Cliff Sear's partner, 1960–62. He was replaced at the club by Dave Bacuzzi.

BEVAN, Frederick Edward Thomas Walter (Forward)
Apps/goals: 9/1 Born: Poplar, London, 27/2/1879 Died: Poplar, 10/12/1935
Career: Millwall St John's, Millwall Athletic, CITY (May 1901-May 1903), Reading, Queen's Park Rangers, Bury, Fulham, Derby County, Clapton Orient, Chatham; retired 1915.

Details: Fred Bevan, who top-scored for City's second XI in his two seasons with the club, did very well after leaving Hyde Road, taking his record in senior football to 119 goals in 320 club appearances, having his best spell with Orient (35 in 118). Reserve to Billy Gillespie, he netted his only goal for City on the opening day of the 1902/03 season in a 3-1 win over Lincoln.

BIANCHI, Rolando (Forward)
Apps/goals: 25/5 Born: Lovere, Italy, 15/2/1983
Career: Albano Sant Allesandro, Atalanta, Cagliari (loan), Reggina, CITY (£8.8 million, July 2007/August 2008), SC Lazio/Italy (loan), Torino.

Details: Rolando Bianchi, 6 foot 2 inches tall with thirteen Italian U21 international caps to his name, was a huge favourite with the City fans, but alas he never settled in, despite scoring on his PL debut against West Ham and following up with a cracker in his next game against Bristol City in the League Cup.

BIGGINS, Wayne (Forward)
Apps/goals: 38/10 Born: Sheffield, 20/11/1961
Career: Lincoln City, Matlock, Kings Lynn, Matlock, Burnley, Norwich City, CITY (£160,000, June 1988/August 1989), Stoke City, Barnsley, Celtic, Stoke City, Luton Town (loan), Oxford United, Wigan Athletic, Leek Town, Stocksbridge Park Steels (player-manager), Buxton; retired 2006.

Details: Wayne Biggins scored 152 goals for his nine League clubs. Signed by Mel Machin, he played alongside Paul Moulden and Trevor Morley in his only season at Maine Road, helping City gain promotion. He won the Second Division with Norwich and the Third Division with Wigan.

BISCHOFF, Mikkel Rufus Mutahi (Defender)
Apps: 2 Born: Copenhagen, Denmark, 3/2/1982
Career: KB Copenhagen, Fremad Amager, Akademisk Boldklub, FC Copenhagen, CITY (£750,000, July 2002–July 2006), Wolverhampton

Wanderers (loan), Sheffield Wednesday (loan), Coventry City, Brondby IF, Lyngby.

Details: A Danish international at Youth and U21 levels, Mikkel Bischoff, 6 foot 4 inches tall, struggled with injuries during his spells with his four English clubs, restricting him to only twenty appearances in five years in the UK.

BISHOP, Ian William (Midfield)
Apps/goals: 101/2 Born: Liverpool, 29/5/1965

Career: Everton, Crewe Alexandra (loan), Carlisle United, AFC Bournemouth, CITY (£465,000, July–December 1989) West Ham United (£500,000 plus Mark Ward), CITY (free, March 1998–March 2001), Miami Fusion/USA, New Orleans Shell Shockers, retired 2005; now resides in Boca Raton, Florida.

Details: In his first spell with City, Ian Bishop, an excellent passer of the ball, helped demolish arch-rivals Manchester United 5-1, scoring the third goal; but despite being popular with the supporters he was sold by manager Howard Kendall to West Ham. Something of a cult hero at Upton Park, he spent the next nine years with the Hammers before returning to City for a second spell, giving up his testimonial to do so. 'Bish' again did well, helping the team stave off relegation and twice gain promotion, to Division One and the Premiership. An integral player to any team, Bishop made almost 650 appearances during his career, 284 with West Ham, and played once for England B.

BLACK, Andrew (Forward)
Apps/goals: 146/52 Born: Stirling, 23/9/1917 Died: c. 1998

Career: Heart of Midlothian; Second World War guest for Aldershot, Chelsea, Chester, Crewe Alexandra, Liverpool and York City; CITY (£7,000, June 1946–August 1950), Stockport County; retired 1953.

Details: Of the many Hearts players who moved from Tynecastle into the Football League during the 1950s, Andy Black was one of the best. A stylish and most gentlemanly player, his first touch was often precise, his passing inch-perfect and when required, he could be as forceful and as aggressive as the next man.

Blessed with a powerful shot, given even half a chance he always seemed to make the opposition goalkeeper work for his money. He was City's top scorer in 1947/48 with seventeen goals.

BLACKSHAW, William (Forward)
Apps: 3 Born: Ashton-under-Lyne, 6/9/1920 Died: c. 2000

Career: Audenshaw United, CITY (May 1937–July 1946), Oldham Athletic, Crystal Palace, Rochdale, Stalybridge Celtic; retired 1955.

Details: Basically a reserve with City, Bill Blackshaw made ninety-nine League appearances after leaving Maine Road.

BLAIR, James (Half-back/inside-left)
Apps/goals: 81/1 Born: Dumfries, 8/9/1885 Died: Dumfries, 12/3/1913

Career: Dumfries Volunteer, Fifth King's Own Highlanders, Kilmarnock, Woolwich Arsenal, CITY (November 1905–May 1910), Bradford City, Stockport County; did not play after First World War.

Details: Jimmy Blair was a smart footballer with an appetite for hard work, who had his best season with city in 1907/08, when he missed only four League matches. He helped Bradford reach the 1911 FA Cup final, having played in two Scottish international trials in 1909 and 1910.

BLAIR, Thomas (Goalkeeper)
Apps: 41 Born: Glasgow, 24/2/1892 Died: 1961

Career: Vale of Clyde, Kilmarnock, CITY (July 1920–May 1922); Edmonton CNR/Canada, Cumberland United/Canada, Boston Wonders Workers FC/USA, Fall River Marksman/USA, Hartford Americans/USA, Pawtucket Rangers/USA, Ayr United, Linfield, Dundee United; retired 1930.

Details: A safe handler, Tommy Blair made all his appearances for City in 1921/22, having taken over from Jim Goodchild. He played in a Scottish international trial in 1922 before going on to star in over 200 games for six North American clubs in six years.

BLEW, Horace Elford (Full-back)
Apps: 1 Born: Wrexham, 1878 Died: Wrexham, 1/2/1957

Career: Grove Park School, Wrexham Old Boys, Rhostyllen, Wrexham, Druids, Bury, Manchester United, Wrexham Victoria, CITY (September 1906), Brymbo; retired 1915; Wrexham (director, 1920s).

Details: An amateur, Horace Blew spent only nineteen days with City, during which time he made one League appearance, replacing Tommy Kelso in the 2-2 draw with Bury. He only managed one outing for United as well!

BOATENG, Jerome (Defender)
Apps: 24 Born: Berlin, Germany, 3/9/1988

Career: Tennis Borussia Berlin, Hertha BSC, Hamburger SV, CITY (£10.64 million, June 2010/July 2011), Bayern Munich (£10 million).

Details: Jerome Boateng made his City debut in a pre-season friendly against Valencia, but soon afterwards suffered a freak injury on international duty with Germany v. Denmark, tearing a tendon in his left knee that he aggravated on the plane home after a collision with a drinks trolley! He made his Premiership debut as a substitute in a 1-0 win over Chelsea in late September 2010, with his first competitive start following in the Europa League draw with Juventus. Unfortunately, he did like playing at right-back and left the Etihad Stadium after just thirteen months. An FA Cup winner in 2011, he has represented his country at U17, U19, U21 and senior levels (twenty-eight full caps) and helped Germany finish third in the 2010 World Cup.

BODAK, Peter (Midfield/forward)
Apps/goals: 17/1 Born: Birmingham, 12/8/1961

Career: Coventry City, Manchester United, CITY (January/October 1983), Royal, Antwerp, Crewe Alexandra, Swansea City, Walsall FC; retired 1991.

Details: Right-sided midfielder Peter Bodak was a good footballer who scored his only goal for City in a 2-2 draw with Nottingham Forest on New Year's Day 1983. He made 134 appearances for his six FL clubs, spending his best years with Crewe.

BOJINOV, Valen Emilov (Striker)
Apps/goals: 12/1 Born: Gorna Oryahovitsa, Bulgaria, 15/2/1986

Career: Pieta Hotspurs, Lecce, Fiorentina, Juventus (loan), CITY (£5.8 million, August 2007–July 2011), Parma (loan), Sporting Clube de Portugal, Lecce (loan), Sporting B, Verona.

Details: Having signed a four-year contract with City, Valeri Bojinov was ruled out for five months after suffering knee ligament damage in the Manchester derby in August 2007. Thereafter he struggled with injuries, being sidelined for another six months from August 2008. He eventually returned to PL action in March 2009 and scored his only City goal in the 2–1 defeat by Tottenham two months later. He has netted six times in forty internationals for Bulgaria.

BOND, Kevin John (Defender)
Apps/goals: 124/12 Born: West Ham, London, 22/6/1957

Career: Bournemouth, Norwich City, Seattle Sounders, CITY (£350,000, September 1981–September 1984), Southampton, Exeter City, Sittingbourne, Dover Athletic; retired 1996; CITY (coach, season 1996/97), Wrexham (coach), Altrincham (coach), Stafford Rangers (manager), West Ham United (scout), Portsmouth (coach/ assistant-manager), Southampton (coach/assistant-manager), Newcastle United (coach/assistant-manager), Bournemouth (manager), Tottenham Hotspur (coach/assistant-manager), Queen's Park Rangers (coach/assistant-manager).

Details: Signed by his father-manager, Kevin Bond was never really accepted by the City fans. Nevertheless, he spent three good years at Maine Road, having his best season in 1982/83 when he appeared in forty-seven senior games as defensive partner to Tommy Caton. In the 3-2 defeat by Huddersfield in April 1984, he scored two penalties in two minutes right on half-time.

Bond made over 600 club appearances at various levels, was capped twice by England 'B' and was in charge at Bournemouth for ninety-five games (2006–08).

BOOK, Anthony Keith (Right-back)
Apps/goals: 315/5 Born: Bath, 4/9/1934

Career: Peasedown Miners FC, Bath City, Toronto City, Plymouth Argyle (£1,500), CITY (£17,000), July 1966, player-caretaker-manager, November 1973–1979; player/assistant-manager to Ron Saunders, November 1973–April 1974; retired as a player, April 1974; manager, April 1974–July 1979; caretaker-manager, October 1980, November–December 1989 and August 1993; then coach); Huddersfield Town (Chief scout, 1997/98).

Details: After making eighty-one League appearances for Plymouth, Tony Book followed Malcolm Allison to Maine Road, where he prospered under the joint-management of Allison and Joe Mercer. He made his City debut in the opening match of 1966/67 against Southampton FC, being a near-permanent fixture in the team for the next seven years with only one interruption due to an Achilles tendon injury in 1968. In his first season at the club he missed just one game and was the inaugural winner of the club's 'Player of the Year award'. In August 1967, Book was named captain following the transfer of Johnny Crossan and was henceforth nicknamed 'Skip' by his teammates. Then, twelve months later he lifted the FA Cup, following up by skippering the Blues to victory in the finals of the League cup European Cup Winners. When he retired as a player Book passed the captaincy to Colin Bell. One of the quickest and certainly the best full-backs in the game between 1966 and 1973, he made 244 Football League appearances for City, and is the club's most successful captain in terms of trophies won. Book was voted the best full-back in Canada while with Toronto City and won the PFA Footballer of the Year' jointly in 1969 with Derby's Dave Mackay.

Book took over as City's temporary manager when Johnny Hart resigned due to ill health in November 1973, and was named assistant to Ron Saunders and when he was sacked after less than six months, Book again took charge of the team, being appointed permanent manager one game later. The first notable victory of management career was a 1–0 win over United in the Manchester derby, made famous by Denis Law's back-heeler! In 1976, Book guided City to victory in the League Cup final, making him the first person to win the competition as both player and manager. He remained in office until 1979, when he was replaced by his former mentor Malcolm Allison. Thereafter he was a loyal stalwart to the club in several other roles until 1997, including another spell as caretaker-boss in 1993. Scout at Huddersfield under manager Brian Horton, Book is Honorary President of Manchester City FC and Life President of the Official Supporters Club. He was also inducted into Manchester City's Hall of Fame in January 2004. Book's brother, Kim, and his son, Steve, were both goalkeepers.

BOOTH, Frank (Forward)
Apps/goals: 107/19 Born: Hyde, Cheshire, autumn 1882 Died: Manchester, 22/6/1919

Career: Hyde, Glossop, Stockport County, CITY (April 1902–January 1907), Bury, Clyde, CITY (July 1911, retired injured, May 1912).

Details: 'Tabby' Booth was a slim and lively winger who hugged the touchline. He made over 100 appearances for City and played in the 1904 FA Cup final victory over Bolton before being sold, with others, following the 1906 bribery 'scandal'. He later took advantage of the FA amnesty and returned to Hyde Road for a second spell, but was only a shadow of the player who had served the club so well during the early part of the twentieth century. After impressing in an England trial, he was capped against Ireland in February 1905, thus becoming the seventh player used by his country in what was then a problematic outside-left position in ten internationals. Booth died in Manchester Royal Infirmary, aged thirty-six.

BOOTH, Thomas Anthony (Defender)
Apps/goals: 491/36 Born: Middleton, Manchester, 9/11/1949

Career: Middleton Boys, CITY (September 1965–October 1981), Preston North End (£30,000; retired 1984; appointed coach, later manager); later worked for TV rental company; lives in Manchester.

Details: Nineteen-year-old Tommy Booth scored a dramatic eighty-ninth-minute winner for City against Everton in the 1969 FA Cup semi-final, duly gaining a winner's medal at Wembley a month later. He then helped City twice win the League Cup (1970 and 1976) and lift the European Cup Winner's Cup (1971) while building up a very impressive total of appearances. In fact, he starred in twenty-six European games for City – the most by an outfield player. Indeed, only six players have made more senior appearances for City than Booth who was described by manager Joe Mercer as being like 'Stan Cullis and Neil Franklin rolled into one'. Making his League debut against Arsenal in October 1968, he remained first choice centre-half until April 1974 and was certainly unlucky not to win full international honours for England, collecting just four U23 caps for his efforts. He managed Preston when the club was suffering financially.

BOOTLE, William (Outside-left)
Apps: 6 Born: Ashton-under-Lyne, 1923 Died: c. 1998

Career: Ashton BC, CITY (June 1943–April 1951), Crewe Alexandra, Wigan Athletic.

Details: A City reserve, Billy Bootle made only half a dozen senior appearances during his eight years with the club, although he did score six goals in thirty-two Second World War fixtures. Over 48,000 fans saw him make his League debut against Newcastle in February 1949.

BOSVELT, Paul (Midfielder)
Apps/goals: 65/3 Born: Doetinchen, Netherlands, 26/3/1970

Career: Go Ahead Eagles Deventer, FC Twente, Feyenoord, CITY (July 2003–July 2005), Heerenveen; (free, retired May 2007).

Details: Defensive midfielder Paul Bosvelt retired at the age of thirty-seven with over 500 League appearances and twenty-four Dutch caps under his belt. He had two solid seasons with City and his influence in the centre of the pitch made him a huge favourite with the supporters.

BOTTOMLEY, William (Half-back)
Apps/goals: 103/2 Born: Mossley, 1886 Died: c. 1952

Career: Edgehill FC, Oldham Athletic, Mossley Britannia, Failsworth, Oldham Athletic, CITY (May 1908 – retired injured, September 1919).

Details: Bill Bottomley, a strong tackling defender, had his best season with City in 1912/13 when he made thirty-four appearances and scored one goal, in a 2-2 draw with Spurs. He made over thirty starts during First World War.

BOWLES, Stanley (Forward)
Apps/goals: 21/4 Born: Manchester, 24/12/1948

Career: CITY (June 1965–September 1970), Bury (loan), Crewe Alexandra, Carlisle United, Queen's Park Rangers, Nottingham Forest, Orient, Brentford, Epping Town; retired 1985; later returned to Brentford (part-time coach); became an after-dinner speaker.

Details: A natural-born footballer with flair and ability, Stan Bowles scored 127 goals in 507 League games for eight different clubs in sixteen years between 1967 and 1983. A colourful character both on and off the field, he top-scored in City's second XI in 1968/69, but found it hard to establish himself in the first team at Maine Road.

He went on to represent the Football League and won five full caps for England, scoring in a 2-0 win over Wales in 1974. Unfortunately, he was not Joe Mercer's favourite player and was dropped by the former City boss from the national team. When he played against Holland in 1977, Bowles wore a Gola boot on his left foot and an Adidas one on his right.

One football fan once remarked, 'If Bowles could pass a betting shop the same way he passes a ball, he'd be a world beater!'

BOWMAN, Walter Wilfred (Utility)
Apps/goals: 49/3 Born: Canada, 1870 Died: Canada, c. 1932
Career: Accrington, CITY (August 1892–June 1900); returned to Canada.
Details: Walter Bowman scored three times in five games for Accrington before becoming the first foreign-born player to sign for City. He spent eight years with the club, during which time he occupied seven different positions, centre-half being by far his best. A scorer on his League debut *v.* Crewe Alexandra in February 1893, he was a reserve for his last six seasons.

BOWYER, Ian (Forward)
Apps/goals: 70/17 Born: Little Sutton, Cheshire, 6/6/1951
Career: Mid-Cheshire Boys, Little Sutton, CITY (June 1966–June 1971), Leyton Orient (£25,000), Nottingham Forest (£40,000), Sunderland (£50,000), Nottingham Forest (£50,000), Hereford United (player, then player-manager), Cheltenham Town (coach), Plymouth Argyle (assistant-manager), Rotherham United (coach), Birmingham City (coach), Nottingham Forest (coach).
Details: A workaholic in midfield, Ian Bowyer's playing career spanned twenty-three years during which time he scored 139 goals in 780 club appearances. His best season with City came in 1969/70 when he had forty-eight outings and gained a League Cup winner's medal. As a Forest player he won the League Cup again (1978), the First Division title and two European Cup finals. In April 1990 Bowyer played alongside his son, Ian, in the same Hereford side.

BOYATA, Anga Dedryck (Defender)
Apps/goals: 24/1 Born: Brussels, Belgium, 8/9/1990
Career: CITY (academy, July 2006 to date), Bolton Wanderers (loan), FC Twente Enschede/Holland (loan).
Details: A Belgian of Congolese decent, Dedryck Boyata developed through City's academy, and was thrust into first-team action in an FA Cup tie against Middlesbrough when he partnered Joleon Lescott in defence in the absent of Kolo Touré who was on duty. He has been capped by Belgium at youth, U21 and senior levels.

BOYER, Philip John (Forward)
Apps/goals: 26/4 Born: Nottingham, 25/1/1949
Career: Musters Road School, Rushcliffe Representative XI, Derby County, York City, AFC Bournemouth, Norwich City, Southampton, CITY (£220,000, November 1980–July 1983), Bulova/Hong Kong, Grantham Town, Stamford, Shepshed Charterhouse, Grantham Town (player/assistant-manager), Spalding; retired,1987; Harrowby Town (manager); Blackpool (scout), Northampton Town (scout); became a bank courier.
Details: Phil Boyer had two wonderfully exciting seasons with Ted MacDougall at Norwich, and as a result played for England against Wales in 1976, his only senior cap, having starred in two U23 internationals prior to that. He scored on his City debut (*v.* Spurs) but unfortunately, with Trevor Francis and Kevin Reeves the regular pairing up front, followed by David Cross, his opportunities were somewhat limited with City, and therefore failed to make an impact. He missed the 1981 FA Cup final through injury, saying it the most 'disappointing moment' of his career. As striker-partners, Boyer and MacDougall scored a total of 195 goals for four different clubs.

BRADBURY, Lee Michael (Striker)
Apps/goals: 46/11 Born: Isle of Wight, 3/7/1975
Career: Cowes, Exeter City (loan), Portsmouth, CITY (record £2.9 million, July 1997/October 1998), Crystal Palace (£1.5 million), Birmingham City Portsmouth, Sheffield Wednesday, Derby County, Walsall, Oxford United, Southend United, Bournemouth (player, retired 2011; then manager), Portsmouth (U14s coach), Havant & Waterlooville (manager).
Details: Lee Bradbury was a major disappointment with City', 'not worth the money' said a lot of people. An England U21 international (3 caps), he worked hard at his game and later gave good service to Palace, Pompey and Bournemouth. He retired with a League record of ninety-two goals in 512 appearances.

BRADFORD, Leo Joseph (Outside-right)
Apps/goals: 5/1 Born: Eccles, 1902 Died: Manchester, c. 1970
Career: Hurst FC, CITY (May 1925–May 1926), Ashton National.
Details: Leo Bradford made his City debut in an 8-3 League win over Burnley in October 1925 when he deputised for Billy Austin who was on duty for England against Wales. His only goal followed seven weeks later in a 4-0 victory over Leeds United.

BRADSHAW, Carl (Utility)
Apps: 7 Born: Sheffield, 2/10/1968
Career: Sheffield Boys, South Yorkshire Boys, Yorkshire Boys, Sheffield Wednesday, Barnsley (loan), CITY (£100,000, September 1988/October 1989), Sheffield United (£50,000), Norwich City, Wigan Athletic, Scunthorpe United, Altrincham; retired 2006.

Details: Although he spent the majority of his career playing as at full-back, Carl Bradshaw also produced some enterprising displays in midfield as well as a forward. He moved to Maine Road in a deal that took Imre Varadi to Hillsborough, but unfortunately never settled at City and left, having made only seven appearances (six as a sub) in just over a year. He won the AGT with Wigan, a Unibond League championship with Alfreton and represented England in four youth internationals. In September 1997, Bradshaw was given a six-month jail sentence for assaulting a taxi driver in Norwich.

BRANAGAN, Kenneth (Full-back)
Apps/goals: 208/3 Born: Salford,
27/7/1930 Died: 9/8/2008
Career: North Salford Youth Club, CITY (November 1948–October 1960), Oldham Athletic; retired 1966.
Details: A loyal servant to City for twelve years, Branagan was safe and self-assured, quick over the ground, who missed only two League games in each of seasons 1952/53 and 1953/54 when forming an excellent partnership with first Eric Westwood and then Roy Little.

Having won Boys' Club caps for England and Great Britain, Branagan was eighteen when he joined City, and after completing his national service in the Army, made his League debut against Sheffield United in December 1950. Unfortunately, he missed both the 1955 and 1956 FA Cup finals, having lost his place to Jimmy Meadows.

Along with two other former City players, Bobby Johnstone and Bert Lister, he helped Oldham gain promotion from Division Four in 1962/63. His son, Jim, also played League football, making over 300 appearances for Blackburn (1979–87).

BRANCH, Paul Michael (Midfield)
Apps: 4 Born: Liverpool, 18/10/1978
Career: Everton, CITY (loan, October-November 1998), Birmingham City, Wolves, Reading (loan), Hull City (loan), Bradford City, Chester City, Halifax Town, Burscough.
Details: Although Michael Branch played senior football for twelve years, he made less than 250 appearances, having his best spells with Everton, Wolves and Chester. Signed by former Everton colleague Joe Royle, his City debut came in a 2-1 win over Colchester. He won England schoolboy, youth and U21 honours. Branch was jailed for seven years at Chester Crown Court in November 2012, after being found with £160,000 worth of cocaine in his possession. He lost an appeal against his sentence in February 2013.

BRAND, Ralph Laidlaw (Forward)
Apps/goals: 22/2 Born: Edinburgh, 8/12/1936

Career: Carricknowe School, Slateford Athletic, Broxburn Athletic, Rangers, CITY (£30,000, August 1965–August 1967), Sunderland (£5,000), Raith Rovers, Hamilton Academical; retired 1972; Darlington (manager), Albion Rovers (coach, then manager), Dunfermline Athletic (coach); became a taxi driver.
Details: Ralph Brand failed to maintain the scoring form he had shown north of the border and was regarded as a 'failure' at Maine Road. It was a pity, because during his time at Ibrox he was outstanding – 206 goals in 317 appearances for Rangers. He helped City win the Second Division championship in 1966, having earlier played in four Scottish Championship-winning teams between 1958 and 1964, helping the Glasgow club complete the treble in the latter campaign. In fact, he won four Scottish League Cup and four Scottish Cup winner's medals, and is the only player to have scored in four consecutive Scottish Cup finals. He netted eight goals in eight full internationals for the Scottish National Football team, his opportunities being limited due to the presence in attack of a certain Denis Law! Brand also gained ten U23 caps and represented the Scottish League.

BRANNAN, Gerard Daniel (Utility)
Apps/goals: 46/4 Born: Prescot, 15/1/1972
Career: Tranmere Rovers, CITY (£750,000, March 1997/October 1998), Norwich City, Motherwell (£378,000), Wigan Athletic, Dunfermline Athletic, Rochdale, Accrington Stanley, Radcliffe Borough, Morecambe, Vauxhall Motors, Burscough; retired 2009.
Details: Ged Brannan made over 300 appearances for Tranmere before moving to Maine Road. A versatile player, he had a good first season with City, scoring three times in thirty-four games, but then lost his way and was eventually transferred to Motherwell after a loan spell with Norwich. He retired with over 600 club appearances under his belt.

BRAY, John (Left-half)
Apps/goals: 279/10 Born: Oswaldtwistle, Lancs,
22/4/1909 Died: Blackburn, 20/11/1982
Career: St Andrew's School/Oswaldtwistle, Clayton Olympia, Manchester Central, CITY (£1,000, October 1929, retired March 1946); Second World War guest for Port Vale, Crewe Alexandra, Blackburn Rovers and Nottingham Forest; Watford (manager), Nelson (coach); played cricket for Accrington (Lancashire League); played cricket for Accrington in the Lancashire League; served in the RAF during Second World War.
Details: The tireless Jackie Bray brought a degree of constructiveness to his performances at left-half and loved to drive forward at every opportunity. An FA Cup and League championship winner with

City in 1934 and 1937, he was also rewarded with six England caps, the first in a 4-0 win over Wales in September 1934 when he laid on a goal for his club-mate Sam Tilson. His last international was against Scotland in April 1937 at Hampden Park, which attracted a record crowd of 149,547. He also played in the unofficial Jubilee match versus Scotland in 1935, starred in three international trials and represented the Football League on five occasions. During the Second World War, Bray scored eleven goals in 181 games for City.

BRENNAN, John (Left-half)
Apps: 60 Born: Manchester, 13/12/1892 Died: 1942
Career: Ancoats Lads' Club, Hollinwood United, CITY (trial, 1910), Denton FC, Glossop, Bradford City, CITY (July 1914–June 1922), Rochdale; retired 1928.
Details: After failing to impress when on trial as a teenager, amateur John Brennan eventually joined City four years later. Although the First World War interrupted his routine at Hyde Road, he gave the club good service, having his best season in 1914/15 when he missed only five League games.

BRENNAN, Mark Robert (Midfield)
Apps/goals: 36/7 Born: Rossendale, 4/10/1965
Career: Ipswich Town, Middlesbrough, CITY (£400,000, July 1990–November 1992), Oldham Athletic.
Details: Mark Brennan made over 350 appearances during his thirteen-year League career (1983–96). He made his City debut against Aston Villa in September 1990 and as a substitute, netted his first goal in his second match to seal a 2-1 win over Norwich.

BRENNAN, Michael (Forward)
Apps: 4 Born: Salford, 17/5/1952
Career: Salford Boys, CITY (July 1968–October 1973), Stockport County (loan), Rochdale.
Details: Micky Brennan was a reserve at Maine Road for four years, top-scoring for City's second XI in 1970/71 and 1972/73 while appearing in two League games in each of those seasons, before joining Rochdale after a loan spell at Edgeley Park.

BRIDGE, Wayne Michael (Left-back)
Apps: 58 Born: Southampton, 5/8/1980
Career: Southampton, Chelsea, Fulham loan), CITY (£10 million, January 2009–June 2013), West Ham United (loan), Sunderland (loan), Brighton & Hove Albion (loan), Reading.
Details: During his time with Southampton, Wayne Bridge's three managers, Dave Jones, Glenn Hoddle and Stuart Gray all predicted he would play for England. They were right – as he went on to gain eight U21 and thirty-six full caps, the first under Sven-Göran Eriksson *v.* the Netherlands in

February 2002. He would surely have won more honours had Ashley Cole not been around! Bridge helped Chelsea win the Premiership title, the League Cup twice and the FA Cup in the space of three years. At May 2013, he was still registered with City and had amassed over 450 appearances at club level.

BRIGHTWELL, David John (Defender)
Apps/goals: 53/2 Born: Lutterworth, 7/1/1971
Career: CITY (April 1988–December 1995), Chester City (loan), Lincoln City (loan), Stoke City (loan), Bradford City (£30,000), Blackpool (loan), Northampton Town, Carlisle United, Hull City, Darlington; retired 2002; now works as a fireman.
Details: David Brightwell, brother of Ian (below) and son of former 1960 British Olympians Ann Packer and Robbie Brightwell, had an excellent career which spanned fourteen years, during which time he appeared in 303 club games, scoring five goals. He had his best season with City in 1993/94 (twenty-four games) and was loaned out three times before finally leaving Maine Road for Bradford City in 1995.

BRIGHTWELL, Ian (Utility)
Apps/goals: 231/17 Born: Lutterworth, 9/4/1968
Career: Midas Junior Club, CITY (July 1985–July 1998), Coventry City (free), Walsall, Stoke City, Port Vale (player, also caretaker-manager), Macclesfield Town (player-coach/caretaker-manager/manager); retired as a player, 2006.
Details: Ian Brightwell won an FA Youth Cup winner's medal in 1986 and gained four England U21 caps, but unlike his brother, David, went on to become a key figure in City's line-up, playing a vital role in the promotion-winning season of 1988/89 when he scored in wins over Brighton, Chelsea, Bradford City and Oxford. He was used more as substitute the following season before switching to right-back in 1990/91. A snapped patella tendon sidelined him for more than a year after that, but he regained full fitness and continued to give City sterling service until his thirteen year association with the club ended with a move to Coventry. Asa Hartford was with Brightwell at Macclesfield, 2006–08.
In February 1992 the Brightwells became the first pair of brothers to play in the same City team since the Futchers in April 1979.

BRISCOE, Lee Stephen (Midfield)
Apps/goals: 5/1 Born: Pontefract, 30/9/1975
Career: Sheffield Wednesday, CITY (loan, February–May 1998), Burnley, Preston North End.
Details: Lee Briscoe scored his only goal for City in a 3-1 win at Huddersfield as the First Division relegation battle hotted up. Unfortunately his presence failed to keep the Blues up! Capped five

times by England at U21 level, he made over 100 League appearances for Burnley.

BROAD, Thomas Higginson (Outside-right)
Apps: 44 Born: Stalybridge, 31/7/1887
Died: Cheshire, 23/2/1966
Career: Redgate Albion, Denton Wanderers, Openshaw Lads' Club, CITY (trial, August 1903), Openshaw Lads' Club, West Bromwich Albion, Chesterfield Town, Oldham Athletic, Bristol City, CITY (March 1919–May 1921), Stoke City, Southampton, Weymouth, Rhyl Athletic; retired May 1928; later worked at a seaside fun fair.

Details: Having been rejected by City as a sixteen-year-old, Tommy Broad went on to make over 300 appearances for four League clubs before finally signing for City in 1919. He partnered Dick Crawshaw on the right wing most of the time. A junior international, he was quick over the ground and once ran 100 yards in 10.6 seconds.

His brother, Jimmy, a utility forward, also a had a trial with City in 1911, and he too failed to impress as a youngster, yet went on to have a long and distinguished career which spanned twenty years, during which time he played for fourteen different clubs and accumulated 258 appearances, scoring ninety-seven goals.

BROADHURST, Charles (Forward)
Apps/goals: 36/26 Born: Moston, 1905
Died: c. 1972
Career: Ashton National, CITY (March 1927–February 1930), Blackpool.

Details: Charlie Broadhurst made a great start to his City career, scoring seven goals in his first seven games, five of them against Darlington – one on his debut (2-2) followed by a majestic four-timer in a 7-0 win in the return fixture three days later. Teaming up well with Tommy Johnson, he continued to find the net during the first two-thirds of the 1927/28 season (bagging another fourteen goals), but following an injury and the arrival of Bobby Marshall and Tommy Tait, he struggled to get into the team and was eventually transferred to Blackpool.

BROADIS, Ivan Arthur (Inside-forward)
Apps/goals: 79/12 Born: Isle of Dogs, Poplar, London, 18/12/1922
Career: Cooper's Company School/Bow, Finchley, Tottenham Hotspur (amateur), Millwall (amateur), Northfleet, Finchley; Second World War guest for Millwall, Manchester United, Tottenham Hotspur, Blackpool, Carlisle United and Bradford Park Avenue; Carlisle United (player-manager), Sunderland (£18,000), CITY (record £25,000, October 1951–October 1953), Newcastle United (£17,500), Carlisle United (£3,500, player-coach), Queen of the South (retired 1960; coach until 1962); served in the RAF during Second World War; engaged as a sports journalist for the *Carlisle Evening News & Star* (1962–84).

Details: Ivor Broadis put a great deal of effort into his inside-forward play. Quick over the ground, with good balance and technique, he made almost 500 club appearances, gained fourteen England caps, being one of the few players to perform in a 7-1 defeat by Hungary in Budapest in 1954, scoring his country's consolation goal, and played in three Inter-League games.

Aged only twenty-three, he was appointed manager of Carlisle (August 1946) and three years later, created history by selling himself to Sunderland.

Having failed to settle in alongside Trevor Ford and Len Shackleton at Roker Park, he joined City in 1949 and made his debut against Spurs just twenty-four hours after signing. He had his best season at Maine Road in 1952/53 when his eight goals in thirty-seven games effectively helped stave off relegation. Eventually sold by City to Newcastle after a 'heart to heart' talk with manager Les McDowall, the money received helped buy Billy McAdams from Distillery. Broadis then played for Newcastle in their 1955 FA Cup final win over City.

BROOK, Eric (Outside-left)
Apps/goals: 493/177 Born: Mexborough, Yorkshire, 27/11/1907 Died: Wythenshaw, Manchester, 29/3/1965
Career: Dolcliffe Road School/Mexborough, Oxford Road YMCA, Swinton Primitives, Mexborough, Wath Athletic, Barnsley, CITY (£6,000, with Fred Tilson, March 1928, retired injured, May 1940); later worked as a coach driver, crane operator and licensee.

Details: Ostensibly an outside-left who also appeared as an inside-forward, Eric Brook was 'full of tricks', an ebullient character with a powerful left-foot shot.

An ever-present for City a record five times, he appeared in 450 out of 474 League games between March 1928 and April 1939, having one unbroken run of 165 matches spread over four years, from November 1929 to October 1933. Only three players have made more League appearances for City than Brook (Oakes, Trautmann and Corrigan), and his overall total of 178 goals (which included thirty-five penalties and eight hat-tricks) and his haul of 159 in the League, are both City records. Only Francis Lee has converted more spot-kicks (forty-six) while Brook and Doherty together netted a total of fifty-four goals in 1936/37.

Brook also had the pleasure of scoring the only goal of a sixth-round FA Cup tie against Stoke before Maine Road's biggest-ever crowd of 84,569 in March 1934.

He won the first of eighteen England caps against Ireland in 1929, but had to wait almost four years for his second *v.* Switzerland. One of his finest hours at international level came in the 'Battle of Highbury' encounter with Italy in 1934, when he scored two goals in the first quarter-of-an-hour, a bullet header from Britton's cross and a thunderbolt free-kick from 20 yards.

Brook played in five international trials, in one wartime international against Wales in 1939, starred in seven Inter League matches, in seven FA XI games and won the FA Cup and First Division championship with City in 1934 and 1937 respectively. He was also a runner-up with City in the 1933 FA Cup final when he became the first player to wear a number 12 shirt! He retired following a wartime car accident. There is a road in Manchester called Eric Brook Close.

BROOKS, George Herbert (Utility)
*Apps/goals: 3/1 Born: Radcliffe, 1888
Died: Armistice Day, 1918*
   Career: Longfield, CITY (January 1911/April 1912), Bury, South Shields, Derby County (until his death).
   Details: Signed as forward cover following excellent performances for Longfield, George Brooks made his City debut in the 1-1 home draw with Aston Villa six weeks after arriving at the club, scoring his only goal in a 3-1 defeat at Bolton in February 1912. He made thirty-three appearances for Derby.

BROOMFIELD, Herbert Charles (Goalkeeper)
*Apps: 4 Born: Audlem, near Nantwich,
11/12/1878 Died: c. 1942*
   Career: Northwich Wednesday, Northwich Victoria, Bolton Wanderers, Manchester United, CITY (July 1908–October 1910), Manchester United; retired 1912; trained a landscape gardener, but later became a painter and decorator; was also associated with the Players' Union from its inception, serving as secretary in 1908/09.
   Details: A reserve at both Manchester clubs, Herbert Broomfield was described in a biography as 'a man who does not waste words, unassuming and a loyal club man.' Deputising for Walter Smith, he conceded nine goals in his four League games for City.

BROWELL, Thomas (Forward)
*Apps/goals: 247/139 Born: Walbottle,
Northumberland, 19/10/1902 Died: Lytham St
Anne's, 5/10/1955*
   Career: Newton Grange, Hull City, Everton (£1,550), CITY (record, £1,780, October 1913–September 1926), Blackpool (£1,150), Lytham (player-coach), Morecambe FC; retired 1940; became a tram driver in Lytham St Anne's.

   Details: After a scoring debut *v.* Sheffield Wednesday, Tommy 'Boy' Browell finished as City joint top-marksman in the 1913/14 season, and after First World War, headed the charts in 1920/21 with thirty-one goals, in 1921/22 with twenty-six and was runner-up in 1925/26 with twenty-eight, which included a five-timer in an 8-3 home League win over Burnley. In between times, he twice topped the scoring charts in second XI football, in 1923/24 jointly with Warner and then in 1924/25, and lies joint second in the list of City's hat-trick heroes with ten.
   Forming deadly partnerships with first Horace Barnes and then Frank Roberts, Browell – clever, witty, willing and full of pluck – was never capped by England, despite scoring 207 goals in 387 League games during his career, but did represent the Football League. He played for City in the 1926 FA Cup final when only a brilliant save by Bolton 'keeper Dick Pym denied him a goal. A street in Manchester is named after City's star player – Tommy Browell Close. His brother, George, played for Hull (1905–11).

BROWN, Harold Robert (Wing-half)
Apps: 2 Born: Tredegar, 1889 Died: c. 1955
   Career: Tredegar, Crewe Alexandra, CITY (October 1910/May 1911), Crewe Alexandra; did not play after First World War.
   Details: Signed as half-back cover, Harry Brown played for City in the drawn games at Middlesbrough and Tottenham on 26 and 27 December 1910. He made over 100 appearances in his two spells with Crewe.

BROWN, John Percival (Outside-left)
*Apps: 6 Born: Liverpool, 1888 Died: Liverpool,
c. 1944*
   Career: Orrell, CITY (September 1908–August 1910), Stoke, Hanley Swifts, Port Vale.
   Details: Stepping in for Jimmy Conlin, Jack Brown set up two of Tom Holford's three goals in City's 4-0 win over Sheffield Wednesday in March 1909 and laid on another for hat-trick hero Lot Jones in a 3-1 victory at Gainsborough the following October.

BROWN, Michael Robert (Midfield)
Apps/goals: 121/4 Born: Hartlepool, 25/1/1977
   Career: Hartlepool Lion Hillcarter FC, CITY (April 1993–December 1999), Hartlepool United (loan), Portsmouth (loan), Sheffield United, Tottenham Hotspur, Fulham, Wigan Athletic, Portsmouth, Leeds United.
   Details: An England U21 international, the tough-tackling, hard-working Michael Brown was a very capable squad member before consolidating his position in City's midfield during Alan Ball's reign as manager. After losing his place and following loan spells with his home town club Hartlepool, he returned to Maine Road and helped

gain promotion to the First Division in 1999. Loaned out to Portsmouth after that success, he was subsequently transferred to Sheffield United by Joe Royle. At May 2013, Brown had made 558 appearances at club level (493 in the League).

BUCHAN, James (Half-back)
Apps/goals: 164/10 Born: Perth, Scotland, 7/7/1881 Died: Glasgow c. 1950

Career: Perth, Hibernian, Woolwich Arsenal, CITY (March 1905-June 1911), Motherwell; retired 1915.

Details: Jim Buchan helped Hibs win the Scottish Cup and League title in 1902 and 1903 respectively before starring in City's 1910 Second Division championship team. A strong player, always keen to 'get stuck in', he played in the 'infamous scandal' League match against Aston Villa in 1905. He went on to perform exceedingly well alongside Tommy Hynds and Jack Banks and then Bill Eadie and Jimmy Blair, as well as Tom Holford and George Dorsett, before becoming surplus to requirements in 1911.

BUCKLEY, Major Franklin Charles (Defender)
Apps: 11 Born: Urmston, 9/11/1882 Died: Walsall, 22/12/1964

Career: Urmston CS, Aston Villa, Brighton & Hove Albion, Manchester United, CITY (September 1907–July 1909), Birmingham, Derby County, Bradford City; retired 1918; became a Major in the Footballers' battalion of the Middlesex Regiment (1916–18); Norwich City (player-manager); commercial traveller; Blackpool (manager), Wolverhampton Wanderers (manager), Notts County (manager), Hull City (manager), Leeds United (manager), Walsall (manager); left football, 1955; became a farmer near Redditch.

Details: An amateur throughout his career, Frank Buckley was a tall, heavily-built defender, hard working and forceful who gained one England cap and won a Second Division championship medal with Derby (1912). After retiring he became a well-respected manager, guiding Wolves into the First Division in 1932 and to the FA Cup final in 1939 Division.

His brother Chris, an amateur with City in 1903, went on to play League football for Aston Villa and Arsenal and was also a director and chairman of Aston Villa in the late 1930s.

BUCKLEY, Gary (Forward)
Apps: 8 Born: Manchester, 3/3/1961

Career: Salford Boys, CITY (May 1977– October 1981), Preston North End, Chorley, Bury, Chorley; retired 1997.

Details: During his career, Gary Buckley, 5 foot 4 inches tall, made seventy-seven League appearances – his first coming with City in a 3-1

win over Tottenham in October 1980 when he played up front with Kevin Reeves.

BURGESS, Charles (Full-back)
Apps: 32 Born: Church Lawton, 25/12/1883 Died: Hartshill, Stoke-on-Trent, 11/12/1956

Career: Butt Lane Swifts, Stoke, CITY (July 1908, retired injured, May 1911).

Details: A cool-headed, solid defender with a tigerish tackle, Charlie Burgess made 195 appearances for Stoke before spending three years with City before a knee injury ended his career. He was signed by Stoke while perched on top of haystack on his father's farm!

BURGESS, Herbert (Left-back)
Apps/goals: 94/2 Born: Openshaw, 12/10/1883 Died: 13/6/1954

Career: Gorton St Francis, Openshaw United, Edge Lane, Moss Side, Glossop, CITY (£250, July 1903–December 1906), Manchester United; retired injured, May 1910; subsequently held coaching positions in Hungary, Spain, Italy, Austria, Denmark and Sweden; returned to UK at Ashton National FC (manager, 1932–34).

Details: Broad-shouldered with an athletic frame, Herbert Burgess was dubbed the 'Mighty Atom' and, despite being only 5 foot 4 inches tall, was still one of the best defenders in the country during the early 1900s. He played in an international trial before becoming the first City player to win a full England cap (1904 *v*. Wales). He later added three more to his tally, represented the Football League on seven occasions, five with City, whom he helped win the FA Cup in 1904. One of a quintet of players who lefty City for rivals United, he won the League title with the Reds in 1908 before a serious knee injury ended his career.

BURRIDGE, John (Goalkeeper)
Apps: 4 Born: Workington, 3/12/1951

Career: Great Clifton School, Workington, Blackpool (loan/signed, £10,000), Aston Villa (£100,000), Southend United (loan), Crystal Palace (£65,000), Queen's Park Rangers (£200,000), Wolverhampton Wanderers (£75,000), Derby County (loan), Sheffield United (£10,000), Southampton (£30,000), Newcastle United (£25,000), Hibernian, Newcastle United, Scarborough, Lincoln City, Enfield (loan), Aberdeen, Newcastle United (loan), Hartlepool United (trial), Barrow (loan), Dunfermline Athletic, Dumbarton, Falkirk (trial), CITY (free, December 1994 – August 1995), Notts County (free), Witton Albion, Darlington, Grimsby Town, Gateshead, Northampton Town, Durham City, Queen of the South, Purfleet, Blyth Spartans, Scarborough, Blyth Spartans (player-manager); China (goalkeeping coach), Blyth Spartans (player-coach; retired as a player, December 1997); Oman national Team (coach), Al Ain FC/UAE (coach), Blackburn Rovers (goalkeeping coach), Leeds United (goalkeeping coach), Newcastle United (goalkeeping coach); columnist for Singapore's *The New Paper*, also TV pundit on Singapore radio.

Details: A fitness fanatic, John Burridge's career spanned four decades and when he finally took off his gloves in 1997, having kept goal for twenty-nine years and been associated with thirty-three different clubs (twenty-three in his last five years as a player), his overall appearance record stood at 1,097, of which 915 were made at senior level. Only Peter Shilton, who he replaced at Southampton in 1987, has made more.

Burridge, well built, agile and commanding inside his area, made his League debut in May 1969 and played his last game of 'serious' football for Blyth Spartans against his former club Blackpool in an FA Cup tie in November 1997, a few days before his forty-sixth birthday. In fact, he spent his best years with Blackpool (134 League starts).

Signed for City by boss Brian Horton as cover for Tony Coton, he made his debut as a substitute (for Coton) against another of his former clubs, Newcastle, on 29 April 1995 and after starting the next two games, he then became the oldest goalkeeper ever to appear in a Premiership match, aged forty-three years, five months and 11 days, when he lined up against yet another of his old clubs, QPR on 14 May.

Details: Burridge, known affectionately as 'Budge' had a wonderful career. He served under several managers, including Terry Venables, who dropped him for the 1982 FA Cup final) and Kevin Keegan, and he won a few prizes, among them the Anglo-Italian Cup with Blackpool (1970), the League Cup with Aston Villa (1977), the Second Division championship with Crystal Palace (1979), the Scottish League Cup with Hibs (1991) and helped Wolves gain promotion (1983). He lined up against eighty-nine out of a possible 101 League clubs, played against twenty-two Scottish teams, conceded 1,080 goals in his 915 League matches, kept 298 clean sheets and was beaten 899 times in his 771 League outings, of which roughly a third (255) were shut-outs. Quite brilliant.

Burridge's wife Janet once said: 'John's so wrapped up in football, I've heard him giving TV commentator Gerald Sinstadt an interview in his sleep.' His book *Budgie* was published in April 2011.

BUSBY, SIR Matthew, CBE (Wing-half/inside-forward)
Apps/goals: 227/14 Born: Bellshill, Lanarkshire, 26/5/1909 Died: Manchester, 20/1/1994
    Career: Orbiston Village FC, Alpine Villa, Denny Hibernian, CITY (February 1928–March 1936), Liverpool (£8,000); Second World War guest for Bournemouth, Brentford, Chelsea, Hibernian, Middlesbrough and Reading; retired October 1945; Manchester United (manager, 1945–69; then administration manager, caretaker-manager, 1970/71, director, club president, life member of club); Football League Management Committee & Football League vice-president; Scotland (manager, 1958/59); once studied for a schoolmaster's appointment.

Details: A moderate inside-forward in his youth, earning initially £5-a-week, Matt Busby developed into a very useful wing-half, skilful and totally committed who played in two FA Cup finals for City, gaining a runner's-up medal in 1933 and winner's prize a year later, collecting his only Scotland cap (*v.* Wales) also in 1933. He made 125 appearances for Liverpool after leaving City and during the hostilities represented his country in wartime internationals, playing for the Army, an FA XI, an All-British XI, the Combined Services and the Scottish Command. Later, he became a brilliant manager with Manchester United, winning five League titles, the FA Cup twice and also the European Cup. Seriously injured in the Munich air crash, he was awarded the CBE in 1958, handed the Freedom of the City of Manchester in 1967 and a year later was knighted. To say 'thank you and goodbye' to one of the great men of Manchester, around 100,000 lined the streets for his funeral in 1994. Busby 'managed' Manchester United for twenty-six years, the same as Sir Alex Ferguson.

C

CAICEDO, Felipe Salvador Corozo (Forward)
Apps/goals: 35/7 Born: Guayaquil, Ecuador, 5/9/1988
    Career: Barcelona SC, Rocafuerte, FC Basle, CITY (£5.2 million, January 2008-July 2011), Sporting SP, Malaga, Levante, Lokomotiv Moscow (£6 million).

Details: The scorer of nine goals in thirty-five internationals for Ecuador, Felipe Caicedo's first ten appearances for City came off the bench, but generally he slipped in and out of contention during his time with the club, although he did net, with a cheeky back-heeler, a PL gamed against WBA and scored a real beauty in a 3-1 UEFA Cup win over Racing Santander in December 2008.

CAINE, James (Wing-half)
Apps: 1 Born: Manchester, 1871
Died: Manchester, c. 1940
    Career: Ardwick Lads' Club, CITY (March 1892–May 1894), Newton Heath.

Details: A reserve right-half, Jim Caine deputised for Harry Middleton in a 2-1 League defeat at Newcastle in October 1893. He didn't figure at all for Newton Heath.

CALDERWOOD, James Cuthbertson (Defender)
Apps: 37 Born: Busby, Lanarkshire,
19/12/1898 Died: 10/6/1968
   Career: Manchester Calico Printers FC, CITY (trial/signed, October 1922–July 1927), Grimsby Town; retired injured, May 1930.
   Details: Able to play in both full-back positions and also at right-half, Jim Calderwood proved an excellent standby for City. He helped Grimsby gain promotion in 1929.

CALLAGHAN, Thomas (Outside-right)
Apps: 2 Born: Brookfield, Glossop, 1885
Died: c. 1944
   Career: Glossop, CITY (June 1907–August 1909), Partick Thistle.
   Details: Tom Callaghan, understudy to George Stewart, made his two League appearances for City in away games at Notts County (0-1) and Bury (0-0) in February 1908, having very little impact.

CALVEY, Mitchell (Centre-forward)
Apps/goals: 7/5 Born: Blackburn, 1870
Died: c. 1951
   Career: Belfast Distillery, Blackburn Rovers, CITY (May 1894/October 1894), Baltimore Orioles, Bacup; retired 1904.
   Details: Mitch Calvey was one of four City players who moved to America in 1894 to join coach A.W. Stewart – the others being Archie Ferguson, Tommy Little and Alec Wallace. Before he left for the States, he scored on his League debut for City in a 4-2 defeat at Bury (the Shakers' first-ever League game) and netted twice in games against Burslem Port Vale (won 4-1) and Rotherham Town (lost 2-3). He was a good player – pity he left!

CAMPBELL, Bernard William (Forward)
Apps/goals: 1/2 Born: Scotland, 1865
Died: c. 1927
   Career: Ayr United, CITY (May 1890–June 1892), Darwen; retired 1900
   Details: Signed with three other Scots – Bill Douglas, John McWhinnie and Davie Robson – Bill Campbell scored twice in City's first-ever FA Cup match, a 12-0 win over Liverpool Stanley in October 1890.

CANN, Sydney Thomas (Right-back)
Apps: 46 Born: Torquay, 30/10/1911
Died: Devon, c. 1998
   Career: Babbacombe County School, Babbacombe FC, Torquay United, CITY (March 1930–June 1935), Charlton Athletic; during the Second World War served in the APTC, also a guest for Aldershot, Bristol City and Torquay United; retired 1946; Southampton (trainer/masseur, assistant-manager, then manager, secretary-manager, secretary), FA coaching post;

Wycombe Wanderers (manager-coach), Norwich City (coach), Sutton United (manager-coach); British College of Physiotherapy (masseur); keen motorist and fisherman.
   Details: England schoolboy international who helped City reach the 1933 FA Cup final, Syd Cann was associated with football for fifty years as a player, coach and manager. He made over 100 club appearances and had his best season with City in 1932/33 when he played in thirty-two competitive games as partner to Billy Dale. He guided Sutton to two FA Amateur Cup finals, losing both, in 1963 and 1969.

CAPEL, Thomas (Forward)
Apps/goals: 13/4 Born: Chorlton-on-Medlock,
Manchester, 27/6/1922 Died: Nottingham,
5/10/2009
   Career: Droylsden, CITY (November 1941–October 1947), Chesterfield, Birmingham City, Nottingham Forest, Coventry City, Halifax Town, Heanor Town; served with the Royal Marines during the Second World War.
   Details: Tommy Capel was a powerful, bustling player who had his best years with Nottingham Forest for whom he scored seventy-two goals in 162 appearances (1949–54). Ironically he made his League debut for City against his future club Chesterfield in January 1947, with his first goal following in his next game, the winner at Millwall. He played with his son, Fred, at Chesterfield.

CARDWELL, Louis (Half-back)
Apps: 45 Born: Blackpool, 20/8/1912 Died: 1986
   Career: Whitegate Juniors, Blackpool, CITY (September 1938–February 1947); Second World War guest for Blackpool, Millwall, Port Vale and West Ham United; Crewe Alexandra; served in the RAF during Second World War.
   Details: Having made 132 League appearances for Blackpool, 'Larry' Cardwell took over at centre-half at Maine Road six games into the 1938/39 season, retaining his place with some fine displays as City finished fifth in the First Division. After playing in forty-five Second World War games, he lost his place to Les McDowall when peacetime football resumed in 1946.

CARRODUS, Frank (Midfield/forward)
Apps/goals: 48/2 Born: Manchester, 31/5/1949
   Career: Manchester & District Schools, Lymm GS Old Boys, Altrincham OB, Heyes Albion, Altrincham, CITY (£5,000, November 1969–July 1974), Aston Villa (£95,000), Wrexham (£70,000); went on 'rebel tour' to South Africa (summer 1982); Birmingham City, Bury, Witton Albion, Runcorn, Altrincham, Macclesfield Town; retired 1988; now lives in Altrincham; runs owns hospitality company and former joint-secretary of

the Manchester City Old Players' Association (with Roy Clarke); he is a pigeon fancier and keen hiker.

Details: Frank Carrodus was employed as a civil servant before becoming a professional footballer. Hard-working with a terrific engine, he made over 350 club appearances during his career, twice winning the League Cup with Aston Villa (1975 and 1977) and collecting a runner's-up prize in same competition with City in 1974, which effectively crowned his best season at Maine Road (twenty-three outings).

CARROLL, Francis (Inside-forward)
Apps: 20 Born: Beesbrook, 11/6/1897
Died: after 1950
Career: Belfast Celtic, CITY (November 1920–May 1925), Newry Town.

Details: Frank Carroll made his first twelve appearances for City in succession between 6 November 1920 and 8 January 1921, ten in the inside-right position. Thereafter he was basically a reserve forward, adding just eight more games to his tally in four years before slipping into non-League football.

CARSON, Adam (Forward)
Apps/goals: 9/3 Born: Glasgow, 1868
Died: c. 1935
Career: Glasgow Thistle, Newton Heath, CITY (March 1893–February 1894), Liverpool.

Details: Highly-rated north of the border, Adam Carson represented the Scottish League before joining Newton Heath for whom he made thirteen appearances. After a run of nine successive League outings for City he spent his last six months in the reserves.

CARTER, Steven Charles (Outside-right)
Apps/goals: 8/2 Born: Great Yarmouth, 23/4/1953
Career: Norfolk Schools, CITY (July 1968–January 1972), Notts County (£18,000), Derby County, Minnesota Kicks (loan), Notts County, Bournemouth, Torquay United, Lymington FC.

Details: Steve Carter was a clever winger who found it increasingly hard to get into City's first team. He finally made his League debut aged seventeen, at Newcastle in April 1971, taking over from Neil Young who was rested ahead of the ECWC semi-final clash with Chelsea. He struck his first goal in a 2-2 draw with Liverpool two weeks later. His expertise from the penalty spot helped Notts County consolidate themselves in the Second Division following a long spell in the lower Leagues. In all, he hit twenty-six goals in 223 games for the Magpies.

CARTWRIGHT, James Ernest (Outside-left)
Apps/goals: 47/5 Born: Lower Walton, 11/12/1888 Died: 1960

Career: Northwich Victoria, CITY (October 1913–June 1921), Crystal Palace, Llanelli; retired 1926.

Details: 'Joe' Cartwright was a sprightly winger, initially reserve to Billy Wallace, who made twenty-five of his appearances during the last season before First World War. After playing sixty games during the hostilities, he was eventually replaced by 'Spud' Murphy in September 1919.

CASSIDY, James Alexander (Inside-right)
Apps: 3 Born: Lurgan, Northern Ireland, 1911 Died: Ireland, c. 1977
Career: Lurgan BC, Newry Town, CITY (October 1935–June 1937), Tranmere Rovers, Dundalk; retired during the Second World War.

Details: Reserve Jim Cassidy made his City debut in a reshuffled forward-line in a 4-0 defeat at Preston in October 1935 when Fred Tilson was away on international duty. His second outing followed in late December, in a 5-1 thrashing at WBA, while his last game was a 0-0 draw with Chelsea in September 1936.

CASSIDY, Joseph (Forward)
Apps/goals: 32/14 Born: Dalziel, Lanarkshire, 30/7/1872 Died: Manchester, c. 1933
Career: Motherwell Athletic, Blythe FC, Newton Heath, Celtic, Newton Heath, CITY (record £250, April 1900/May 1901), Middlesbrough (£75), Workington (player-coach); retired 1908.

Details: Joe Cassidy earned £4 a week with City and he did very well, scoring some decisive goals, but the management thought he was earning too much money so he was sold to Middlesbrough at a loss!

He netted 100 goals in 174 games for Newton Heath and followed with another thirty-four in 135 starts for Middlesbrough, having the pleasure of scoring the first-ever goal at Ayresome Park.

Sadly, Cassidy had a mental breakdown in April 1916.

CASTILLO, Nery Alberto Canfalonieri (Forward)
Apps: 9 Born: San Louis Potosi, Mexico, 13/6/1984
Career: Danubio, Olympiacos, Shakhtar Donetsk, CITY (loan, January-May 2008), Dnipro (loan), Chicago Fire (loan), Aris (loan/signed), Pachuca (loan), Léon.

Details: Pacy Mexican international, capped twenty-one times (six goals scored), Nery Castillo made his City debut in the FA Cup against West Ham soon after starting his loan spell with the club.

CATON, Thomas Stephen (Defender)
Apps/goals: 198/8 Born: Kirkby, Liverpool, 6/10/1962 Died: Oxford, 30/4/1993

Career: Merseyside Schools, Liverpool Boys, CITY (July 1979-December 1983), Arsenal (£500,000), Oxford United (£80,000), Charlton Athletic (£100,000).

Details: Tommy Caton made his League debut as a sixteen-year-old against Crystal Palace in August 1979 – qualifying as one of the club's youngest players (with Paul Simpson and Glyn Pardoe). Taking over from Dave Watson, he never missed a match that season (playing in all forty-seven games), making him one of the game's youngest footballers ever to complete his first full term in senior football while still a teenager.

He reached the milestone of 100 First Division games on 6 March 1982, at the age of nineteen years and five months – the youngest player in Football League history to achieve this feat. Also named City's 'Player of the Year' in 1981/82, two of his eight goals for City were scored against his future club Arsenal in December 1982. Following relegation from the top flight in 1983 – when David Pleat's Luton Town won at Maine Road on the final day of the season – Caton was unwilling to remain with the club and handed in a transfer request. He eventually left for Highbury having played two games short of 200 for City. An England schoolboy and youth international, Caton went on to win fourteen U21 caps (ten with City) and was a loser in both the 1979 Youth and 1981 FA Cup finals with the Blues. He sadly collapsed and died near his home when still a Charlton player. Four years earlier, he had escaped death after falling through a plate glass window when saving a young boy from serious injury. He had forty-eight stitches and two skin grafts to his left arm. Caton's brother, Paul, was associated with City in 1983/84.

CHADWICK, Graham (Half-back)
Apps: 14 Born: Oldham, 8/4/1942

Career: Manchester Boys, CITY (September 1959–July 1964), Walsall, Chester City.

Details: Graham Chadwick made thirty-three League appearances during his career, being a reserve with each of his three clubs. He made his City debut against Ipswich Town in September 1962, playing his last game against Southampton some two years later.

CHANNON, Michael Roger (Striker)
Apps/goals: 94/30 Born: Orcheston, 28/11/1948

Career: Shrewton U/11s, Amesbury Secondary Modern School, Salisbury & Wiltshire Schools, Southampton, Durban Celtic/South Africa (loan), CITY (record, £300,000, July 1977–September 1979), Cape Town City/South Africa (loan), Southampton, Newcastle KB United/Australia (loan), Gosnells City (loan), Caroline Hills/Hong Kong (loan), Newcastle United, Bristol Rovers, Norwich City, Durban City (loan), Miramar

Rangers, Portsmouth, Finn Harps/Ireland; retired May 1987); has been a successful racehorse trainer since 1990, having stables at West Isley near Newbury.

Details: A big, strongly-built forward with good pace and powerful shot, Mick Channon scored twenty-one goals in forty-six full internationals for England between 1972 and 1977, being the player capped most times by boss and former City player Don Revie.

His transfer to Maine Road in 1977 led to the departure of Joe Royle, but he soon made his mark, netting fourteen goals in his first season and top-scoring with fifteen in 1978/79, finishing with an average of one goal every three games during his two full seasons at the club, although his confidence ebbed away slightly after his first.

Well-known for his swirling arm 'windmill celebration' after scoring, Channon made over 850 appearances in all competitions and bagged almost 300 goals. In fact, he became the first Southampton player to reach the milestone of 200 goals when he scored against City in January 1980.

In the Football League alone, Channon netted 232 times in 717 appearances, won the FA Cup with Saints (*v.* Manchester United) in 1976 and the League Cup with Norwich (and Asa Hartford) in 1985. He also gained nine England U23 caps and twice represented the Football League.

Among the owners who have their horses trained at Channon's stables are two former City managers, Kevin Keegan and Alan Ball, and also Sir Alex Ferguson.

CHANTLER, Christopher (Midfield)
Apps: 1 Born: Cheadle Hulme, 16/12/1990

Career: CITY (June 1998, professional, December 2007–January 2012), Carlisle United (loan/signed).

Details: Chris Chantler was signed by City at the age of seven, spotted by former player Neil Young. Graduating from the club's Reserves and Academy he was in the elite development squad when he made his senior debut as a late substitute in the 2010 Europa League game against Juventus FC on his twentieth birthday in 2010.

CHAPELOW, Herbert (Outside-right)
Apps: 7 Born: Cheshire, 1888 Died: c. 1961.

Career: Chorley, CITY (May 1909–August 1911), Middlesbrough.

Details: Signed as cover for Stewart, Bert Chapelow made his City debut at inside-left in a 2-1 home defeat by Blackpool on the opening day of the 1909/10 season. His other six outings were all on the wing, with his best display coming in the 6-0 win over Wolves a week before Christmas when he assisted in two of Irvine Thornley's three goals.

CHAPLIN, John Fowler (Left-back)
Apps: 17 Born: Dundee, 10/10/1882 Died: after 1945

Career: Dundee Wanderers, Dundee, Tottenham Hotspur, Dundee, CITY (November 1910–November 1913), Leeds City; retired during the First World War.

Details: Well-built with a good, strong kick, Jack Chaplin took over from the injured Frank Norgrove and held the left-back position comfortably until the aforementioned defender returned in mid-March.

CHAPMAN, Thomas (Centre-half)
Apps/goals: 28/3 Born: Newtown, Monmouthshire, 1871 Died: 1929

Career: Newtown Excelsior, Newtown, CITY (April 1895/May 1896), Grimsby Town, Chatham, Maidstone United.

Details: A Welsh international (seven caps) Tom Chapman also represented the Football League and won the Welsh Cup with Newtown in 1895. He was a sturdy player who kicked, headed and tackled with equal power and judgement. Made his City debut in a 1-0 win over Woolwich Arsenal in September 1895 and scored his first goal a month later in 4-1 victory over Darwen.

CHAPPELL, Trevor (Goalkeeper)
Apps: 8 Born: Leicester, 1873 Died: Manchester, c. 1935

Career: Leicester Fosse, West Manchester, CITY (March 1896, retired injured, July 1900).

Details: Trevor Chappell provided excellent cover for Charlie Williams, producing solid performances when called into the first team, especially in goalless draws with his former club, Leicester Fosse, and Burton Swifts and in the 9-0 home battering of the Swifts during the last month of the 1897/98 season.

CHARVET, Laurent Jean (Right-back)
Apps/goals: 23/1 Born: Beziers, France, 8/5/1973

Career: Cannes, Chelsea, Newcastle United (£750,000), CITY (£1 million, October 2000–October 2002), Sochaux/France.

Details: Bought by manager Joe Royle as a replacement for out of form Richard Edghill, Laurent Charvet failed to be the right-back many City fans had hoped for and lost his place in the team. In the following season, after Kevin Keegan had taken over from Royle, Charvet was given a second chance, but found it difficult to fit into the 3-5-2 formation adopted by 'KK', and in the end Shaun Wright-Phillips was preferred to the Frenchman in the right-wing back position, as was a rejuvenated Edghill. Charvet won the ECWC in 1998 with Chelsea and played in the 1999 FA Cup final for Newcastle. After recovering from a broken hand sustained in a domestic accident, he opted to sever his ties with City and move back to France.

CHEETHAM, Roy Alexander John (Defender)
Apps/goals: 143/6 Born: Eccles, 21/12/1939

Career: Manchester Boys, CITY (July 1955–January 1968), Detroit Cougars/USA, Charlton Athletic, Chester City.

Details: Roy Cheetham was the first substitute used by City – introduced in place of Mike Summerbee in the 4-2 League win at Wolves on 30 August 1965. Ever reliable, he gave the club excellent service, and after his initial games alongside Dave Ewing in 1957/58, he was in and out of the first team over the next ten years, having his best prolonged spells in League action in 1959/60, 1961/62 and 1953–64. His last outing for City was at WBA in December 1967.

CHRISTIE, John (Right-back)
Apps: 10 Born: Manchester, 1879 Died: c. 1955

Career: Sale Holmefield, Manchester United, CITY (May 1904–September 1907), Bradford Park Avenue, Croydon Common, Brentford; retired 1914.

Details: Due to the good form of Johnny McMahon and also Tommy Kelso, John Christie managed only ten League appearances for City in three seasons, although his debut was as an emergency left-half in a 1-0 win over Stoke in January 1905.

CHRISTIE, Trevor John (Centre-forward)
Apps/goals: 10/3 Born: Newcastle, 28/2/1959

Career: Leicester City, Notts County (£80,000), Nottingham Forest (£165,000), Derby County (£100,000), CITY (August–October 1986), Walsall (£30,000), Mansfield Town (£30,000), Kettering Town, Rugby Town, Hucknall Town (player-coach), Arnold Town; retired 1996; became a salesman in Mansfield.

Details: Signed in a part-exchange deal involving Mark Lillis, Trevor Christie spent only ten weeks at Maine Road, during which time he led the attack in all ten games he played in, scoring on his debut in a 3-1 win over Wimbledon, while netting twice in a 2-2 draw with Norwich. During a lengthy career he bagged 147 goals in 497 League appearances, helping Notts County, Derby and Walsall all gain promotion.

CLARE, Thomas (Full-back)
Apps: 1 Born: Congleton, Cheshire, 12/3/1865 Died: Ladysmith, Vancouver, Canada, 27/12/1929

Career: Congleton Schools, Talke Rangers, Goldenhill Wanderers, Burslem Port Vale, Stoke, Burslem Port Vale, CITY (trial, March 1898), Burslem Port Vale (player-coach; retired April

1899; later secretary-manager); emigrated to Canada, summer 1907.

Details: A right-back of thoughtful bent, Tommy Clare was quick and resolute, good in the air and strong on the ground. Hardly ever 'roasted' by a winger who had one outing for City, as trialist in a 2-0 defeat at Newcastle. He gave Stoke excellent service for thirteen years, making 251 appearances and playing in the Potters' first-ever League game *v.* WBA in September 1888. Capped by England four times (1889–94), he also represented the Football League.

CLARK, Gordon Vincent (Right-back)
Apps: 64 Born: Gainsborough, 16/4/1914 Died: London, 18/10/1997

Career: Goldthorpe United, Southend United, Denaby United, CITY (January 1936–April 1947); Second World War guest for Accrington Stanley, Stockport County and Wrexham; Hyde United, Waterford (player-manager); Distillery (manager), Aldershot (manager), West Bromwich Albion (chief scout, assistant-manager, then manager), Sheffield Wednesday (assistant-manager), Peterborough United (manager), Arsenal (chief scout), Fulham (assistant-manager), Philadelphia Fury/USA (coach), Queen's Park Rangers (assistant-manager).

Details: Gordon Clark was signed as cover for Billy Dale and eventually took over the right-back position to form a useful partnership with Sam Barkas. A City player for eleven years, he made 180 appearances during Second World War and as a manager took Peterborough into the semi-final of the League Cup (1966).

CLARKE, Jeffrey Derrick (Defender)
Apps: 15 Born: Hemsworth near Pontefract, 18/1/1954

Career: Pontefract Schools, CITY (August 1971–June 1975), Sunderland, Newcastle United, Brighton & Hove Albion (loan), MKE Ankaragucu/Turkey, Whitley Bay; retired 1988; Newcastle United (Community Officer, later assistant-coach); qualified as a physiotherapist under the PFA scheme in 1995.

Details: Jeff Clarke made over 300 League appearances for the two North East clubs after leaving City. Ideally built, he was a good old-fashioned stopper centre-half who found it tough to get into the first XI at Maine Road.

CLARKE, Royston James (Outside-left)
Apps/goals: 370/79 Born: Crindau, Newport, South Wales, 1/6/1925 Died: Sale, Cheshire, 13/3/2006

Career: Albion Rovers, Cardiff City, CITY (record £12,000, April 1947–September 1958), Stockport County (player, then player-coach,

caretaker-manger), Northwich Victoria, Whalley Grange; retired 1963; later ran his own sports business; CITY (social club manager to 1988; also joint-secretary of the Manchester City Old Boys Association (with Frank Carrodus); served with the ATC during the Second World War.

Details: Roy Clarke played three consecutive League games in three different Divisions in 1947 – for Cardiff *v.* Exeter City in the Third Division (S) on 17 May 1947, for City in the Second Division against Newport County on 14 June and for City again *v.* Wolves in the First Division on 23 August.

Fast and clever, and lightweight (barely 10 stone 4lbs), he was City's top scorer in 1949/50 with ten goals, netted ten more in 1951/52 and struck another ten in 1954/55, one a brilliant diving header to beat Sunderland in the Villa Park mud in the 1955 FA Cup semi-final.

Capped twenty-two times at senior level by Wales (1949–56) he also made one Second World War international appearance.

As a teenager, Clarke played international baseball for Wales. His brother, William played for Ipswich Town and Wales as an amateur.

CLARKE, Wayne (Striker)
Apps/goals: 23/2 Born: Willenhall, 28/2/1961

Career: West Midlands Boys, Wolverhampton Wanderers, Birmingham City, Everton (£500,000), Leicester City, CITY (January 1990–July 1992), Shrewsbury Town (loan), Stoke City (loan), Wolverhampton Wanderers (loan), Walsall, Shrewsbury Town, Telford United (player-manager); retired November 1996; became a postman.

Details: Well past his best when he joined City, Wayne Clarke came off the bench fourteen times for City, scoring his two goals as a substitute at Nottingham Forest (won 3-1, December 1990) and at home to West Ham (won 2-0, April 1992). Capped by England at schoolboy and youth team levels, Clarke's three brothers Allan (a full England international), Derek and Frank, all played professional football. Wayne himself netted over 150 goals in more than 500 appearances during his fifteen-year career, winning the League with Everton in 1987.

CLAY, John Harfield (Inside-forward)
Apps: 2 Born: Stockport, 22/11/1948

Career: Stockport Boys, CITY (July 1962–July 1968), Macclesfield Town.

Details: Registered with City for six years, John Clay made his two League appearances in his last season at Maine Road – as a substitute *v.* Wolves in October and as Colin Bell's deputy in a 2-0 defeat at WBA in December.

CLAYTON, Rex (Centre-forward)
Apps/goals: 4/2 Born: East Retford, Notts, 1916 Died: c. 1980
Career: Retford Locomotive, Retford Town, CITY (November 1935–June 1938), Bristol City (£750), Lincoln City; retired during Second World War.
Details: Rex Clayton arrived at City as a raw-boned nineteen-year-old. A reserve during his time at Maine Road, he was one of six players used in the centre-forward position during the 1937/38 season, scoring on his debut in a 6-1 win over Derby County.

CLEMENTS, Kenneth Henry (Defender)
Apps/goals: 282/2 Born: Middleton, 9/4/1955
Career: Middleton YC, Oldham Athletic ('B' team), CITY (July 1972–September 1979), Oldham Athletic (record, £200,000), CITY (loan, March 1985, signed for £20,000, June 1985–March 1988), Bury, Limerick (player-manager), Shrewsbury Town, Curzon Ashton; retired 1992; opened a driving school near Oldham, resumed his interest in painting and now works as a chauffeur for Manchester property tycoon Aneel Mussarat at MCR Property Ltd in Rusholme, Manchester UK.
Details: A decidedly good, honest footballer, strong in the air, Kenny Clements gave as good as he got and produced some sterling performances during his two spells at Maine Road. After establishing himself in the team in 1975/76, accompanying Willie Donachie at full-back, he continued as first-choice alongside the Scot until breaking his leg in a clash with the Ipswich defender Kevin Beattie in November 1978. This set him back, and by the time he had regained full fitness, Ray Ranson had taken over his position. A Football League representative, Clements left for Oldham in a record deal and after making 182 League appearances for the Latics, returned to Maine Road where he spent another three years.

CLICHY, Gael (Left-back)
Apps: 74 Born: Toulouse, France, 26/7/1985
Career: Hersoise, Cugnaux, Muret, Tournefeuille, Cannes (all France), Arsenal, CITY (£7 million, July 2011).
Details: After 187 Premiership appearances for Arsenal, Gael Clichy moved to City on a four-year deal. He made his first competitive appearance against Manchester United in the FA Community Shield, and his first Premier League start against Swansea straight after. Sent off in his eleventh PL game against Chelsea, he returned to become a key player in the championship-winning season, thus collecting his second winner's medal in this competition, following his first with Arsenal in 2004. He also won the FA Cup with the Gunners in 2005. An attacking full-back with good recovery skills, he was capped by his country at every level from U15 to U19, and also at U21, and has now played in seventeen full internationals.
At the age of fifteen while playing for Cannes, Clichy nearly died. After climbing over a metal fence surrounding the club's ground, a ring he was wearing got caught in the framework that resulted in the skin and tissue from the fourth finger of his right hand being completely torn off. During the seven-hour operation to repair the finger, Clichy's heart stopped beating due to a problem with his lungs. It restarted after fifteen seconds. The doctor who led the operation described his survival as 'a miracle.'

CLIFFORD, Hugh (Half-back)
Apps: 4 Born: Glasgow, 4/5/1866 Died: Glasgow, 1942
Career: Renton, Carfin Shamrock, Stoke, Celtic, CITY (July 1895/March 1896); retired injured.
Details: Hughie Clifford was banned from playing football for two years following illegally signing for Celtic after walking out on Stoke in a raging temper. He attempted to resurrect his career with City but failed.

CLOUGH, Nigel Howard (Forward)
Apps/goals: 43/5 Born: Sunderland, 19/3/1966
Career: AC Hunters FC, Heanor Town, Nottingham Forest, Liverpool, CITY (£1.5 million, January 1996–May 1998), Nottingham Forest (loan), Sheffield Wednesday (loan), Burton Albion (player, then player-manager); Derby County (manager).
Details: Son of Brian, Nigel Clough played in all of City's remaining fifteen PL (plus three FA Cup ties) following his arrival at Maine Road in 1996, but his efforts could not stave off relegation and after more twenty-five appearances the following season, when he also lost his place in the team due to injury, he was loaned out to his former club, Nottingham Forest. Although he returned to City, he did not play for the club again. During a fine career with his four major League clubs, Clough scored 145 goals in 499 appearances, 131 in 412 outings for Forest alone. He gained two League Cup and two FMC winner's medals while at The City Ground and after entering non-League football with Burton, he won the NPL and Conference titles in 2002 and 2009. After playing in fifteen U21 internationals for England, he made his senior debut in May 1989 *v.* Chile, collecting his fourteenth and final cap four years later *v.* Germany. He also played in three 'B' internationals.

CODLING, Rowland James (Left-half)
Apps: 5 Born: Durham, 7/10/1879 Died: 1940
Career: Durham YC, Stockton, Swindon Town, Stockport County, Clapton Orient, Aston Villa,

Northampton Town, Croydon Common, CITY (August 1910/May 1911), Denton; retired 1914.

Details: Sturdy defender Roly Codling was almost thirty-one when he joined City, signed to strengthen the squad after promotion, having five outings in a row in September/October 1910. During his sixteen-year career, he made over 200 first-class appearances, helping Villa to runner's-up spot in the First Division.

COLBRIDGE, Clive (Forward)

Apps/goals: 65/12 Born: Hull, 27/4/1934

Career: Hull City, Leeds United, York City, Workington, Crewe Alexandra, CITY (May 1959–February 1962), Wrexham.

Details: Clive Coldridge scored thirty goals in 112 games in four seasons of lower League football before joining City.

A neat and tidy footballer with strong shot, he replaced Ray Sambrook on the left-wing and, adapting quickly to First Division football, he had an excellent 1959/60 campaign, netting nine times in forty games, relegation being avoided by just three points. He only managed twenty-one starts in 1960/61 and hardly any the following session due to the presence of Dave Wagstaffe. He went on to score thirty-six goals in 133 games for Wrexham (to May 1965).

COLE, Andrew (Striker)

Apps/goals: 23/10 Born: Nottingham, 15 October 1971

Career: Arsenal, Fulham (loan), Bristol City (loan, then signed for £500,000), Newcastle United (£1.75 million), Manchester United (£7 million), Blackburn Rovers (£7.5 million), Fulham (free), CITY (free, July 2005/August 2006), Portsmouth, Birmingham City (loan), Sunderland, Burnley (loan), Nottingham Forest; retired November 2008; MK Dons (coach), Huddersfield Town (coach), Manchester United (assistant-coach).

Details: Perhaps the finest goal-scoring predator of his era, Andy Cole had everything – pace, control, strength and, above all, a wonderful knack of knowing where the net was, even with his back to goal and marked by six defenders!

The second-highest scorer in PL history (behind Alan Shearer with 260), Cole netted 187 times in the top flight and shares the record with Shearer for netting thirty-four goals in a single campaign. In a superb career he scored for six different PL clubs and overall struck off 290 goals in 646 club appearances. He won the First Division title with Newcastle, five Premierships, two FA Cups, two Charity Shields, the European Champions League and in the Intercontinental Cup with Manchester United and the League Cup with Blackburn. He was voted the PFA's Young Player of the Year and won the Golden Boot award in 1993/94. He is

one only four players to have netted five goals in a PL game (for Manchester United *v.* Ipswich in 1995), gained four full caps for England under four different managers (1995–99), played in eight U21 internationals (four goals scored), in one 'B' team game, as well as several schoolboy and youth matches.

A born-again Christian, Cole and Nick Barmby were the first two graduates from the FA's National School of Excellence to win a full cap for England (*v.* Uruguay in 1995).

It was a pity he chose United instead of City, for he only spent thirteen months with the Blues against his near seven years at Old Trafford. He missed the closing stages of his season with City due to injury, but not after he had scored some fine goals, as usual!

In 2000, Cole visited Zimbabwe and later returned to set up his own charity foundation called the Andy Cole Children's Foundation which helped AIDS orphans. He is also a distant relation of Mariah Carey.

COLEMAN, Anthony George (Forward)

Apps/goals: 104/16 Born: Ellesmere Port, 2/5/1945

Career: Marine, Ellesmere Port, Stoke City, Tranmere Rovers, Preston North End, Bangor City, Doncaster Rovers, CITY (£12,000, March 1967–October 1969), Sheffield Wednesday (£20,000), Blackpool, Cape Town & Durban City/South Africa, Southport, Stockport County, Macclesfield Town; retired 1992; ran a café in Waterloo, Liverpool, sold ice-cream on Crosby beach; now lives in Australia, employed as a driver for the State railway.

Details: A much-travelled winger, who served with fifteen different clubs, Tony Coleman was sometimes regarded as a problem boy, but nevertheless he was a fine footballer who created several chances for Neil Young, Colin Bell and Franny Lee. He certainly played his best football under Joe Mercer and the influential Malcolm Allison with City, and seven of his eight League goals proved crucial when the First Division title was won in 1968, while the two he scored in an FA Cup win at Blackburn the following season took City into the quarter-finals, with a Wembley triumph following in due course. Unfortunately, after an internal disagreement Coleman moved to Sheffield Wednesday.

COLOSIMO, Simon (Right-back)

Apps: 7 Born: Australia 24/8/1980

Career: South Melbourne, CITY (£800,000, July 2001/January 2002), KRC Genk.

Details: An Australian international with four Youth and thirteen full caps to his credit, Simon Colosimo started only one game of his seven outings for City – in a League Cup tie against Notts County. He was released after just six months.

COMRIE, Malcolm (Inside-forward)

Apps/goals: 17/1 Born: Denny, 1905
Died: before 1980

Career: Denny Hibernian, Brentford, CITY (July 1932–May 1934), Burnley, Crystal Palace, York City, Bradford City.

Details: Malcolm Comrie's career spanned ten years, ending on the outbreak of Second World War. He partnered Eric Brook on City's left-wing in a third of the matches in 1932–33, scoring his only goal for the club in a 4-1 win over Wolves the November. He had his best spell with York, netting twenty goals in seventy-nine League games between 1936 and 1938.

CONLIN, James (Outside-left)

Apps/goals: 175/30 Born: Durham,
6/8/1881 Died: Flanders, France, 23/6/1917

Career: Captain Colts Rovers, Cambuslang, Hibernian, Falkirk, Albion Rovers, Bradford City, Broadheath CITY (July 1906–September 1911), Birmingham, Airdrieonians, Broxburn United; killed while serving with the Highland Light Infantry.

Details: A diminutive winger, one of the smallest players of his era, Jimmy Conlin was continually under the hammer from the bigger and more bruising defenders who opposed him, but he always had a smile on his face – more so after he had created a chance, or even scored a goal! A born footballer, he was a wonderful crosser of the ball and was never afraid to cut inside and have a crack at goal. His played for England in the 2-1 defeat by Scotland at Hampden Park in 1906. A real character, he twice represented the Football League and won the Second Division championship with City in 1910.

CONLON, Barry John (Forward)

Apps: 8 Born: Drogheda, 1/10/1978

Career: Junior football, Carrick Rangers, Stella Maris, Dundalk, Carrick Rangers, Queen's Park Rangers, CITY (August 1997/September 1998), Plymouth Argyle (loan), Southend United (£95,000), York City (£100,000), Colchester United (loan), Darlington (£60,000), Barnsley, Rotherham United (loan), Darlington, Mansfield Town, Bradford City, Grimsby Town, Chesterfield, Stockport County, ROC de Charleroi-Marchienne/Belgium, Dundalk.

Details: Shortly before signing for City, Barry Conlon played for the Republic of Ireland internation under-nineteen team in the 1997 UEFA under-eighteen international championship finals in Iceland, scoring and getting sent off against Switzerland. He made his City debut in September 1997, as a late 'sub' for Georgi Kinkladze in a 6-0 win over Swindon Town FC. But his first-team appearances were limited to just one League start and six more substitute appearances before being released at the end of his year-long contract.

A 6-foot 3-inch, strong-running, left-footed player with good control, Conlon became a soccer journeyman after leaving Maine Road, going on to serve fourteen other clubs. At 2013 his overall record stood at 123 goals in 473 senior appearances – and he also played in seven U21 internationals for his country.

CONNOR, David Richard (Utility)

Apps/goals: 168/10 Born: Wythenshaw,
27/10/1945

Career: Manchester Boys, CITY (August 1962–January 1972), Preston North End (£40,000), CITY (March 1974/May 1975), Macclesfield Town (player, then manager).

Details: Dave Connor made only 130 League starts in his first ten years with City, but still gained many admirers for his enthusiasm and dedication, whereby he stood firm, turning down several opportunities to join another club. A versatile performer, he occupied every position except goalkeeper and centre-half and made ten appearances when City won the League title in 1967/68. Some say he had his best game for the Blues in the 1969 FA Cup semi-final win over Everton, his efforts earning him the substitute's spot in the final. After returning to Maine Road, he spent just over a season playing in the reserves.

CONSTANTINE, James (Centre-forward)

Apps/goals: 22/16 Born: Ashton-under-Lyne,
16/2/1920 Died: c. 1999

Career: Ashton National, Rochdale, CITY (April 1945–August 1947), Bury, Millwall, Tonbridge; retired 1955.

Details: Strong and forceful with a receding hairline, Jimmy Constantine, after top-scoring in 1945/46 with twenty-nine goals, got his City League career off to a great start by netting a hat-trick on his debut against his future club Millwall in September 1946. He later broke an ankle, but by then had already notched twelve goals, which went a long way in helping City win the Second Division title. Dubbed 'Connie' he later scored eighty-three goals in 153 appearances for the Lions, being top-striker three seasons running, and was Bury's leading marksman in 1947/48 with fourteen, including a hat-trick in a 7-1 win over Millwall at snow-bound Den in mid-February.

A Grenadier guardsman who was also a welterweight boxing champion in 1940/41, Constantine was knocked out playing for Ashton National in a local League game, and while in hospital was signed by Rochdale manager Ted Goodier.

CONWAY, James Patrick (Outside-right)
Apps/goals: 16/1 Born: Dublin, 10/8/1946
Career: Bohemians, Fulham, CITY (August 1976–January 1978), Portland Timbers; retired injured, 1979; Oregon State University (football coach).

Details: Jim Conway's winner at Coventry in May 1977 confirmed City as runner's-up in Division One. An Irish international at amateur and senior levels (winning twenty full caps) he was the only non-Englishman to feature in the 1975 FA Cup final, for Fulham *v.* West Ham before following coach Bill Taylor to Maine Road. Conway's son Paul played for Carlisle.

COOKE, Terence John (Wide-midfield)
Apps/goals: 42/8 Born: Marston Green, Birmingham, 5/8/1976
Career: Manchester United, Sunderland (loan), Birmingham City (loan), Wrexham, CITY (£1 million, January 1999–March 2002), Wigan Athletic (loan), Sheffield Wednesday (loan, two successive spells), Grimsby Town, Sheffield United (loan), Grimsby Town (free), Sheffield Wednesday (free), Chesterfield, Barnsley, Peterborough United, Kidderminster Harriers, Oldham Athletic, Colorado Rapids.

Details: An FA Youth Cup winner with Manchester United, Terry Cooke played for England at youth and U21 levels, but found it tough to gain regular first-team football with any of the clubs he served, a knee injury causing him a lot of problems.

COOKSON, Samuel (Full-back)
Apps/goals: 306/1 Born: Manchester, 22/11/1896 Died: 12/8/1955
Career: Stalybridge Celtic, Macclesfield, CITY (October 1918–September 1928), Bradford Park Avenue; retired 1933; returned with Barnsley; retired again, 1935.

Details: A former miner, Sammy Cookson, small, with powerful physique which proved deceptive to opponents, formed a long-term partnership with Eli Fletcher, the pair earning the accolade as 'best uncapped full-backs of the era.'

Initially paid 10s (50p) a week by City, he scored his only goal for the club in a 3-3 FA Cup draw with the Corinthians in January 1926. He later helped Barnsley win the Third Division (N) title at the age of thirty-nine. There is a road in Manchester called Sammy Cookson Close. His brother, Jimmy, a prolific goalscorer with Chesterfield and West Bromwich Albion, was a City reserve before his release in 1925.

COOPER, Paul David (Goalkeeper)
Apps: 17 Born: Brierley Hill, 21/12/1953
Career: Kingswood SM School, Staffs County Boys, Boney Hay Juniors, Cannock Athletic, Sutton Town, Birmingham City, Ipswich Town, Leicester City, CITY (£20,000, March 1989/August 1990), Stockport County; retired 1992; worked for a nut and bolt company in Liverpool.

Details: A very capable goalkeeper, agile and confident, Paul Cooper won the FA Cup and UEFA Cup with Ipswich and promotion with Stockport. He amassed over 500 club appearances and was an expert at saving penalties.

CORBETT, Frank William (Right-back)
Apps: 15 Born: Birmingham, 8/10/1909 Died: Birmingham, 20/11/1974
Career: Worcester City, Torquay United, CITY (March 1930–June 1936), Lincoln City; retired May 1939; became a fireman in Birmingham.

Details: Described as being 'very sound and steady' Frank Corbett (brother of Vic, below) failed to hold down a first-team place during his six years with City, having his best spell in the team halfway 1932/33 when he deputised for Syd Cann on seven occasions.

CORBETT, Victor John Samuel (Full-back)
Apps: 6 Born: Birmingham, 1908 Died: after 1950
Career: Bromsgrove Rovers, Worcester City, Hereford United, CITY (May 1933–May 1935), Southend United, Brierley Hill; retired 1939.

Details: Like his kid brother, Vic Corbett also struggled to get into City's first team, although he was only at the club for two years. He had a nightmare in a 4-1 defeat at Derby on Christmas Day in 1933. The Corbetts played together in City's second XI on several occasions.

CORLUKA, Vedran (Right-back)
Apps/goals: 47/1 Born: Derventa, Bosnia, 5/2/1986
Career: Inter Zapresic, Dinamo Zagreb, CITY (£7 million, August 2007/September 2008), Tottenham Hotspur (£8.5 million), Bayer Leverkusen (loan), Lokomotiv Moscow.

Details: Versatile 6-foot 3-inch Croatian international Vedran Corluka, who has forty-two intermediate and sixty full caps to his name, initially signed a five-year contract with City but left the club after barely 12 months! A consistent player, he was totally committed and despite a nightmare blunder during City's shocking 6–0 defeat to Chelsea FC, he remained strong during his first season in England when occasionally he was also used as a defensive midfielder, proving to be a factor for opposing attackers. He scored his only City goal in the 4–2 defeat by Aston Villa on the opening weekend of the 2008/2009 Premier League, but he also netted in the dramatic 4-2 penalty shoot-out victory over Midtjylland in a UEFA 2008/9 game. He played his last game for City against Sunderland AFC in August 2008, throwing his shirt into the crowd at the final whistle.

CORRADI, Bernardo (Striker)
Apps/goals: 29/3 Born: Sienna, Italy, 30/3/1976

Career: Siena, Poggibonsi, Ponsacco, Cagliari, Montevarchi, Fidelis Andra, Chievo, Inter Milan, SCC Lazio, Parma, Valencia, CITY (£2 million, July 2007/Jukly 2008), Parma (loan/signed), Reggina, Udinese, Montreal Impact.

Details: Experienced Italian striker with thirteen caps to his name, Bernardo Corradi never really hit it off at City. He was sent off twice – on his debut against Chelsea and in the Manchester derby – and his goal celebrations were quite bizarre!

CORRIGAN, Thomas Joseph (Goalkeeper)
Apps: 605 Born: Manchester, 18/11/1948

Career: Sale, CITY (September 1966–March 1983), Seattle Sounders, Brighton & Hove Albion, Norwich City (loan), Stoke City (loan); retired February 1985; left club, March 1985; later engaged as goalkeeping coach by Celtic, Middlesbrough, Tranmere Rovers, Barnsley, Liverpool and West Bromwich Albion.

Details: Joe Corrigan, 6 foot 4½ inches tall, became City's number one 'keeper in 1969 and, after losing his place and being transfer-listed, he buckled down to business and returned to the side. He was a permanent fixture between the posts from March 1975 until May 1982, having one superb run of 198 consecutive League appearances from 8 November 1975 to 23 August 1980. In fact, during his time with City, Corrigan was an ever-present four times. He gained European Cup Winner's Cup and League Cup winner's medals in 1971 and 1976, played in the 1981 FA Cup final, won nine full, one U23, three U21 and ten 'B' caps for England, represented the Football League, the FA and played for an England XI. Only Alan Oakes (680) has appeared in more senior games for City than 'Big Joe', who was voted City's 'Player of the Year' a record three times and holds the club record for most appearances in European competitions with twenty-seven. A braver, more efficient custodian would be hard to find.

COTON, Antony Philip (Goalkeeper)
Apps: 194 Born: Tamworth, 19/5/1961

Career: Mile Oak Rovers, Birmingham City, Watford (£330,000), CITY (£1 million, July 1990–January 1996), Manchester United, Sunderland; retired 1997; Manchester United (goalkeeping coach).

Details: Tony Coton saved a penalty with his first touch in League football – playing for Birmingham against Sunderland in 1980. Tall and strong with good reflexes and a safe pair of hands, he replaced Andy Dibble at Maine Road and had five-and-a-half excellent seasons between the posts for City before moving to Old Trafford, following the arrival of Eike Immel. Coton played once for England 'B'.

COUPE, Douglas (Full-back)
Apps: 1 Born: Worksop, 1886 Died: c. 1953

Career: Worksop, CITY (January 1908–May 1910); non-League football.

Details: Relatively unknown defender Doug Coupe's only game for City was in the 2-0 home League win over Grimsby in December 1909, when he deputised for Tommy Kelso.

COUPLAND, Clifford Arthur (Right-half)
Apps/goals: 27/2 Born: Grimsby, 29/5/1900 Died: 30/1/1969

Career: Haycroft Rovers, Grimsby Town, Mansfield Town, CITY (March 1925–July 1927), Grimsby Town, Caernarfon Town, Sittingbourne, Crystal Palace; retired 1932.

Details: A fine constructive wing-half with 'good speed, clever footwork and shooting power', Cliff 'Baggy' Coupland did well with Mansfield before replacing Harry Sharp at City, retaining his position for quite a while before Charlie Pringle was switched over from the left following the arrival of Jimmy McMullan.

COWAN, Samuel (Half-back)
Apps/goals: 407/24 Born: Chesterfield, 10/5/1901 Died: Haywards Heath, Sussex, 4/10/1964

Career: Ardwick Juniors, Huddersfield Town, Denaby United, Bullcroft Main Colliery, Doncaster Rovers, CITY (December 1924–October 1935), Bradford City (£2,000), Doncaster Rovers, Mossley; retired June 1938; Brighton & Hove Albion (coach); CITY (manager, November 1946-June 1947); set up his own physiotherapy practice in Brighton, being engaged by Sussex CCC and by the MCC, on tour to Australia, 1962/63; a keen motorist and swimmer, he also enjoyed boxing.

Details: Sam Cowan never kicked a football in earnest until he was seventeen, and in his first 'trial game' for Ardwick Juniors he only wore one boot! He became a great motivator who captained City for three years (1932–35), leading the team to successive FA Cup finals, winning the second in 1934. An international trialist, he gained three England caps (1926–31) and represented the Football League. An ever-present in 1934/35, he did not play at all the following season and was then sold to Bradford.

While refereeing a charity football match on behalf of the Sussex and England wicketkeeper-batsman Jim Parks, Cowan (aged sixty-two) collapsed on the pitch and died in the dressing room a few minutes later. There is a road in Manchester called Sam Cowan Close.

COWAN, William Duncan (Inside-forward)
Apps/goals: 23/11 Born: Edinburgh, 9/8/1896 Died: Scotland, c. 1962

Career: Tranent Juniors, Dundee, Newcastle United (£2.250), CITY (£3,000, May 1926/May 1927), St Mirren, Peebles Rovers, Northfleet, North Shields, Hartlepool United, Darlington, Bath City; retired 1933.

Details: Billy Cowan won the FA Cup with Newcastle and gained a Scottish cap before joining City. With ability in both feet, he possessed a potent shot and was always looking to have a crack at goal, scoring some fine goals including two in a 4-1 home win over Notts County in March 1927 as City pressed for promotion. One pen-picture described him as being 'a mazy dribbler with the leather.'

COWIE, Andrew (Outside-left)
Apps/goals: 11/3 Born: Lochee, 1879 Died: 1955

Career: Thames Ironworks, Gravesend United, CITY (June 1898–May 1900), Queen's Park Rangers, Woolwich Arsenal.

Details: A clever winger with good pace, Andy Cowie started very well with City, scoring and making goals, but injury intervened, and after George Dougal was switched from inside to outside-left he never got another chance.

COX, Walter (Goalkeeper)
Apps: 1 Born: Southampton, 1878 Died: 1945

Career: Southampton St Mary's, Bristol St George's, Bedminster, Millwall Athletic, CITY (May 1900/May 1901), Bury, Preston North End, Dundee; retired 1908.

Details: Wally Cox made his debut for Southampton as an outfield player before becoming a capable goalkeeper. His only game for City was against Preston in February 1901 when he deputised for Charlie Williams in a 3-1 win.

CRAWSHAW, Richard Leslie (Inside-forward)
Apps/goals: 26/6 Born: Manchester, 21/9/1899 Died: Manchester, 23/10/1977

Career: Stockport County, CITY (June 1919–July 1922), Halifax Town, Nelson, Stalybridge Celtic, Mossley; retired 1932; served in the Navy during Second World War; swimming, cricket and tennis were his pastimes.

Details: Dick Crawshaw formed part of a very good City frontline that included with Ernie Goodwin, Tommy Browell and Matt Barrass. He bagged all his goals in 1921/22, including a debut strike against Bolton. On Nelson's tour of Spain in 1923, Crawshaw netted against both Racing Santander and Real Madrid.

His nephew, Dick Duckworth, played for Chesterfield, Rotherham and York City.

CREANEY, Gerard Thomas (Forward)
Apps/goals: 25/5 Born: Coatbridge, 13/4/1970

Career: Celtic Boys' Club, Celtic, Portsmouth, CITY (£1 million, September 1995/1996), Oldham Athletic (loan), Ipswich Town (loan), Burnley (loan), Chesterfield (loan), St Mirren, Notts County, TPV/Finland, Raith Rovers, Queen of the South, Clydebank; retired 2001; Bellshill Athletic (manager).

Details: City swapped Paul Walsh for Scottish 'B' and U21 international Gerry 'Trigger' Creaney, but the striker never really bedded in at Maine Road and after loan spells with four Football League clubs he joined St Mirren. His career realised 105 goals in 303 club appearances.

CROFT, Lee David (Forward)
Apps/goals: 32/1 Born: Billinge Higher End, Wigan, 21/6/1985

Career: Garswood United, CITY (July 2001–August 2006), Oldham Athletic (loan), Norwich City (£585,000), Derby County, Huddersfield Town (loan), St Johnstone, Oldham Athletic.

Details: England youth and U20 international Lee Croft, a competent reserve with City, made his first-team debut in March 2005 against Bolton, coming on as a substitute in Kevin Keegan's final game in charge. With over 250 club appearances to his name, he was in the Oldham team that knocked Liverpool out of the FA Cup in January 2013.

CROOKS, Lee Robert, LAC (Midfield)
Apps/goals: 91/2 Born: Wakefield, 14/1/1978

Career: CITY (June 1994–March 2001), Northampton Town (loan), Barnsley (£190,000), Bradford City, Notts County (loan), Rochdale, Guiseley, Ossett Town; quitted football in 2000.

Details: Lee Crooks was a combative and versatile defender or midfielder, whose career was littered with foot and ankle injuries, yet he still amassed 222 appearances in the top three Divisions, including 196 in the Football League. A product of City's youth system, Crooks spent seven years at Maine Road during a turbulent period of promotion or relegation, including the 1999 Second Division Play-off Final against Gillingham FC. He played for England at youth and the FL U21 levels, the latter against their Italian counterparts, and made his League debut against Port Vale in September 1996. At the age of thirty-two, he embarked on a new career in the British Armed Forces, joining the infantry unit of the RAF.

CROSS, David (Striker)
Apps/goals: 38/13 Born: Heywood, Lancashire, 8/12/1950

Career: Heywood GS, Rochdale, Norwich City (£40,000), Coventry City (£150,000), West Bromwich Albion (£150,000), West Ham United (£200,000), CITY (£125,000, August 1972–April 1983), Vancouver Whitecaps (£75,000), Oldham Athletic, Vancouver Whitecaps, West Bromwich Albion, Bolton Wanderers, Bury (loan), Blackpool,

Heywood Old Boys; retired 1990; Oldham Athletic (U15s coach & assistant manager), Rochdale (scout); president of the Heywood Cricket Club; also a financial advisor for Allied Dunbar.

Details: A fine marksman in his day, David Cross netted over 200 goals in more than 600 club games during his career, finishing as City's leading striker in 1982/83 with thirteen goals, including one inside the first against his former club Norwich. He won the FA Cup and Second Division title with West Ham (1980 and 1981), gained promotion with the Canaries (1972) and helped the Whitecaps to the NASL Western title (1984).

CROSSAN, John Andrew (Midfield)
Apps/goals: 110/28 Born: Londonderry, Northern Ireland, 29/11/1938
Career: Derry City, Coleraine, Sparta Rotterdam/Holland, Standard Liege/Belgium, Sunderland (£27,000), CITY (£40,000, January 1965–August 1968), Middlesbrough (record £30,000), KSK Tongeren/Belgium; retired 1975.

Details: The recipient of twenty-four caps for Ireland (ten with City), Johnny 'Jobby' Crossan was a very skilful footballer with an eye for goal. As captain he helped City gain promotion in 1966, but when his place came under threat from Messrs Bell and Young, he switched to Ayresome Park. He later became injury prone and needed medical attention after suffering a severe bout of insomnia. He ended his career with more than 400 club appearances and 104 goals to his credit.

In January 1959, Crossan was handed a 'life time' suspension (from English football) by the FA for accepting an illegal payment from Derry City, but this was lifted when he joined Sunderland in 1962.

CUMMING, James Ferguson (Outside-right)
Apps/goals: 41/3 Born: Alexandria, 1890
Died: Scotland, 1961
Career: Clydebank Juniors, CITY (April 1913–March 1920), West Ham United; played non-League football from 1921.

Details: Jim Cumming had his best season with City in 1913/14, scoring three times in twenty-eight appearances when partnering Harry Taylor on the right-wing. His third goal was the winner in the Manchester derby in front of 36,000 fans at Old Trafford. He made fifteen appearances for the Hammers in their first season of League football.

CUNLIFFE, Robert (Inside-forward)
Apps/goals: 3/1 Born: Manchester, 17/5/1945
Career: CITY (July 1960–June 1965), York City.
Details: Reserve Bobby Cunliffe, who understudied Derek Kevan and Jimmy Murray at Maine Road, scored on his debut in a 1-1 draw with Plymouth Argyle in October 1963. Brother David was a City reserve, 1966–69.

CUNLIFFE, Robert Arthur (Outside-left)
Apps/goals: 49/10 Born: Ashfield-in-Makerfield, 27/12/1928
Career: Bryn, Garswood St Andrew's, CITY (September 1945–June 1956), Chesterfield, Southport; retired 1959.

Details: Bob Cunliffe top-scored for City's second XI in 1950/51, before going on to average a goal every five games for the first team, including strikes against Aston Villa (2-2) and WBA (won 2-0) in August and October 1955.

CUNNINGHAM, Anthony Eugene (Forward)
Apps/goals; 24/4 Born: Kingston, Jamaica, 12/11/1957
Career: Kidderminster Harriers, Stourbridge, Lincoln City (£20,000), Barnsley (£80,000), Sheffield Wednesday, CITY (£100,000, July 1984/February 1985), Newcastle United (£75,000), Blackpool (£25,000), Bury (£40,000), Bolton Wanderers (£70,000), Rotherham United (£50,000), Doncaster Rovers, Wycombe Wanderers, Gainsborough Trinity; retired 1995.

Details: In fifteen years of League football, Tony Cunningham scored 116 goals in 495 games with eleven different clubs, having by far his best spell with his first, Lincoln City (thirty-two in 123). He didn't complete the 1984/85 season with City, scoring his only League goal in a 3-0 win at Cardiff, plus three in the League Cup, two in a second-round win over his future club, Blackpool.

CUNNINGHAM, Gregory Richard (Left-back)
Apps: 5 Born: Carnmore, County Galway, 31/1/1991
Career: Cregmore FC, Mervue United, CITY (June 2007–May 2012), Leicester City (loan), Nottingham Forest, Bristol City.

Details: Selected by the Republic of Ireland at U17 and U21 levels, Greg Cunningham had three full caps to his name at May 2013, having gained his first against Armenia three years earlier. He played for City in four different competitions, making his senior debut as a substitute in a 5-1 win over Birmingham in April 2009.

CURLE, Keith (Defender)
Apps/goals: 204/13 Born: Bristol, 14/11/1963
Career: Bristol Rovers, Torquay United, Bristol City, Reading, Wimbledon, CITY (record £2.5 million, August 1991–August 1996), Wolverhampton Wanderers (£650,000, later player-coach), Sheffield United (player-coach), Barnsley, Mansfield Town (player-manager; retired as a player, 2005); Chester City (manager), Torquay United (manager), Notts County (manager).

Details: Keen-tackling defender Keith Curle, who skippered City for five years and was a huge favourite with the fans, amassed 827 appearances in a wonderful career. Britain's most expensive defender when signed from Wimbledon, Curle took over from Colin Hendry in City's back four and was outstanding in his first season at Maine Road, missing only three games, as the Blues finished fifth in the table. His form earned him a call-up to the England squad, debuting in April 1992 as a substitute in a 2–2 draw with the CIS in Moscow. After starting in a further warm-up game (*v.* Hungary) he was selected for Euro 92 where he covered at right-back in an opening goalless group game with Denmark. He won three full caps and played in four 'B' internationals. Nine of Curle's thirteen goals for City were penalties.

He was voted WBA's 'Player of the Year' in 1997/98 – after his own-goal when playing for Wolves, which won the Black Country derby at The Hawthorns!

CURRIER, James (Centre-forward)
Apps/goals: 113/84 (wartime only)
Born: Wednesbury, 20/1/1915 Died: c. 1981.

Career: Wednesbury BC, West Bromwich Albion (trial), Cheltenham Town, Bolton Wanderers, CITY (guest, April 1940–April 1943); also guest for Blackburn Rovers, Chester, Crewe Alexandra and Manchester United; retired 1946.

Details: Jim Currier is included because of his terrific scoring record for City as a Second World War guest. Of his eighty-four goals, forty-seven came in forty-two games in 1940/41, the same season which saw him bag six of his ten hat-tricks for the Blues, two of them five-timers, in 9-1 and 6-1 home and away wins over Rochdale in the space of seven days in January. Currier actually found the net in twenty-two of City's thirty-five North Regional League matches in 1940/41, having started off by scoring eleven times in four outings in 1939/40. He also struck twenty-six goals in 1942/43. For Bolton, he netted fourteen times in twenty-six First Division matches.

D

DABO, Ousmane (Midfield)
Apps: 18 Born: Laval, France, 8/2/1977

Career: Stade Rennais, Inter Milan, Vicenza (loan), Parma, AS Monaco, Vicenza (loan), Atalanta, SS Lazio, CITY (July 2006–January 2008), SS Lazio.

Details: A French international with three caps to his credit, Ousmane Dabo's spell with City was hampered by suspension and injury, resulting in only ten League starts in his first season and none in his second!

DALE, William (Full-back)
Apps: 271 Born: Manchester 17/2/1905 Died: Manchester, 12/6/1987

Career: Hugh Oldham Lads' Club, Sandbach Ramblers, Manchester United, CITY (December 1931–May 1938), Ipswich Town, Norwich City; retired during Second World War; was a fan of greyhound racing.

Details: Billy Dale joined City with Harry Rowley and Bill Ridding, plus a small fee going across town to United. He played in two FA Cup finals with City, gaining a winner's medal in the second (1934), and followed up with a First Division championship medal in 1937, playing in thirty-six of the forty-two matches as partner to Sam Barkas. One of the best uncapped full-backs of his day, Dale was 'cool and stylish, quick in recovery and cultured in distribution'.

DALEY, Stephen (Midfield)
Apps/goals: 54/4 Born: Barnsley, 15/4/1953

Career: Wolverhampton Wanderers, CITY (record £1.347 million, September 1979–February 1982), Seattle Sounders, Burnley, Walsall, San Diego Sockers, Lye Town, Kettering Town, Old Wulfrunians; retired 1995; worked in a brewery; later Telford United (manager), Bromsgrove Rovers (manager), Bilston Town (manager); now a publican in Birmingham.

Details: As a Wolves player, Steve Daley represented England at youth and 'B' team levels, and during his seven years at Molineux scored forty-three goals in 244 appearances, helping the Wanderers reach the 1972 UEFA Cup final and beat his future club, Manchester City in the League Cup final of 1974. He spent 2½ seasons at Maine Road, but was he worth the money? Some say not. He scored twice in thirty-six outings in his first season and twice in eighteen after that.

Daley's father, Alan, played for Mansfield, Hull, Coventry, Doncaster and others (1946–61).

DALZIEL, Gordon (Striker)
Apps: 6 Born: Motherwell, 16/3/1962

Career: Rangers, CITY (December 1983/September 1984), Partick Thistle, East Stirlingshire, Raith Rovers, Ayr United (player; retired 1998; manager); Glenafton Athletic (manager, two spells), Raith Rovers (manager).

Details: Gordon Dalziel, a stop-gap acquisition by manager Billy McNeill, made only half a dozen first-team appearances for City, his debut coming in a 1-0 League win at Chelsea forty-eight hours after signing. Dalziel's greatest success as a player was achieved at Raith where he became the club's top goal scorer of all time, winning the Scottish League Cup in 1994/5 as well as two Scottish Football League First Division titles. In his first managerial job, he guided Ayr to the Scottish League Cup final and Scottish Cup semi-final in the same year (2002). He was later sacked after failing to get the club into the Scottish Premier League.

DANIELS, Arthur W. C. (Outside-left)

Apps: 32 Born: Mossley, 9/5/1901

Career: Salford Lads' Club, Mossley, CITY (August 1920–May 1926), Watford, Queen's Park Rangers.

Details: Arthur Daniels played in City's second XI for 2½ years before making his League debut (in place of 'Spud' Murphy) in a 3-1 defeat at Tottenham in March 1923. He was in and out of the team thereafter and went on to score eighteen goals in 136 League games for Watford.

DANIELS, Bernard Joseph (Forward)

Apps/goals: 14/2 Born: Salford, 24/11/1950

Career: Manchester United (junior), Ashton United, CITY (March 1973–July 1975), Chester, Stockport County.

Details: Barney Daniels was twenty-two when he joined City and was top scorer for second XI in successive Central League seasons of 1973/74 and 1974/75, while his two senior goals came in a 4-1 win over Leicester. Unfortunately, he failed to make headway in the first team due, no doubt, to the form of Messrs Law, Lee, Bell and Marsh!

DARTNELL, Herbert (Forward)

Apps: 4 Born: Northampton, c. 1879 Died: after 1945

Career: Wellingborough, CITY (April 1900/ December 1901), Barnsley, Wellingborough; retired 1907.

Details: Normally an outside-left, Bert Dartnell was leading scorer for City's second XI in 1900/01. He made the first of his four League starts in a 4-0 win over West Bromwich Albion eleven days after signing.

DAVIDSON, Alexander (Forward)

Apps/goals: 7/1 Born: Beith, Ayrshire, 1879

Career: Beith FC, Third Lanark, Glossop, CITY (March 1899–June 1901), Reading, West Ham United, Luton Town, Fulham, New Brompton, Kilmarnock; retired 1915.

Details: Alex Davidson's lonely goal for City clinched a 2-0 win over his former club Glossop in March 1900. He spent only a month with Fulham, but still made over 200 appearances in the Southern League after leaving City.

DAVIDSON, David (Half-back)

Apps: 1 Born: Govan Hill, Scotland, 20/8/1934

Career: Glentyne Thistle, CITY (August 1951–July 1958), Workington.

Details: Dave Davidson had virtually a seven-year hitch at Maine Road, spending the majority of City days in the reserves. His solitary first-team appearance came in a 3-2 defeat at Bolton in October 1953 when he deputised for Roy Paul, who was on international duty with Wales.

DAVIDSON, Duncan (Forward)

Apps/goals: 7/1 Born: Elgin, Scotland, 5/7/1954

Career: Sea Bee/Hong Kong, CITY (September 1983/July 1984); entered Highland League football.

Details: Duncan Davidson's only goal for City proved to be the winner at home to Swansea (2-1) in October 1983. He made his first four League appearances as a substitute, his debut coming in a 6-0 win over Blackburn.

DAVIDSON, Robert (Full-back)

Apps: 32 Born: West Calder, Scotland, 1877 Died: Scotland, c. 1940

Career: Celtic, CITY (August 1902–October 1904), Airdrieonians.

Details: Bob Davidson went straight into City's first team, having a sound debut in a 3-1 win over Lincoln. He played in twenty-six out of thirty-four League games in 1902/03, occupying both full-back positions with four different partners. He lost his place when Herbert Burgess arrived from Glossop.

DAVIES, Frank (Goalkeeper)

Apps: 6 Born: Birkenhead, 1886 Died: after 1945

Career: Birkenhead, Derby County, Glossop, CITY (June 1906–October 1909).

Details: Third choice behind Billy Hall and Walter Smith, Frank Davies conceded thirteen goals in his first two League games for City – 4-1 and 9-1 defeats against Woolwich Arsenal and Everton respectively in September 1906. He made sixty-one League appearances for Glossop.

DAVIES, Gordon (Inside-forward)

Apps/goals: 13/5 Born: Manchester, 4/9/1932

Career: Ashton United, CITY (December 1951–June 1957), Chester, Southport; played non-League football from 1959.

Details: Reserve to several star players including Ivor Broadis, Don Revie and Johnny Hart during his time with City, Gordon Davies was twice top scorer for City's second XI in 1953/54 and 1954/55. Surprisingly, he netted only eleven goals in forty-six League appearances in his eight-year career.

DAVIES, Gordon John (Forward)

Apps/goals: 42/15 Born: Merthyr Tydfil, 3/8/1955

Career: CITY (June 1972–May 1974), Merthyr Tydfil, Fulham (£5,000), Chelsea (£90,000), CITY (£70,000, October 1985–October 1986), Fulham (£50,000), Wrexham; retired 1992; became a pest control officer for Rentokil in Leighton Buzzard.

Details: Released as a teenager, Gordon 'Ivor the Engine' Davies returned to Maine Road as a thirty-year-old and scored in four different competitions for City in 1985/86, including a hat-trick in a FMC win over Leeds United as he finished up as leading marksman with fifteen goals. A Welsh international (twenty-two caps won), he had an excellent career, netting a total of 161 goals in 391 appearances for his five League clubs. Keen at golf and squash, he was awarded a testimonial by Fulham in 1991.

DAVIES, Ian Claude (Left-back)
Apps: 8 Born: Bristol, 29/3/1957

Career: Cleveland Juniors/Bristol, Norwich City, Detroit Express, Newcastle United, CITY (August 1982–August 1984), Bury, Brentford, Cambridge United, Carlisle United, Exeter City, Bath City, Bury Town, Diss Town, Yeovil Town, Bristol Rovers, Swansea City, Gloucester City; was also a cricketer on Somerset's books.

Details: Welsh U21 international, Ian Davies was Norwich's youngest-ever debutant in 1974. He then made eighty-two appearances for Newcastle before his career fizzled out and, in fact, having been initially signed by City as cover for Bobby McDonald, he was loaned to three clubs before eventually moving to Carlisle. He made his debut for City in the 2-2 draw with Sunderland a month after moving to Maine Road.

DAVIES, Joseph (Utility forward)
Apps/goals: 38/13 Born: Chirk, 1866
Died: Chirk, 1943

Career: Chirk, Everton, Chirk, CITY (February 1891–January 1894), Sheffield United, CITY (1895-May 1896), Millwall Athletic, Reading, CITY (August 1900/August 1901), Stockport County, Chirk; retired May 1905.

Details: Joe Davies scored City's first hat-trick in the Football League, in a 7-0 win over Bootle in September 1892.

Alert, with a good technique, but rather selfish at times, he averaged a goal every three games during his three spells at Hyde Road. Capped eleven times in total, he was City's first Welsh international (*v.* England in 1891) having won his first cap in February 1890 against Scotland when with Everton for whom he played in the first season of League football in 1888/89. At Sheffield United he found himself in trouble with the club's directors for taking lodgings in a public house and was suspended for two weeks. He played in the same forward-line as Billy Meredith with Chirk, City and Wales.

A relative, Stan Davies, played for Preston North End, Everton, WBA, Birmingham, Cardiff City, Rotherham and Wales 1919–30.

DAVIES, Robert (Half-back)
Apps: 6 Born: Stone, 1890 Died: c. 1950

Career: Stafford Rangers, CITY (August 1911/June 1912), Pontypridd.

Details: Bob Davies started the 1911/12 season as City's first-choice right-half, but after five consecutive outings which included a 6-2 home defeat by Aston Villa, he slipped into the reserves and made only one more appearance before departing.

DAVIES, Ronald Wyn (Striker)
Apps/goals: 52/9 Born: Caernarfon, 20/3/1942

Career: Caernarfon BC, Llanberis FC, Caernarfon Town, Wrexham, Bolton Wanderers, Newcastle United (£80,000), CITY (£52,000, August 1971/September 1972), Manchester United (£25,000), Blackpool, Crystal Palace (loan), Stockport County, Arcadia Shepherds/South Africa, Crewe Alexandra, Bangor City; retired 1979; became a baker in Bolton; now lives in his home town of Caernarfon.

Details: An excellent target man and the perfect foil for Franny Lee, Wyn 'The Leap' Davies was terrific in the air and played exceedingly well during his only season at Maine Road. In fact, City were on course to win the League title, but some say that the introduction of Rodney Marsh led to the team faltering in the home straight! Welsh-speaking Davies had an excellent career overall, scoring almost 200 goals in 650 club appearances, including 164 in 576 League games. He had his best spells with Bolton and Newcastle, winning the Fairs Cup with the Magpies. Capped at youth and U23 levels, he went on to net six goals in thirty-four full internationals for Wales between 1964–74.

DE JONG, Nigel (Midfield)
Apps/goals: 137/2 Born: Amsterdam, 30/11/1984

Career: Ajax, Hamburger SV, CITY (£18 million, January 2009–August 2012), AC Milan (£3.5 million).

Details: Combative international midfielder Nigel De Jong had ten U21 and sixty-seven full caps to his name (one goal) at May 2013. He won the FA Cup and Premiership title with City and was the first Blues player to appear in a World Cup final when picking up a runner's-up medal for Holland *v.* Spain in 2010. Deployed in the role of centre-field enforcer in a team whose defence badly needed securing, he made his Premiership debut against Newcastle soon after moving from Germany and became a firm favourite with the fans, but had to wait until May 2011, in his ninety-third match, before scoring his first City goal in a 2–1 win over West Ham. He was joined at AC Milan by ex-City star Mario Balotelli in January 2013.

DELLOW, Ronald William (Outside-right)
Apps/goals: 10/4 Born: Crosby near Liverpool, 13/7/1914 Died: c. 1982.

Career: Bootle St Mary's, Blackburn Rovers, Mansfield Town, CITY (£1,300, January 1935/March 1936), Tranmere Rovers; Second World War guest for Tranmere Rovers, New Brighton,

CITY (March–September 1942), Everton, Southport, Wrexham and Blackburn Rovers; Carlisle United, Ards (player-manager); coached in Holland for twenty-one years, 1948–69, spending the last six with FC Vollendam.

Details: Ron Dellow was a fast and tricky winger who, deputising for Ernie Toseland, scored on his City debut in a 2-1 win at Derby, netted twice in his third game. When Toseland returned, he moved inside and was on target in his last outing, a 4-2 defeat at Portsmouth. Dellow won the Third Division (N) title with Tranmere (1938).

DENNISON, James (Forward)
Apps/goals: ½ Born: Sale, Cheshire, 1881 Died: c. 1950
Career: Sale Holmfield, CITY (February 1903–October 1906); played non-League football until the First World War.

Details: Standing in for Billy Gillespie, Jim Dennison scored twice in his only League game for City – a 5-2 win at Blackburn in March 1904.

DENNISON, Robert (Forward)
Apps/goals: 10/4 Born: Arnold, 6/10/1900 Died: 1973
Career: Arnold St Mary's, Norwich City, Brighton Hove Albion, CITY (May 1925/August 1926), Clapton Orient, Chesterfield, Yarmouth Town; retired 1939.

Details: One of several useful reserves registered with City in the mid-1920s, Bob Dennison scored in three successive matches in November/December 1925 and in a fine career, netted eighty-three goals in 248 League appearances, including thirty-four in 117 for Norwich and twenty-nine in seventy outings for Orient.

DEYNA, Kazimierz (Forward)
Apps/goals: 43/13 Born: Starograd, Gdanski, 23/10/1947 Died: San Diego, USA, 1/9/1989
Career: Wlokniarz Starograd Gdanski, LKS Lodz, Legia Warsaw, CITY (November 1978–January 1981), San Diego Sockers (NASL & indoor League); retired 1988.

Details: Poland's World Cup captain Kazimierz Denya was one of the first wave of overseas players to play in the England. However, things didn't run smoothly for him at Maine Road: a spate of injuries and off-field problems resulting in him making only forty-three appearances in all competitions. An exceptionally gifted playmaker, he became a cult figure with City fans, and there is no doubt that his seven goals in the last eight games of 1978/79 season were crucial in the team's successful relegation battle. Deyna scored forty-one times in ninety-seven internationals for his country (1968–78) and 159 in 449 club games. He won five NASL titles with San Diego Sockers

and appeared in the 1981 film *Escape To Victory* as Paul Wolcheck. In 1994, Denya – known as 'Kazzy'– was chosen by the Polish Football Association (PZPN) and the readers of all Polish sports-related newspapers as the Polish Football Player of All Time. Killed in a car accident at the age of forty-one, he is buried in Warsaw's military Powazki Cemetery.

DIBBLE, Andrew Gerard (Goalkeeper)
Apps: 141 Born: Cwmbran, Monmouthshire, 8/5/1965
Career: Llantarnum Comprehensive School, Torfaen Schools, Cardiff City, Luton Town (£125,000), Sunderland (loan), Huddersfield Town (loan), CITY (£240,000, July 1988–February 1991), Aberdeen (loan), Middlesbrough (loan), Bolton Wanderers (loan), West Bromwich Albion (loan), Glasgow Rangers, Middlesbrough (trial), Luton Town, Middlesbrough, Altrincham, Hartlepool United, Carlisle United (loan), Stockport County, Wrexham; retired 2003.

Details: Before losing his place to Tony Coton, Andy Dibble had two excellent seasons at Maine Road, helping City gain promotion in 1989. A Welsh international at schoolboy, youth (5), U21 (1) and senior levels (3), he stood 6 feet 3 inches tall and at times weighed around sixteen stone. He made over 400 appearances as a professional.

DICKOV, Paul (Striker)
Apps/goals: 200/41 Born: Livingston, West Lothian, 1/11/1972
Career: Arsenal, Luton Town (loan), Brighton & Hove Albion (loan), CITY (£1 million, August 1996–February 2002), Leicester City (£500,000), Blackburn Rovers (£150,000), CITY (free, July 2006–August 2008), Crystal Palace (loan), Blackpool (loan), Leicester City (free), Derby County (loan), Leeds United (free); retired May 2010; Oldham Athletic (player-manager; retired as a player, May 2011), Doncaster Rovers (manager).

Details: With the club in turmoil, Paul Dickov became Alan Ball's last signing for City. An impish striker, keen and aggressive, he started off by playing a supporting role to Shaun Goater before finishing as leading marksman with nine goals in 1997/98 – the joint lowest since 1910/11. The following season, he scored one of City's greatest-ever goals, a dramatic late equaliser in the Play-off final against Gillingham, which took the game into extra-time before the Blues won on penalties. Earlier, he netted a crucial leveller in the semi-final encounter with Wigan. Injuries plagued the diminutive Scot after that, and when Premier League status was regained in 2000, some thought that his chances of playing would be limited as City signed former FIFA World Player of the Year George Weah and Costa Rican star Paolo Wanchope. But Dickov earned a place in the team, his performances attracting the attention of Scotland manager Craig Brown, who duly called him into his squad for the first time. Having represented his country at schoolboy, youth and U21 levels, he went on to collect four full caps. He helped Arsenal win the ECWC and Leicester clinch the League One title, suffered two promotions and two relegations and during an excellent career, scored 118 goals in 474 club appearances. He was called off the bench a record sixty-nine times by City (fifty-eight in the League). As boss of Oldham, and facing the sack, he saw his team pull off a brilliant FA Cup win over Liverpool in January 2013.

DISTIN, Sylvain (Defender)
Apps/goals: 206/6 Born: Bagnolet, France, 16/12/1977

Career: Joué-les-Tours, FC Tours, Guegnon, Paris St Germain, Newcastle United (loan), CITY (£4 million, July 2002–July 2007), Portsmouth (free), Everton.

Details: Following the loan spell at St James' Park, Newcastle wanted to sign Sylvain Distin permanently, but he instead opted to sign for City where he knew he would be allowed to play in his preferred position of centre-half rather than left-back. The transfer fee involved set a club record for a defender. Consistent performances in his first season with the Blues resulted in Distin being named the club's Player of the Year for the 2002/03 season, and at the start of 2003/04 he was named captain following the retirement of Ali Benarbia. Remaining at the club for five years, Distin played alongside several different partners at the 'back' and there's no doubt that he and Richard Dunne were the best duo. He left for Portsmouth saying he wanted 'a fresh challenge', and in his first season at Fratton Park gained an FA Cup winner's medal. He reached the milestone of 600 club appearances with Everton in 2012/13.

DITCHFIELD, James Charles (Full-back)
Apps/goals: 15/1 Born: Lancashire, 1870
Died: after 1925

Career: Accrington, Rossendale, CITY (December 1895/November 1896).

Details: Charlie Ditchfield played over thirty games for Accrington before dropping out of League football in 1894, only to return with City where he partnered Davie Robson in his first two games and Dick Ray in his last thirteen before being released.

D'LARYEA, Jonathan Amar (Midfield)
Apps: 1 Born: Manchester, 3/9/1985

Career: CITY (June 2001–October 2005), Mansfield Town (loan/signed), Northwich Victoria, Eastwood Town, Gainsborough Trinity.

Details: Strong tackling midfielder, Jonathan D'Laryea, of Ghanaian descent, actually signed for City at the age of nine, before graduating the rough the club's academy scheme after leaving school. He made only one first-class appearance, in a League Cup defeat by Arsenal in October 2004. He had 162 League outings for Mansfield, receiving an England 'C' call up while at Field Mill. His twin brother Nathan was a junior with City, but failed to make the grade.

DOBING, Peter Alan (Forward)
Apps/goals: 94/32 Born: Manchester, 1/12/1938

Career: Crewe Rangers, Blackburn Rovers, CITY (July 1961–August 1963), Stoke City (£37,500); retired injured, May 1973; ran his own crockery business; a good cricketer, who was twelfth man for Lancashire v. Yorkshire.

Details: City's leading scorer in 1961/62 with twenty-two goals, including a hat-trick to no avail in a 5-3 defeat at West Ham, Peter Dobing was an honest worker, blessed with a terrific engine who gave excellent service to each of this three League clubs, scoring 230 goals in 671 appearances. He was superb in his two seasons with City, and, after leaving Maine Road, he did exceedingly well with Stoke. Unfortunately, his disciplinary record left a lot to be desired. In 1970 he served a nine-week ban (while recovering from a broken leg) and during his professional career was sent off four times.

Capped by England seven times at U23 level, he also represented the Football League (scoring a hat-trick v. the League of Ireland), played in the 1960 FA Cup final for Blackburn and as captain, won the League Cup with Stoke in 1972. His father was a Rugby League professional.

DOCHERTY, Michael (Full-back)
Apps: 13 Born: Preston, 29/10/1950

Career: Burnley, CITY (April–December 1976), Sunderland; retired injured, 1979; appointed coach, then caretaker-manager); Hartlepool United (manager), Rochdale (manager), Gillingham (joint caretaker-manager); Huddersfield Town (coach), Burnley College (coach).

Details: An England Youth international, Mick Docherty made 153 League appearances for Burnley before spending eight months with City. A confident full-back, he was signed after Willie Donachie had been injured, and made his debut in the Manchester derby on the last day of the 1975/76 season. Replacing Kenny Clements at the start of the next campaign, he then lost his place to the same player and within two months was on his way to Roker Park. He made seventy-three League appearances for Sunderland before retiring through injury.

His father was Tommy Docherty, ex-Preston and Scotland wing-half who managed Chelsea, Aston Villa and Manchester United, among others.

DOHERTY, Peter Dermont (Inside-forward)

Apps/goals: 131/80 Born: Magherafelt, 5/6/1913 Died: Poulton-le-Fylde near Blackpool, 6/4/1990

Career: Station United/Coleraine, Coleraine, Glentoran, Blackpool (£1,500), CITY (record £10,000, February 1936–December 1945); served in the RAF during Second World War, also guest for Birmingham City, Blackburn Rovers, Brentford, Derby County, Grimsby Town, Lincoln City, Liverpool, Manchester United, Port Vale, Walsall and West Bromwich Albion; Derby County (£6,000), Huddersfield Town, Doncaster Rovers (player-manager; retired as a player, 1953); Northern Ireland (manager); Bristol City (manager), Notts County (joint advisor), Aston Villa (chief scout), Preston North End (assistant-manager/coach), Sunderland (assistant-manager), Blackpool (scout).

Details: Peter Doherty was a sixteen-year-old County Derry bus conductor when he impressed in a ten-minute trial for the Irish League club Coleraine! The watching manager and coaches had no doubt that he would become a star player – and that's precisely what happened!

The flame-haired Doherty made rapid progress and, blessed with one of the most astute tactical brains of all time, he became one of the cleverest, trickiest and most entertaining inside-lefts of the late 1930s. He could tackle, dribble, shoot and create chances for others, and was no mug with his head either.

The club's first five-figure signing, he was City's top scorer in 1936/37 (with thirty-two goals) and in 1937/38 (with twenty-six), he actually found the net in each of the last seven League games in 1936/37.

He helped Glentoran win the Irish Cup in 1930, City clinch the League championship in 1937, Derby beat Charlton in the 1946 FA Cup final and Doncaster lift the Third Division (N) title in 1950, as well as winning one Victory and sixteen full caps for his country – far fewer than he deserved, although Second World War didn't help matters!

Described by some as the 'best' player ever to come out of Northern Ireland (perhaps until George Best appeared on the scene), Doherty has certainly been City's greatest-ever star, and was named in the top greatest fifty players of the twentieth century. He was the first City player to manage his country (1951/52).

DONACHIE, William (Defender)

Apps/goals: 438/2 Born: Glasgow, 5/10/1951

Career: Glasgow Amateurs, CITY (October 1968–March 1980), Portland Timbers (£200,000), Norwich City, Burnley, Portland Timbers, Oldham Athletic (player-coach); CITY (coach, seasons 1998–2001), Everton (assistant-manager/coach).

Details: Willie Donachie was first spotted by City playing in midfield, and within sixteen months of joining the club he made his League debut as a substitute (for Tony Book) against Nottingham Forest, starting his first game two months later against Crystal Palace. Eventually securing a regular place in the team at the end of the 1970/71 season, he remained there as a permanent fixture for eight years. Playing at left-back, he missed only eighteen League games out of a possible 347 between March 1971 and May 1979, being an ever-present twice. Only Asa Hartford, with thirty-six, has won more caps for Scotland that Donachie's total of thirty-five, who also represented his country in three U23 internationals. He played in two League Cup finals for City, losing in 1974, winning in 1976. He worked under former City star Joe Royle at Oldham, Maine Road and Everton.

DONALDSON, Alexander Pollock (Outside-right)

Apps: 7 Born: Barrhead, East Renfrewshire, 4/12/1890 Died: Chorley, c. 1960.

Career: Belgrade, Balmoral United, Riply Athletic, Sheffield United (trial), Bolton Wanderers (£50); First World War guest for Leicester Fosse & Port Vale; Sunderland, CITY (May 1923/May 1924), Crystal Palace, Chorley, Ashton National, Chorley; retired May 1931; became licensee of the Gardener's Arms, Bolton.

Details: A Scottish international, six caps gained (one goal scored) between 1914 and 1922, Alex Donaldson was a clever ball player with good pace who spent his best years with Bolton (six goals in 146 appearances, 1912–21). Reserve to winger Hugh Morris during his season with City, he made his debut against the team that rejected him, Sheffield United! Recovering from a fractured kneecap (suffered *v.* Preston in February 10921) Donaldson played until he was forty and was instrumental in raising the standard of Lancashire Combination while with Chorley.

DONNELLY, Robert (Centre-half/left-back)

Apps/goals: 37/1 Born: Craigneuk, 1913 Died: Scotland, after 1960

Career: Partick Thistle, CITY (June 1935–July 1937), Morton; did not play after Second World War.

Details: After some fine displays for Partick, Bob Donnelly came south and replaced Sam Cowan at the heart of the City defence. Making his debut against the previous season's FA Cup finalists WBA two months after signing, he had an excellent first season at Maine Road before losing his place to Bobby Marshall. His last game for City was at left-back in a 5-2 win at Preston in April 1937.

DORAN, John Francis (Centre-forward)
Apps/goals: 3/1 Born: Belfast: 3/1/1896
Died: 1940

Career: Gillingham, Pontypridd, Newcastle Empire, Coventry City, Norwich City, Brighton & Hove Albion, CITY (August 1922–January 1924), Crewe Alexandra, Mid-Rhondda United, Shelbourne, Boston Town; retired 1934.

Details: Jack Doran had a varied career, playing for clubs in England, Ireland and Scotland, having his best spell with Brighton, for whom he netted forty-four goals in seventy-one League games: 1920–22. As a replacement for the injured Tom Johnson, he made his three appearances for City at the start of the 1922/23 season, scoring in the 3-3 draw with Sheffield United. He played regularly for the reserves after that.

DORSETT, George (Winger/half-back)
Apps/goals: 211/65 Born: Brownhills,
9/8/1881 Died: Manchester, 15/4/1943

Career: Brownhills Schools, Shireoaks Athletic, Small Heath, Shrewsbury Town, Brownhills Albion, West Bromwich Albion, CITY (joint record £450, December 1904); retired May 1912).

Details: The majority of George 'Sos' Dorsett's 100 appearances for West Bromwich Albion came on the left-wing, but with Frank Booth already established in that position for City, he became something of a utility player at Hyde Road, occupying every front-line berth as well as lining up at wing-half. Taking over from Billy Meredith at outside-right, he netted fifteen goals in 1905/06 before having a good, prolonged spell at left-half. Unfortunately, a leg injury ruined his last season with City. Dorsett won Second Division championship medals with both WBA and City and represented the Football League. His brother, Joe (below) was also with the Albion.

DORSETT, Joseph Arthur Harold (Forward)
Apps/goals: 145/20 Born: Brownhills,
19/4/1888 Died: Eccles, Manchester, 15/3/1951

Career: Brownhills Albion, West Bromwich Albion, CITY (May 1910–January 1920), Colne, Southend United, Millwall Athletic; retired May 1923.

Details: A nimble winger, similar to his brother, Joe Dorsett joined West Bromwich Albion three years after George; yet they were together at Hyde Road for two seasons, appearing in nineteen games as forward-line colleagues. The younger by seven years, Dorsett junior was a one-touch player who always tended to hug the touchline, right or left, and had his best scoring season in 1911/12 with seven goals, including two against Spurs. He played for an England XI in 1914.

Dicky Dorsett, who played for Wolves and Aston Villa in the 1930s/40s, was the nephew of George and Joe.

DOUGAL, George (Inside/outside-left)
Apps/goals: 77/13 Born: Edinburgh, 1873
Died: before the Second World War

Career: Hibernian, CITY (March 1898–May 1901), Glossop.

Details: George Dougal partnered Jimmy Whitehead initially and then Fred Williams on City's left flank and he did well, creating and scoring some important goals, two coming in his first four outings when promotion was still a reality. Dougal contributed again in 1898/99 when the Second Division championship was won, netting in a 4-0 win in the Manchester derby. He moved to Glossop once Fred Threlfall started to impress.

DOUGLAS, William (Goalkeeper)
Apps: 63 Born: Dundee, 1870;
Died: Dundee, c. 1950

Career: Dundee Old Boys, CITY (May 1890–January 1894), Newton Heath, Derby County, Blackpool, Warmley, Dundee; retired 1914.

Details: Bill Douglas was hardly troubled in City's first-ever game in the FA Cup – when Liverpool Stanley were battered 12-0 in October 1890. A tall goalkeeper, cocky at times, he often raced out of his 'area', tackled an opposing forward and cleared the ball downfield with one of his mighty kicks. He also kept a clean sheet in City's first League game, a 7-0 win over Bootle in September 1892 and was an ever present in the Alliance season of 1891/92 and in the Division Two campaign of 1892/93. He was suspended sine die by Newton Heath – following a humiliating 5-2 defeat by Fairfield in the 1896 Manchester Cup final.

DOWD, Henry Williams (Goalkeeper)
Apps/goals: 219/1 Born: Salford, 4/7/1938

Career: ICI/Blackley, CITY (January 1958–December 1970), Stoke City, Charlton Athletic, Oldham Athletic; retired 1974; became area-manager for JW Lees Brewery, Middleton.

Details: One of the few City goalkeepers to score in a competitive game, Harry Dowd, playing up front after breaking his finger, netted the equaliser against Bury in February 1964. Aged nineteen when he joined the club, he eventually took over from Bert Trautmann and went from strength to strength, helping City win the Second Division title in 1966, played in seven games (four wins) early on in City's 1967/68 League championship-winning season, and gained an FA Cup winner's medal in 1969.

After three outings for Stoke, he played 131 games for Oldham, with whom he twice won promotion, from Divisions Four and Three respectively in 1971 and 1974. Dowd retired from football on his thirty-sixth birthday.

DOYLE, Michael (Defender/midfielder)
Apps/goals: 572/41 Born: Manchester,
25/11/1946 Died: Ashton-under-Lyne, 27/6/2011
   Career: Stockport Boys, CITY (May 1962–June 1978), Stoke City (£50,000), Bolton Wanderers (£10,000), Rochdale; retired May 1984; became sales manager for sports company Slazenger; also pundit on local radio.
   Details: Mike 'Tommy' Doyle – currently third in the club's list of appearance makers behind Alan Oakes and Joe Corrigan – gave City wonderful service for sixteen years and after leaving Maine Road played 128 times for Stoke. The recipient of Second and First Division championship medals in 1966 and 1968, he helped City win the FA Cup in 1969, the League Cup twice in 1970 (when he scored the equaliser in the final *v.* WBA) and 1976, and the European Cup Winner's Cup, also in 1970, plus two Charity Shield prizes and a League Cup runner's-up medal. After some solid performances during the 1965/66 and 1966/67 campaigns, he played in 363 League games out of a possible 426 between March 1967 and March 1977 – and at the same time scored vitally important goals.
   Capped five times by England, Doyle played in eight U23 internationals, twice represented the Football League and also played for an England XI (*v.* Team America in 1976) and Young England. Strong and workmanlike, who could also put in a decent shift in midfield, Doyle was replaced by Paul Futcher in City's defence. In his first two games for Bolton, he conceded an own-goal and was also sent off.

DRUMMOND, Duncan David (Inside-forward)
Apps/goals: 28/6 Born: Glasgow, 1879
Died: Glasgow, c. 1942
   Career: Bellshill Athletic, Celtic, CITY (February 1902–May 1904), Partick Thistle.
   Details: After just four outings for Celtic, Duncan Drummond joined City with Willie McOustra. He did well as Fred Threlfall's partner on the left flank before being replaced by Sandy Turnbull. His first goal for the Blues was a beauty, in a 2-2 draw at Villa Park in March 1902.

DUNFIELD, Terence (Defender)
Apps: 1 Born: Vancouver, Canada, 20/2/1982
   Career: CITY (May 1997–December 2002), Bury (loan/signed), Worcester City (loan), Macclesfield Town, Shrewsbury Town.
   Details: After impressing in City's intermediate and reserve matches, Terry Dunfield made his only first-team appearance as a twenty-third-minute substitute in the final Premiership game of the 2000/01 season at Chelsea, replacing the injured Jeff Whitley. Soon afterwards he scored the best goal of the game as City beat rivals United in the Manchester Senior Cup final. He made almost

200 club appearances after leaving City. Dunfield played for both Canada and England's youth teams before winning full and U21 caps for the country of his birth.

DUNKLEY, Maurice Edward Frank (Outside-right)
Apps/goals: 58/6 Born: Kettering,
19/2/1914 Died: Northampton, 27/12/1989
   Career: Kettering Town, Northampton Town, CITY (March 1938–May 1947); served in RAF during Second World War, also guest for Leicester City, Millwall, Northampton Town, West Bromwich Albion and West Ham United; Kettering Town, Northampton Town, Corby Town; retired 1950; played cricket for Northamptonshire.
   Details: Maurice Dunkley, blessed with good pace and plenty of skill, had an excellent 1946/47 season with City, scoring four goals in thirty-two League games. He was replaced at Maine Road initially by Jackie Wharton and then Billy Linacre.

DUNNE, Leo (Left-back)
Apps: 3 Born: Dublin, 1908
   Career: Drumcondra, CITY (August 1933–June 1935), Hull City, Drumcondra; retired 1939.
   Details: Reserve to Billy Dale for two seasons, Leo Dunne was the first City player to win a full cap for the Republic of Ireland, gaining two in 1935. A first-class defender, he made almost sixty appearances for the Blues' second team before moving to Hull.

DUNNE, Richard Patrick (Defender)
Apps/goals: 352/8 Born: Tallaght, Dublin,
21/9/1979
   Career: Home Farm, Everton, CITY (£3 million, October 2000–September 2009) Aston Villa (£6 million).
   Details: Signed with Laurent Chavery in 2000 after right-back Richard Edgehill had suffered from a dip in form, Richard Dunne made a traumatic start to his City career after serious breaches of club discipline. But after that he became a real 'diamond' at the heart of the defence, amassing over 350 appearances in nine years. Strong and mobile, good in the air and on the ground, Dunne helped City win the Second Division title in 2002. Continuing to impress with his defending, he was voted the club's Player of the Year for four seasons in a row, 2004–08, became captain in 2006, replacing Sylvin Dustin, and in July 2008 signed a new four-year contract. However, in August 2008, Gary Cook, the club's Chief Executive said 'China and India are gagging for football content to watch and we're going to tell them that City is their content. We need a superstar to get through that door and Richard Dunne doesn't roll off the tongue in Beijing.' Dunne was sold to Aston Villa a

year later. In his last season with City, the Irishman made forty-seven appearances and was sent off three times, bringing his tally of red cards to eight – an unwanted record he shares with Patrick Vieira and Dun Ferguson. Capped seventy-six times by the Republic of Ireland (eight goals scored), Dunn played in the 2002 World Cup finals and has also represented his country in two 'B' internationals. In 2012/13 he reached the milestone of 500 club appearances.

DYER, Frank George (Defender)
Apps/goals: 37/3 Born: Bishopbriggs, Strathclyde, 5/8/1870 Died: 1940
    Career: Clydebank Boys, Chryston FC, Bolton Wanderers, Warwick County, West Bromwich Albion , Woolwich Arsenal, CITY (August 1893, retired through ill-heath and injury, May 1898).
    Details: A diligent, dexterous and hard-pressing defender, Frank Dyer amused the fans with his war cry of 'that's mine' when going for the ball. His best season with City was his first when he scored a fine goal from left-back in a 4-2 win over Northwich Victoria in January. He made over 100 first-class appearances during a shortened career.

DYSON, John (Inside-forward)
Apps/goals: 73/29 Born: Oldham, 8/7/1934 Died: Oldham, 22/11/2000
    Career: Nelson, CITY (October 1951–March 1961), Stirling Albion; played cricket for Lancashire and Staffordshire.
    Details: England U23 international and FA representative, Jackie Dyson scored for City in their 1956 FA Cup final win over Birmingham. A competent forward with good technique and a strong shot, he spent four years in the reserves before making his mark in the first team during the second half of the 1955/56 season as Roy Clarke's left-wing partner. Retaining his place the following term, he then slipped back into the second XI and played his last League game for City in March 1960. As a cricketer Dyson was a right-handed batsman and off-spin bowler, who scored 4,499 runs and took 161 wickets in 150 games in two spells for Lancashire between 1954 and 1965. A controversial figure throughout his sporting career, he was a free spirit and it ended up costing him his job at Lancashire in 1960 when the committee charged him with 'a serious breach of discipline and an act of insubordination and insolence to the captain'. Dismissed, he joined Staffordshire in the Minor Counties League, before returning to Old Trafford in September 1963 after the aforementioned committee had been overthrown.

DŽEKO, Edin (Striker)
Apps/goals: 109/40 Born: Sarajevo, SFR Yugoslavia, 17/3/1986

Career: Željezničar, Teplice, Usti-nad Labem (loan), VfL Wolfsburg, CITY (£27 million, January 2011).
    Details: After scoring twenty-four goals in sixty-three games in his first eighteen months in English football, collecting both FA Cup and Premier League winner's medals in the process, giant striker Edin Džeko became City's 'super-sub' during the first half of the 2012/13 season, coming off the bench to bag some crucial goals. Manager Roberto Mancini continued to use him diligently as one of his substitutes until Sergio Aguero was injured and Mario Balotelli lost his form. The second highest-priced footballer signed by City (behind Robinho) Džeko's transfer fee was also a record for any player from the former Yugoslavia. Capped five and four times at U19 and U21 levels respectively by Bosnia & Herzegovina, he has now scored a record twenty-nine goals in sixty-two full internationals for his country. A Bundesliga winner in 2009 with Wolfsburg (for whom he struck sixty-six goals in 111 appearances in three-and-a-half seasons) Džeko became Bosnia's first UNICEF ambassador later that same year, and will study sport and physical education at the University of Sarajevo when his playing career ends. His father was also a professional footballer.

E

EADIE, William Phillips (Centre-half)
Apps/goals: 205/6 Born: Greenock, 1882 Died: Scotland before 1960.
    Career: Greenock Morton, CITY (August 1906–June 1914), Derby County; retired 1915.
    Details: Bill Eadie, although tall and slender, was a tough, strong-kicking defender who feared no-one. One of several players signed by City in the wake of the bribery and subsequent suspension scandal, he took over from Tommy Hynds and spent eight years at Hyde Road, helping City win the Second Division championship in 1909/10, following his Lancashire Combination Division 2 winner's medal he collected the previous season. After leaving City, Eadie starred in Derby's promotion-winning campaign of 1914/15.

EASTWOOD, Eric (Defender)
Apps: 16 Born: Heywood, Lancs, 24/3/1916 Died: Bolton, 12/10/1991
    Career: Chorley Road Congregationalists, Little Lever, Westhoughton, Heywood St James , CITY (April 1935–March 1947); Second World War guest for Blackburn Rovers, Bolton Wanderers, Manchester United and Rochdale; Port Vale; retired 1951.
    Details: A well-built, hard-tackling centre-half, Eric Eastwood's career was unfortunately disrupted by Second World War, during which time he made 163 appearances for City.

EDELSTON, Joseph (Wing-half)
*Apps: 6   Born: Appleby Bridge near Wigan,
27/4/1891 Died: London, 10/3/1970*
   Career: St Helens Recreationalists, Hull City,
CITY (June/November 1920), Fulham (retired
May 1926; joined backroom staff at Craven
Cottage; assistant-manager); later engaged by
Brentford and Clapton Orient; Reading (manager,
1939–47).
   Details: A well-proportioned half-back of proven
ability, Joe Edelston was signed by City on his
return from touring South Africa with the FA. He
made his City debut at Liverpool in August 1920
– this being one of only seventy-one appearances
he made at club level during his career. His
son, Maurice Edelston, was an England amateur
wartime international and BBC commentator.

EDEN, James (Left-back)
*Apps: 1   Born: Manchester, c. 1890 Died: after
1945*
   Career: CITY (October 1911/May 1912);
released.
   Details: Signed from local non-League football,
Jim Eden's only game for City was in the 2-0 defeat
at Woolwich Arsenal in March 1912, after Billy
Henry withdrew through injury.

EDGE, Alfred (Forward)
*Apps: 1   Born: Hanley, Stoke-on-Trent,
1866 Died: 10/4/1941*
   Career: Goldenhill, Stoke, Newton Heath
(£100), Nottingham Jardine's Athletic, Stoke,
Northwich Victoria, CITY (January/May 1894),
Macclesfield.
   Details: A short-term acquisition, Alf Edge's
only outing for City was against his former club,
Northwich Victoria, twelve days after signing. He
was one of thirteen different players who appeared
at inside-left in 1893/94.
   One of Stoke's early professionals, he played
in the Potters' first-ever League game (v. WBA)
and was awarded a gold medal for his services
to the Staffordshire club and setting a record for
most goals scored in an FA Cup tie, five against
Caernarfon Wanderers in 1886.

EDGHILL, Richard Arlon (Full-back)
Apps/goals: 210/1 Born: Oldham, 23/9/1974
   Career: Junior football, CITY (June 1990–June
2002), Birmingham City (loan), Wigan Athletic
(free), Sheffield United, Queen's Park Rangers,
Bradford City, Macclesfield.
   Details: After making his debut against
Wimbledon FC in 1993, Richard Edghill's progress
was hampered by several serious injuries, missing
the entire 1996/7 season due to a knee problem.
He recovered and featured regularly in City's
first XI for the next three seasons, scoring in the

1999 Play-off final penalty shoot-out victory over
Gillingham his first professional goal! Edghill
then skippered City to promotion back to the
Premiership, but unfortunately, after a poor start to
2000/01 when he conceded a calamitous own goal
in a 2–1 defeat by Coventry, he lost his place and
was loaned to Birmingham. Manager Joe Royle
then signed Richard Dunne and Laurent Charvert,
at which point Edghill thought his City days were
over, but after a bad run of results he was recalled.
However, following relegation and the arrival of
new boss Kevin Keegan and right-sided defender
Sun Jihai, Edghill's opportunities became fewer,
leading to his departure to Wigan, having made
over 200 appearances and played for England at
U21 and 'B' team levels.

EDMONDSON, John Henry (Goalkeeper)
Apps: 40 Born: Accrington, 1882 Died: c. 1960
   Career: Accrington, CITY (May 1902–
December 1906), Bolton Wanderers (£600);
retired May 1915.
   Details: Signed as cover for Jack Hillman, Harry
Edmondson's first three League games for City
resulted in wins. He had his best run in the side in
1905/06, making twenty-eight appearances. One
of the players suspended in the illegal payments
scandal, after leaving Hyde Road he played 259
first-class games for Bolton, being an ever-present
when the Trotters won the Second Division
championship in 1909.

EGAN, Thomas William (Forward)
Apps: 7 Born: Chirk, 1872 Died: 1946
   Career: Denbighshire Schools, Chirk, Fairfield/
Manchester, CITY (November 1893/March 1894),
Burnley, Ashton North End, Sheffield United,
Lincoln City, Birdwell, Altofts FC, Darwen,
Royston United, Stockport County.
   Details: A Welsh international, capped against
Scotland in 1892, Tom Egan was a tenacious
forward, fast and clever, but unfortunately he
never settled with any one club. City suffered four
defeats in the seven games in which he played, his
debut ending in a 3-0 reverse at Liverpool.

EKELUND, Ronald (Midfield)
Apps: 4 Born: Glostrup, Denmark, 21/8/1972
   Career: Brondby IF, Barcelona, Southampton
(loan), CITY (loan, December 1995/January
1996), Coventry City (loan), Lyngby (loan),
Odense Boldklub, Toulouse, Walsall, San Jose
Earthquakes, California Cougars; retired 2007;
San Jose Earthquakes (technical advisor).
   Details: Injuries limited Ronnie Ekelund's playing
time at Maine Road. A soccer nomad, serving with
eleven different clubs, he played fifty-one times
for Denmark at U17, U19 and U21 levels and
appeared in the 1992 Olympic Games. His best

years were spent with Barcelona and San Jose Earthquakes. He won the Danish Cup twice with Brondby and the MSL on two occasions with the Earthquakes.

ELANO, Blumer Ralph (Midfield)
Apps/goals: 38/10 Born: Iracemápolis, Brazil, 14/6/1981
Career: Guarani/Brazil, Limeira's Internacional, Santos, Shakhtar Donetsk, CITY (£8 million, August 2007–July 2009), Galatasaray, Santos, Gremio.
Details: Playmaker Elano made an impressive debut for City in August 2007 against West Ham, scoring his first goal, a brilliant 30-yard drive, soon afterwards past the Newcastle 'keeper Shay Given. He later helped knock the Hammers out of the FA Cup, and scored penalties against Birmingham, Sunderland AFC, and Bolton, while also collecting five yellow cards in his first season in English football! Versatile enough to play in several positions, including full-back, he had a decent 2008/09 campaign, but with the high-profile return of Shaun Wright-Phillips and the signing of his fellow Brazilian Robinho, he eventually moved to pastures new in Turkey. He won five trophies with Santos, three with Donetsk and two with Brazil for whom he scored nine goals in fifty internationals.

ELLEGAARD, Kevin Stuhr (Goalkeeper)
Apps: 7 Born: Copenhagen, Denmark, 23/5/1983
Career: Brondby IF, Hvidovre IF, BK Sollerod-Vodbaek, KB Copenhagen, Farum BK, CITY (£750,000, July 2002–July 2005), Blackpool (loan), Hertha BSC/Berlin, Randers FC, SC Heerenveen, IF Elfsborg.
Details: In 2003/04, Kevin Ellegaard made four League appearances for City, twice as a substitute when he replaced David Seaman. Then, once David James had arrived, his chances diminished, eventually leading to his transfer to Hertha Berlin. Capped fifty-six times by Denmark at U16–21 levels, Ellegaard helped Elfsborg win the Swedish Cup in 2012.

ELLIOTT, Andrew (Midfield)
Apps: 1 Born: Ashton-under-Lyne, 21/11/1963
Career: Derby Boys, CITY (April 1980–May 1982), Sligo Rovers, Chester City.
Details: Reserve midfielder Andy Elliott's only game in a City shirt came in the 0-0 League draw at Middlesbrough in March 1982. He deputised for Asa Hartford.

ELLIOTT, Stephen William (Forward)
Apps: 2 Born: Dublin, 6/1/1984
Career: Belvedere FC, Stella Maris, CITY (December 1999–August 2004), Sunderland (£225,000), Wolverhampton Wanderers, Preston North End, Norwich City (loan), Heart of Midlothian, Coventry City.
Details: After scoring five goals in thirty minutes of a trial game for Stella Maris, nippy striker Stephen Elliott was signed by City boss Joe Royle. Unfortunately, he suffered with a back injury during his time at Maine Road, making only two substitute appearances in Premiership games against Bolton and Middlesbrough in February and May 2004. Selected by the Republic of Ireland twenty-three times in four categories of intermediate football, he has nine full caps to his name, scored fifteen goals when Sunderland won the championship in 2005, and at May 2013 his club record stood at fifty-three goals in 274 appearances.

ELWOOD, James Hugh (Defender)
Apps: 32 Born: Belfast, 12/6/1901 Died: Ireland, 1937
Career: Glentoran, CITY (March 1924–July 1927), Chesterfield, Bradford Park Avenue, Derry City; retired 1939.
Details: Jimmy Elwood, tall and strong, made twenty-three League appearances for City between March and December 1924 before losing his place to Sam Cowan. A competent reserve thereafter, he went on to make 119 appearances for Bradford with whom he gained two caps for Northern Ireland in 1929.

EMPTAGE, Albert Taylor (Inside-forward/left-half)
Apps/goals: 144/1 Born: Grimsby, 26/12/1917 Died: 1997
Career: Scunthorpe & Lindsay United, United, CITY (March 1937–January 1950); Second World War guest for Manchester United and Portsmouth; Stockport County; retired 1953; served in the Royal Navy during Second World War.
Details: Albert Emptage was at Maine Road for thirteen years, during which time he made 178 first-team appearances, thirty-four during the Second World War, helping City win the Second Division title in 1947. A willing worker, he switched to left-half after the hostilities where he performed excellently alongside Les McDowall and then Joe Fagan. He represented the Football League v. the Irish League in 1947.

ESPIE, John (Wing-half)
Apps: 1 Born: Hamilton, 1868 Died: Scotland, c. 1939
Career: Rangers, Motherwell, Queen's Park, Burnbank, Swifts, Burnley, CITY (February/May 1896), Dundee; retired, 1900.
Details: Having done well north of the border, and also with Burnley (nine goals in 95 appearances), Jock Espie made his only League start for City in March 1896, in the 1-1 home draw with Burton Swifts when George Mann was absent.

ETHERINGTON, Robert Dilworth (Outside-right)
Apps: 12 Born: Croston, 19/6/1899 Died: 1981
   Career: Leyland, CITY (August 1921–June 1924), Rotherham County.
   Details: Reserve first to Billy Meredith and then to Hugh Morris, Bob Etherington made his League debut for City in a 2-0 home win over Burnley in April 1922. He made ten appearances the following season, but none at all in 1923/24 when Alex Donaldson acted at he stand-in right-winger.

ETUHU, Dickson Paul (Midfield)
Apps: 13 Born: Kano, Nigeria, 8/6/1982
   Career: CITY (August 1997–January 2002), Preston North End (£300,000), Norwich City (£450,000), Sunderland (£1.5 million), Fulham (£1.5 million), Blackburn Rovers.
   Details: Hardworking and honest, 'ET' never really made an impact with City, but did exceedingly well with Preston, for whom he made 149 appearances, following up with seventy for Norwich. He has now won seventeen caps for Nigeria. He is the elder brother of Kelvin (below).

ETUHU, Kelvin Peter (Winger)
Apps/goals: 15/1 Born: Kano, Nigeria, 30/5/1988
   Career: CITY (July 2004–January 2012), Rochdale (loan), Leicester City (loan), Cardiff City (loan), OA Kavala/Greece (trial), Portsmouth, Barnsley.
   Details: Unlike his brother, Kelvin Etuhu chose to play for England at youth team level and became the twenty-fourth graduate from City's Academy to break into the first XI when he made his debut as a substitute in the League Cup victory over Norwich in 2005. He never reached the same heights as Dickson, and in July 2010, was arrested and charged with assault following an incident at a Manchester casino five months earlier when three people were injured. Etuhu was found guilty and handed an eight-month jail sentence, causing City to cancel his contract.

EVANS, Chedwyn Michael (Striker)
Apps/goals: Born: St Asaph, Denbighshire, 28/12/1988
   Career: Rhyl Athletic, Chester City, CITY (July 2007–July 2009), Norwich City (loan), Sheffield United (£3 million).
   Details: Ched Evans progressed through the ranks with City, but failed to make an impression in the first team and, after a loan spell with Norwich, moved to Sheffield United. After two sub-standard seasons with the Blades, he hit the headlines by scoring thirty-five goals in 2011/12 while also taking his tally of full caps for Wales to thirteen. In April 2012, Evans was sentenced to five years imprisonment for rape. Six months later the Court of Appeal rejected an appeal against his conviction.

EWING, David (Centre-half)
Apps/goal 303/1 Born: Logierait near Perth, 10/5/1929 Died: Stockport, 17/7/1999
   Career: Luncarty Juniors, CITY (June 1949–July 1962), Crewe Alexandra; CITY (coach, seasons 1965–70), Sheffield Wednesday (coach), Bradford City (coach), Crystal Palace (coach), Hibernian (manager), CITY (reserve team manager/coach, seasons 1973–79); ran a hardware shop in Reddish, Stockport, for many years.
   Details: A real old-fashioned stopper centre-half, as tough as iron, the anchorman at the back, Scotsman Dave Ewing gave City wonderful service as a player. He had to wait four years before making his debut, taking over the number five shirt from Jack Rigby in January 1953. An ever-present the following season, he retained his position until 1959, when John McTavish became first choice. Ewing missed only twenty-seven games in six seasons, helped City reach two FA Cup, gaining a winner's medal in 1956, and when he returned to Maine Road for a third spell in the late 1970s, he guided the second XI to their first-ever Central League title. Ewing's only goal for City came in a 2-1 League win over Portsmouth in September 1957, while on a personal note he had the misfortune to concede a record ten own-goals during his Maine Road career. He died in 1999 after a long illness.

EYRES, Stanley Sydney (Centre-forward)
Apps/goals: 1/1 Born: Droylsden, 1885 Died: Cheshire, c. 1950
   Career: Failsworth, CITY (April 1907/ September 1908), Colne, Crewe Alexandra; retired 1915.
   Details: Twenty-four hours after signing, Stan Eyres made a scoring debut for City in a 3-2 defeat at Sunderland on the last day of the 1906/97 campaign. He played in the reserves throughout 1907/08 before re-entering non-League football.

F

FAGAN, Fionan (Outside-right)
Apps/goals: 165/35 Born: Dublin, 7/6/1931
   Career: Shamrock Rovers Schoolboys, Transport FC, Hull City, CITY (15,000, December 1953–March 1960), Derby County (£8,000), Altrincham (player-manager), Northwich Victoria, Mossley, Ashton United; retired 1967; became a driving instructor, and was a founder of City's Former Players Association in the early 1990s.
   Details: The son of Irish international and Shamrock Rovers outside-left John Fagan, Fionan started his League career with Hull, signed by Raich Carter. He joined City on Christmas Eve 1953, played in the reserves twenty-four hours later and made his senior debut on Boxing Day, in 2-1

home win over Sheffield United FC. Establishing himself as a first-team regular in 1954/55, as part of the tactical system known as the 'Revie Plan', this season proved his most successful for City. He scored eleven goals in forty-two games, including a hat-trick against Manchester United FC at Old Trafford, and helped City reach the FA final. He missed the following year's final and a winner's medal! Fagan, who lost his place to Colin Barlow, played in one 'B' and two full internationals for Eire as a City player and later added six more full caps to his tally with Derby (five goals scored). A knee ligament injury forced him to retire.

FAGAN, Joseph Francis (Centre-half)
Apps/goals: 158/2 Born: Liverpool, 12/3/1921 Died: Liverpool, 30/6/2001
   Career: Earlestown Bohemians, CITY (October 1938–August 1951); Second World War guest for Portsmouth; Nelson, Bradford Park Avenue, Nelson (player-manager); retired 1953; Rochdale (trainer), Liverpool (coach, assistant-manager, manager); served in the Royal Navy during Second World War.
   Details: Making his City debut on New Year's Day 1947 *v.* Fulham, Joe Fagan – a solid, dependable centre-half – soon assured himself of a regular first-team place by his cool and consistent play. After appearing at right-half, he moved to the heart of the defence, where his sound positional judgment, strong headwork and general reliability soon marked him out as a player of solid worth. He had an unbroken run of 121 consecutive League appearances from his baptism through to November 1949. He helped City win the Second Division championship in 1947 and as Liverpool's manager won the treble (League, League Cup and European Cup) in 1984.

FAIRCLOUGH, Albert (Centre-forward)
Apps/goals: 5/1 Born: St Helens, 4/10/1891 Died: Stockport, 5/11/1958
   Career: Windle Villa, St Helens Town, St Helens Recreationalists, Eccles Borough, CITY (April 1913–May 1920), Southend United, Bristol City, Derby County, Gillingham; retired 1929.
   Details: The career of Albert Fairclough, brother of Peter (below), was disrupted considerably the First World War. Nevertheless, he was top scorer for City's Central League side in 1913/14, 1914/15 and 1919/20, the latter jointly with Ernie Lievesley. He did very well with each of his next four clubs, scoring eighty-eight goals in 163 League games before retiring. He netted twice in Southend's first-ever League game (a 2-0 win over Brighton in August 1920) and was also suspended by the Bristol City directors for allegedly 'not trying' and for breaches of training regulations.

FAIRCLOUGH, Peter (Forward/left-half)
Apps/goals: 5 Born: St Helens, 1893 Died: 1963
   Career: Eccles Borough, CITY (April 1913–May 1920), Tranmere Rovers.
   Details: The First World War also interrupted Peter Fairclough's League career with City, although he did play in over 100 games during the hostilities. Initially a reserve centre-forward (making his debut in that position in a 4-1 defeat at Aston Villa in April 1915), he developed into a very competent left-half, yet played just twice in the same City team as his brother, in home and away Second World War games against Stoke in April 1919.

FARRELL, Thomas (Inside-left)
Apps: 3 Born: Earlstown, 1882 Died: Scotland, c. 1951
   Career: Woolwich Arsenal, CITY (September 1905–January 1908), Airdrieonians.
   Details: A reserve with City for two-and-half seasons, Tom Farrell's three appearances were made in 1906/97 when he deputised twice for Irvine Thornley and once for Jimmy Conlin. He failed to start a game with Arsenal.

FASHANU, Justinus Soni (Striker)
Apps: 2 Born: Hackney, 19/2/1961 Died: Shoreditch, London, 2/5/1998
   Career: Stropham, Attleborough, Peterborough United (junior), Norwich City, Adelaide City/Australia (loan), Nottingham Forest (£1 million), Southampton (loan), Notts County (£150,000), Brighton & Hove Albion, Los Angeles Heat/USA, (player-manager), Edmonton Brickmen/Canada, CITY (October/November 1989), West Ham United, Leyton Orient, Hamilton Steelers/Canada, Southall (player-coach), Toronto Blizzard/Canada, Newcastle United (trial), Leatherhead, Torquay United, Airdrieonians, Trelleborg/Sweden, Heart of Midlothian, Atlanta Ruckus/USA, Miramar Rangers/New Zealand; retired 1997; Ellicott City/USA(coach); was an ABA heavyweight boxer before joining Norwich as a professional in 1978.
   Details: Although his career was marred by a niggling back injury, Justin Fashanu scored over 150 goals (some of them quite spectacular, including 'goal of the season' for Norwich *v.* Liverpool) in 425 appearances during his career. However, his spell with City was short and sweet, his two substitute appearances coming in defeats of 2-0 by Aston Villa and 6-0 at Derby. He represented England at Youth, U21 (eleven caps won) and 'B' team levels. And Kevin Keegan gave him a trial at Newcastle.
   Known for his off the field activities that included an alleged affair with TV actress Julie Goodyear (Coronation's Street's bar maid Bet Lynch) in 1992, Fashanu was listed at number ninety-nine in the Top 500 Lesbian and Gay Heroes in The

Pink Paper. And until former French international Olivier Rouver came out in 2008, Fashanu was still the only professional footballer in the world to disclose that he was gay. In March 2009 a football team, The Justin Fashanu All-stars, supported by the FA, was christened at a special event in Brighton. The team, created by the Justin Campaign against homophobia in football, promoted the inclusion of openly gay players in football. When living and coaching in Maryland, USA, Fashanu was charged with sexually assaulting a teenage boy. Disillusioned, he returned to England and sadly was found dead in a lock-up garage in Shoreditch, having apparently hanged himself. In April 2012, John Read's biography of Justin Fashanu was published. His younger brother John Fashanu, played for Norwich, Crystal Palace, Lincoln, Millwall, Wimbledon, Aston Villa and England.

FAULKNER, Roy Vincent (Inside-left)
Apps/goals: 7/4 Born: Manchester, 28/6/1935
  Career: CITY (December 1952–September 1957), Walsall, Wellington Town; retired injured, 1965; became a salesman for a Midlands engineering company.
  Details: Top scorer in City's 1955/56 Central League season, Roy Faulkner also made his s even senior appearances during this same season, netting on his debut in a 4-3 defeat at Birmingham and later netting the winner at Blackpool. With so much forward talent at Maine Road, he moved to Walsall, for whom he struck forty-three goals in 105 appearances, helping the Saddlers win the Fourth Division championship. He remained a semi-professional throughout his career.

FAYERS, Frederick Leslie (Half-back)
Apps/goals: 77/5 Born: King's Lynn, 29/1/1890 Died: Yorkshire, 4/2/1954
  Career: Northern Nomads, St Albans City, Watford, Huddersfield Town, Stockport County, CITY (May 1920–May 1923), Halifax Town (player-coach).
  Details: Fred 'Tiny' Fayers, only 5 feet 4 inches tall, was a committed footballer, a gritty performer who gave nothing less than 100 per cent every time he took to the field. He joined City with more than 200 senior appearances under his belt, and continued to impress during his first two seasons at Hyde Road. Playing across the middle with Max Woosnam and Micky Hamill, he missed only two League games in 1920/21 and ten the following term, before losing his place to Sammy Sharp. Fayers gained nine England amateur caps, scoring three goals.

FELTON, William (Full-back)
Apps: 83 Born: Heworth, Gateshead, 1/8/1900 Died: Manchester, 22/4/1977

  Career: Pelaw Albion, Pandon Temperance, Pelaw Albion, Wardley Colliery, Jarrow (May 1919), Grimsby Town, Sheffield Wednesday (£1,450), CITY (March 1929–March 1932), Tottenham Hotspur, Altrincham; retired June 1936; was also a very fine golfer.
  Details: Before joining City, former miner Bill Felton won the Second Division title with Sheffield Wednesday in 1926, and after leaving Maine Road he skippered Spurs to promotion to the top flight in 1933. A lusty right-back, quick in recovery with a solid tackle, he proved an excellent partner to first Jack Ridley and then Billy Dale in City's defence. Unfortunately, it was Felton's mistake in the last minute of the 1932 FA Cup semi-final against Arsenal led to Cliff Bastin's winning goal. Unfortunately, he never played for City again! He won his only England cap *v.* France in Paris in May 1925.

FENTON, Nicholas Leonard (Defender)
Apps: 20 Born: Preston, 23/11/1979
  Career: CITY (August 1996-September 2000), Notts County (loan), Bournemouth (loan, two spells), Notts County (£150,000), Doncaster Rovers, Grimsby Town, Rotherham United, Morecambe.
  Details: Nick Fenton, an England Youth international, played right-back and centre-half for City, producing several inspired performances before leaving the club in 2000. He had amassed over 525 League appearances at May 2013, including 168 for Notts County and 115 for Rotherham. One that got away as far as City are concerned – possibly so!

FERGUSON, Archibald (Left-back)
Apps: 2 Born: Edinburgh, c. 1865 Died: USA, c. 1930
  Career: Heart of Midlothian, Preston North End, CITY (July/October 1894), Baltimore Orioles/USA.
  Details: After only two first-team appearances for City, against Walsall and Grimsby Town in September 1894, Archie Ferguson left Hyde Road for the States with three other players, Mitch Calvey, Tommy Little and Alec Wallace.

FERNANDEZ, Gelson (Midfield)
Apps/goals: 59/4 Born: Praia, Cape Verde, 2/9/1986
  Career: FC Sion, CITY (£4.25 million, July 2007–July 2009), St Etienne/France, Chievo (loan), Leicester City (loan), Udinese (loan), Sporting Clube de Portugal, FC Sion (loan).
  Details: Combative midfielder Gelson Fernandez won four U21 and eleven full caps for Switzerland before becoming a record outgoing transfer by a Swiss club. After making his City debut in a League

Cup tie against Bolton, he went on to have a decent first season with the Blues, starting twenty-four of the thirty-two games he played in, and scoring two goals, but after an influx of midfielders, he was used mainly as a substitute in 2008/09, coming off the bench no less than eighteen times. He didn't like that and moved to France!

Later signed again by manager Sven-Göran Eriksson, this time for Leicester in August 2011, at May 2013, Fernandez had upped his tally of senior caps to forty (two goals scored) and had also made over 250 club appearances.

FIDLER, Dennis John (Inside/outside-left)
Apps/goals: 5/1 Born: Stockport, 232/6/1938
   Career: Stockport Schools, Manchester United (amateur), CITY (November 1956–May 1960), Port Vale, Grimsby Town (£2,000), Halifax Town, Darlington (£3,500), Macclesfield Town; retired; became a fishmonger.
   Details: Dennis Fidler was a reserve with City for almost four years. He made his debut (in place of Fionan Fagan) in a 2-2 home draw with Luton in October 1957, and scored his only goal in a 4-0 win at Leeds in February 1959. He spent his best years with Halifax, scoring forty goals in 143 League appearances between 1963 and 1966.

FINNERHAN, Patrick (Inside-right)
Apps/goals: 89/27 Born: Northwich,
23/3/1872 Died: Sale, c. 1941
   Career: Chirk, Northwich Victoria, CITY (June 1894–May 1897), Liverpool (£150), Bristol City.
   Details: Pat Finnerhan partnered Billy Meredith on the right-wing at Northwich, before doing likewise with City, for whom he gave wonderful service for three seasons, being an ever-present in his first two and top-scoring with fifteen goals in 1894/95. He represented the Football League in 1895 and was an England international trialist the following year.

FINNIGAN, Richard Prythderch (Goalkeeper)
Apps: 8 Born: Wrexham, 16/5/1904
Died: Halton, Cheshire, 1979
   Career: Oswestry Town, Holyhead Town, Connah's Quay & Shotton, Wrexham, Holyhead Town, Connah's Quay & Shotton, CITY (May 1926/May 1927), Accrington Stanley, Connah's Quay & Shotton, Wrexham, Colwyn Bay United, Chester, Stockport County, Winsford United; retired 1937.
   Details: A Welsh international (one cap gained *v.* Ireland in 1930) Dick Finnigan, of gypsy extraction, was reputedly discovered by Wrexham in a circus! His form could vary from brilliant to erratic, and during his season at Maine Road, he covered for Jimmy Goodchild and Bert Gray, keeping a clean sheet on his debut in a 2-0 win at Port Vale in

October. He made 118 appearances for Wrexham, with whom he twice won the Welsh Cup.

FISHER, James Albert (Inside-forward)
Apps/goals: 5/2 Born: Glasgow, 12/2/1881
Died: Nottingham, 4/12/1937
   Career: East Stirlingshire, St Bernard's, Celtic, Aston Villa, Fulham, Bristol City, Brighton & HA, CITY (June 1906/May 1907), Bradford PA, Coventry City, Caledonians/Scotland, Merthyr Town (player-manager), Notts County (secretary-manager); quit football, 1927.
   Details: After top-scoring for Bristol City in 1904/05 and failing to impress with Brighton, Albert Fisher was signed by City as cover for Irvine Thornley and Billy Jones. He scored on his debut (in a 9-1 drubbing at Everton) and netted in his final game at Middlesbrough, but thereafter played in the second XI.

FLEET, Stephen (Goalkeeper)
Apps: 6 Born: Urmston, 2/7/1937
   Career: Manchester Boys, Lancashire Schools, CITY (August 1953–June 1963), Wrexham, Stockport County; retired 1968; CITY (coach, 1970s).
   Details: After turning professional with City in February 1955, Steve Fleet was a reserve for eight years, mainly to Bert Trautmann and at times to John Savage. He made the first of his six appearances in a 4-3 home League defeat by Wolves in November 1957 and his last in a 3-0 win over Birmingham in February 1960, replacing the German 'keeper both times. He made a total of 142 appearances for his other two League clubs.

FLEMING, Gary James (Full-back)
Apps: 19 Born: Londonderry, Northern Ireland,
17/2/1967
   Career: Nottingham Forest, CITY (£150,000, August 1989/March 1990), Notts County (loan), Barnsley (£85,000); retired injured, June 1997.
   Details: Gary Fleming was a very efficient full-back and also a sweeper (when required), strong in all aspects of defensive play who partnered Andy Hinchcliffe during the first half of the 1989/90 season before City's new manager Howard Kendall brought in Alan Harper who had played under him at Everton.
   Fleming gained one U23 for his country and thirty-one at senior level and during a fine career, he made in excess of 350 club appearances, having by far his best years with Barnsley from 1990.

FLETCHER, Eli (Full-back)
Apps/goals: 327/2 Born: Tunstall, Staffs,
15/12/1887 Died: 1954
   Career: Hanley Swifts, Crewe Alexandra, CITY (May 1911–June 1926), Watford (player/assistant-

manager), Sandbach Ramblers, Ards; retired 1930.

Details: The ever-reliable Eli Fletcher, who made most appearances for City during the First World War (133), was the club's first choice left-back from the day of his debut *v.* Newcastle United in September 1911 until April 1922, missing only eighteen out of a possible 266 League matches. One of the club's longest-serving players of all time (fifteen years in total), at one point he was playing so well that local pundits thought he might oust Jesse Pennington from the England team. It was not to be, and all Fletcher had to show for his efforts was to represent the Football League on three occasions. He was replaced in City's line-up by Philip McCloy.

FLETCHER, Leonard (Centre-forward)
Apps/goals: 5/1 Born: Helsby, 1909
Died: c. 1970
Career: amateur football, CITY (November 1932–May 1935), Watford, Runcorn; retired during the Second World War.

Details: Signed as cover for Bobby Marshall and Fred Tilson, Len Fletcher made his City debut in a 3-0 home win over Everton in February 1933, was reserve for that season's FA Cup final and scored his only goal in a 2-1 win at Middlesbrough in September 1934. He netted twenty-two goals in thirty-six League games for Watford.

FLITCROFT, Garry William (Midfield)
Apps/goals: 141/15 Born: Bolton, 6/11/1972
Career: Turton High School, Bolton Boys, Lilleshall School of Excellence; CITY (July 1989–March 1996), Bury (loan), Blackburn Rovers (£3.5 million), Sheffield United (loan); retired injured, July 2006; Leigh Genesis FC (manager), Chorley Town (manager).

Details: As a twelve-year-old, Garry Flitcroft rejected Manchester United's overtures in favour of a move to Manchester City. He spent two years honing his skills at Lilleshall Hall, before signing professional forms at Maine Road. Following a brief spell with Bury in 1992, he made his League debut for City as a substitute in a 3-3 draw at Oldham in August 1992, and thereafter, as a strong, aggressive midfielder, went on to appear in over 140 competitive games. At a time when City were going through financial difficulties, club chairman Francis Lee told manager Alan Ball Jnr to sell his most profitable player. That was Flitcroft, who went to Blackburn!

An England schoolboy and youth international, he gained ten U21 caps, and after leaving City made 280 first-class appearances for Blackburn with whom he won the League Cup in 2002.

His younger brother David played for Preston, Lincoln, Chester and Rochdale in the 1990s.

In September 2011, Flitcroft was named as a 'core participant' in the Leveson inquiry into the News International phone hacking scandal.

FLOOD, William Robert (Midfield)
Apps/goals: 18/2 Born: Dublin, 10/4/1985
Career: Cherry Orchard FC/Dublin, CITY (April 2001–August 2006), Rochdale (loan), Coventry City (loan), Cardiff City (£200,000), Dundee United (loan, two spells), Celtic, Middlesbrough, Dundee United.

Details: 'Willo' Flood represented the Republic of Ireland ten times at youth team level before going on to win sixteen U21 caps. A wide midfielder, just 5 feet 6 inches tall, with good pace and skill, he made his debut for City in the UEFA Cup game *v.* The New Saints (TNS) in 2003, but was always on the edge of regular first-team football, despite being voted his country's U19 'Player of the Year' in 2004.

Sent off on his debut for Dundee United (for taking a free-kick too quickly), he followed up with the SPL 'Goal of the Season' for the Tannadice club in a 3-0 win over St Mirren in December 2007. He played in six SPL games for Celtic in 2009/10, the first in the Old Firm derby against Rangers.

In December 2005, Flood's home in Wythenshawe was the subject of a burglary in which Flood himself was threatened and taunted at knife point for over twenty minutes by a twenty-nine-year-old man wearing a Manchester City shirt. The ordeal left Flood with recurring nightmares, resulting in him needing counseling and being unable to live alone.

FOE, Marc-Vivien (Midfield)
Apps/goals: 38/9 Born: Yaoundé, Cameroon, 1/5/1975 Died: Lyon, France, 26/6/2003
Career: Union Garoua/Camerloon, Canon Yaoundé, Lens/France, West Ham United (£4.2 million), Lyon (£6 million), CITY (loan, for £550,000, August 2002/May 2003).

Details: Known as the 'Gentle Giant', Marc-Vivien Foe was wanted by Manchester United in 1998, but his club, Lens, turned down Alex Ferguson's bid of £3 million and a year later he joined West Ham, moving back to France with Lyon in 2000.

Already a world class international midfielder when he signed for City, Foe made his debut for the Blues on the opening day of the 2002/03 season in a 3–0 defeat by Leeds, scoring his first goal at Sunderland four months later. And by sheer coincidence, his ninth and final goal for City was also against the Wearsiders and was, in fact, the last ever scored at Maine Road, on 21 April 2003. A first-team regular under manager Kevin Keegan, he played in thirty-eight of the club's forty-one matches during his season on loan.

As part of the Cameroon squad for the 2003 FIFA Confederations Cup he played against Brazil's

National Football Team and the Turkish National Football team, but was rested for the match against the USA, before returning to action for the semi-final against Colombia on 26 June 2003. In the seventy-second minute, Foé collapsed in the centre circle with no other players near him. After attempts to resuscitate him failed on the pitch, he was stretchered off where he received mouth-to-mouth resuscitation and oxygen. Medics spent forty-five minutes attempting to restart his heart, and although he was still alive upon arrival at the stadium's medical centre, sadly he died shortly afterwards. The initial autopsy did not determine an exact cause of death, but a second concluded that Foé's death was heart-related, as it discovered evidence of hypertrophic cardiomyopathy, a hereditary condition known to increase the risk of sudden death during physical exercise. His tragic death caused a profound shock. Numerous tributes to his joyous personality and infectious humor were expressed in the media. A tribute plaque lies outside the Etihad Stadium.

Foe left this world in his prime, having scored twenty-eight goals in 234 club matches and eight in sixty-four internationals. He won the French League championship and League Cup in successive seasons with Lyon.

FORD, Albert Arthur (Outside-right)
Apps: 4 Born: Newcastle-upon-Tyne,
2/8/1901 Died: Peterborough, 24/3/1976
Career: Spen Black & White, Seaton Delaval, CITY (May 1921–June 1923), Norwich City, Peterborough & Fletton United; later worked as a mechanical engineer.
Details: Albert Ford was only twenty when he made his League debut for City (in place of Pat Kelly) in a 2-1 win at Bradford City in February 1922. A speedy winger, he played in the next three games when City failed to score a single goal. He made just one appearance for Norwich v. Reading in May 1924.

FORRESTER, Thomas (Forward)
Apps/goals: 10/2 Born: Stoke, summer
1864 Died: Stoke, 1950
Career: Trentham, Stoke, Stoke St Peter's, CITY (October 1892–May 1894), Tunstall/Stoke-on-Trent.
Details: Tom Forrester was twenty-eight when he joined City, signed initially as cover for Hugh Morris and David Weir. Making his League debut in a 1-1 home draw with Burton Swifts in November 1892, he scored in his second game at Lincoln and in his last v. Walsall Town Swifts before returning to the Potteries.

FOSTER, Clifford Lake (Outside-left)
Apps: 3 Born: Rotherham, 1904

Career: Scunthorpe United, Rotherham County, Bournemouth & Boscombe Athletic, Morecambe, CITY (April 1927/April 1928), Oldham Athletic, Halifax Town; retired injured, May 1930.
Details: Much-travelled reserve Cliff Foster deputised for George Hicks in successive League games against Barnsley, Wolves and Barnsley again, halfway through the 1927/28 season. He had his best spell with Halifax.

FOSTER, Harold Arthur (Outside-left)
Apps/goals: 8/1 Born: Manchester, 1875
Died: before 1945
Career: local football, CITY (August 1896/March 1898), Darwen.
Details: Harry Foster was one of eleven different players used on the left-wing in the two seasons he was with City. He appeared in six Leagues in 1896/97, scoring his only goal in a 1-1 home draw with Loughborough.

FOSTER, John Colin (Right-back)
Apps: 16 Born: Blackley, 19/9/1973
Career: YTS, CITY (August 1989/March 1998), Carlisle United, Bury, Hyde United.
Details: England schoolboy international John Foster had to wait until 1994 before making his senior debut for City, away at Newcastle in the Premiership. A well-built defender, he was always in reserve and after six-and-a-half years with the club moved to Carlisle.

FOWLER, Robert Bernard (Striker)
Apps/goals: apps/goals: 92/28 Born: Toxteth,
Liverpool, 9 April 1975
Career: Liverpool, Leeds United, CITY (£3 million, January 2003–January 2006), Liverpool (free), Cardiff City (free agent), Blackburn Rovers (free), North Queensland Fury/Australia, Perth Glory/Australia, Bury (assistant-manager), Muangthong United/Thailand (player-manager), MK Dons (coach); invested in racehorses; media work for Abu Dhabi Sports Channel, Sky Sport and TV; with a net wealth of £28 million, was named in the Sunday Times Rich List as one of the 1,000 wealthiest Britons in 2005.
Details: Robbie Fowler joined Manchester City FC following a protracted transfer saga that resulted in Chairman David Bernstein leaving the club. Encouraged to sign by manager Kevin Keegan, Fowler made a moderate start to his City career, scoring just twice in his first thirteen matches. He struggled with his fitness in 2003/04, but did score against his old club Liverpool in a 2–2 home draw. The arrival of close friend, Steve McManaman, gave Fowler hope, but the pair failed to rekindle their prolific partnership from their time at Anfield, and received criticism from the fans and tabloids regarding their huge salaries,

alleged to be excessive, as well as being named and shamed in a sex scandal covered by the *News of the World* that year. Thankfully, Fowler rallied and showed a marked improvement during the second half of 2004/05, scoring his 150th Premiership goal in the 3–2 win over Norwich in February, but alas his failure to convert a ninetieth-minute penalty kick against Middlesbrough on the last day of the campaign, denied City a place in the UEFA Europa League. Nevertheless, he still finished as the club's joint top score, thus gaining the approval of the fans. Injured again, he made only two substitute appearances in the first four months of 2005/06 before bagging a sixteen-minute hat-trick against Scunthorpe in the FA Cup, following up with a goal in a 3-1 win in the Manchester derby.

In a terrific career, Fowler netted 252 goals in 589 club matches, and only Shearer, Andy Cole and Thierry Henry have scored more than his 163 in the Premiership. He also holds the record for scoring the fastest hat-trick in PL history, for Liverpool *v.* Arsenal in 1993.

The recipient of twenty-six England caps (seven goals), Fowler was unlucky inasmuch that there were some great strikers around at the same time, including Alan Shearer, Teddy Sheringham and Michael Owen, although a serious injury, suffered in February 1998, hit him hard and ruled him out of that year's World Cup. Honoured as a schoolboy, he also appeared in one unofficial, one 'B' and eight U21 internationals, starred in England's UEFA Youth Cup triumph in 1993, was twice PFA 'Young Player of the Year' (1995 and 1996), played in two League Cup-winning teams for Liverpool (1995 and 2001), and was an unused substitute in the triumphant FA Cup and UEFA Cup finals of 2001. And with North Queensland Fury in 2010, Fowler was named 'Player of the Year' and Players' 'Player of the Year' and also won the Golden Boot award. His book, *Fowler, an Autobiography*, was published in September 2005.

FRANCIS, Trevor John (Forward)
Apps/goals: 29/14 Born: Plymouth, Devon, 19/4/1954
Career: Ernesettle Youth Club/Plymouth, Plymouth Boys, Birmingham City, Detroit Express/USA (loan), Nottingham Forest (£975,000 plus Vat and Levy = £1 million), Detroit Express (loan), CITY (£1.2 million, September 1981/July 1982), Sampdoria/Italy (£800,000), Atalanta/Italy (£900,000), Glasgow Rangers, Queen's Park Rangers, Woologong City/Australia, Queen's Park Rangers player-manager), Sheffield Wednesday (free, February 1990, retired as a player, May 1991, then manager); soccer pundit on Sky Sport; Birmingham City (manager), Crystal Palace (manager); now football match summariser for Asian TV networks.

Details: Utility forward Trevor Francis – Britain's first £1 million footballer – had a wonderful playing career, scoring 225 goals in 752 club appearances as well as netting twelve times in fifty-two internationals for England, making his debut *v.* Holland at Wembley in 1977.

He headed the winning goal in the 1979 European Cup final, won the Scottish League Cup with Rangers and as a manager guided Sheffield Wednesday to both the FA Cup and League Cup finals in 1993 and Birmingham to the 2001 League Cup final and into the First Division play-offs four seasons running. He also won England Youth honours and played five times for his country's U23 team. The deal to bring Francis to City caused behind-the-scenes friction at Maine Road. During negotiations, chairman Peter Swales informed manager John Bond that the club could not afford the transfer fee. Bond then issued an ultimatum, 'If Francis doesn't sign, I will resign.' He signed.

After a promising start, scoring two goals against Stoke City on his debut, he was frequently injured, spending a lot of time on the treatment table, but still tucked away fourteen goals in twenty-nine games and made the England squad for the 1982 World Cup in Spain. However, back at Maine Road, financial problems were again an issue. Francis' contract gave him a salary of £100,000 plus bonuses, which the club could no longer afford to pay to a player who regularly sustained injuries, and as a result he was sold to Sampdoria.

FREEMAN, Raymond Henry (Forward)
Apps/goals: 4/1 Born: Droitwich, Worcs, 1913 Died: after 1975
Career: Bromsgrove Rovers, CITY (November 1935–May 1939), Exeter City; retired 1945.
Details: After scoring plenty of goals for Bromsgrove, Ray Freeman was signed as a reserve striker by City, but with the regular strike-force doing the business he found it hard to get into the first team, making only four starts in three-and-half seasons; his only goal coming in a 3-2 League win at Tottenham in March 1939 when he deputised for Jack Milsom.

FRONTZECK, Michael (Left wing-back)
Apps: 25 Born: Mönchengladbach, Germany, 26/3/1964
Career: Spvgg Odenkirchen, Borussia Mönchengladbach, VfB Stuttgart, VfL Bochum, Borussia Mönchengladbach, CITY (January 1996/January 1997), SC Frieburg (£80,000), Borussia Mönchengladbach (retired as a player, 2000; assistant-coach), Hannover (assistant-coach), Alemannia Aachen (manager), Arminia Bielefeld (manager), Borussia Mönchengladbach (manager), FC Pauli (manager).

Details: A strong, attacking player, Michael Frontzeck amassed over 550 career appearances and won six U21 and nineteen full caps for Germany. An Alan Ball signing, like his teammates, he battled in vain as City were relegated from the Premiership, and continued to perform after that before getting 'homesick' and returning to Germany.

FROST, Ronald Albert (Winger)
Apps/goals: 2/1 Born: Hazel Grove, Cheshire, 16/1/1947
    Career: Stockport Boys, CITY (July 1962–June 1965), Kettering Town.
    Details: Reserve Ron Frost played twice for City in three seasons, scoring on his debut in a 4-3 defeat at Charlton in March 1964 when he deputised for Neil Young on the right-wing.

FROST, Samuel (Half-back)
Apps/goals: 112/4 Born: Poplar, London, 1879 Died: Isle of Dogs, London, 1/3/1926
    Career: Millwall St John's, Millwall Athletic, CITY (May 1901–March 1907), Millwall Athletic; retired injured, April 1913.
    Details: An able-bodied wing-half, Sammy Frost, in fact, made his City debut as Billy Meredith's right-wing partner in a 3-1 defeat at Everton, but after a season in the reserves, he bedded himself into the middle line, replacing Bobby Moffatt and holding his place for three years, collecting a Second Division championship-winning medal in 1903. He duly returned to The Den, upped his total of appearances for the Lions to an impressive 177 and also represented the Southern League in 1911, having appeared for the football League as a City player. A damaged knee ended his career, and as a result Frost went to Bow County Court and claimed under the Workmen's Compensation Act. He won his case and was awarded £1-a-week for life!

FÜLÖP, Márton (Goalkeeper)
Apps: 3 Born: Budapest, 3/5/1983
    Career: BKV Elöre/Hungary, BFC Siofok, MTK Hungaria, Tottenham Hotspur (£65,000), Chesterfield (loan), Coventry City (loan), Sunderland (£500,000), Leicester City (loan), CITY (loan, April/May 2010), Ipswich Town, West Bromwich Albion, Asteras Tripoli.
    Details: The recipient of ten U21 and 24 full caps for Hungary, and possibly the tallest City player ever at 6 feet 6 inches, goalkeeper Márton Fülöp answered an emergency call when Shay Given was sidelined with a dislocated shoulder, and played in the last three Premiership games of the 2009/10 season, which included the 'so called Champions League play-off' against Tottenham.

FURR, George Maurice (Outside-right)
Apps: 3 Born: Watford, 1885 Died: after 1945

Career: Watford, CITY (August 1909/November 1910), Watford, Croydon Common; retired 1915.
    Details: Winger George Furr spent fifteen months with City. He made three appearances in place of George Stewart towards the end of the 1909/10 season, playing well on his debut in a 3-1 win over Gainsborough Trinity.

FUTCHER, Paul (Defender)
Apps: 46 Born: Chester, 25/9/1956
    Career: Chester, Luton Town (£100,000), CITY (record £350,000, June 1978/July 1979), Oldham Athletic (£150,000), Derby County, Barnsley, Halifax Town, Grimsby Town, Dundalk, Droylsden, Gresley Rovers (player-manager), Southport (player-coach); retired as a player, Ashton United (manager), Huddersfield New College (coach).
    Details: Paul Futcher, the defensive half of twin brothers, was the most expensive defender in England when joined City for a record fee in 1978. With eleven England U21 caps under his belt, he replaced club stalwart Tommy Booth in the side, but failing to live up to expectations, he attracted criticism. Booth won his place back, and at the end of the season Futcher was sold to Oldham for a cut-price fee of £150,000. During his three years with Grimsby (1991–94) Futcher was voted 'man of the match' in nearly every game he played, and is one of the club's all time legends. He made over 900 appearances during his career (798 for his League clubs) and was twice chosen for the senior England squad, but each time was denied the chance of winning a full cap by a road accident. His son, Ben Futcher, played for Oldham, Doncaster, Lincoln, Grimsby, Peterborough and Bury, while Paul is the uncle of Danny Murphy, ex-Liverpool and Fulham.

FUTCHER, Ronald (Striker)
Apps/goals: 20/7 Born: Chester, 25/9/1956
    Career: Chester, Luton Town, CITY (August 1978/April 1979), Minnesota Kicks, Portland Timbers, Southampton, Tulsa Roughnecks, NAC Breda, Barnsley, Oldham Athletic, Bradford City, Port Vale, Barnsley, Crewe Alexandra, Boston United; retired 1993; Bradford City (Community Officer), Oakland University/USA (coach), RSL Florida (coach); also involved in a sportswear business in the North-east of England.
    Details: Ron Futcher left Kenilworth Road for City after David Pleat was appointed manager of the Hatters. He played alongside his twin brother at Maine Road under Tony Book, but never really settled, starting only ten League games – although he did scored a hat-trick in a 4-1 win at Chelsea in September 1978. During a fine career, Futcher scored almost 300 goals in 705 club appearances with a League record of 269 in 607 matches.

An elder Futcher brother, Graham (born in 1953) played for Chester ... and the four Futchers, together, made a grand total of 2,134 appearances at all levels of football!

G

GARCIA, Francisco Javier Fernandez (Midfield)
Apps/goals: 33/2 Born: Mula, Spain, 8/2/1987
Career: Real Madrid (from the age of nine), Osasuna (£2.25 million), Real Madrid (£3.6 million), Benfica (£6.7 million), CITY (£15.8 million, August 2012).
Details: Hard-working midfielder Javi Garcia spent twelve years in two spells at the Bernabeu Stadium. He played in the club's youth, 'B', reserve and senior sides, and helped Real win the Spanish Super Cup in 2008. With Benfica he won the Portuguese League title three times and the League Cup once before moving to City, for whom he made an impressive Premiership debut by scoring from a Carlos Tévez free-kick in a 1-1 draw with Stoke. Capped by his country forty-seven times at various levels from U16 to U21, he's so far appeared in one full international *v.* Serbia in 2012.

GARNER, William Walter (Half-back)
Apps: 5 Born: Manchester, c. 1890 Died: before 1980
Career: Heaton Park, CITY (August 1912–May 1919), Southport.
Details: A reserve throughout his seven-year spell with City, Billy Garner did well in his five starts but unfortunately the arrival of the First World War didn't do him any favours!

GARRIDO, Javier Behobide (Left-back)
Apps/goals: 62/2 Born: Irun, Spain, 15/3/1985
Career: Real Sociedad, CITY (£1.75 million, August 2007–July 2010), SS Lazio/Italy, Norwich City (loan).
Details: A very competent left-back, Javier Garrido's displays are characterised by his constant overlapping runs. He played a big part in the most successful Premier League start in City's history with four victories and four clean sheets from the opening six games in August/September 2007, but was replaced by Michael Ball just before Christmas. He scored his first City goal direct from a free-kick in a 3-2 defeat by Liverpool FC in October 2008 and his second with a fantastic free-kick *v.* Wolves a year later, However, he found it increasingly hard to gain a place in the first team until Roberto Mancini took over as manager, only to struggle again in 2009/10 which led to him leaving for Italy. The winner of twenty-four youth and nine U21 caps for Spain, Garrido helped his country with the UEFA U19 tournament in 2004.

GARTLAND, Peter (Left-back)
Apps: 1 Born: Seaham, c. 1890 Died: before 1960
Career: Seaham Harbour, CITY (March 1914–May 1917).
Details: Peter Gartland's only appearance for City was in the 2-1 home League win over Chelsea on Boxing Day 1914 when he deputised for Eli Fletcher. Sadly, he lost a leg in battle in France in 1917.

GAUDINO, Maurizio (Forward)
Apps/goals: 20/3 Born: Bruhl, West Germany, 12/12/1966
Career: TSG Reinhau, SV Waldhof Mannheim, VfB Stuttgart, Eintracht Frankfurt, CITY (loan, December 1994/May 1995), Club America (loan), FC Basel, VfL Bochum, Antalysapor, SV Waldhof Mannheim; retired 2004.
Details: Loanee Maurizio Gaudino helped City end the 1994/95 season with some magnificent performances, including a 3-2 victory over the League champions Blackburn Rovers FC, as well as scoring with a magnificent winning header against Liverpool, which helped secure top-flight status. Before his short spell with City, Gaudino scored thirty goals in 171 Bundesliga games for VfB Stuttgart with whom he won the German League title. In 1993, he gained five full caps for his country.

GAUGHAN, William Bernard (Outside-left)
Apps: 10 Born: Devonport, 20/11/1892 Died: South Wales, 1956
Career: Devonport BC, Cardiff City, CITY (June 1914–July 1919), Newport County.
Details: After failing to make the grade with Cardiff, nippy winger Bill Gaughan tried his luck with City. Deputising for Joe Dorsett in nine of his ten outings, the First World War unfortunately interrupted his progress. He later played over 100 games for Newport (1920–24).

GAYLE, Brian Wilbert (Defender)
Apps/goals: 66/3 Born: Kingston, 6/3/1965
Career: Wimbledon, CITY (£325,000, July 1988–January 1990), Ipswich Town (£330,000), Sheffield United, Exeter City, Rotherham United, Bristol Rovers (loan), Shrewsbury Town; retired June 1999.
Details: After making exactly 100 appearances for Wimbledon and helping them reach the 1988 FA Cup final, Brian Gayle was signed by City Mel Machin to play alongside Steve Redmond. He was superb in his first full season at Maine Road, missing only five League matches, and scoring vital goals against Plymouth and Swindon as City gained promotion to the First Division. However, after fourteen outings during the first half of 1989/90 he was replaced by Colin Hendry

and quickly moved to Ipswich, before having 138 outings for Sheffield United (1991–96). He retired in 1999 with 493 club appearances to his name.

(GEOVANNI), Deiderson Gomez Geovanni Mauricio (Forward)
Apps/goals: 23/3 Born: Aciaca, Brazil, 11/1/1980
Career: Cruzeiro, America Brazil, Barcelona, Benfica, Cruzeiro, Portsmouth (trial), CITY (free, July 2007/July 2008), Hull City (free), San Jose Earthquakes/USA, Vitoria, America-MG/USA.
Details: Signed on a Bosman deal, the skilful Geovanni scored on his debut for City in a 2–0 victory over West Ham a month after signing and then netted the only goal in the Manchester derby as City continued their 100 per cent start to the season, making him a huge hit with the fans! He was also on target against Wigan in early December, but after that his outings were mainly via the subs' bench and at the end of the season he was released. The likeable Geovanni played in six U23 internationals for Brazil, won his first full cap *v.* Mexico in 2001 and represented his country at the 2000 Olympic Games.

GIBBONS, Sydney (Centre-half)
Apps: 11 Born: Darlaston, Staffs, 24/3/1907 Died: West London, 14/7/1953
Career: Wolverhampton Wanderers, Walsall, Cradley Heath, CITY (April 1927–May 1930), Fulham, Worcester City (player-manager); retired during the War; Fulham (scout); ran a tobacconist's shop in Putney until his death.
Details: The son of a Black Country foundry worker, Syd Gibbons was as tough as they come and due to his imposing image, was nicknamed 'Carnera', after the famous boxer. A Junior international, capped for England against Scotland in 1926, and having failed to make headway at Molineux and Walsall, he spent a season in non-League football before joining City, initially as cover for Sam Cowan for whom he deputised when making his debut in a 3-1 home win over Oldham in October 1927. Unable to get regular first-team football, he left Maine Road for Fulham. Forming a terrific half-line with Albert Barrett and Len Oliver, he made 318 senior appearances in eight years, helping the Cottagers win the Third Division (S) title and reach the FA Cup semi-final.

GIBSON, Thomas Duncan (Centre-forward)
Apps/goals: 2/2 Born: Glasgow, 1901 Died: Glasgow, before 1975
Career: Bridgetown Waverley, CITY (July 1926/May 1927), South Shields.
Details: A one-season reserve to Frank Roberts, Tom Gibson scored twice in his second game for City, in a 5-2 home League win over Fulham in January 1927. He made only four appearances for South Shields.

GIDMAN, John (Right-back)
Apps/goals: 71/3 Born: Garston, Liverpool, 10/1/1954
Career: Garston Schoolboy football, Liverpool, Aston Villa, Everton (£650,000), Manchester United (£450,000), CITY (free, October 1986–August 1988), Stoke City (free), Darlington (player/assistant-manager); retired as a player, 1989; King's Lynn (manager); moved to Marbella, Spain to run a café/bar.
Details: An attacking right-back, capped once by England against Luxembourg in a World Cup qualifier in March 1977, John Gidman's presence in City's defence couldn't prevent them from slipping into the Second Division at the end of his first season at Maine Road. His three goals for the club came in different competitions, including a ninety-seventh-minute equaliser in an FA Cup tie *v.* Huddersfield in January 1988.
He twice helped Aston Villa win the FA Youth Cup, the League Cup twice and the Third Division championship. He also played in three youth and four U23 internationals. While with Villa, he suffered eye damage from an exploding firework and was sent off in a UEFA Cup tie against Barcelona in the Nou Camp in 1978. He made 432 League appearances during his career, including eighty-five for United and 197 for Villa.

GILL, Raymond (Defender)
Apps: 9 Born: Manchester, 8/12/1924 Died: Rochdale, 17/9/2001
Career: Local football, CITY (December 1941–June 1951), Chester, Hyde United, Altrincham, Winsford United.
Details: A wartime signing by City, aged seventeen, Ray Gill was registered with the club for ten years and had to wait until March 1949 before making his League debut, at right-half in place of Billy Walsh in a 1-1 draw with the FA Cup finalists Wolves in front of 45,000 fans at Molineux. He did superbly well with Chester, making 406 League appearances in eleven years – a club record that still stands today.

GILLESPIE, William Jardine (Inside-forward)
Apps/goals: 231/132 Born: Strathclyde, 2/10/1873 Died: Lyn, Massachusetts, USA, 1942
Career: Strathclyde, Lincoln City, CITY (January 1897–May 1905); emigrated to the USA; Harvard University (soccer coach).
Details: Billy Gillespie, a brawny Scot, formed a wonderful right-wing eight-year partnership with Welshman Billy Meredith. In his first half-season with City, he netted four goals in eleven appearances and was leading scorer with nineteen in 1897/98 when the Second Division championship was won. He continued to add to his goal tally, having his best-scoring campaign in 1902/03 when, having

fought off a challenge from Joe Cassidy two seasons earlier, he bagged a total of thirty as City, relegated the previous season, regained top-flight status at the first attempt. In 1903/1904, Gillespie was once again City's top League marksman with eighteen goals as the team finished second behind Sheffield Wednesday. In that same season City won the FA Cup with Gillespie in the team.

At the end of the 1904/05 campaign, the Football Association conducted an investigation into the financial activities of Manchester City and discovered that players had been paid extra money. It was ruled that manager Tom Maley should be suspended from football for life while seventeen players, including Meredith and Gillespie, were fined and suspended until January 1907. Gillespie refused to pay his fine, and instead emigrated to the States where he remained for the rest of his life. Even then he hit the sports pages when, in the summer of 1906, he was fined a further £50 and further suspended by the FA for alleged transfer irregularities. Gillespie averaged fourteen goals a season for City and had the pleasure, and honour, of scoring the club's first top-flight hat-trick, a four-timer in fact, in a vital game against Blackburn Rovers in April 1902. His brother, Matt Gillespie, played for Lincoln, rivals Newton Heath, Blackburn and Accrington.

GILLIES, Alexander (Forward)
Apps: 5 Born: Cowdenbeath, 1874
Died: Lochgelly, Scotland, 1921
    Career: Lochgelly United, Bolton Wanderers, CITY (February/May 1896), Lochgelly, Heart of Midlothian, Sheffield Wednesday (£100), Leicester Fosse, Dumbarton (two spells), Lochgelly United (two spells).
    Details: With the Second Division title race hotting up, Alex Gillies, signed as forward cover, played his part in vital end-of-season matches, but alas, City missed out on promotion by losing two of the four Test Matches.

GIVEN, Séamus John James (Goalkeeper)
Apps: 69 Born: Lifford, County Donegal, 20/4/1976
    Career: Lifford Celtic, Glasgow Celtic, Blackburn Rovers, Swindon Town (loan), Sunderland (loan), Newcastle United (£1.5 million), CITY (£7 million, February 2009–July 2011), Aston Villa.
    Details: After signing for City on a four-and-a-half-year-contract, Shay Given criticised Newcastle's management for not trying hard enough to keep him at the club. A terrific shot-stopper, the Irishman was quite brilliant on his City debut in February 2009, making at least four superb saves in a 1–0 win over Middlesbrough. With Joe Hart going out on loan, he immediately established himself the posts,

making the 400th League appearance of his career nine months later against his future club Aston Villa. With captain Kolo Touré away on international duty, Given was given the captain's armband by manager Roberto Mancini, who described him as 'one of the five best 'keepers in the world'. A dislocated shoulder, suffered during a match against Arsenal in April 2010, ruled Given out for the rest of the season and surprisingly, after regaining full fitness, he was dropped for the opening Premiership game of 2010/11 v. Tottenham, replaced by the returning Hart who bedded down to become City's permanent first-choice 'keeper, although Given played enough during the season to receive an FA Cup winner's medal. After five starts in the U21s, Given is his country's second most decorated player with 125 senior caps to his name. He won the First Division title with Sunderland and the InterToto Cup with Newcastle, and had made 593 club appearances at May 2013.

GLÁUBER, Leandro Honorato Berti (Left-back)
Apps: 1 Born: São José do Rio Preto, Brazil, 5/8/1983
    Career: Atletico Mineiro, Palmeiras, FC Nuremberg, CITY (August 2008/May 2009), São Caetano, Rapid Bucharest, Columbus Crew/USA.
    Details: Brazilian international (capped v. Guatemala in 2005) 'Berti' Gláuber's only outing for City was an eighty-fourth-minute substitute v. Bolton on the last day of the 2008/09 season. He played his best football in the Bundesliga with Nuremberg.

GLEGHORN, Nigel William (Midfield)
Apps/goals: 39/11 Born: Seaham, 12/8/1962
    Career: Deneside Junior & Northlea Senior Schools, Seaham Red Star, Ipswich Town (£5,000), CITY (£47,500, August 1988/September 1989), Birmingham City (£175,000), Stoke City (£100,000), Burnley (free), Brentford (loan), Northampton Town (loan), Altrincham, Witton Albion, Nantwich Town (player-manager); England U14 (coach), England U21 (scout); became senior sports lecturer at South Trafford College, Manchester; played cricket for Durham at U18 and U21 levels, having a top-score of 135; also had a trial with Middlesex as a batsman/wicketkeeper.
    Details: Former fireman Nigel 'Gleggy' Gleghorn scored in four different competitions in his only season with City. An intelligent midfielder with a delicate touch and a terrific engine, he possessed a powerful left-foot which he used to great effect. Surprisingly, he did not sign professional forms until he was twenty-three, but over a period of thirteen years in top-line soccer, he bagged 105 goals in 571 club appearances, having his best spell with Stoke (thirty-one strikes in 208 games). He

won the Leyland DAF Cup with Birmingham in 1991 and the Second Division championship with Stoke in 1993.

GLENNON, Christopher David (Forward)
Apps: 5 Born: Manchester, 29/10/1949
Career: Manchester Boys, CITY (August 1965–July 1971), Tranmere Rovers (loan), Northwich Victoria.

Details: A City reserve, Chris Glennon made his League debut as second-half substitute for Neil Young in a 1-0 defeat at Nottingham Forest in March 1969. A year later, he started three games as leader of the attack, having earlier tasted European football for the first time against Academica Coimbra in the ECWC.

GOATER, Leonardo Shaun, MBE (Striker)
Apps/goals: 212/103 Born: Hamilton, Bermuda, 25/2/1970
Career: North Village, Boulevard, North Village, Manchester United (free), Rotherham United (free), Notts County (loan), Bristol City (£175,000), CITY (£400,000, March 1998–August 2003), Reading (£500,000), Coventry City, Southend United, Bermuda Hogges, North Village Rams; retired 2011.

Details: Leading scorer in 1998/99 (with twenty-two goals) and again in 1999/2000 (with twenty-nine), the 'Goat' found the net in four different competitions during his first full season with City, including a thirty-fourth-minute hat-trick in a 4-0 win over Gillingham, on the way to promotion to the Premiership. His hundredth City goal came in the last-ever Maine Road Manchester derby in November 2002 (won 3-1). After giving his all, he was put under pressure when Nicolas Anelka arrived on the scene and as a result, his first-team opportunities reduced, and as a result was transferred to Reading.

During his career, Goater – admired by many fellow professionals for his attitude and commitment – notched 282 goals in 724 appearances, including 221 in 556 at League level alone. He also scored twenty-two goals in thirty-six games for Bermuda. In June 2003, he was awarded the MBE for services to youth sport in his home country.

GODFREY, Joseph (Half-back)
Apps/goals: 9/1 Born: Walleswood, Sheffield, 5/9/1894 Died: Sheffield, after 1945
Career: Kiveton Park, Brighton FC/Sheffield, Nottingham Forest, Birmingham, Coventry City, CITY (November 1919/May 1920), Merthyr Town, Rotherham Town, Beighton Recreationalists, Denaby United, Mexborough, Denaby United.

Details: Mainly a reserve with every major club he served, 'Joby' Godfrey made only twenty-five League appearances during his career. His only goal for City earned two points against Preston North End in March 1920 (1-0).

A former Yorkshire miner, he scored twenty-six goals in wartime football for Birmingham for whom his brother, Bruce, also played.

GODWIN, Verdi (Forward)
Apps/goals: 8/3 Born: Blackburn, 17/2/1926
Career: Blackburn Rovers, CITY (June 1948/June 1949), Stoke City (£3,000), Mansfield Town (£8,000), Middlesbrough, Grimsby Town, Brentford, Southport, Barrow, Tranmere Rovers, Kings Lynn, Macclesfield Town, Netherfield, New Brighton; retired April 1964; thereafter scout for Blackpool, Chelsea, Plymouth Argyle, Liverpool, Vancouver Whitecaps, Bolton Wanderers & Wimbledon, to 1985.

Details: A useful forward, Verdi Godwin scored twenty-eight goals in 143 appearances in ten years of League football, having his best spells with Blackburn and Mansfield. A reserve with City, he netted on his senior debut at Preston (won 3-1) and struck twice in his next game at Charlton. After retiring he became a successful scout, 'spotting' the talent of Steve Heighway, Paul Mariner and Tony Waiters among others. Presumably his parents were keen patrons of opera as they named their son after the famous Italian composer, Guiseppe Verdi! It is thought that Godwin is still alive, making him one of City's oldest former players.

GOLAC, Ivan (Full-back)
Apps: 2 Born: Kuprivnica, Croatia, FPR Yugoslavia, 15/6/1950
Career: Partizan Belgrade, Southampton, Bournemouth (loan), Southampton (£50,000), CITY (loan, Match 1983), Bjelasica/Yugoslavia, Southampton, Portsmouth (loan), FC Zumen (player-coach; retired as a player, 1988; Partizan Belgrade (coach, then manager), Croatia (national team manager), Torquay United (manager), Dundee United (manager), IA Akranes/Iceland (manager), Sartid Smederevo (manager), Karpaty Lviv (manager); ran a chocolate factory in Belgrade.

Details: Ivan Golac was the first 'foreigner' to appear in a League Cup final at Wembley – for Southampton against Nottingham Forest in 1979. Saints lost 3–2 to the holders, who were also the First Division champions. After making over 150 appearances under Lawrie McMenemy at The Dell, the relationship between player and manager turned sour in 1982 following a contract dispute. This led to Golac going out on loan to first Bournemouth and then City. A terrific professional who trained well and loved 5-a-sides particularly in the small gym, Golac's two League outings for City were against Swansea and his former club Southampton, both games ending in 4-1 defeats!

GOMERSALL, Victor (Full-back)
Apps: 39 Born: Manchester, 17/6/1942
Career: Junior football, CITY (May 1958–
August 1966), Swansea Town.

Details: After spending eight years at Maine
Road, Vic Gomersall went on to score six goals
in 178 appearances for Swansea before dropping
out of League football in 1971. Well proportioned
and strong in the tackle, he made his First Division
debut for City against Chelsea in November 1961,
deputising for Cliff Sear but had to wait until
1964/65 before having a decent run in the side,
partnering Dave Bacuzzi at full-back in twenty-
nine League matches.

GOODCHILD, Andrew James (Goalkeeper)
Apps: 217 Born: Southampton, 4/4/1892
Died: Eastleigh, Hampshire, 2/10/1950
Career: St Paul's Athletic, Southampton,
Southampton Common, CITY (December 1911–
August 1927), Guildford City; retired 1930.

Details: Ex-dock worker, and discarded by
Southampton, Jimmy Goodchild saved a penalty
on his City debut, in an FA Cup tie against Preston
in 1912 (won 1-0). Safe if not spectacular, he vied
with Walter Smith for a first-team place in his early
days at Hyde Road and was an ever-present in
1920/21, conceding fifty goals, when City claimed
second spot in the First Division. Selected for
the Central League XI against the North Eastern
League in 1920, six years later he played in
City's FA Cup final defeat by Bolton. Goodchild,
who spent almost sixteen years with City, made
the second highest number of First World War
appearances for the club (130).

GOODWIN, Ernest William (Outside-right)
Apps/goals: 21/5 Born: Chester-le-Street,
Durham, 1891 Died: c. 1960
Career: Spennymoor United, Leeds City, CITY
(October 1919–May 1921), Rochdale.

Details: A useful forward with powerful right
foot shot, Ernie Goodwin scored three goals in
twenty League games for Leeds City before the
Yorkshire club folded. He joined City as a reserve
to Tommy Broad and started off well by scoring on
his debut in a 4-2 win over Sheffield Wednesday.
He had sixteen starts in 1919/20 and only five the
following season moving to Rochdale.

GORRINGE, Frederick Charles (Forward)
Apps/goals: 1/2 Born: Salford, 1903 Died: 1965
Career: St Cyprians, Manchester Ship Canal,
CITY (September 1926–July 1928), Lincoln City,
Crewe Alexandra, Bolton Wanderers, Reading;
retired injured, 1932.

Details: A reserve with all his five League clubs
except Crewe, Charlie Gorringe scored twice in
his only game for City, in a 7-3 home win over
Barnsley in January 1928 when he deputised for
Charlie Broadhurst. He also netted in his first game
for Lincoln.

GOULD, William (Outside-right/left)
Apps/goals: 8/2 Born: Burton-on-Trent,
1886 Died: after 1945
Career: Burton United, Leicester Fosse, Bristol
Rovers, Glossop, Bradford City, CITY (May
1909–May 1912), Tranmere Rovers; did not play
after the First World War.

Details: Quick and lively, Billy Gould made
over 100 club appearances before joining City
as cover for George Stewart. He played in the
last six League games of 1909/10, scoring on his
debut against his former Glossop, and also against
Burnley, making his last two towards the end of the
following season.

GOW, Gerald (Midfield)
Apps: 36/6 Born: Glasgow, 29/5/1952
Career: Bristol City, CITY (October 1980–
January 1982), Rotherham United, Burnley, Yeovil
Town (player-manager), retired as a player, 1988;
Weymouth (manager).

Details: An experienced campaigner, signed
by John Bond, Gerry Gow made 375 League
appearances for Bristol City before spending
fifteen months at Maine Road, during which time
he produced some energetic displays in midfield
alongside Tommy Hutchison and Steve Mackenzie.
A Scottish U23 international, he netted his first
City goal in his fourth game in a 3-0 home win
over Southampton.

GRANT, Anthony James (Midfield)
Apps: 25 Born: Liverpool, 14/11/1974
Career: Everton, Swindon Town (loan),
Tranmere Rovers, CITY (£450,000, December
1999–October 2001), West Bromwich Albion
(loan), Burnley (£250,000).

Details: An England U21 international, the
strong-tackling Tony Grant made over 150 club
appearances during his career, playing for Everton
in the annual FA Charity Shield game at Wembley
in 1995. With several other quality midfield players
around, he had to fight for first-team football
with City, having his best spell in the first team in
2000/01 (twelve outings).

GRANVILLE, Daniel Patrick (Full-back)
Apps/goals: 80/3 Born: Islington, London,
19/1/1975
Career: Cambridge United, Chelsea (£300,000),
Leeds United (£1.6 million), CITY (loan, August-
September 1999, signed £1 million, October
1999–December 2001), Norwich City (loan),
Crystal Palace (£500,000), Colchester United,
Leyton Orient, Hemel Hempstead Town.

Details: Danny Granville made 114 appearances for Cambridge United before moving to Stamford Bridge. He won both the League Cup and European Cup Winner's Cup with Chelsea in 1998, but failed to make an impact at Elland Road. He struggled at times with City and was pushed onto the bench before spending a month on loan at Norwich. He then returned to Maine Road and helped City retain top-flight status. Between 2001 and 2007, the thrice-capped England U21 left-back made 138 appearances for Palace.

GRATRIX, Roy (Defender)
Apps: 15 Born: Salford: 9/2/1932
Career: Taylor Brothers, Blackpool, CITY (September 1964/April 1965), Toronto/Canada.

Details: Playing behind the likes of Stan Matthews and Stan Mortensen, centre-half, Roy Gratrix made 436 appearances for Blackpool, won one England 'B' cap and represented the Football League during his eleven years at Bloomfield Road. He took over from Roy Cheetham at the heart of the City defence, and produced some sterling performances before Michael Batty claimed the number five spot, albeit for only a short while.

GRAY, Albert (Goalkeeper)
Apps: 75 Born: Tredegar, Wales, 23/9/1900
Died: Blackpool, 16/12/1969
Career: Rhyl Athletic, Ebbw Vale, Oldham, Athletic, CITY (January 1927–August 1930), Manchester Central, Coventry City, Tranmere Rovers, Chester, Waterford, Congleton Town; retired 1939; also good at tennis and golf, winning the Merseyside Footballers' Open Championship in 1933; became a sergeant-instructor during the Second World War; later a bookmaker in Cleveleys near Blackpool.

Details: Welsh international goalkeeper Bert Gray, 6 feet 3 inches tall and capped times by his country between 1924 and 1938, was 'cool, safe and inspired confidence in his defenders.' He took over from Jimmy Goodchild for City and after a good run in the first team during which time he produced some fine performances, he handed over his gloves to Lewis Barber. In a fine career, which saw him accumulate over 450 club appearances, Gray also presented the Southern League *v.* the Irish League and toured Canada with the FAW party in 1929.

GRAY, Matthew (Forward)
Apps/goals: 101/23 Born: Renfrew, Scotland, 11/7/1936
Career: Third Lanark, CITY (February 1962–April 1967), Port Elizabeth/South Africa; retired 1972.

Details: The first substitute to score for City – doing so in a 4-3 League defeat at Cardiff in September 1965 – Matt Gray was a skilful footballer who made his mark at Maine Road during the second half of the 1962/63 season, following up with some outstanding displays the following term when acting as an aide and reliable ally to strikers Derek Kevan and Jimmy Murray. He faded from the scene during the Second Division championship- winning season of 1965/66, and made only three appearances in 1966/67, before emigrating to South Africa where he continued playing for five more years.

GREALISH, Anthony Patrick (Midfield)
Apps: 15 Born: Paddington, London, 21/9/1956 Died: Ilfracombe, Devon, 23/4/2013
Career: Wilberforce Junior & Rutherford Secondary Modern Schools/Paddington, Leyton Orient, Luton Town (£150,000), Brighton & Hove Albion (£100,000), West Bromwich Albion (£80,000), CITY (trial, September 1986, signed for £20,000 plus Robert Hopkins, October 1986-August 1987), Rotherham United, FC Salgueros/Portugal (loan), Walsall (player-coach), Bromsgrove Rovers (player, assistant-manager/ coach, then manager), Atherstone Town (assistant-manager/coach), Sandwell Borough (player); assisted West Bromwich Albion Old Stars; worked in Sutton Coldfield and lived near Marbella, Costa del Sol, Spain until his death, from cancer, aged fifty-six.

Details: An aggressive central midfielder who seemed to cover every blade of grass during the course of a game, Tony Grealish, who won forty-seven caps for the Republic of Ireland (eight goals scored) often played with a healthy beard, making him look more fearsome than he really was! He played in the 1983 FA Cup final for Brighton *v.* Manchester United), won the Fourth Division championship with Rotherham, and made over 600 appearances during a lengthy career. His stay with City was short and sweet – fifteen outings in total, his debut coming in the Manchester derby three days after arriving at Maine Road.

GREENACRE, Christopher Mark (Striker)
Apps/goals: 9/1 Born: Halifax, 23/12/1977
Career: Schoolboy football, CITY (June 1994–November 1999), Cardiff City (loan), Blackpool (loan), Scarborough (loan), Mansfield Town (free), Stoke City, Tranmere Rovers, Wellington Phoenix/ New Zealand.

Details: A quick-thinking, nippy striker, a penalty-box predator, Chris Greenacre found it hard to establish himself in City's first team and after loan spells with three different clubs, he joined Mansfield for whom he scored fifty-nine goals before switching to Stoke in 2002. After adding another forty-six goals to his tally with Tranmere, he moved to New Zealand in 2009 with 416 appearances and 126 goals under his belt.

GREENWOOD, John Jones (Half-back)
Apps: 1 Born: Manchester, 22/1/1921
Died: Yorkshire, 25/11/1994
   Career: CITY (September 1946-June 1949), Exeter City, Aldershot, Halifax Town (to May 1952).
   Details: In senior football for six years, Jack Greenwood made just forty-four League appearances for his four clubs, thirty-one with Exeter. His only game for City (in three post-war seasons) came in the 1-0 defeat away to Aston Villa in March 1949, when he deputised for Billy Walsh.

GREGG, Willis (Left-back)
Apps: 9 Born: Woodhouse, 21/7/1908 Died: 1989
   Career: Mexborough Town, Chesterfield, Torquay United, Accrington Stanley, CITY (April 1937/November 1938), Chester; retired during the Second World War.
   Details: Able to play in both full-back positions, Will Gregg made his League debut for Chesterfield in 1932. After good service with Torquay and Accrington, he joined City as cover for Sam Barkas for whom he deputised twice during his first full season at Maine Road, and in seven games in succession in September/October 1938.

GREGORY, Charles Frederick (Half-back)
Apps/goals: 21/2 Born: Doncaster,
24/10/1911 Died: 1985
   Career: Brodsworth Colliery, Doncaster Rovers, CITY (March 1930–March 1934), Reading, Crystal Palace, Hartlepool United, Rotherham United; retired 1947.
   Details: Although the Second World War seriously interrupted Charlie Gregory's playing career, he still managed to appear in 228 League games, having his best years with Reading (1933–37).

GREGORY, Julius Reginald (Full-back)
Apps: 3 Born: Romiley, 1881 Died: France, 1916
   Career: Unsworth FC, Bury, CITY (May 1905/ May 1906), Brighton & Hove Albion, Luton Town (until his death).
   Details: A strong, confident defender, Julius Gregory could play on either flank and after fourteen League games with Bury, he spent a season with City, making just three first-team appearances, at Preston and at home to Derby County and Sunderland. He did much better in the Southern League with Brighton and Luton. He was killed in action during the First World War.

GRIEVE, Robert Bruce (Forward)
Apps/goals: 46/19 Born: Greenock, Scotland,
28/3/1888 Died: after 1945
   Career: Greenock Morton, CITY (August 1906– November 1911), Accrington, Leicester Fosse, Southport; retired during the First World War.

Details: Bob Grieve made his City debut against Woolwich Arsenal in September 1906 and played his last game against Newcastle in February 1909. He was a reserve for over two-and-a-half years thereafter, due to the form of Messrs. Thornley, Jones and Holford. A clever little player, Grieve had his best scoring spree with City in 1907/08 when he netted eleven times, including a hat-trick on the opening day of the season against Sunderland (won 5-2) and braces against Notts County and Everton.

GRIFFITHS, Carl Brian (Forward)
Apps: 21/4 Born: Oswestry, 16/7/1971
   Career: Shrewsbury Town, CITY (£500,000, October 1993–August 1995), Portsmouth (£200,000), Peterborough United (£225,000), Leyton Orient (loan/signed), Wrexham (loan), Port Vale, Leyton Orient, Luton Town, Harlow Town, Braintree Town, Brentwood Town (player-manager), Maldon Town, Barkingside; retired May 2010; Aveley (manager).
   Details: After being named in the PFA's Team of the Year for 1992/93 and no doubt for scoring sixty-two goals in 170 games during a difficult period with Shrewsbury (where he played under Asa Hartford's management), City manager Brian Horton lured Carl Griffiths to Maine Road. Unfortunately the move into the Premiership proved a bit too much for the Welsh youth, U21 and 'B' international striker who netted just four times in eighteen League games for the Blues. However, during a fine career in senior football, he netted 144 goals in 395 appearances.

GROENENDIJK, Alfons (Midfield)
Apps: 13 Born: Leiden, Holland, 17/5/1964
   Career: UVS, FC Den Haag, Roda JC, Ajax, CITY (July 1993/May 1994), Sparta Rotterdam; retired 2001; Jong Ajax (manager), VV Katwijk (manager), Willem II (assistant-manager), FC Den Bosch (manager).
   Details: Alfons Groenendijk made over 400 League appearances in Dutch football, winning the UEFA Cup (1992) and League title (1993) with Ajax. He had just thirteen outings, wore the number 2, 6, 7, 9, 11 and 12 shirts and made his debut in a 1-0 defeat by Everton in August 1993.

GUIDETTI, John Albert Fernando Andres Luigi Olaf (Striker)
Apps: 1 Born: Stockholm, Sweden, 14/4/1992
   Career: Brommapojkarna, Impala Bromman Boys, Mathare YSA, Ligi Ndogo/Niarobi, Brommapojkarna, CITY (April 2008), Brommapojkarna (loan), Burnley (loan), Feyenoord/Holland (loan).
   Details: The player with the longest name in City's history (forty-one letters!), John Guidetti trained with Lionel Messi at a summer camp before having an excellent first season in the

Blues' U18 team, scoring thirteen goals in thirteen appearances. He also marked his reserve team debut with a brilliant hat-trick against Burnley, for whom he would later play. After featuring in City's pre-season tour of the USA, he was handed his senior debut in a League Cup tie against WBA in September 2010. Guidetti, who has one Swedish cap to his credit, is on contract at the Etihad Stadium until 2015.

GUNN, John (Inside-left)
Apps/goals: 25/5 Born: Lancashire, 1873 Died: c. 1940
    Career: Bolton Wanderers, CITY (record £30, October 1896/April 1897), Clyde.
    Details: After an excellent season, when he had four different partners on the left-wing, John Gunn surprisingly left City to continue his career in Scotland. He scored his first City goal in his third game, a 3-1 win over Burton.

GUNNING, James Michael (Forward)
Apps: 15 Born: Helensburgh, Scotland, 25/6/1929 Died: 1993
    Career: Hibernian, CITY (November 1950–July 1954), Weymouth, Barrow.
    Details: Jim Gunning was one of ten different outside-rights used by City during his time at Maine Road. Initially understudy to John Oakes, he made five appearances in his first season, three in his second and seven in his third.

H

HAALAND, Alf-Inge Rasdal (Midfield)
Apps/goals: 45/3 Born: Stavanger, Norway, 23/11/1972
    Career: Bryne/Norway, Nottingham Forest, Leeds United (£1.6 million), CITY (£2.5 million, June 2000; retired July 2003); returned with Rosseland FC/Norway.
    Details: Alfie Haaland is remembered for his feud with Roy Keane that started in September 1997. With Manchester United a goal down at Leeds, Keane injured his anterior cruciate ligament and while lying on the ground, Haaland criticised the midfielder for an attempted foul and suggested that he was feigning injury to avoid punishment. Three-and-a-half years later, in April 2001, when Haaland was a City player, Keane hacked the Norwegian, high up on his right knee during the Manchester derby. Keane was red-carded for the eighth time as a United player, and was initially fined £5,000 and handed a three-match ban. However, later in his biography he said that he 'wanted to 'hurt' Haaland as revenge for the criticism he received years previously. After this revelation, Keane found himself subject to an FA inquiry and received an additional five-match ban

and massive £150,000 fine. Never the same player again, Haaland retired from senior football in July 2003 after failing to regain full fitness. City terminated his contract after reviewing medical reports. A youth international and winner of 29 U21 and thirty-four full caps for Norway, Haaland was highly competitive himself, receiving over twenty yellow cards during his career which were realised in 279 appearances and twenty-one goals.

HADDINGTON, William Raymond (Forward)
Apps/goals: 7/4 Born: Scarborough, 18/11/1923 Died: 1994
    Career: Bradford PA; Second World War guest for Halifax, Exeter City, Plymouth Argyle and Portsmouth; Bradford City, Oldham Athletic, CITY (November 1950/December 1951), Stockport County, Bournemouth, Rochdale, Halifax Town, Bedford Town, Juventus FC/Australia; retired 1960.
    Details: A terrific striker of a dead ball, Ray Haddington, playing alongside Dennis Westcott, scored in each of his first four League games for the Blues, against Leeds (1-1), West Ham (2-0), Blackburn (1-4) and Southampton (2-3). He had earlier netted sixty-three goals in 117 Third Division (N) matches for Oldham.

HALL, Joseph Edward (Centre-forward)
Apps: 1 Born: Boldon, 1890 Died: after 1945
    Career: Preston North End, Jarrow Croft, Barnsley, CITY (May 1913–May 1915), Bristol Rovers, Newport County, Bristol Aeroplane Co.
    Details: A reserve for two seasons, Joe Hall's only first-team appearance for City was against his former club Bradford on the last day of the 1914/15 season, deputising for Fred Howard in a 3-1 defeat.

HALL, William (Goalkeeper)
Apps: Born: Bolton, 1881 Died: after 1945
    Career: Bolton Wanderers, Bristol Rovers, CITY (September 1906/March 1907), Crystal Palace.
    Details: Signed after Frank Davies had conceded thirteen goals in the first two matches of the 1906/07 season, Bill Hall took over between the posts for the next eleven League games before he was replaced by a fit-again Walter Smith in late November.

HALLIDAY, David (Centre-forward)
Apps/goals: 82/51 Born: Dumfries, Scotland, 19/12/1901 Died: Aberdeen, 5/1/1970
    Career: Queen of the South Wanderers, Queen of the South, St Mirren, Dundee, Sunderland (£4,000), Arsenal (£6,500), CITY (£5,700, November 1930–December 1933), Folkestone, Clapton Orient, Yeovil & Petters United (player-manager), Aberdeen (manager), Leicester City

(manager; then scout); later hotelier in Aberdeen; was a fine billiards player.

Details: Having lost his way at Highbury, Dave Halliday regained his form with City, netting fourteen goals in his first season and top-scoring in his second with thirty-two, including a ten-minute hat-trick against his former club Sunderland in January 1932.

Generally a brilliant marksman, he struck 386 goals in 507 League and Cup games north and south of the border, including a record forty-three for Sunderland in 1928/29 when he was also the First Division's leading striker and 101 in four seasons with Dundee. Only five players in the history of the game have scored more League goals than Halliday. One of the best centre-forwards in the game, he represented the Scottish League in 1924, but was never capped by his country (why?). As manager he guided Aberdeen to the SL title in 1955 and to three Cup finals, winning in 1947, and as Leicester boss he won the Second Division championship in 1957. His brother, Bill, played for Queen of the South, Newcastle and Third Lanark.

HALLOWS, Herbert (Half-back)
Apps: 1 Born: Southport, 1879 Died: Southport, c. 1939

Career: Southport Central, CITY (May 1900/ May 1901), Southport Central.

Details: A one-season and one-match wonder, Bert Hallows made his only appearance for City in January, deputising for Billy Smith in a 4-2 defeat at Nottingham Forest.

HAMANN, Dietmar (Midfield)
Apps/goals: 71/1 Born: Waldsasse, West Germany, 27/8/1973

Career: FC Wacker Munchen, Bayern Munich, Newcastle United (£4.5 million), Liverpool (£8 million), Bolton Wanderers, CITY (£400,000, July 2006–July 2009), MK Dons (player, player-coach), Leicester City (coach), Stockport County (manager); became a TV pundit with RTÉ Sport.

Details: Didi Hamann never kicked a ball for Bolton. In fact, he was at the club for less that a day and after a controversial agreement, his unusual transfer from the Reebok Stadium paid dividends for City, especially in his first two seasons when his cool, calm temperament and cultured play made him a stand-out figure in midfield. Unusually tall for a player in his position (6 feet 3 inches), he won three U20, ten U21 and fifty-nine full caps for Germany (five goals scored) and generally had an excellent career, making almost 600 club appearances (538 in League competitions). His only goal for City – a superb long range effort – came in a UEFA Cup game against EB/Streymur in 2008. He won the Bundesliga title twice and UEFA once with Bayern Munich and with Liverpool he

collected two FA Cup, two League Cup, two Super Cup, Champions League and UEFA Cup winner's medals. Before leaving City he had talks with Preston, QPR and Notts County, but chose MK Dons in the end. He worked under former City manager Sven-Göran Eriksson at Leicester.

HAMBLETT, John Gordon (Half-back)
Apps: 1 Born: Manchester, 1883 Died: after 1945

Career: St Francis Gorton, CITY (July 1905– May 1908), St Helens Rangers.

Details: A City reserve for three seasons, Gordon Hamblett's only outing for the club was against Sunderland (h) on the last day of the 1906/07 season when Bill Eadie and Jim Buchan were both absentees.

HAMILL, Michael (Half-back)
Apps/goals: 128/2 Born: Belfast, 19/1/1885 Died: Belfast, 23/7/1943

Career: St Paul's Swifts, Belfast Rangers, Manchester United, Belfast Celtic, CITY (£1,000, September 1920–August 1924), Fall River/USA, Boston Wonders Workers/USA, New York Giants/USA, Coats FC/USA, Belfast Celtic; retired 1928; Belfast Distillery (manager), Belfast Celtic (manager).

Details: Micky Hamill was a good, all-round footballer, although some critics thought he lacked the 'vital spark' which would have turned him into an exceptional player. Certainly one of City's first major influences of the early 1920s, he spent four years at Maine Road before trying his luck in America. He represented the Irish League on three occasions and gained seven full caps for Ireland, helping his country win the Home International Championship in 1913/14. Hamill was mysteriously found dead in a Belfast canal.

HAMMOND, Geoffrey (Full-back)
Apps/goals: 36/2 Born: Sudbury, 24/3/1950

Career: Ipswich Town, CITY (trial, September 1974, signed October 1974–April 1976), Charlton Athletic, Connecticut Bi-Centennials, Hadleigh United, Bury Town.

Details: Geoff Hammond made almost sixty appearances for Ipswich before partnering Willie Donachie in City's defence. He lost his place to Kenny Clements. He teamed up with his former coach at Charlton, Malcolm Musgrave in America.

HANNAH, George (Inside-forward)
Apps/goals: 131/16 Born: Liverpool, 11/12/1928 Died: Sale, 5/5/1990

Career: Liverpool City Boys, Everton (amateur), Linfield; Second World War guest for Mansfield Town and Nottingham Forest; Newcastle United (£23,000 with Alf McMichael), Lincoln City,

CITY (£10,000 plus John McClelland, September 1958–July 1964), Notts County (£2,000), Bradford City (£1,000); retired May 1966; ran a newsagents shop in Manchester and later worked for British Telecom.

Details: George Hannah captained Liverpool City boys, but was rejected by Everton who considered him too frail. National Service took him to Ireland where he became a professional with Linfield. Then, after representing the Irish League *v.* the Scottish League at Ibrox Park in September 1949, he was signed by Newcastle. And then, in 1955, he scored for the Magpies in their FA Cup final win over his future club, Manchester City!

With no physical advantages, he developed into an industrious and skilful inside-forward, a one-touch player, who became very popular with the fans. And his presence, and experience, certainly went along way in helping City escape relegation in 1959. A first-team regular for three years, he lost his place in 1961/62.

Hannah's career realised 404 appearances and sixty-seven goals. He went on FA tours to South Africa in 1957 (two outings), the Far East in 1961 (eleven games) and New Zealand in 1964 (twelve appearances) and also played twice for the FA XI.

HANNAWAY, John (Full-back)
Apps: 66 Born: Bootle, 22/10/1927
   Career: Seaforth Fellowship, CITY (April 1950–June 1957), Gillingham, Southport.
   Details: After a season in the reserves, Jack Hannaway took over from Eric Westwood in City's first team and made a big impression, appearing in thirty-seven senior games in 1951/52 before Westwood returned. He had the occasional outing afterwards before going on to play in 126 League matches for Gillingham.

HANNEY, Edward (Half-back)
Apps/goals: 78/1 Born: Tilehurst, Reading, 19/1/1889 Died: after 1945
   Career: Workington Town, Reading, CITY (November 1913–November 1919), Coventry City, Reading, Northfleet; retired 1925.
   Details: Having used four different centre-halves in the first eleven weeks of the 1913/14 season, Ted Hanney was recruited to become the sixth, holding his position unchallenged until the outbreak of the First World War. He played in only seven League games after the hostilities before having thirty-two outings for Coventry and forty-one for Reading.

HANVEY, Keith (Defender)
Apps: 1 Born: Manchester, 18/1/1952
   Career: CITY (June 1968–July 1972), Swansea City, Rochdale, Grimsby Town, Huddersfield Town, Rochdale; retired 1986.

Details: Keith Hanvey's only game for City was in a Texaco Cup tie against Airdrieonians in September 1971. After leaving Maine Road, he made 205 League appearances for Huddersfield and 136 for Rochdale.

HAREIDE, Age Fridtjof (Defender)
Apps: 25 Born: Isle of Haried, Norway, 23/9/1953
   Career: Hødd, Molde, CITY (October 1981–July 1983), Norwich City, Molde (player-manager; retired as a player, 1987), Helsingborgs IF (manager), Brøndby IF (manager), Rosenborg (manager), Norway (national team manager), Orgryte (manager), Viking (manager), Helsingborgs IF I(caretaker-manager); also manager for the Volvo car company and occasional commentator for Norwegian broadcasting company.
   Details: Strong and totally committed, Age Hareide preferred a defensive role and made seventeen appearances (eight as a substitute) in his first season with City. He played in over 300 club games during his career, while also winning fifty caps for Norway (five goals).
   As a manager, he won three League titles in three different countries – Denmark, Sweden and Norway.

HARGREAVES, James (Outside-left)
Apps: 8 Born: Blackburn, 1870
   Career: Blackburn Rovers, Northwich Victoria, CITY (December 1893/April 1894), Blackburn Rovers.
   Details: Jim Hargreaves made his City debut in place of Bob Milarvie in a 3-2 home win over Rotherham on Boxing Day 1893, having his last outing against Walsall Town Swifts on the final day of the season.
   NB: Four players named Hargreaves were registered with League clubs in the 1890s and it is possible that three could have been related, and also their respective statistics may have been confused.

HARGREAVES, Owen Lee (Midfield)
Apps/goals: 4/1 Born: Calgary, Alberta, Canada, 20/1/1981
   Career: Calgary Foothills FC (junior), Bayern Munich, Manchester United (£17 million), Manchester City (free, August 2011, released, May 2012).
   Details: Born to a Welsh mother and an English father, Owen Hargreaves was eligible to represent Canada, Wales and England. He chose the latter, and went on to play in three U21, one 'B' and forty-two full internationals, being the 1,111th player to be capped at senior level. The first footballer so far to have played for England without having previously

lived in the UK, he's also the second, only after Joe Baker, to have done so without having previously played in the English League system.

Hard-working and a strong tackler, he once held the record for making most substitute appearances for England (twenty-five) and, in fact, was called off the bench no less than fouteen consecutive times. A Premier and Champions League winner with Manchester United in 2008, he made a scoring debut for City against Birmingham in a League Cup tie in September 2011 – only his sixth game in more than three years, as injuries seriously affected his career from 2008 onwards. He helped Bayern win four Bundesliga titles, the DFB-Pokol three times and the UEFA Champions League, Intercontinental Cup and DFB-Ligapokal all once. Thirty-nine of his England caps came as a Munich player.

His father played for Bolton Wanderers' youth team and also for Calgary Kickers in Canada.

HARLEY, Alex (Striker)
Apps/goals: 49/32 Born: Glasgow, 28/4/1936 Died: Birmingham, 13/3/1969

Career: Maryhill, Third Lanark, CITY (£19,500, August 1962/August 1963), Birmingham City (£42,500), Leicester City, Toronto City/Canada, Dundee, Portadown, Cape Town City/South Africa, Newton Unity/ Birmingham Works League; became a croupier in a Birmingham casino.

Details: A very useful centre-forward, strong and mobile, Alex Harley netted sixty-eight times in eighty-five League games for Third Lanark before topping City's scoring charts in 1962/63 with thirty-two goals, including an eighty-ninth minute in the Manchester derby at Old Trafford. His last for the club was the equaliser in the return fixture at Maine Road. He died from a heart attack in a Birmingham hotel.

HARPER, Alan (Right-back/midfield)
Apps/goals: 62/2 Born: Liverpool, 1/11/1960

Career: Liverpool, Everton (£100,000), Sheffield Wednesday (£275,000), CITY (£150,000, December 1989–August 1991), Everton (£200,000), Luton Town, Burnley, Cardiff City (loan); retired 1996; Everton (youth coach), Bolton Wanderers (scout), Liverpool (chief scout).

Details: The versatile Alan Harper made 340 League appearances during his career. An England youth international, he won two League titles with Everton and during his time at Maine Road occupied both full-back positions, played as a defensive midfielder and also as an emergency forward. His two City goals were scored in a 4-0 LC win over Torquay in September 1990 and the 2-0 League victory over Coventry eleven days later. Harper played under manager Howard Kendall at both Everton (two spells) and City.

HARPER, John (Full-back)
Apps: 35 Born: Mid Wales, c. 1871 Died: after 1930

Career: Newtown, CITY (August 1895–May 1898), Chatham.

Details: Said to have been a 'tough character', Jack Harper partnered Davie Robson at full-back in his first season with City who finished runners-up in Division Two, but missed promotion after two Test Match defeats. He then lost his place to Charlie Ditchfield and after long periods in the second XI, he moved south to Chatham.

HARPER, William George (Goalkeeper)
Apps: 4 Born: Bothwell, South Lanarkshire, 15/11/1900 Died: after 1945

Career: Wishaw FC, Sunderland, CITY (May 1923/May 1924), Crystal Palace, Luton Town, Weymouth; retired 1932.

Details: Replacing the injured Jim Mitchell, Bill Harper conceded ten goals in four outings for City, his debut ending in a 3-1 home defeat to Nottingham Forest. He made 120 League appearances during his career that was cut short through injury.

HARRISON, John Richardson (Outside-left)
Apps/goals: 2/1 Born: Rhyl, 1908

Career: Rhyl YC, Llandudno Junction, Rhyl Athletic, CITY (February 1929/June 1930), Sheffield United Brighton & Hove Albion; at school was good at boxing and athletics.

Details: A Welsh junior international, Jack Harrison – reserve to Eric Brook – failed to make the grade with City, despite scoring in his second game, in a 3-1 win over Middlesbrough in November 1929.

HART, Charles Joseph John (Goalkeeper)
Apps: 217 Born: Shrewsbury, 19/4/1987

Career: Oxon Primary School, Meole Brace Science College, Shrewsbury Town, CITY (£600,000, May 2006), Tranmere Rovers, Blackpool (loan), Birmingham City (loan); also a good club cricketer.

Details: Joe Hart was rated as one of the best goalkeepers in world football in 2012. A terrific shot-stopper, he is now England's number one – and injuries permitting will remain so for a few more years to come!

Standing 6 feet 5 inches tall and tipping the scales at almost 13 stone, Hart – who replaced Shay Given – has been superb between the posts for City over the last three seasons, helping the Blues win the FA Cup and the Premiership title, while also upping his tally of senior caps to thirty-two, having previously played for his country in five Youth and 21 U21 internationals. He won the Premiership 'Golden Glove' award in 210/11 for the most clean sheets (twenty-nine), a new club record previously held by Nicky Weaver with twenty-six. He then won the same award again in 2011/12 when City won their first League title in forty-four years and was top man again in 2012/13. Hart is on contract with City until 2016.

HART, John Paul (Inside-forward)
Apps/goals: 178/73 Born: Golborne, Cheshire,
8/6/1928
  Career: Longton Youth Club, CITY (December 1944), retired injured, May 1963; assistant-manager, manager, March 1973; retired October 1973).
  Details: City's leading second XI scorer in 1947/48, Johnny Hart followed up by finishing joint top marksman in the first team in 1951/52 (with Dennis Westcott) and again in 1954/55 (with Joe Hayes). Unfortunately, he broke his leg against Huddersfield a week before the 1955 FA Cup final, which also denied him the chance of playing in the following year's final.
  Registered as a City player for more than eighteen years, injuries seriously affected his game. It was a particularly cruel blow because Hart was, without doubt, a very fine footballer. After just twenty-four outings up to 1949, he followed up with a terrific spell between 1950 and 1955, before ending his days at Maine Road with only eleven starts up to 1961. Hart retired following a pancreatic attack.

HARTFORD, Richard Asa (Midfield)
Apps/goals: 321/36 Born: Clydebank, Scotland,
24/10/50
  Career: Fairfley Primary & Clydebank High Schools, Dunbartonshire Boys, Drumchapel Amateurs, West Bromwich Albion, Leeds United (for twenty-four hours), CITY (£225,000, August 1974–July 1979), Nottingham Forest (£450,000), Everton (record £500,000), CITY (£375,000, October 1981–May 1984), Fort Lauderdale Sun (free), Wolverhampton Wanderers (trial), Norwich City, Norway (coaching), Bolton Wanderers (player-coach), Stockport County (player-coach), Oldham Athletic, Shrewsbury Town (player, coach, manager), Boston United (player-manager); retired May 1991, aged forty; Blackburn Rovers (coach, assistant-manager), Stoke City (coach, caretaker-manager), CITY (coach, assistant-manager, caretaker-manager, 1994–1997), Blackpool (coach), Macclesfield Town (assistant-manager), Accrington Stanley (junior coach), Birmingham City (scout), Norwich City (scout); played for WBA Old Stars (1990s).
  Details: Asa Hartford made his League debut for WBA at the age of seventeen – the first of 823 senior appearances he would amass during his long career. An energetic midfielder with a terrific engine, he was here, there and everywhere. Initially replacing Franny

Lee, he impressed on his debut (in a 4-0 win over West Ham), and went on to give City great service as a player in two spells covering eight years. He gained fifty Scotland caps, thirty-six with City (five goals scored), played in the 1978 and 1982 World Cups and also represented his country at Youth, U21 and U23 levels. Having appeared for WBA against City in the 1970 League Cup final, he then won the trophy with the Blues in 1976 and again with Norwich in 1985, when his deflected shot gave the Canaries victory over Sunderland. He acted as City's caretaker-manager during August–October 1996, before Steve Coppell took over, guided City's second XI to the Pontins League title in 2000 and during his 'coaching' career worked with Kenny Dalgalish at Blackburn, Joe Jordan and Lou Macari at Stoke, and Alan Ball and Stuart Pearce at City. A heart problem resulted in his move to Leeds in November 1971 being cancelled at the eleventh hour. His subsequent career made nonsense of the fears occasioned by Leeds' doubting staff! Christened Asa after the celebrated American singer Al Jolson, Hartford is included in the Scotland international team's *Roll of Honour* and also in the *Scottish Football Hall of Fame* and was at Macclesfield with another former City player, Ian Brightwell.

HARVEY, Howard (Forward)
Apps/goals: 7/1 Born: Wednesbury,
5/4/1875 Died: Birmingham, 1938
  Career: Wolverhampton Road Council School, Walsall Town Swifts, Small Heath, Aston Villa, Burslem Port Vale (£50), CITY (£180, January 1900/May 1901), West Bromwich Albion (reserves), Burton United, Watford, Glentoran, Darlaston; retired May 1905.
  Details: Described as a 'cool central forward', Howard Harvey failed to make headway with any of his three West Midland clubs, but did well with Port Vale, striking thirty goals in sixty-five appearances, top-scoring in his last half-season in the Potteries. His only goal for City was in a 2-0 win at Glossop in March 1900.

HAYDOCK, Joseph (Full-back)
Apps: 1 Born: Bolton, c. 1866
  Career: Bolton Wanderers, CITY (July 1890/ May 1891).
  Details: Played in City's first-ever FA Cup qualifying tie, a 12-0 win over against Liverpool Stanley in October 1890. He made fifty appearances for Bolton.

HAYDOCK, William Edward (Forward)
Apps/goals: 3/1 Born: Salford, 19/1/1936
  Career: Buxton Town, CITY (March 1959–March 1961), Crewe Alexandra, Grimsby Town, Stockport County, Port Elizabeth/South Africa, Southport; retired 1972; Cork City (assistant-manager), Blackburn Rovers (physiotherapist).

Details: Billy Haydock top-scored for City's second XI in 1959/60, but failed to make an impression in the first team, netting his only senior goal on his debut against Blackpool in March 1960 (lost 3-2). He did much better with Crewe (thirty goals in 142 League appearances), and after switching to full-back, played in 287 first-class matches for Stockport (1965–71). He retired with 434 League appearances under his belt.

HAYES, Joseph (Inside-forward)
Apps/goals: 364/152 Born: Kearsley near Bolton, 20/1/1936 Died: 4/2/1999
Career: Bolton Sunday League football, CITY (August 1953–June 1965), Barnsley, Wigan Athletic, Lancaster City (player-manager); retired 1970.

Details: Joe Hayes, one of the best goal-poachers in League football during the 1950s, topped City's scoring charts on three occasions – in 1954/55 (jointly with Johnny Hart), in 1955/56 and again in 1957/58, and he also netted City's goal in the 1956 FA Cup final. Arriving at Maine Road for a trial with his boots wrapped in brown paper, he went out and netted four goals. He was signed almost immediately, and in October 1953 made his League debut against Tottenham Hotspur. Capped twice by England at U23 level, Hayes also played for Young England and an FA XI and it was a knee injury, suffered at Bury in 1964, which resulted in him leaving City. Hayes currently lies fourth in City's all-time list of goalscorers, behind Eric Brook, Tom Johnston and Colin Bell.

HEALE, James Arthur (Forward)
Apps/goals: 92/41 Born: Bristol, 19/9/1914 Died: 23/5/1997
Career: Bristol City, CITY (January 1934–May 1945), Doncaster Rovers; retired 1946; employed as a fireman during the Second World War.

Details: Jimmy Heale won Gloucestershire County honours before joining Bristol City for whom netted eight goals in twenty-six League games. He quickly bedded himself in at Maine Road and played in fourteen League games (scoring twice), yet had to sit and watch City beat Portsmouth in the FA Cup final because he was cup-tied! He continued to serve City well and besides his senior record, he also netted thirty-three goals in forty-two Wartime fixtures.

HEALEY, Ronald (Goalkeeper)
Apps: 39 Born: Manchester, 30/8/1952
Career: Manchester Boys, CITY (November 1966–May 1974), Altrincham (loan), Coventry City (loan), Preston North End (loan), Cardiff City; retired May 1982; returned to work at Manchester airport.

Details: Ron Healey made only thirty-nine League appearances with his first three clubs before amassing 216 with Cardiff. Understudy in the main to Joe Corrigan, he got a decent run in City's first XI towards the end of the 1970/71 season, keeping three clean sheets in nine games. He had further mini-spells in the team in March/April 1972 and two in 1972/73, as well as enjoying loan spells at Coventry and Preston, before moving to Ninian Park. Quite acrobatic at times, Healey was capped twice by the Republic of Ireland.

HEANEY, Neil Andrew (Winger/wing-back)
Apps/goals: 21/2 Born: Middlesbrough, 3/11/1971
Career: Arsenal, Hartlepool United (loan), Cambridge United (loan), Southampton (£300,000), CITY (£500,000, November 1996–August 1999), Charlton Athletic (loan), Bristol City (loan), Darlington (free, Dundee United (£175,000), Plymouth Argyle (free); retired January 2003.

Details: After five years as a professional with Arsenal and loan spells with two lower League clubs, Neil Heaney had a very good eighteen months with Southampton before joining City, for whom he scored a debut goal *v.* Watford in the FA Cup. Unfortunately, after a decent start, he never got into his stride at Maine Road, and after being used at times as a wing-back he moved down the League ladder to Darlington. An England youth team player, Heaney gained six U21 caps and when he retired in 2003, his career had produced sixteen goals in 196 club appearances.

HEATH, Adrian Paul (Forward)
Apps/goals: 89/6 Born: Stoke-on-Trent, 17/1/1961
Career: Stoke City, Everton (£700,000), Espanyol/Spain, Aston Villa (£360,000), CITY (February 1990–March 1992), Stoke City, Burnley, Sheffield United, Burnley (non-contract; retired as a player, then manager), Sheffield United (assistant-manager), Sunderland (coach, scout).

Details: Nicknamed 'Inchy' because of his size, Adrian Heath was a sharp-shooting, instinctive marksman who pounced on the half-chance in front of goal. He had a fine career, netting 120 goals in 525 League games in England alone, while playing eight times for England at U21 level and once for he 'B' team.

He never quite reached the scoring form expected of him at Maine Road, although he did work well alongside Niall Quinn and David White, and scored winners in League games against Sheffield Wednesday and Norwich in April 1990 and against his former club Everton four months later, as well as striking twice in a 3-1 League Cup win over QPR.

In the space of three years with Everton (1984–87), he won the League title twice, the FA Cup and the European Cup Winner's Cup, plus four

FA Charity Shields. Unfortunately, he failed as a manager.

HEDLEY, Foster (Outside-left)
Apps/goals: 2/2 Born: Monkseaton, Northumberland, 6/1/1908 Died: 1983
Career: St Andrew's/Newcastle, South Shields, Corinthians/Newcastle, Jarrow, Hull City, Nelson, CITY (March 1930/July 1931), Chester, Tottenham Hotspur, Millwall, Swindon Town; retired during the Second World War.
Details: Signed as reliable cover for Eric Brook, Foster Hedley scored in each of his two League outings for City, the winner on his debut *v.* Sheffield United (2-1) and in the 4-1 defeat at Birmingham two weeks later. After leaving City, Hedley became one of the most dangerous wingers in Third Division football, scoring twenty-nine goals in eighty-eight games for Chester (1931–33).

HEINEMANN, Geoffrey Henry (Half-back)
Apps: 24 Born: Stafford, 17/12/1905
Career: Stafford Rangers, CITY (October 1928–May 1931), Coventry City, Crystal Palace, Clapton Orient, Wellington Town.
Details: A confident defender with a biting tackle, Geoff Heinemann did very well after leaving City, making over 160 League appearances for the three 'C' clubs before joining Wellington in 1938. Taking over, when required from Jimmy McMullan, he had his best spell in City's first team either side of Christmas, 1929.

HÉLAN, Jérémy (Left-back/left-winger)
Apps: 1 Born: Clichy-la-Garenne, France, 9/5/1992
Career: AS Jeunesse d'Aubervilliers, Clairfontaine, Stade Rennais, CITY (February 2009), Carlisle United (loan), Shrewsbury Town (loan), Sheffield Wednesday (loan, two spells).
Details: Jérémy Hélan controversially signed for City after deciding to see out the remainder of his professional contract with Rennes, and as a result was suspended from international football for a month. For the remainder of the 2008/09 season and during the next two campaigns, he established himself as a regular in City Elite Development Squad before making his only appearance for the Blues in September 2012 as a 106th-minute substitute for Luca Scapuzzi in a third-round League Cup-tie defeat by Aston Villa.

HENDERSON, John (Centre-forward)
Apps/goals: 5/1 Born: Scotland, 1/2/1879
Career: Abercorn, CITY (November 1901/May 1902); returned to Scotland.
Details: A relatively unknown reserve to Billy Gillespie, John Henderson scored his only goal for City - set up by Billy Meredith - in his second League outing - a 3-3 draw away to Bolton on New Year's Day 1902.

HENDERSON, John Alfred (Centre-half)
Apps/goals: 5/1 Born: Kelty, Scotland, 1890
Career: Kelty Rangers, Cowdenbeath Hibernians, Abercorn, St Bernard's/Edinburgh (April 1914–May 1920), CITY, Southend United, Mid-Rhondda, Gillingham, Dunfermline Athletic; retired 1927.
Details: Reserve to Ted Hanney, Jock Henderson played in thirty-three games for City during the First World War, before making his League debut in a 3-1 home win over Oldham in September 1919. He played eighty games for Gillingham (1922–24).

HENDREN, (O'Hanrahan), Elias, Henry (Forward)
Apps: 2 Born: Turnham Green, Chiswick, 5/2/1889 Died: Whittington Hospital, Highgate, 4/10/1962
Career: Sandersons FC, Queen's Park Rangers, Brentford, CITY (March 1908/October 1909), Coventry City, Brentford; Middlesex CCC (1907–37); Harrow School (cricket coach), Sussex CCC (coach).
Details: 'Patsy' Hendren, better known for his exploits on the cricket field than as a footballer, did exceptionally well, second time round, with Brentford, scoring fifteen goals in 138 League appearances between 1920–27. His two outings for City were against Nottingham Forest and Sheffield United in successive First Division matches at the end of the 1908/09 relegation season when deputised for the injured David Ross. He also played for England against Scotland in a Victory international in 1919.
One of Middlesex and England's greatest-ever batsmen, his fifty-one Test Matches realised a total of 3,525 runs, including seven centuries and a top-score of 205 not out. For Middlesex, he amassed 57,611 runs (av. 50.80), struck 170 centuries and 301 not out his best highest-score. In fact, only one other cricketer, Sir John Hobbs, hit more centuries than Hendren and only two, Hobbs and Frank Woolley, exceeded his tally of runs in county cricket. He died from Alzheimer's disease, aged seventy-two.

HENDRY, Edward Colin James (Defender)
Apps/goals: 77/10 Born: Keith, Scotland, 7/12/1965
Career: Islavale FC, Dundee, Blackburn Rovers (£30,000), CITY (£700,000, October 1989–November 1991), Blackburn Rovers (£700,000), Glasgow Rangers.
Details: One of manager Mel Machin's last signings for City, Colin Hendry took over from Brian Gayle at the heart of the defence, and for two years produced some terrific displays before being replaced by Keith Curle. He made his debut in a

sky blue shirt in a 3-0 home defeat by Nottingham Forest, but thereafter, once bedded in, he and Steve Redmond played splendidly together, helping City finish fifth in the top flight in 1990/91.

The heartbeat of the Blackburn defence for many years, Hendry won the FMC and the Premiership title with Rovers in 1987 and 1995 and gained one 'B' and thirty-five full caps for Scotland. In his two spells at Ewood Park he scored thirty-five goals in 408 first-class appearances.

HENRY, Anthony (Midfield)
Apps/goals: 93/12 Born: Houghton-le-Spring, 26/11/1957

Career: Durham Boys, CITY (July 1974– September 1981), Bolton Wanderers, Oldham Athletic, Stoke City, Mazda/Japan, Shrewsbury Town, Witton Albion; retired 1994; became a financial advisor for the Prudential Insurance Company; lives in Bicton, Shrewsbury.

Details: In his day, Tony Henry was a very effective playmaker, whose career spanned twenty years during which time he appeared in well over 480 club games and scored eighty goals, having by far his best spell with Oldham (1983–87). After a steady start at Maine Road, he made his debut for City as a substitute, for Jimmy Conway, in a 2-0 League win at Sunderland in September 1976 and scored his first two goals in a 2-1 League Cup victory over Sheffield Wednesday three years later. He also netted in the 2-0 win in the Manchester derby in October 1979.

HENRY, William Armstrong (Full-back)
Apps/goals: 183/1 Born: Glasgow, 6/9/1894 Died: c. 1960

Career: Blantyre Celtic, Glasgow Rangers, Falkirk, Leicester Fosse, CITY (November 1911– July 1920), St Bernard's FC/Edinburgh.

Details: A tall, strong-kicking full-back, Billy Henry took over from Tommy Kelso in City's first XI as soon as he arrived at Hyde Road, and held his position unchallenged until the outbreak of the First World War. Even then he continued to play with grim determination and added a further twenty-five appearances to his tally during the hostilities.

HENSON, Philip Michael (Midfield)
Apps: 20 Born: Manchester, 30/3/1953

Career: Brookdale YC, CITY (May 1969– February 1975), Swansea City (loan), Sheffield Wednesday £44,000), Sparta Rotterdam/Holland, Stockport County, Rotherham United (player, then assistant-manager, manager and also general manager).

Details: Phil Henson's League career realised twenty-nine goals in 249 appearances, his best years coming with his last club, Rotherham, having struggled with injuries at Hillsborough. He never really got a chance with City, owing to the presence of so many talented midfield players and, in fact, from his debut day as a substitute against Crystal Palace in January 1972, he made only three appearances in just over two years before having a decent run in the first team under Tony Book during the first half of the 1974/75 campaign.

HERD, Alexander (Inside-forward)
Apps/goals: 288/125 Born: Bowhill, Fife, 8/11/1911 Died: Dumfries, 21/8/1982

Career: Cardenden Saints, Hearts of Beith, Hamilton Academical, CITY (February 1933– March 1948); served in Army during the Second World War; also guest for Stockport County, Chelsea, Manchester United and Newcastle United; Stockport County (signed); retired 1951; worked as sales representative for an asphalt company in Cheshire before moving back to Scotland.

Details: Alec Herd certainly made a dramatic entry into English football! Within fifteen months of signing for City, he had played in two FA Cup finals, collecting a winner's medal in the second (*v.* Portsmouth in 1934) while also scoring twenty-eight goals. A very clever player, who invariably tried to bring the ball out of defence before 'feeding' his forwards, he was a key figure in what some say has been City's greatest-ever teams, that of 1936/37, when he made thirty-six appearances and scored eighteen goals, including the winner in the home Manchester derby in January, as City swept to their first Football League championship. Partnering Ernie Toseland on the right wing, with Peter Doherty and Eric Brook linking up on the left and Fred Tilson driving through the middle, Herd created chances galore for the last three named as City bagged a total of 117 goals.

His career with City carried on throughout the Second World War, during which time he netted sixty more goals in ninety appearances when on leave from the Army. He was almost forty years of age when he retired in 1951, having netted forty-one goals in 119 appearances for Stockport and over 200 in more than 500 club games at senior level. Surprisingly, Herd never represented his country at senior level, although he did play for Scotland in a Second World War international and also starred for a Scottish League XI.

His brother Andrew played for Hearts and Scotland, while his son, David Herd, was a centre-forward with Arsenal, Manchester United, Stoke City, Stockport and Scotland. In fact, Alec and his son played in the same Stockport team against Hartlepool United (home) on 5 May 1951, David scoring in a 2-0 win.

HESHAM, John Frank (Forward)
Apps: 3 Born: Hyde, Manchester,
11/12/1880 Died: France, 17/11/1915
Career: Gorton St Francis, CITY (November 1896–June 1901), Crewe Alexandra, Accrington Stanley, Stoke, Leyton, Oldham Athletic, Preston North End, Croydon Common, Crewe Alexandra, Newton Heath Alliance (until his death).

Details: Reserve forward Frank Hesham – described as being 'an earnest and conscientious player' – made just three League appearances in five years for City – although he did finish up as top-scored for the second XI in 1897/98. He was killed while on active duty with the Royal Garrison Artillery in France.

HESLOP, George Wilson (Defender)
Apps/goals: 204/3 Born: Wallsend, 1/7/1940
Career: Dudley Welfare, Newcastle United, Everton, CITY (£25,000, September 1965–August 1972), Cape Town City/South Africa (loan), Bury £3,000), retired 1974; Northwich Victoria (manager), Bury (coach); became a licensee of the Hyde Road Hotel and City Gates pub, Manchester.

Details: City's tall, well-built blond defender George Heslop was outstanding at the heart of the defence during his first three seasons at Maine Road, when he deservedly won both Second Division and then First Division championship winner's medals (1966 and 1968). After an uneasy 1968/69 campaign when Tommy Booth took over at centre-half, which resulted with him missing the FA Cup final triumph over Leicester, Heslop was back in the thick of the action in 1969/70, helping City complete the League Cup and European Cup Winner's Cup double. He understudied England international Brian Labone at Everton for three years.

HICKS, George Wolstenholme (Forward)
Apps/goals: 135/48 Born: Weaste near Salford,
30/4/1902 Died: Manchester, after 1945.
Career: Salford Lads' Club, Droylsden, Manchester Central, CITY (November 1923–October 1928), Birmingham, Manchester United, Bristol Rovers, Swindon Town, Rotherham United, Manchester North End; retired May 1936.

Details: An FA Cup runner-up in 1926 and a Second Division championship winner two years later, the slimly-built George Hicks was a clever ball-playing left-winger with good pace and strong shot. He certainly proved his worth with City, averaging a goal every three games while producing many excellent performances. Replacing 'Spud' Murphy during the second half of the 1924/25 season, he created chances aplenty for Tom Johnson and Frank Roberts, and in 1926/27 netted twenty-two goals himself – only Johnson bagged more than season. Hicks scored over seventy goals in 252 career appearances.

HIGGS, Frank Jary (Goalkeeper)
Apps: 1 Born: Willington-on-Tyne,
Northumberland, 2/9/1910 Died: Cumbria, 1956
Career: Willingham Quay, Bedlington United, Seaton Delaval, Chelsea, Linfield, Barnsley, CITY (June 1932/May 1933), Aldershot, Walsall, Carlisle United, Southend United, Barrow; retired 1939.

Details: In his eleven-year professional career, goalkeeper Frank Higgs managed only ninety-nine League appearances, forty-nine with Carlisle and thirty-five with Barnsley. Competent enough, with safe hands, he was third in line behind Len Langford and Nicholls during his stay at Maine Road. His one outing was in a 3-2 home defeat by Middlesbrough early in the season.

HILDERSLEY, Ronald (Midfield)
Apps: 1 Born: Kirkcaldy, Fife, 6/4/1965
Career: Kirkcaldy Schools, CITY (June 1981–June 1984), Chester City (initially on loan), Rochdale, Preston North End, Cambridge United (loan), Blackburn Rovers, Wigan Athletic, Halifax Town.

Details: Ron Hildersley who was just 5 feet 4 inches tall, made 140 League appearances during his ten-year career. A City reserve for three seasons, his only first-class outing came in a 4-1 defeat at Swansea in March 1983, when he was substituted by Andy May.

HILEY, Scott Patrick (Right-back)
Apps: 9 Born: Plymouth, 27/9/1968
Career: Exeter City, Birmingham City, CITY (loan, February 1996, signed for £250,000, July 1996–December 1999), Southampton, Portsmouth (£200,000), Exeter City, Crawley Town, Tiverton Town, Cullumpton Rangers; retired 2009, aged forty-one.

Details: An over-lapping right-back with good pace, Scott Hiley was already a vastly experienced footballer with 318 League and Cup appearances under his belt when he joined City in 1986. He spent two-and-a-half years at Maine Road – mainly in the reserves – and in all played just nine times in the first XI, five as a substitute. He won the Fourth Division title with Exeter in 1990.

HILL, Andrew Roland (Right-back)
Apps/goals: 113/6 Born: Maltby, Yorkshire,
20/1/1965
Career: Schoolboy football, Manchester United, Bury, CITY (December 1990–August 1995), Port Vale (£150,000); retired June 1998.

Details: England Youth international Andy Hill was released by Manchester United as a teenager and went on to make 317 appearances for Bury, before switching to Maine Road at the age of twenty-five. Composed and committed, he stayed with City for over four-and-a-half years, having his best season in 1990/91, when he missed only six First Division matches as Neil Pointon's full-back partner. Hill, who could also play in other defensive positions, retired with over 550 club games under his belt.

HILL, Frederick (Midfield)
Apps/goals: 41/3 Born: Sheffield, 17 January 1940
Career: Sheffield Schools, Bolton Wanderers, Halifax Town, CITY (May 1970–August 1973), Cape Town City/South Africa (loan), Peterborough United, Cork Hibernians/Ireland, Droylsden, Radcliffe Borough; retired May 1978; became a licensee in Peterborough.

Details: A strong-running, skilful inside-forward with loads of ability, Freddie 'The Fox' Hill took over from Ian Bowyer in City's first XI and played in twenty-eight games in his first season, but only thirteen in his next two.

Capped by England in ten U23 and two full internationals (versus Northern Ireland and Wales in October/November 1962) he spent his best years with Bolton for whom he scored seventy-nine goals in 412 appearances (1957–69). He helped Peterborough win the Fourth Division title in 1974.

HILL, Percy (Full-back)
Apps: 40 Born: Hampshire, c. 1884 Died: 1955
Career: Southampton, Everton, CITY (November 1906–November 1909), Airdrieonians, Swindon Town.

Details: Strongly-built, Percy Hill was a reserve at Southampton before making his League debut for Everton in 1905. One of several excellent full-backs at Hyde Road, he made twenty-three of his senior appearances in his first season with City, partnering either Frank Norgrove or Tommy Kelso.

HILL, Robert (Forward)
Apps/goals: 22/9 Born: Edinburgh, 1870
Career: Linfield, Sheffield United, CITY (November 1895, released, May 1897)

Details: Bob Hill was born in Scotland, started his career in Ireland and made his League debut in England. He scored twenty-one goals in fifty-eight games for the Blades before spending eighteen months with City, deputising for Messrs McReddie, Rowan and Sharples, among others. Hill netted the winner in the Manchester derby in December 1895, netted against the foe in the 2-1 Christmas Day defeat of 1896, and bagged two more goals in his final outing versus Woolwich Arsenal in April 1897.

HILLMAN, John (Goalkeeper)
Apps: 124 Born: Tavistock, Devon, 30/10/1870 Died: Burnley, summer 1955
Career: Tavistock Juniors, Burnley, Everton, Dundee, Burnley, CITY (January 1902–December 1906), Millwall Athletic; retired elbow injury,

1908; Burnley (trainer/coach); ran confectionary ship in Burnley for many years.

Details: Second in stature only to the giant Billy 'Fatty' Foulke (Chelsea and Sheffield United) Jack Hillman, 6 feet tall and weighing around 16 stone, was on par regarding ability with most goalkeepers in League football during the early 1900s. He effectively took over between the posts from Charlie Williams and held his position until September 1905, when Jack Edmonson replaced him. Capped once by England in a 13-2 win over Ireland in 1899, Hillman gained Second Division championship and FA Cup winner's medals with City in 1903 and 1904. He retired with over 350 club appearances to his name.

HINCE, Paul Frank (Forward)
Apps/goals: 11/4 Born: Gorton, Manchester, 2/3/1945
Career: Old Drive Primary & Burnage Grammar Schools/Manchester, Manchester Boys, Reseda FC, Pinnington Celtic, CITY (June 1966–February 1968), Charlton Athletic, Bury, Crewe Alexandra, Macclesfield; retired and became a reporter, covering Oldham Athletic's matches for the *Manchester Evening News*, having initially trained in journalism in the mid-1960s.

Details: Paul Hince once described himself as a 'chain-smoking, drink-sodden heathen from Gorton' and was frisked by his manager at Charlton and Bury. After turning down offers from Bury and Burnley, he signed for City at the age of twenty-one and scored twice on his debut in a 2-2 draw with WBA in March 1967. He made a further six appearances early in the championship-winning season that followed (before Francis lee arrived on the scene) and bagged two more goals, in wins over Newcastle and Coventry. However, in a relatively short career, he claimed just eleven goals in ninety-four League appearances.

HINCHCLIFFE, Andrew Gordon (Defender)
Apps/goals: 139/11 Born: Manchester, 5/2/1969
Career: Manchester Boys, CITY (July 1985–July 1990), Everton (£800,000 plus Neil Pointon), Sheffield Wednesday; retired March 2002; now engaged as a commentator by Sky Sport.

Details: After two seasons playing for the intermediates and reserves, wholehearted and enthusiastic left-back, and occasional midfielder, Andy Hinchcliffe established himself as City's first choice left back in 1987/88, playing in forty-two of the forty-four League matches. A scorer in the Manchester derby in September 1989 when City won 5-1, he remained a first-team regular in the first team until injury laid him low in March 1990. Four months later, he was off to Goodison Park. An FA Cup and Charity Shield winner with Everton in 1995, he gained seven England caps

(1996–99), having the honour of never being on the losing side (four wins, three draws). And when he lined up against Switzerland in 1998, he became the first Sheffield Wednesday player for five years to represent England at senior level. He also represented his country at youth and U21 levels. Hinchcliffe retired with a serious Achilles heel injury in 2003 with 463 club appearances under his belt.

HINDMARSH, James (Half-back)
Apps/goals: 35/2 Born: Whitburn near Sunderland, 19/4/1885 Died: 1959
Career: Whitburn Colliery, Sunderland, Fulham, Watford, Plymouth Argyle, Stockport County, CITY (December 1912–September 1919), Newport County; retired 1922.
Details: Tall and strong, Jimmy Hindmarsh made his League debut for Sunderland in 1905, spent five years in the Southern League and played seventy-four games for Stockport before joining City. After six months in the reserves, he eventually replaced Tom Holford in the first XI and produced some excellent performances alongside Ted Hanney, until losing his place to John Brennan. Hindmarsh represented the Southern League as a Fulham player.

HITCHCOCK, Ernest (Inside-right)
Apps: 1 Born: Birmingham, 1885
Career: Aston Villa, CITY (March/May 1909), Halesowen, Cradley Heath.
Details: After failing to break into the first team at Villa Park, Ernie Hitchcock tried his luck with City but made only one senior appearance – in a 3-1 League defeat at Leicester.

HOAD, Sidney James (Outside-right)
Apps/goals: 69/2 Born: Eltham, Middlesex, 27/12/1890 Died: 1973
Career: St Anne's FC/Blackpool, Blackpool, CITY (May 1911–May 1920), Rochdale, Nelson, Hurst; retired 1928.
Details: Sid Hoad's career with City effectively ended when League football was suspended in 1915. Prior to that, although not a first-team regular at the time, he produced some fine displays, especially in 1911/12, when he played in thirty-nine out of forty League and Cup games. His first goal came in a 2-0 win over Bolton in September 1912, his second in a 4-0 FA Cup win over Birmingham in January 1913.

HODGETTS, John (Forward)
Apps/goals: 1/2 Born: Manchester, 1864 Died: Manchester, c. 1929
Career: Gorton, CITY (August 1886–May 1891), Manchester East End.
Details: The club's first professional, John Hodgetts was paid five shillings-a-week (25p) in 1887. He scored twice in City's first-ever FA Cup qualifying tie against Liverpool Stanley in 1890 (won 12-0).

HODGKINSON, Derek John (Outside-right)
Apps/goals: 1/1 Born: Weston-Super-Mare, 30/4/1944
Career: Barnwell YC, Margate, CITY (August 1961–June 1964), Stockport County.
Details: A City youth team player and reserve for three years, Derek Hodgkinson will never forget his League debut – he scored in a 1-1 draw at Bury in September 1963 when deputising for Neil Young. He netted eleven goals in fifty-three outings for Stockport.

HODGSON, Ronald (Centre-half)
Apps: 1 Born: Birkenhead, 11/1922 Died: 26/8/2009
Career: Tranmere Rovers, CITY (October 1944–June 1947), Southport, Crewe Alexandra.
Details: Chosen to play alongside Billy Walsh when Les McDowall was absent, Ron Hodgson's only senior game for City came in a 7-2 home League win over Bradford in September 1946. He made forty-two League appearances for Southport and thirty-one for Crewe.

HOEKMAN, Daniel (Midfield)
Apps: 3 Born: Nijmegen, Holland, 21/9/1964
Career: Va-Nec Oss, NEC Nijmegen, Roda JK, VVV-Venlo, ADO Den Haag, CITY (non-contract, September–November 1991), Blackburn Rovers (trial), Southampton, ADO Den Haag, NEC Nijmegen; retired 1997; FC Mameenlinna/ Finland (coach), NEC TOP Oss/ Holland (coach), A-Jazeera Club/Abu Dhabi (coach), Bonner SC (coach), Al-Ahli SC (coach), Racing Mechelen/ Belgium (coach), A-Mesaimeer SC (coach).
Details: Left-sided midfielder Danny Hoekman made just three 'sub' appearances for City – the first in a 3-1 League win at Notts County two weeks after joining. As a teenager, he suffered a serious knee injury (following a clash with FC Utrecht goalkeeper Jan Willem van Ede). Regarded at the time as one of the greatest talents in Holland, his knee was so badly damaged he was sidelined for eighteen months. Civil proceedings against van Ede followed. Hoekman eventually made over 200 appearances in Dutch football.

HOGAN, William James (Outside-right)
Apps: 3 Born: Salford, 9/1/1924 Died: Truro, Cornwall, 6/3/2013
Career: CITY (May 1942–August 1949), Carlisle United (£4,000); retired 1956.
Details: After just three First Division outings for City (all at the end of the 1948/49 season against Wolves, Arsenal and Huddersfield), Billy Hogan's

career took off under manager Bill Shankly at Carlisle for whom he scored twenty-seven goals in 220 appearances. A soldier in the Army during the Second World War, Hogan suffered from Alzheimer's disease for many years prior to his death.

HOLDEN, Richard William (Outside-left)
Apps/goals: 58/5 Born: Skipton, 9/9/1964
   Career: Carnegie College, Burnley (non-contract), Halifax Town, Watford, Oldham Athletic, CITY (£900,000, August 1992/October 1993), Oldham Athletic, Blackpool; retired injured, 1996; became head of the outpatient physiotherapist department at Nobles Hospital/Isle of Man; also managed Manx club Peel FC; went into private practice at the Mount Murray Hotel/I-o-M; Barnsley (assistant-manager/physio); now runs Island Physiotherapy/I-o-M.
   Details: Occasionally a target of the Maine Road boo-boys, Rick Holden was a first-team regular during his fifteen months with City, playing in forty-nine of the fifty games possible in 1992/93. Strong and direct, he returned to Boundary Park, after being out of favour with manager Brian Horton. During an excellent career Holden scored sixty-five goals in 458 club appearances and won the Second Division championship with Oldham in 1991.

HOLFORD, Thomas (Defender)
Apps: Born: Hanley, Stoke-on-Trent, 28/1/1878 Died: Blurton, Stoke-on-Trent, 6/4/1964
   Career: Granville's night School, Cobridge, Stoke, CITY (April 1908–May 1914), Port Vale (player-manager); conscripted into forces, 1917 (served with the Royal Artillery First World War guest for Nottingham Forest; retired May 1923; Port Vale (trainer, then manager, later scout, trainer again).
   Details: A hard worker, totally committed, Tom Holford was only 5 feet 5 inches tall, and although, he tended to give the ball 'too much air' when clearing his lines, his defending was second to none. Known affectionately as 'Dirty Tommy', he bolstered up City's defence to a certain degree, but also gave a good account of himself in attack when playing centre-forward. His twelve goals, including hat-tricks against Bradford City and Everton in the space of three weeks in January, helped City win promotion in 1910.
   His career effectively covered twenty-six years, during which time he appeared in 513 first-class matches (479 in the League), scored seventy-two goals and played in every position except goal. In 1924, at the age of forty-six, he came out of retirement to assist Port Vale in an emergency. His overall record was quite remarkable, inasmuch that he lost four years due to the war. He won one England cap *v.* Ireland in 1903.

HOLMES, William Marsden (Half-back)
Apps/goals: 166/4 Born: Darley Hillside, Derbyshire, 1875 Died: London, 22/2/1922
   Career: Matlock BC, Chesterfield, CITY (July 1896–August 1905), Clapton Orient (player-manager; retired as a player, 1908).
   Details: Big and strong, Billy Holmes had a biting tackle and feared no-one, making him one of the best defenders in the game. Known as 'Doc' he spent nine years with City, but the last four were not happy ones as injuries resulted in only thirty-two appearances out of a possible 149. He was left out of City's 1904 FA Cup final team, having played in the quarter and semi-final wins over Middlesbrough and Sheffield Wednesday. In fact, so angry and upset was he when told that amateur Sutcliffe would be replacing him at left-half against Bolton, that he reacted by slinging his boots through the dressing room window! A Second Division championship winner with City in 1899, Holmes represented the Football League (*v.* the Irish League) in 1897 and also gained a Lancashire Combination League winner's medal with the reserves in 1901/02. It was a shock to everyone associated with Clapton Orient when he collapsed and died while still manager. His brother, Sammy Holmes, played for Derby County between 1889/90.

HOPE, James Gibson (Outside-left)
Apps: 7 Born: Glasgow, 11/9/1919 Died: Glasgow, c. 1990
   Career: Ardeer Recreationalists, CITY (February 1939–February 1947), Queen of the South; served in the Army during the Second World War.
   Details: After returning from war duties, Jim Hope, just 5 feet 4 inches tall, made seven League appearances on City's left-wing during the first half of the 1946/47 season, before switching his allegiance back to his native Scotland.

HOPKINS, Robert Arthur (Midfield/winger)
Apps/goals: 9/1 Born: Hall Green, Birmingham, 25/10/1961
   Career: Pitmaston School, South Birmingham Schools, West Midlands County Boys Aston Villa, Birmingham City, CITY (£130,000, September-October 1986), West Bromwich Albion (£60,000 (plus Imre Varadi), Birmingham City (£25,000), Shrewsbury Town, South China/Hong Kong, Instant Dictionary FC/Hong Kong, Solihull Borough, Colchester United (non-contract), Solihull Borough (player-coach), Bromsgrove Rovers, Paget Rangers; retired 2003; Pelsall FC (coach); also played for WBA Old Stars.
   Details: Robert Hopkins' early career was littered with disciplinary problems – due to his total commitment on the pitch! A right-sided midfielder,

he even played at full-back at times, and when he joined South China in 1992, he had already amassed 354 appearances (307 in the Football League) for his six English clubs. He spent just six weeks at Maine Road, making his debut in a 2-2 draw with Norwich City and scoring his only goal in his sixth outing *v.* Leicester, lost 2-1.

An FA Youth Cup winner with Aston Villa, he had the pleasure of scoring with his first kick in League football, as substitute for Villa *v.* Norwich in 1980. He helped Birmingham gain promotion in 1985.

HORLOCK, Kevin (Midfield)
Apps/goals: 232/42 Born: Erith, 1/11/1972

Career: West Ham United, Swindon Town, CITY (£1.25 million, January 1997–August 2003), West Ham United (£300,000), Ipswich Town (free), Doncaster Rovers (loan), Scunthorpe United, Mansfield Town (loan), Needham Market FC.

Details: Kevin Horlock failed to make a single appearance in his first spell with West Ham, but did exceptionally well with Swindon, scoring twenty-six goals in 199 League and Cup games before his transfer to Maine Road, being manager Frank Clark's first signing. His greatest strength was his willingness to follow up his own forward passes and also his shooting power – he scored some stunning goals at times. A regular for City during his first three seasons at the club, he starred in the 1996 Second Division and 2002 Division One championship winning teams, and was eventually replaced in the engine-room by Joey Barton.

The recipient of two 'B' and thirty-two full caps for Northern Ireland, Horlock moved into non-League football in April 2008, having netted seventy goals in 546 appearances for his seven League clubs.

HORNE, Alfred (Half-back/inside-forward)
Apps/goals: 11/2 Born: Stafford, 13/6/1903
Died: Nottinghamshire, 13/4/1976

Career: Alvechurch, West Bromwich Albion (amateur), Stafford Rangers, Hull City, Southend United, CITY (March 1928/September 1929), Preston North End, Lincoln City, Mansfield Town; retired 1938.

Details: Unable to make headway with WBA, Alf Horne moved into non-League football with Stafford Rangers where his scoring exploits attracted scouts from several clubs. However, he struggled with Hull and Southend and managed only eleven outings for City – although he did set up two of Frank Roberts' five goals against Clapton in March 1928 and two of Bobby Marshall's three against Southampton four weeks later. After forty outings for Preston (five goals) he had an excellent spell with Lincoln, netting thirty-six times in 315 senior matches. A penalty expert, he scored a hat-trick of spot-kicks for the

Imps *v.* Stockport in September 1935, and during his career, appeared in 350 first-class matches, 315 in the Football League.

HORNE, Stanley Frederick (Full-back/half-back)
Apps: 66 Born: Clanfield, Oxfordshire, 17/12/1944

Career: Bampton YC, Aston Villa, CITY (September 1965–February 1969), Fulham (£18,000), Chester City (£2,000), Rochdale; retired 1975.

Details: Stan Horne was advised to give up the sport while at Villa Park. However, he defied doctor's orders and, as a hard-working grafter, went on to amass over 200 League appearances for his next four clubs. The first black footballer to play for City, he appeared at left-back and right-half for the Blues, having his best season in 1966/67 (thirty-eight outings).

HORRIDGE, Peter (Full-back)
Apps: 3 Born: Manchester, 31/5/1935
Died: Manchester, 10/4/2010

Career: Newton Heath Parish, CITY (October 1951–June 1959), Crewe Alexandra.

Details: A reserve full-back, Peter Horridge made three first-team appearances in almost eight years for City, marking Stanley Matthews out of the game on his debut *v.* Blackpool in November 1958 (0-0), partnering Cliff Seal against Aston Villa two weeks later and lining up against Everton, away, in January 1959. He failed to get a game with Crewe.

HORSWILL, Michael Frederick (Defender/midfield)
Apps: 15 Born: Annfield Plain, Durham, 6/3/1953

Career: County Durham junior football, Sunderland, CITY (with Dennis Tueart plus £25,000, March 1974/July 1975), Plymouth Argyle (£30,000), Hull City (£15,000), Happy Valley/Hong Kong, Carlisle United; retired 1984; became a licensee in Boldon, Tyne & Wear.

Details: Mick Horswill won the FA Cup with Sunderland at the age of twenty. Competent in defence or midfield, he made his debut, with Dennis Tueart, in the goalless Manchester derby at Maine Road forty-eight hours after joining City. Unfortunately, niggling injuries affected his game after that. He made almost 300 club appearances during his career.

HOSIE, James (Half-back)
Apps/goals: 43/3 Born: Glasgow, 1876
Died: after 1935

Career: Glasgow Perthshire, Reading, Blackburn Rovers, CITY (January 1901/October 1902), Stockport County, Bristol City; retired 1910.

Details: A strong, well composed defender, Jamie Hosie made his League debut for Blackburn in

1900. He joined City as back up for Holmes and a month later played his first game for the club in a 5-2 defeat at Everton. He missed only one game the following season when he scored his three goals – his first, the winner, versus Aston Villa (home), his second in a 4-0 victory over Sheffield United and his last in a 3-1 defeat at Nottingham Forest. Hosie made over eighty appearances after leaving City.

HOWARD, Frederick James (Centre-forward)
Apps/goals: 91/43 Born: Walkden, 1893
Died: Wales, c. 1964
   Career: Walkden Wednesday, CITY (September 1912–May 1920), Mid-Rhondda, Pontypridd, Gillingham, Dundee Hibernians, Ayr United (trial), Clyde, Port Vale, New Brighton, Wrexham, Welshpool Town, Holyhead Town; retired 1928.
   Details: After four months in City's second XI, Fred Howard – taking over from Harry Taylor – scored four goals on his League debut in a 4-1 win over Liverpool in January 1913. In fact, he loved playing against the Merseysiders, netting three more goals past them in 1913/14 and two more in 1914/15. Powerfully built, robust with a strong right foot, he finished second in City' scoring charts in his first season with the club, came joint top with Tommy Browell in his second (which saw him net a treble at Derby) and topped the list in the last campaign before the First World War. Army duties kept him out of football for almost four years, and unfortunately he was never the same player after that, plying his trade around the UK with a variety of clubs.

HOWE, Frederick (Centre-forward)
Apps/goals: 6/5 Born: Bredbury, Cheshire,
24/9/1912 Died: 1984
   Career: Wilmslow FC, Stockport County (amateur), Hyde United, Liverpool (£2,000), CITY (June/October 1938), Grimsby Town; Second World War guest for Stockport County & Watford; Oldham Athletic; retired May 1947.
   Details: A natural opportunist, Fred Howe was leading scorer for Liverpool in 1934/35. He joined City after netting thirty-six goals in ninety-four appearances for the Anfield club, but unfortunately he didn't stay too long at Maine Road – despite netting in four of his six League matches, including a debut goal in a 5-0 win over Swansea. Howe was a plumber by trade.

HOWEY, Stephen Norman (Defender)
Apps/goals: 103/11 Born: Sunderland,
26 October 1971
   Career: Newcastle United, CITY (£2 million, August 2000–July 2003), Leicester City (£300,000), Bolton Wanderers (free), New England Revolution/USA, Hartlepool United; retired 2006; Crook Town (manager),

Middlesbrough (coach), Bishop Auckland (part-time player-coach); became co-presenter of Total Sport on BBC Newcastle with Marco Gabbiadini and Simon Pryde; East Durham College Football Development Centre (coach).
   Details: Initially a striker, Steve Howey was converted into a centre-back at Newcastle and went on to represent England in that position, gaining four full caps. He also played in one unofficial international and was in his country's squad for Euro 96. Powerful in the air and on the ground, he made almost 370 club appearances, working under manager Kevin Keegan at both Newcastle and City. He forged a fine partnership with Richard Dunne in his first season at Maine Road, which saw him score a dramatic eighty-fourth-minute equaliser in the Manchester derby in April 2001 – a game best remembered for the clash between Alf-Inge Haaland and Roy Keane! Excellent alongside Dunn, Lucien Mettomo and also Sylvain Distin after that, he remained a regular in the side up to March 2003 when a combination of injury and loss of form saw him miss the closing stages of the campaign. He gained Division One championship medals with Newcastle (1993) and City (2002). His brother, Lee, played for Sunderland, Ipswich, Burney and Northampton.

HOYLAND, Jamie (Midfield)
Apps/goals: 3/1 Born: Sheffield, 23/1/1966
   Career: Sheffield Schools, CITY (July 1982–July 1986), Bury, Sheffield United, Bristol City (loan), Burnley, Carlisle United (loan), Scarborough; retired 2000; Rochdale (assistant-manager), Bolton Wanderers (coach), Preston North End (coach), Sheffield United (academy coach).
   Details: An England youth international, Jamie Hoyland made his debut for City at the age of seventeen, scoring to celebrate the occasion in a 6-0 League Cup victory over Torquay United in October 1983. He played only twice more for the club – in League games against Oldham in 1985 and Derby in 1986. After leaving Maine Road, Hoyland did very well, amassing a further 483 club appearances, having his best years with Bury for whom he played 205 times. His son Tommy played for Sheffield United and Bradford City.

HUCKERBY, Darren Carl (Forward)
Apps/goals: 82/31 Born: Nottingham, 23/4/1976
   Career: Lincoln City, Newcastle United (£400,000), Millwall (loan), Coventry City (£1 million), Leeds United (£56 million), CITY (£3.38 million, December 2000–September 2003) Nottingham Forest (loan), Norwich City (loan/signed, £1 million), San Jose Earthquakes/USA; retired September 2009.
   Details: City, struggling at the bottom end of the Premiership when they signed Darren Huckerby,

were subsequently relegated, but the striker stayed loyal to the club, helping the Blues win the Football League First Division championship in 2001/02 when he and Shaun Goater bagged a total of forty-eight League goals, fifty-eight in all games. Huckerby contributed twenty-six, including a hat-trick in successive home wins over Nottingham Forest (3-0) and Barnsley (5-1) in the space of eight days. He then headed the opening goal of the next season, to beat his former employers, Newcastle. However, the arrival of Nicolas Ankela and Jon Macken meant less playing time for 'Huckers', who eventually ended the season on-loan to Nottingham Forest FC, being part of the team that reached the Division One playoffs. In a fine career, Huckerby scored forty-three goals in 529 club appearances, won four England U21 caps, played in one 'B' international and helped Norwich reach the Premiership in 2004.

HUGHES, Edwin (Wing-half)
Apps/goals: 89/3 Born: Wrexham, 1886
Died: Montgomery, 17/4/1949
   Career: Wrexham & St Giles, Wrexham Victoria, Wrexham, Nottingham Forest, Wrexham, CITY (December 1912–May 1920), Aberdare Athletic, Colwyn Bay, Llandudno Town; retired 1925; became a licensee, also worked as a stone mason and fine cricketer, representing Denbighshire.
   Details: Stylish wing-half and long throw expert Eddie Hughes could also deliver 'the precise, defence-splitting pass through to his forwards'. After a six-month 'breaking-in' period, during which time he made his City debut in a 4-1 win over Liverpool in January 1913 (the day Fred Howard scored all four goals) he won a regular place in the middle-line in 1913/14, replacing Bill Bottomley. However, the First World War arrived and completely disrupted his League career, although he did make sixty-five appearances for the club during the hostilities, won two caps for Wales in Victory internationals and later played with Lot Jones at Aberdare. A Second Division championship winner with Nottingham Forest, for whom he made 176 appearances, he gained sixteen full caps for Wales (1906–14). His brother Richard played for Wales as an amateur.

HUGHES, John (Outside-left)
Apps: 2 Born: Manchester, 1873
   Career: Local junior football, CITY (March 1894/May 1895)
   Details: John Hughes made his two appearances for City against Lincoln City and Crewe Alexandra at the end of the 1893/94 season – one of six players to fill the left-wing position that term.

HUGHES, Michael Eamonn (Midfield)
Apps/goals: 33/1 Born: Larne, 2/8/1971

Career: Carrick Rangers, CITY (May 1988–July 1992), RS Strasbourg/France (record £450,000), West Ham United (loan/signed), Wimbledon (£1.6 million), Birmingham City (loan), Crystal Palace (free), Coventry City, St Neot's Town (player-coach); retired 2010; Carrick Rangers (manager).
   Details: Capped at schoolboy and youth team levels, and City's Young Player of the Year in 1990, Michael Hughes went on to play in one U21, two U23 and 71 full internationals for Northern Ireland, while also amassing almost 550 club appearances (473 in the League). Having his best years with Wimbledon (130 games) and Palace (141), he marshalled the midfield with confidence while scoring some stunning goals. Making his League debut for City as a seventeen-year-old at Plymouth in October 1988, he was only a first-team regular in his last season at Maine Road when he also netted his only goal for the club, in a 3-2 home win over Sheffield United. He played with his former international teammate Steve Lomas at St Neot's.

HUMPHREYS, Reginald (Right-back)
Apps: 3 Born: Oswestry, 1888
   Career: Oswestry Town, CITY (May 1910–May 1912), Oswestry Town.
   Details: A reserve for two seasons Reg Humphreys, stepping in for Tommy Kelso, made his League debut in a 2-1 League defeat at Bristol City in December 1910. His three appearances were all away.

HUNTER, Robert (Right-back/right-half)
Apps: 7 Born: Manchester, 1876
   Career: CITY (March 1898–March 1903), Stockport County.
   Details: Another reserve, Bob Hunter, hardly got a look in during his five years with City. He made the first of his seven League appearances in a 0-0 draw at Notts County in March 1901 and played his last game against Stoke in April 1902. He didn't do much with Stockport either.

HURST, Daniel James (Outside-left)
Apps: 15 Born: Pemberton, Wigan, 9/11/1876 Died: c. 1950
   Career: Black Diamonds FC/Workington, Blackburn Rovers, Workington, CITY (May 1901/May 1902), Manchester United.
   Details: After making his debut against Everton on the opening day of the season, Danny Hurst played in roughly half of City's fixtures in 1901/02. Partner to both Drummond and Williams on the left-wing, he made his last appearance for City against Aston Villa in February 1902, before joining the newly constructed Manchester United three months later. He was Blackburn's top scorer in 1898/99.

HUSSEIN, Yasser El-Mohammodi Abdulrahman (Midfield)
Apps: 1 Born: Doha, Qatar, 9/10/1982
    Career: Al-Rayyan, Manchester United, Royal Antwerp (loan), AEL Limassol, Al-Sadd, CITY (August 2005/January 2006), Al-Rayyan, Sporting Braga, Boavista, Al-Ahly, Zamalek, Lierse.
    Details: Manager Stuart Pearce signed Yasser Hussein on the recommendation of former player Ali Benarbi who was playing with him in Qatar. However, Hussein made only one first-team appearance for City – in a League Cup tie against Doncaster Rovers. He said he that leaving City was 'the biggest mistake of his life'.
    Hussein scored twenty goals in sixty-nine internationals for Qatar and is the second-longest named player (thirty-five letters) ever to be associated with the club. He failed to get a game with United, and won two Egyptian League titles and the CAF Cup with Al-Ahly (2008–10).
    His father played in Egypt and coached in Qatar, while brothers Ahmed and Mohammed won caps for Qatar at U/20 and senior levels respectively.

HUTCHINSON, George Walter (Goalkeeper)
Apps: 7 Born: Manchester, c. 1872
    Career: local football, CITY (May 1894–May 1896).
    Details: Reserve to Charlie Williams, George Hutchinson conceded four goals at Woolwich Arsenal on his City debut in September 1894 and let in another nineteen in his next six outings including two fives, at Newcastle and at home to Newton Heath in the Manchester derby. That effectively was the end of his senior career!

HUTCHISON, Thomas (Wing-forward)
Apps/goals: 60/5 Born: Cardenen, Scotland, 22/9/1947
    Career: Dundonald Bluebells, Alloa Athletic, Blackpool, Coventry City, Seattle Sounders, CITY (£47,500, October 1980–July 1982), Bulova/Hong Kong, Burnley, Swansea City (initially as player-manager), Merthyr Tydfil; retired 1995; later PFA Youth Development Officer for the Merthyr & Taff Ely Borough Council; Bristol City (Football Development officer); also ran Pontypridd residential sports camp; now lives in Scotland.
    Details: John Bond's first signing as manager at Maine Road, Tommy Hutchison had the 'displeasure' of scoring twice in the hundredth FA Cup final in 1981 – for City followed by an equaliser for Tottenham Hotspur. He was not the first to do this, however – Bert Turner had netted for Charlton and opponents Derby County in the 1946 final. Gary Mabbutt followed suit for Spurs and Coventry in 1987.
    Tall and lanky, he was a fine ball-player whose 'individual traits were there for all to see as he weaved and wriggled his way past defenders with sleight of foot'. A real character, he had an excellent spell with City. Debuting against Brighton (away) just after signing, he scored his first two goals for the club in a 4-0 homer win over Wolves two months later and in fact he played in sixty out of a possible sixty-seven games before injury ended his days at Maine Road in February 1982.
    Hutch' had a wonderful career which spanned thirty years (1965–95) during which time he appeared in 863 League games. Only three players have bettered that – Peter Shilton 1,005, Tony Ford 931 and Scotsman Graeme Armstrong 909. And in all competitions, he played in over 1,000 competitive matches, including seventeen internationals for Scotland (1973–75). He represented his country in the 1974 World Cup finals, but was surprisingly omitted from the tournament in Argentina four years later when he was arguably playing the finest football of his career.
    He won the Anglo-Italian Cup with Blackpool (1971), the NASL/Conference (West) championship with Seattle Sounders (1980), the Hong Kong Cup with Bulova (1983) the Welsh Cup with Swansea (1989) and an FA Cup runner's-up medal with City (1981). 'Hutch' played under former City boss Joe Mercer at Coventry.

HYNDS, Thomas (Centre-half)
Apps/goals: 172/9 Born: Hurlford, Kilmarnock, 20/5/1880 Died: 1944
    Career: Hurlford Thistle, Celtic, Bolton Wanderers (loan), Clyde (loan), CITY (September 1901–December 1906), Woolwich Arsenal (£100), Leeds City (£50), Heart of Midlothian, Ladysmith FC/Canada, Musselburgh/Scotland; retired May 1911; later coached in British Columbia/Canada and Italy.
    Details: Tom Hynds – a terrific defender, strong and commanding – missed only sixteen League games in his five seasons with City before becoming embroiled in the 1906 bribery scandal, resulting in a £75 fine and ban until New Year's Day 1907. Then, when the seventeen players were put up for auction at the Queen's Hotel, Manchester, it was Woolwich Arsenal who stepped in to sign the centre-half for just £100. Hynds won the Second Division championship and FA Cup with City and represented the Scottish League in 1901. His brother, John, was a City reserve in 1910/11.

I

IBRAHIM, Abdisalam (Midfield)
Apps: 3 Born: Guriceel, Somalia, 4/5/1991
    Career: Øyer-Tretten/Norway, Lørenskog/Norway, Fjellhamer/Norway, CITY (July 2007 to date), Scunthorpe United (loan), Stromsgodset/Norway (loan), NEC/Holland (loan), Strømsgodset (loan).

Details: Two years after starring in City's FA Youth Cup-winning team, tall Somalian Abdi Ibrahim made his senior debut as a substitute in an FA Cup tie against Scunthorpe in January 2010, came off the bench against Liverpool in a Premiership game soon afterwards and made his first start in the League Cup encounter *v.* WBA early the next season. Regarded as a 'great prospect' and with a style of play similar to that of Patrick Vieira, he is on contract with City until May 2014. Between 2006 and 2012, Ibrahim played for Norway at every level from U15 to U23, gaining a total of thirty-five intermediate caps. His brother, Abdrashid, played for FC United of Manchester and Rossendale.

IMMEL, Eike (Goalkeeper)
Apps: 50 Born: Stadtallendorf, West Germany, 27/11/1960
    Career: Margburg BC, Borussia Dortmund, VfB Stuttgart, CITY (£400,000, August 1995; retired May 1997); Fenerbahçe/Turkey (coach).
    Details: A very competent goalkeeper, with good positional sense and the ability to throw the ball out accurately and long to a colleague, Eke Immel played in the Bundesliga for seventeen seasons before joining City, on the recommendation of former striker Uwe Rosler and with sound references from no other than Bert Trautmann. With three 'keepers injured, he was an ever-present in his first season at Maine Road. However, after starting as first choice the following season, an ongoing shoulder injury flared up once more and he was allowed to return to Germany (at his own expense) for treatment. The operation was not a success, and he duly announced his retirement. Immel who played twenty-seven times for his country at intermediate level, gained nineteen full caps. He gained a winner's medal at Euro 1980 and collected two WC runner's-up prizes in 1982 and 1986. He also won the Bundesliga with Stuttgart in 1992 and currently holds the dubious record for conceding most goals in German League history – 829 in 534 matches. In January 2008, Immel was a contestant in *Holt Mich Hier Raus!*, the German edition of *I'm a Celebrity, Get Me Out of Here!*

INGEBRIGTSTEN, Kåre Hedley (Midfield)
Apps/goals: 17/3 Born: Trondheim, Norway, 11/10/1965
    Career: Rosenborg BK, CITY (January 1992–May 1994), Rosenborg BK, Strømsgodset, Lillestrøm SK, Rosenborg BK, Lillestrøm SK; retired injured, 1998; Rannheim FC (coach), Rosenborg BK (assistant-coach), Boda-Glimt (manager), Viking FC (assistant-coach).
    Details: Joining the club midway through the 1992/93 campaign, he did not play at all as City finished ninth in the League. He made all of his seventeen appearances the following season, and thought he had scored his first goal against Ipswich

in January 1994, but shortly after his 'goal' the game was called off due to a waterlogged pitch with City leading 2–0. However, he finally opened his account a week later in sensational style by netting a hat-trick in third-round FA Cup win over Leicester. At the end of the season, after failing to establish himself in the first team, he returned to Rosenborg. Ingebrigtsen won twenty-three caps for Norway, scoring one goal.

INGHAM, Thomas Walter (Forward)
Apps/goals: 2/1 Born: Chorlton-cum-Hardy, 7/6/1896 Died: 1972
    Career: CITY (December 1921–May 1923), Chesterfield.
    Details: Reserve to Tommy Browell, Matt Barras and Frank Roberts, Tom Ingham made his League debut for City in a 0-0 draw at Chelsea in March 1922 and scored in his second game, a 5-1 defeat at Newcastle five weeks later. He had no joy at Chesterfield either!

INGRAM, Rae (Centre-half/left-back)
Apps: 28 Born: Manchester, 6/12/1974
    Career: CITY (June 1992–May 1998), Macclesfield Town (loan/signed), Port Vale, Bangor City; retired 2004; now employed as a firefighter.
    Details: Rae Ingram signed professional forms at Maine Road in July 1993, was named Young Player of the Year in 1994 and made his senior debut, under manager Alan Ball, in August 1995 against Everton. A centre-half, he was forced to play out of position at left-back due to a lack of specialist full-backs at the club and featured twenty-two times in 1996/97, finding a first-team place from January onwards under new boss Frank Clark who had replaced short-term employee Steve Coppell. He fell out of the first-team picture though in 1997/98, and finished the season on loan at Sammy McIlroy's club, Macclesfield Town whom he helped gain promotion. He was one of fourteen professionals released by City in 1998. Ingram recovered from a bout of ME.

IRELAND, Stephen James (Midfield)
Apps/goals: 176/23 Born: Cork, 22/8/1986
    Career: Cobh Rangers, CITY (August 2001–August 2010), Aston Villa (£13 million, plus James Milner), Newcastle United (loan).
    Details: Stephen Ireland scored the fastest-ever Cup goal for City – after just thirty-five seconds of the UEFA Cup clash with Hamburg in April 2009. One of several fine and important goals he bagged for the club, he smacked home a real beauty late on to beat Reading and likewise against Sunderland, both in 2007. He dropped his shorts to reveal a superman logo on his underpants after his effort against the Wearsiders.

In December 2009, Mark Hughes was replaced as City manager by Roberto Mancini and with Nigel De Jong and Patrick Vieira showing good form, Ireland spent most of the second half of the season as a substitute, despite being voted the club's 'Player of the Year' in 2008/09 after playing in fifty matches.

Ireland and Mancini had words and in the summer of 2010 the Irish international moved to Villa Park. Having played for his country at youth and U21 levels, Ireland now has six full caps to his credit (four goals).

ISAKSSON, Andreas (Goalkeeper)
Apps: 20 Born: Symgehamn, Sweden, 3/10/1981

Career: Trelleborg, Juventus, Djurgardens IF, Rennes, CITY (£2 million, August 2006–July 2008), PSV Eindhoven, Kasimpasa SK/Turkey.

Details: One of the few goalkeepers in world football to top the century mark in international appearances, Andreas Isaksson has so far won 104 caps for Sweden (2002–13). Tall and agile, he was signed by City to replace David James, but knee and ankle injuries kept him sidelined until December 2006 when he took over from Nicky Weaver for his Premiership debut in the Manchester derby. After that, a broken thumb and another knee problem meant he missed more matches than he played and after making his twentieth and final appearance for the club in an 8-1 thrashing at Middlesbrough (where he played exceedingly well!), he switched to Holland.

J

JACKSON, Bertram Harold (Full-back)
Apps: 101 Born: Manchester, 1884

Career: Luton Town, CITY (May 1907–May 1911), Stalybridge Celtic; retired during the First World War.

Details: A well-built defender, good in the air, Bert Jackson was City's regular left-back (mainly as Tommy Kelso's partner) from December 1907 until October 1908. He was then used on both flanks, missing only five League games in 1909/10 before Jack Chaplin and Frank Norgrove came to the fore, resulting in his transfer to Stalybridge Celtic.

JACKSON, Gary Andrew (Midfield)
Apps: 8 Born: Swinton, 30/9/1964

Career: Manchester Boys, CITY (July 1981–September 1985), Exeter City, SK Torhout/Belgium.

Details: A City player for four years, Gary Jackson played well in the second XI before making his debut as a substitute in a 2-0 defeat in front of 46,000 spectators at Tottenham in February 1982, and played his last game *v.* Sunderland three months later. He donned six different numbered jerseys in his eight outings for City. He made thirty-five League appearances for Exeter before switching to Belgian football.

JACKSON, Harold (Centre-forward)
Apps/goals: 9/3 Born: Blackburn, 30/12/1918 Died: Blackburn, 1984

Career: Darwen, Burnley, CITY (June 1946/December 1947), Preston North End, Blackburn Rovers, Chester; retired 1951.

Details: Basically a reserve with all of his League clubs, Harry Jackson was City's top scorer in the first Central League season after the Second World War, but despite his efforts he made only nine first appearances, netting three goals, including one on his debut away at Leicester City (won 3-0). He had his best spell with Chester (twenty-one League outings and ten goals).

JAMES, David Benjamin, MBE (Goalkeeper)
Apps: 100 Born: Welwyn Garden City, Hertfordshire, 1/8/1970

Career: Sir Frederic Osborn School, Watford, Liverpool (£1 million), Aston Villa (£1.8 million), West Ham United (£3.5 million), City (£1.3 million, January 2004–August 2006), Portsmouth (£1.2 million), Bristol City, Bournemouth, IBV/Iceland (player-coach; retired as a player, May 2013).

Details: Deeply involved in charity work and AIDS awareness, he set up The David James Foundation; was a model for Giorgio Armani and H&M as well as working as a global ambassador to the Special Olympics. He is also an occasional columnist for *The Observer* newspaper, his illustrations feature in the children's book, *Harry's Magic Pockets: The Circus* and he's worked/trained with the Miami Dolphins (AMFA). He now resides in Chudleigh, Devon.

Despite there being the fear that he is never more than a shot or cross away from dropping a clanger, David James's sheer presence between the posts has, over the years, added that little extra assurance to most defences, including England's!

He began his League career with Watford in August 1990 and was still going strong twenty-three years later! After fine spells with Liverpool, Villa and West Ham, he made his City debut in January 2004, in a 1-1 home draw with Blackburn. During the second half of that season the Blues won only four of the seventeen matches that James started, two of which came after he had saved penalties against Wolves and Leicester. On the last day of the following season, City needed to beat Middlesbrough to qualify for the UEFA Cup and with five minutes remaining, and the scores level at 1-1, manager Stuart Pearce took off Claudio Reyna and brought on substitute 'keeper Nicky Weaver, sending the giant 6-foot-4½-inch figure of James into the attack for the remainder of the game. The unusual tactic almost worked when, in injury-time, 'Boro defender Franck Queudrue conceded a penalty by handling a cross-aimed at James. However, Robbie Fowler's spot-kick was saved by Mark Schwarzer, leaving City licking their UEFA Cup wounds! Three months later James left City for Portsmouth on a two-year deal.

On his retirement in May 2013, James had appeared in 924 club games. He also holds the distinction of twice having been the record holder for consecutive Premier League appearances, with 159 during his Liverpool days, 1994–98, and 166 while playing for City and Portsmouth, 2006–08. These streaks were eventually topped by Chelsea FC's Frank Lampard and Aston Villa's Brad Friel respectively. In February 2009, James set a new Premier League record of 535 appearances; eventually taking his tally to 572 (only Ryan Giggs has made more) and he's also the record holder for most clean sheets in Premiership and Championship football (173).

An FA Youth Cup winner with Watford, he won the League Cup with Liverpool in 1995 and the FA Cup with Portsmouth in 2008. He gained five Youth, two 'B', ten U21 and 53 full caps for England and was awarded the MBE in 2012 for services to football and charity.

James once pulled a muscle in his back when reaching for a television remote control and was forced out of matches. He also missed a match at Liverpool suffering from a RSI injury to his thumb that he blamed on his excessive computer-game habit!

JAMES, Francis Edward (Centre-forward)
Apps: 2 Born: Halesowen, 1886
Died: Stourbridge, c. 1952
Career: Halesowen Town, Brownhills Albion, CITY (July 1909/July 1910), Exeter City; retired 1919.

Details: Frank James – top scorer for City's second team in his only season with the club – made two his two League appearances in 1-1 away draws at Birmingham and Barnsley when he deputised for Tom Holford.

JARVIS, Harold (Half-back)
Apps: 2 Born: Manchester, c. 1898
Career: CITY (October 1919–May 1921).

Details: Reserve with City for almost two seasons, Harry Jarvis was one of eight players who occupied the right-half berth in 1919/20, making his debut in the goalless draw League draw with Newcastle in April. His second outing was against Arsenal five months later.

JEFFRIES, Derek (Defender)
Apps/goals: Born: Longsight, 22/3/1951
Career: Manchester Boys, CITY (July 1967–September 1973), Crystal Palace, Peterborough United (loan), Millwall (loan), Chester City, Telford United; retired 1983.

Details: Nurtured along in the second and third teams for two seasons, Derek Jefferies made his League debut for City as a substitute in a 2-1 home win over WBA in October 1969. He made nine appearances that season, including two in the ECWC competition, twenty-eight in 1970/71 and fourteen the following season, before making an impressive forty-one in 1972–73 when he partnered Tommy Booth at the heart of the defence. He also played once for England at U23 level. Surprisingly to some, Jefferies was then transferred to Crystal Palace. In the summer of 1977, Jeffries linked up with his former colleague at Maine Road, Alan Oakes, who was manager of Chester.

JENSEN, Niclas Christian Monberg (Left-back)
Apps/goals: 56/2 Born: Copenhagen, 17/8/1974
Career: B93, Lyngby, PSV Eindhoven, FC Copenhagen, CITY (£550,000, January 2002/July 2003), Borussia Dortmund (£750,000), Fulham, FC Copenhagen; retired 2010.

Details: Following his transfer from Copenhagen, Niclas Jensen played in the remaining eighteen games of the 20010/02 season, helping City win promotion to the Premiership. Then, after returning from the World Cup, he appeared in thirty-three out of the thirty-eight top-flight games of 2002/03, scoring with a spectacular 30-yard volley to win the game against Leeds United. He played in forty-four games at intermediate level for Denmark before going on to win sixty-two full caps, 1998–2008.

JIHAI, Sun (Wing-back/midfield)
Apps/goals: 117/4 Born: Dalian, Liaoning, China, 30/9/1977
Career: Dalian Wanda, Crystal Palace (loan), CITY (£2 million, February 2002–July 2008), Sheffield United, Chengdu Blades (loan), Guizhoiu Renhe.

Details: The first East Asian player to sign for City, Sun Jihai made his debut in a 4–2 win over Coventry as the promotion race from the First Division hotted up. The following season as his game went from strength to strength, his solid defence and dangerous attacking forays winning over many City fans. On his first goal for City in October 2002, he became the first Chinese player to score in the Premiership when he headed home City's opening goal in a 2–0 win over Birmingham. Following a fine 2003/04 season, unfortunately early in 2004/05 he damaged his cruciate ligaments in a tackle with the Chelsea striker Eidur Gudjohnsen and missed the rest of the season. After recuperating and following a strict physical regimen devised by his father, Sun retuned as a regular starter in City's line up. However, he was rocked by another injury in February 2007 against Portsmouth and following the arrival of manager Sven-Göran Eriksson, who rarely used Sun in 2007/08, preferring Vedran Corluka at right-back with Michael Ball in the centre of the defence. As a result Sun was transferred to Sheffield United. Capped seventy-eight times by China (1996–2008) Sun played in the 2002 World Cup and won six club trophies with Dalian Wanda. In 2012, he reached the milestone of 600 appearances in senior football.

On 1 January 2003, an estimated three hundred million TV viewers tuned to see, for the first time ever, two Chinese footballers – Jihai (City) and Li Tie (Everton) – play against each other in a Premiership match.

JOBLING, Leonard Walter (Outside-right)
Apps: 2 Born: Sunderland, c. 1885

Career: Carlisle United, Norwich City, CITY (February 1912/May 1913), Hartlepool United; retired 1919.

Details: Signed as cover for Sid Hoad, Len Jobling had to wait eleven months, until January 1913, before making his League debut against Notts County (home), having a hand in two of the goals in the 4-0. His second game followed forty-eight hours later at Villa Park (lost 2-0). He scored twice in sixty-three appearances for Norwich.

JOBSON, Richard (Defender)
Apps/goals: 57/4 Born: Hull, 9/5/1963

Career: Birmingham City (trial), Burton Albion, Watford (£22,000), Hull City (£40,000), Oldham Athletic (£460,000), Leeds United (£1 million), Southend United (loan), CITY (free, March 1998–December 2000), Watford (loan), Tranmere Rovers (loan/signed), Rochdale (player-coach); retired May 2003; became Chairman of PFA; now senior executive of the PFA player management department.

Details: After 255 games for Hull and 225 for Oldham, Richard Jobson moved to Leeds a year after the Latics' relegation from the Premiership, but his career at Elland Road was disrupted by injury and after a loan spell at Southend, he was reunited with his former boss Joe Royle at Maine Road. Again, Jobling suffered with injuries, but still helped City reach the Premiership with two successive promotions. Royle then decided that his thirty-seven-year-old defender was too old for top-flight football and after loaning him to Watford and Tranmere, he transferred him to the latter club in 2000. He played his last League game six days before his fortieth birthday. In his long career, the ever-dependable Jobson made scored thirty-nine goals in 694 club appearances and won two 'B' caps for England. He succeeded Nick Cusack as PFA Chairman.

JOHNSON, Adam (Forward)
Apps/goals: 97/15 Born: Sunderland, 14/7/1987

Career: Middlesbrough, Leeds United (loan), Watford (loan), CITY (£7 million, February 2010), Sunderland (£10 million, August 2012).

Details: An FA Youth Cup winner with Middlesbrough, left-sided midfield, with good pace, plenty of skill and strong shot, Adam Johnson joined City on a four-and-a-half year contract and made his first appearance for the club on soon afterwards, as substitute for Stephen Ireland against Hull City. Three days later, he made his first start against Bolton, playing on the right side of a three-man attack alongside Carlos Tévez and Emmanuel Adebayor. He scored his first goal for the Blues against his home town club Sunderland AFC in the ninety-third minute, curling a left footer into the top corner to earn a last-gasp 1-1 draw. This performance led English National Football team manager Fabio Capello to publicly praise him and consider him for selection! He actually chose him, awarding him his first cap as an eighty-fourth-minute substitute for City teammate James Milner in a 3-1 win over Mexico in May 2010. At 2013 he had played twelve times for his country at senior level (two goals) having earlier played for England's youth team and on nineteen occasions for the U21s. On New Year's Day, 2011, Johnson scored City's PL winner at Blackpool F and dedicated his goal to Dale Roberts, his close friend and Rushden Diamonds goalkeeper, who committed suicide just three weeks earlier. He ended the season with an FA Cup winner's medal and followed up by helping City clinch the Premiership title twelve months later. Then he was off, going north to Wearside with still two years of his City contract left to run. Earlier in his career, Johnson had scored sixteen goals in 120 appearances for Middlesbrough.

JOHNSON, David Edward (Forward)
Apps/goals: 6/1 Born: Liverpool, 23/10/1951

Career: Everton, Ipswich Town, Liverpool (record £200,000), Everton (£100,000), Barnsley (loan), CITY (March/May 1984), Tulsa Roughnecks/USA, Preston North End (non-contract), Naxxar Lions/Malta, Barrow AFC (player-manager); Liverpool (corporate lounge host, Anfield); also BBC Radio Merseyside as a match summariser.

Details: An exciting player at the peak of his career, David Johnson could shoot, head, dribble, chase back, tackle and create chances. He netted 156 goals in 540 club games in fourteen years, and actually scored on his debut in six different competitions for Everton, doing likewise in his first game for Ipswich and England. He went on to gain eight full caps (six goals), having earlier played in nine U23 internationals. The first player to score for both clubs in a Merseyside derby, he won five League titles, three European Cup finals, the League Cup twice and the European Super Cup while at Goodison Park and Anfield. In his brief spell with City, his solitary goal came on his debut in a 2-1 home win over Cardiff City.

JOHNSON, Jeffrey David (Midfield)
Apps: 9 Born: Cardiff, 26/11/1953

Career: Clifton Athletic, CITY (August 1970–January 1974), Swansea City (loan), Crystal Palace, Sheffield Wednesday, Newport County, Gillingham, Port Vale, Barrow; retired 1986; became a taxi driver.

Details: A Welsh schoolboy, youth and U23 international, Jeff Johnson top-scored for City's second XI in 1971/72, but failed to make headway after that and with nine senior outings to his credit, moved to Crystal Palace. He went on to make over 500 club appearances in his career, 211 for Sheffield Wednesday, with whom he gained promotion from the Third Division in 1980 before a broken leg resulted in early retirement.

JOHNSON, Michael (Midfield)
Apps/goals: 45/3 Born: Urmston, 3/3/1988

Career: CITY (June 2004–released, January 2013)

Details: Michael Johnson was released from his £40,000-a-week contract with City five years after being regarded as one of the brightest young talents in English football, destined for full international honours. Blighted by injuries, including a serious one to his right knee, he gained more pounds (in weight) than he made appearances, and after receiving a £5,500 fine for two drink-driving offences in 2012, manager Roberto Mancini said enough's enough. Johnson made his Premiership debut at the age of eighteen, and by doing so became the twentieth graduate from the club's academy to break into the first team. He gained youth and U21 honours before it all went wrong!

JOHNSON, Nigel Meridon (Defender)
Apps: 7 Born: Rotherham, 23/6/1964

Career: Rotherham United, CITY (June 1985–May 1987), Rotherham United.

Details: Central defender Nigel Johnson made 264 League appearances in his two spells with Rotherham, scoring ten goals. Strong and reliable, he stood in for Mick McCarthy and Kenny Clements at Maine Road, making his debut on the opening day of the 1985/86 season in a 1-1 draw at Coventry. He was perhaps just a tad short of being a top First Division player.

JOHNSON, Thomas Clark Fisher (Centre-forward)
Apps/goals: 354/166 Born: Dalton-on-Furness, 19/8/1901 Died: Monsall Hospital, Manchester, 29/1/1973

Career: Dalton Athletic, Dalton Casuals, CITY (trial, May 1918, signed February 1919–March 1930), Everton (£6,000), Liverpool, Darwen; retired May 1937.

Details: A former shipyard apprentice riveter, Tommy 'Tosh' Johnson scored in eight successive League games for City during February and March 1929 and ended the season with a club record thirty-eight, including a five-timer against Everton in September, another club record he shares with George Smith. Johnson also netted in twenty-three of the forty games he played in. His overall tally of City goals included twenty-one successful penalties and nine hat-tricks. Only Eric Black has scored more League and senior goals for City – 159 and 178 against Johnson's 158 and 166.

Johnson was spotted and recommended to the club by Eli Fletcher, but at first City weren't all that keen on signing a non-League player. Fletcher, however, was adamant that Johnson would be a 'great asset' and threatened to resign if they didn't secure his services. In the end all was settled, and Johnson became an instant hot by scoring on his debut in a Lancashire Section wartime game against Blackburn Rovers, following up soon afterwards with a hat-trick against Port Vale. But when League football resumed after the First World War, Johnson was not in the first team and, in fact, had to wait until mid-February 1920 before making his first competitive appearance in the sky-blue strip, celebrating with both goals in a 2-0 win over Middlesbrough. He didn't actually gain a regular place in the first XI until halfway through the 1921/22 campaign, but after that there was no stopping him as the goals flowed thick and fast with his feet and head, right up until his transfer to Everton. And there is no doubt that City fans were shocked when he was sold, severely criticising the board of directors for their decision. It got worse when Johnson scored for Everton against City in the 1933 FA Cup final. With so many talented marksmen around at the same time, Johnson won only five caps for England, scoring five goals, one on his debut against Belgium in 1926 (won 5-3), two against Wales in 1929 (6-0) and two more against Spain in 1931 (7-1). An international trialist (1925), he played twice for the Football League and once for an FA XI before switching to Goodison Park. His record with Everton was sixty-four goals in 159 games and for Liverpool eight in thirty-nine. The humorist of the side, Johnson was a cricket, golf, boxing and curling enthusiast and a pretty useful snooker player to boot.

JOHNSTONE, Robert (Forward)
Apps/goals: 139/51 Born: Selkirk, Scotland, 7/9/1929

Career: Newtongrange Bluebell, Newtongrange Star, Selkirk FC, Hibernian, CITY (£20,700, March 1955–September 1959), Hibernian (£6,500), Oldham Athletic, Witton Albion; retired 1965; worked in the building trade, was a part-time driver for an Oldham-based seafood company, was an excellent crown green bowler and played for Saddleworth cricket club.

Details: Bobby Johnstone was brilliant in manoeuvring the ball and making that decisive defence-splitting pass or move only the thoughtfully gifted can regularly manage. At times he was compared with Wilf Mannion and Peter Doherty as a schemer and ball artist. He spent nine years with Hibs before joining City, gaining two League championship winning medals in successive seasons, 1950–52, while collecting the first thirteen of what would be a grand total of seventeen full caps for Scotland. He also represented the Scottish League on six occasions and played for Great Britain against the Rest of Europe.

At the end of the 1954/55 season, he scored for City in their FA Cup final defeat by Newcastle, but a year later he was a happy chappie when, after netting the crucial semi-final winner against Spurs, he was on target at Wembley again, this time helping City lift the trophy with a 3-1 victory over Birmingham. In his four-and-a-half years at Maine Road, Johnstone – known as 'Bobby Dazzler' – was at times, quite superb, topping the scoring charts in 1956/57 with nineteen goals, including a hat-trick in a thrilling 5-4 League win over Everton in December – when he could well have scored a second treble.

In a wonderful first-class career, north and south of the border, for Hibs, City and Oldham, Johnstone scored 190 goals in 502 appearances, 183 in 466 League matches.

JONES, Arthur (Forward)
Apps/goals: 2/1 Born: Llandudno, 5/6/1870
Career: Small Heath/Birmingham, CITY (July 1893/May 1894).
Details: Archie Jones failed to get a game with Birmingham and only managed two with City, scoring on his League debut in a 6-1 demolition of Middlesbrough in September 1893. He was one of thirty-five players used by City in 1893/94 – twenty-four of whom had at least one game in the forward-line!

JONES, Christopher Harry (Forward)
Apps: 3 Born: Jersey, Channel Islands, 18/4/1956
Career: Jersey Boys, Jersey & Guernsey Schools, Tottenham Hotspur, CITY (August-November 1982), Crystal Palace, Charlton Athletic, Leyton Orient, St Albans City; retired 1988; St Peter's FC/Jersey (manager).
Details: Chris Jones, who scored forty-two goals in 185 first-class games in eleven seasons at White Hart Lane, spent barely three months at Maine Road, during which time he played in just three League appearances. He made his debut against his former club Spurs, contributing to a 2-1 win until being substituted.

JONES, Christopher Martin Nigel (Centre-forward)
Apps/goals: 7/2 Born: Altrincham, 19/11/1945
Career: Cheshire Boys, CITY (December 1962– July 1968), Swindon Town, Oldham Athletic (loan), Walsall, York City (£7,000), Huddersfield Town, Doncaster Rovers, Darlington (loan), Rochdale; retired 1980; worked as a supply teacher at Tadcaster Grammar School (RE and PE); also co-commentator on BBC Radio York.
Details: Chris Jones was the first teenager to score an FA Youth Cup hat-trick for City in a 6-1 win over Middlesbrough in January 1964. He was also leading marksman in City's second XI from 1965 to 1968. Acting initially as reserve to Derek Kevan, Jimmy Murray and suchlike, he had to wait until December 1966 before making his first-team debut in place of Mike Summerbee, in a 1-1 draw with Nottingham Forest. He netted his first City goal in his second game, a 3-0 win at WBA, but found it hard to get into the League side. However, after leaving Maine Road he did very well, netting more than 100 goals in 350 appearances up to his retirement in 1980.

JONES, David (Full-back)
Apps/goals: 118/1 Born: Trefonen near Oswestry, 11/12/1867 Died: Bolton, 27/8/1902
Career: Oswestry, Chirk, Newton Heath, Bolton Wanderers, CITY (September 1898, until his death).
Details: A cool, two-footed, resolute defender with a timely tackle, Di Jones was only fifteen when he helped Oswestry win the Shropshire County Cup and two years later captained Chirk to Welsh Cup glory. Employed as a miner, he gave that up when he joined Newton Heath but was released to Bolton at the age of twenty. He never looked back, going on to win fifteen caps for Wales, debuting in an 11-0 thrashing of Ireland at Wrexham in 1888. He amassed 255 appearances for the Wanderers, missed the club's first penalty (*v.* Everton in January 1892), played in the 1894 FA Cup final and in September 1895 was awarded a benefit match – the first game ever to be played at Burnden Park. After trying to persuade Billy Meredith to join him at Bolton, in October 1898 it was Jones who switched clubs, moving across Lancashire to City who he helped win the Second Division title. A consistent performer over a period of four seasons, Jones sadly died at the age of thirty-four. He suffered a gashed knee in a pre-season friendly in mid-August 1902. The wound was stitched at the local hospital, but turned septic, tetanus set in and Jones was dead within ten days; such was the ignorance surrounding such injuries during that era.

JONES, Richard Thomas William (Inside-forward/outside-left)
Apps/goals: 12/2 Born: Montgomeryshire, 2/4/1879 Died: Lambeth, London, 20/11/1943

Career: Millwall St John's, Millwall, CITY (May 1901/May 1902), Millwall, until retiring in 1910; remained at club as assistant-trainer, then trainer until 1935.

Details: A Welshman, brought up in the Isle of Dogs, London, Dick Jones was the first Millwall player to win a full international cap for eleven years when he appeared against Scotland and Ireland in 1906.

A Southern League footballer for most his career – he scored eighty-five goals in 385 games for Millwall – Jones spent just the one season with City, scoring on his debut in a 3-1 win over Nottingham Forest in November 1901 when deputising for Fred Williams. Described in the press as 'a vigorous forward with rare dribbling skills' he won the S/L Professional Cup and both the Western League and London League titles with the Lions for whom his brothers Edward and Will also played.

JONES, Robert Samuel (Half-back)
Apps: 18 Born: Wrexham, 1868 Died: Salford, 25/5/1939

Career: Challenger Boys FC/Wrexham, Wrexham Grosvenor, Everton, CITY (June 1894; retired May 1895); became a labourer at Blackpool's south shore dockyard.

Details: Rob Jones played in Everton's first-ever League game against Accrington in September 1888. A burly defender, able to play at right-back or centre-half, he was a reliable reserve with the Merseyside club before moving to City, soon after gaining his first cap for Wales *v.* Ireland. However, a year later he broke his right leg playing in a Manchester Senior Cup tie against Bolton that forced him into early retirement.

JONES, William John Beattie (Centre-forward)
Apps: 3 Born: Liverpool, 6/6/1924 Died: 17/4/1995

Career: CITY (May 1948–June 1951), Chester.

Details: Top scorer in City's second XI in 1949/50, Billy Jones made only three senior appearances, two at the end of his first season at Maine Road when deputised for George Smith in a 1-1 draw with FA Cup winners Wolves on his debut in front of 45,000 fans, and in the 3-0 home defeat by the then reigning League champions Arsenal.

JONES, William Lot (Inside-right)
Apps/goals: 302/74 Born: Chirk, 8/4/1882 Died: Chirk, 13/7/1941

Career: Rushton Druids, Bolton Wanderers (trial), Chirk, Druids, CITY (January 1903– August 1919), Southend United, Aberdare Athletic (player-manager), Wrexham, Oswestry Town, Chirk (player-manager); retired 1926, aged forty-four; served in France with the 'Sportsman's battalion' during WW; ran a greengrocery business in Chirk and Oswestry until his death.

Details: After top-scoring in City's second XI in successive seasons (1903–05) Lot Jones launched himself into a long and exciting career which went on and on and on! One of the fittest players of his era, one scribe remarked 'his cleverness in control of the ball, his awareness, bigness of heart, making one oblivious to the smallness of his stature.' Besides his uncanny skill, Jones was also a grafter, a workhorse, yet at times was erratic with his shooting. One reporter said he had 'one of the worst shots I have ever seen'.

Nevertheless, Jones drew up a tremendous record with City, claiming a goal every four matches. He gained a Second Division championship medal in 1910 and won nineteen of his twenty Welsh international caps while at Hyde Road. His benefit match (*v.* Middlesbrough in 1908) raised £835. His nephew was Di Jones (q.v.).

JORDAN, Stephen Robert (Left-back/centre-half)
Apps: 64 Born: Warrington, 6/3/1982

Career: CITY (June, 1997–July 2007), Cambridge United (loan), Burnley (free), Sheffield United, Huddersfield Town (loan), Rochdale.

Details: 6-foot-tall defender Stephen Jordan broke into City's first team in 2004 following a handful of substitute appearances, most notably when he kept his side in the Manchester derby at Old Trafford, courageously hooking the ball off the line to deny United a certain goal. Unfortunately he couldn't secure a place in the first team once Michael Ball had settled in at left-back.

K

KANCHELSKIS, Andrei (Winger)
Apps/goals: 11/1 Born: Kirovograd, USSR, 23/1/1969

Career: Kirovograd SC, Dynamo Kiev, Shakhtar Donetsk, Manchester United, Everton, Fiorentina, Glasgow Rangers, CITY (loan, January/April 2001), Southampton, Al-Hilal, Saturn Moscow Obtast, Krylia Sovetova; retired 2007; sporting director FC Nosta Novotroitsk; manager Torpedo-Zil Moscow, FC Ufa, FC Volga Nizh Novgorod (assistant-manager).

Details: The only player in history to have scored in each of the Glasgow, Manchester and Merseyside derbies, Andrei Kanchelskis was an outstanding winger, fast, clever with the ability to score goals. Unfortunately, he spent his first seven years in England at Old Trafford and Goodison Park instead of Maine Road! On loan with City, he scored a fine goal in an FA Cup tie against Liverpool before having his last outing in the 1-1 draw with his former club in the Manchester derby in April 2001.

During a much-travelled career, he scored 125 goals in 535 club appearances, including seventy-two in 397 League games. He was capped seven times by Russia, on six occasions by the CIS and played in thirty-six full internationals for Russia. He won the Russia Cup (with Kiev, 1990), two PL titles, the FA Cup, League Cup and Super Cup with United and two SPL championships, three Scottish Cups and two League Cups with Rangers.

In his autobiography, *Managing My Life*, Alex Ferguson alleged that he was offered a £40,000 bribe to sell Kanchelskis. When this was refused, he claimed that death threats were made to Martin Edwards, chairman of Manchester United at the time.

KARL, Steffen (Midfield)
Apps/goals: 6/1 Born: Hohenmolsen, East Germany, 3/2/1970

Career: Medizin Halle-Nietleben, Empor Halle, Hallescher FC, Stahl Heltstedt, Borussia Dortmund, CITY (loan, March-April 1994), FC Sion, Hertha BSC, FC St Pauli, Valerenga, Lokomotiv Sofia, Chemnitzer FC, Fortuna Chemnitz; retired 2008.

Details: Soon after his loan spell at Maine Road was over, Steffen Karl had a dust-up with his coach Ottmar Hitzfeld at Borussia, for whom he had been a reserve for virtually four-and-a-half years. A defensive midfielder, his only goal for City was a brilliant eighty-fifth-minute winner at Southampton in April 1994.

Karl scored seventeen goals in a League career that covered 331 games and won one U21 cap for his country.

KAVELASHVILI, Mikhail (Striker)
Apps/goals: 29/3 Born: Tbilisi, Georgia, 22/7/1971

Career: Dinamo Tbilisi, Sporting Vladikavkaz (loan/signed), CITY (£1.4 million, March 1996–May 1998), Grasshoppers (loan), FC Zurich, FC Sion, Aarau, Sporting Vladikavkaz (loan), FC Basel; retired 2007.

Details: Skilful striker, strong and mobile, Mikhail Kavelashvili scored a fine opportunist goal on his City debut in the Manchester derby in April 1996, bagging two more goals in a 3-2 win at Southend six months later before his work permit ran out.

In his nineteen-year career, he scored 166 goals in 396 League appearances, having his best spell with his first club, Dinamo Tbilisi, with whom he won four League championships, while also helping Grasshoppers clinch the Swiss League title. He netted eight times in forty-five full internationals for Georgia.

KEARY, Albert (Forward)
Born: Liverpool, 1889

Career: Violet FC/West Derby, Bootle, African Royal/Liverpool, Liverpool Dominion, Accrington Stanley, CITY (May 1911/May 1912), Port Vale; retired May 1912.

Details: A smart footballer, but perhaps out of his depth at League level, Bert Keary – playing instead of Lot Jones–scored in his second game for City, in a 3-1 win over Bolton.

KEEGAN, Gerard (Midfield/right-back)
Apps/goals: 50/3 Born: Bradford, 3/10/1955

Career: Schoolboy football, CITY (August 1971–February 1979), Oldham Athletic, Mansfield Town, Rochdale, Altrincham; also an excellent golfer; became an insurance agent and later worked as a car-park attendant at Manchester airport.

Details: Ged Keegan was a hard worker, efficient and strong, who made his debut for City in March 1975, in a 2–1 defeat by Carlisle. However, his most memorable game in a blue shirt came in the 1976 League Cup final victory over Newcastle. Keegan also played in the first ever England U21 international *v.* Scotland in 1977 and netted five goals in 144 League appearances for Oldham.

KELLY, Patrick J. (Forward)
Apps/goals: 29/3 Born: Kilcoo, Northern Ireland, 7/9/1896

Career: Belfast Celtic, CITY (October 1920–July 1923), West Ham United, Fordsons FC; retired 1926.

Details: Irish international Paddy Kelly, the first City player to win a full cap (*v.* England in October 1920), made thirteen League appearances in his first season at Hyde Road and eleven in his second, deputising for initially Tommy Broad and then for Billy Meredith. He scored his first goal in a 2-1 win over Huddersfield in January 1922.

KELLY, Raymond (Striker)
Apps: 1 Born: Dublin, 29/12/1976

Career: Athlone Town, CITY (£30,000, August 1994–December 1998), Wrexham (loan, two spells), Bohemians; retired 2001 to become an airline pilot.

Details: Eire U21 international Ray Kelly's only first-team appearance for City was against Huddersfield Town in November 1997. After returning 'home' he excelled, scoring five goals for the 'Bohs' who reached the Irish Cup final, losing in a replay to Shelbourne.

KELLY, William Bainbridge (Forward)
Apps: 10 Born: Newcastle, 1891

Career: Benwell Adelaide/Newcastle, Balmoral/Newcastle, Blaydon, North Shields Athletic, Watford, Newcastle United, CITY (£405, November 1911–August 1913), Blyth Spartans.

Details: A useful reserve at Newcastle (six appearances), Bill Kelly had difficulty getting into City's first team owing to the form of Messrs

Thornley, Jones, Taylor and Wynn. He made his debut in a 2-1 defeat at Preston forty-eight hours after his transfer.

KELSO, Thomas (Full-back)
Apps/goals: 151/3 Born: Renton, Dunbartonshire, 24/6/1888 Died: after 1945

Career: Third Lanark, CITY (August 1906–February 1913), Dundee (signed, having been on trial since October 1912), Glasgow Rangers; retired during the First World War.

Details: A big man, standing 6 feet 2 inches tall, Tommy Kelso made good use of his rangy physique, his long legs proving vital in many last ditch challenges. He helped City win the Second Division title in 1910 and played in two Scotland trials during his time at Hyde Road before deservedly collecting his only full cap with Dundee v. Wales in 1914, having played in two international trials as a City player. Two of his three goals were scored in the first half of City's 2-2 draw at Liverpool in September 1911. His uncle, Bob, was a Scottish international who played for Renton and Dundee.

KENNEDY, Mark John (Left-back/forward)
Apps/goals: 77/11 Born: Clonsilla, Dublin, 15/5/1976

Career: Millwall, Liverpool, Queen's Park Rangers, Wimbledon, CITY (£1 million, July 1999–July 2001), Wolverhampton Wanderers £2 million), Crystal Palace, Cardiff City, Ipswich Town; retired 2012; appointed coach at Portman Road.

Details: Mark Kennedy won promotion to the Premier League in his first season with City who were relegated the following year. Manager Jon Royle was sacked, replaced by Kevin Keegan who, seeking to rebuild the squad, decided Kennedy was not part of his plans and sold him to Wolves.

Able to play as a wing-back or left-winger, Kennedy made 538 appearances at club level and won one U17, flour U21 and thirty-four full caps for Eire.

KENNEDY, Robert (Full-back/wing-half)
Apps/goals: 254/9 Born: Motherwell, 23/6/1937

Career: Coltness United, Queen of the South (trial), Clyde (trial), Kilmarnock, CITY (£45,000, July 1961–March 1969), Grimsby Town (£9,000, player-coach), Drogheda United; retired 1974; Grimsby Town (manager, Bradford City (manager), Blackburn Rovers (coach).

Details: After overcoming serious illness, which sidelined him for eight months, Bobby Kennedy went on to gain League, SFA Cup and League Cup runner's-up medals with Kilmarnock before moving to Maine Road for a then record fee for a wing-half. Following a tough first season with City he was converted into a full-back and in 1965/66 helped the team regain top-flight status. Capped

once by Scotland at U21 level, he played in over 450 club games during his career.

In June 1968, City Chairman Albert Alexander, hearing on the 11 o'clock news the news that Bobby Kennedy (the US politician) had been shot, said 'Well, it's his own fault for being out so late'! Kennedy's daughter, Lorraine, managed Bradford City women's football team.

KERNAGHAN, Alan (Defender/midfield)
Apps/goals: 78/2 Born: Otley, West Yorkshire, 25/4/1967

Career: Bangor BC, Middlesbrough, Charlton Athletic (loan), CITY (£1.6 million, September 1993–September 1997), Bolton Wanderers (loan), Bradford City (loan), St Johnstone (loan/signed), Brechin City, Clyde (player-manager), Livingston, Falkirk, Dundee (player-manager); retired 2007; Glasgow Rangers (coach), Brentford (coach).

Details: Initially switched from centre-forward to centre-half by Middlesbrough, Alan Kernaghan eventually became a solid, reliable defender who went on to have an excellent career. He played superbly alongside Keith Curle in City's back-four and at times was equally effective as a midfield anchorman.

Capped six times at schoolboy level by Northern Ireland, he later played in twenty-two full internationals for Eire (1992–96) and amassed almost 500 club appearances, 266 coming in eight years at Ayresome Park.

KERR, Andrew (Utility)
Apps: 10 Born: Lugar, Ayrshire, 29/6/1931 Died: Ayrshire, 24/12/1997

Career: Wishaw High School, Lugar Boswell Thistle, Partick Thistle, CITY (£11,000, May–December 1959), Kilmarnock (£6,000), Sunderland (£22,250), Aberdeen (£8,000), Glentoran, Inverness Caledonian Thistle; retired 1968; later worked for the Rolls Wood Group (Aberdeen).

Details: Andy Kerr, who won one 'B' and two full caps for Scotland, and twice represented the Scottish League, spent six months with City. Able to play in defence or attack, unfortunately, despite some decent performances early on, especially as Cliff Sear's left-back replacement, he never settled at Maine Road and was back in Scotland within seven months. A prolific marksman with Kilmarnock, scoring 103 goals, he was a five-time losing Cup finalist north of the border.

KERR, David William (Right-back)
Apps: 6 Born: Dumfries, Scotland, 6/9/1974

Career: Maxweltown Thistle/Dumfries, CITY (September 1990–July 1996), Mansfield Town (loan/signed), Chester City, Droylsden; retired 2003.

Details: After gaining a Lancashire FA Youth Cup winner's medal in 1992, strong-tackling full-back Davy Kerr – voted Young Player of the Year in 1993 – was a regular in City's second XI before making his League debut against Everton halfway through the 1993/94 season. Unfortunately, he couldn't hold down a place in the first team and eventually moved to Field Mill.

KEVAN, Derek Tennyson (Centre-forward)
Apps/goals: 76/56 Born: Ripon, Yorkshire, 6/3/1935 Died: Birmingham, 4/1/2013
Career: Ripon Secondary Modern School, Harrogate & District Schools, Ripon YMCA, Ripon City, Sheffield United (trial), Bradford Park Avenue, West Bromwich Albion (£3,000), Chelsea (record £50,000), CITY (£35,000, August 1963–July 1965), Crystal Palace (free), Peterborough United, Luton Town, Stockport County, Macclesfield Town, Boston United, Stourbridge, Ansells FC, West Bromwich All Stars (player & manager); became a publican in Birmingham; also worked as a lottery agent for WBA.
Details: Derek Kevan had two excellent seasons with City. Forming a fine partnership with Jimmy Murray, together they bagged a total of ninety-one goals, Kevan top-scoring with thirty-six in 1963/64 and twenty the following term. Big and strong, and nicknamed 'The Tank', he was fired by City manager Joe Mercer for 'cheating in training.'
Capped fourteen times by England (eight goals), Kevan won promotion with Chelsea and the Fourth Division championship with Stockport. An during his career netted 235 times in 440 club games, heading the First Division scoring charts in 1961/62.

KIDD, Brian (Inside-forward)
Apps/goals: 130/59 Born: Collyhurst, Manchester, 29 May 1949
Career: St Patrick's & Collyhurst Schools, Manchester Schoolboys, Manchester United, Arsenal (£110,000), CITY (£100,000, July 1976–March 1979), Everton (£150,000), Bolton Wanderers (£110,000); Atlanta Chiefs/USA (loan), Fort Lauderdale Strikers/USA, Minnesota Strikers/USA; retired July 1984; Barrow (manager), Swindon Town (coach/assistant-manager), Preston North End (coach/assistant-manager, then manager), Manchester United (junior coach, Director of School of Excellence, youth development officer, assistant-manager), Blackburn Rovers (manager), Leeds United (Director of Football/assistant-manager), England (coach/assistant-manager), Sheffield United (assistant-manager), Portsmouth (assistant-manager), CITY (Academy coach, Technical Advisor, early 2009, assistant-manager, July 2009; caretaker-manager, May 2013).

Details: Brian Kidd top-scored in his first season at Maine Road with twenty-three goals and headed the charts again in 1977/78 with twenty. A strong, hard-running, highly effective striker, he struck a four-timer in a 5-0 League win over Leicester in January 1977, and his overall record for City was exceptional, considering that at the time, the game was going through one of the most dour defensive periods for some considerable time.
'Kiddo' first hit the headlines on his nineteenth birthday when scoring for Manchester United in the 1968 UEFA Champions Leage final 4-1 win over Benfica. Overall he had a terrific career, netting over 300 times in more than 600 appearances in England and the USA, with 152 of his goals coming in 461 Football League matches. He represented England at Youth, U23 and senior levels (two full caps gained) and also played for the Football League XI.
He won eight trophies (including the double twice) while coach and assistant-manager at Old Trafford and since then he's 'won' the FA Cup and Premiership title with City. Kidd, who attended the same school (Collyhurst) as Colin Barlow and Nobby Stiles, acted as City's caretaker-manager for the last two matches of the 2012/13 season (*v.* Reading away and Norwich at home) following the sacking of Roberto Mancini.

KILLEN, Christopher John (Forward)
Apps: 3 Born: Wellington, New Zealand, 8/10/1981
Career: Rongotai College, Miramar Rangers/New Zealand, CITY (March 1999–July 2002), Wrexham (loan), Port Vale (loan), Oldham Athletic (£200,000), Hibernian (free), Glasgow Celtic (free), Norwich City (loan), Middlesbrough, Shenzhen Ruby/China, Chongqing/China.
Details: Chris Killen had to wait two-and-a-half years before making the first of his three substitute appearances for City, coming on for Danny Tiatto against Rotherham United in November 2001. Unable to make inroads, he eventually moved to nearby Oldham and later won the SPL title with Celtic (2008). Capped by New Zealand at U21 and U23 levels, he had scored fourteen goals in forty-six full internationals since 2001.

KINKLADZE, Georgiou (Midfield)
Apps/goals: 121/22 Born: Didube, Tiblisi, Russia, 6/11/1973
Career: Mrekebi Tiblisi, Dynamo Tiblisi, Saarbrücken (loan), Boca Juniors (loan), CITY (£2 million, July 1995–May 1998), Ajax Amsterdam (£4.9 million), Derby County (loan/signed), Anorthosis, Rubin Kazan; retired 2006; became a sports agent, based in Moscow.
Details: Georgi Kinkladze, by far, has been one of the most popular City players over the last twenty-five years. Spotted by Chairman Francis Lee on TV,

playing for Georgia against Wales at Cardiff when he scored a quite stunning goal, he signed on the same day that Alan Ball became manager. Difficult to dispossess, he was outstanding in his first two seasons at Maine Road, scoring some wonderful goals, including two beauties in a 4-1 win at Oxford (Frank Clark's first game in charge). His best City goal, however, was the one at West Ham in an FA Cup replay in 1998. Unable to a regular place in Joe Royle's team, the fans were perplexed when the 'Georgian magician' was sold to Ajax. He won fifty-seven caps for Georgia (seventeen with City) and scored nine international goals. His club and international career realised 499 appearances and 102 goals. He won seven medals at club level.

KINSEY, Stephen (Forward)
Apps/goals: 115/18 Born: Gorton, Manchester, 2/1/1963
   Career: Manchester Boys, CITY (May 1979–October 1986), Chester City (loan, two spells), Minnesota Strikers/USA, Fort Lauderdale Strikers, Los Angeles Lazers, Dallas Sidekicks, Miami Freedom, Tacoma Stars, Tampa Bay Rowdies, Rochdale, St Mirren, Coleraine, Fort Lauderdale Strikers, Molde SK, Milwaukee Wave, Detroit Neon, Tampa Bay Terror, Richmond Kickers, Buffalo Blizzard; retired 1997; also ran summer soccer school in Florida where he still lives.
   Details: Steve Kinsey produced some outstanding performances for City. He made his debut in a 3-1 win at Wolves in April 1981 and after making fifty-seven appearances over the next three seasons, he had his best spell in the first team in 1984/85, scoring eight goals in forty-one games, helping City clinch promotion to the top flight. He also netted in the 5-4 FMC defeat by Chelsea at Wembley in 1986.
   After leaving Maine Road, Kinsey went on to play indoor and outdoor football for twelve different USA clubs, having his best spell with Minnesota Strikers for whom he scored sixty-three goals in ninety-nine games (1986–88).

KIRKMAN, Alan John (Forward)
Apps/goals: 7/6 Born: Bolton, 21/6/1936
   Career: Bacup Borough, CITY (October 1955–February 1959), Rotherham United, Newcastle United, Scunthorpe United, Torquay United, Workington, Netherfield (player-manager), Rossendale; retired 1972; Horwich RMI (manager, two spells); became transport manager of a haulage company in Bolton.
   Details: Top scorer for City in successive Central League campaigns in the mid-fifties, Alan Kirkman netted twice on his senior debut to earn a 3-3 draw at Birmingham in April 1957. Eight months later, he struck two more in a thrilling 5-4 win at Sheffield Wednesday. However, with so much forward talent

at the club, he moved on and eventually ended his career with a record of eighty-one goals in 303 League appearances, fifty-eight coming in 144 starts with Rotherham, including one in the very first League Cup final *v.* Aston Villa (1961).

KNOWLES, Frank (Left-half)
Apps: 2 Born: Hyde, Cheshire, 23/3/1891
   Career: Hyde United, Stalybridge Celtic, Manchester United; First World War guest for Hyde United, Arsenal & Oldham Athletic; Hartlepool United, CITY (October 1919/May 1920), Stalybridge Celtic, Ashington, Stockport County, Newport County, Queen's Park Rangers, Ashton National, Macclesfield; retired 1927; served with the RGA (Aldershot) during the First World War.
   Details: Frank Knowles left his work in a cotton mill to become a professional footballer. After a slow start, he went on to have a decent career, accumulating over 200 appearances at various levels. His two outings for City came in successive Manchester derbies soon after signing for the club, a 3-3 home draw on his debut followed by a 1-0 defeat at Old Trafford.
   In November 1912, Knowles escaped, but two other passengers were killed in a car crash near Rudyard Lake, Staffs.

KOLAROV, Aleksandar (Defender)
Apps/goals: 94/11 Born: Belgrade, 10/11/1985
   Career: Cukaricki/Serbia, OFK Belgrade, SC Lazio, CITY (£16 million, July 2010).
   Details: Serbian international Aleksandar Kolarov – 6 feet 2 inches tall – made thirty-seven appearances in his first season with City, gaining an FA Cup winner's medal in the progress. Twelve months later he helped the Blues win the Premiership, although the arrival of Gael Clichy greatly reduced his opportunities as first-choice left-wing back. A tough competitor who enjoys driving forward, he has scored some fine goals, including two in Champions League fixtures – the equaliser at home to Napoli in September 2011 and another against Real Madrid in September 2012. Kolarov has forty-one full caps to his credit (two goals scored).

KOMPANY, Vincent (Defender/midfield)
Apps/goals: 206/7 Born: Brussels, Belgium, 10/4/1986
   Career: RSC Anderlecht, SV Hamburg, CITY (£6 million, August 2008).
   Details: Signed by Mark Hughes, and initially a holding midfielder, Vincent Kompany is now regarded as one of the best defenders in European football. A commanding figure, strong in the tackle, quick over the ground, a born leader, he helped City win the FA Cup and Premiership title in successive seasons while at the same time adding to his total of full internationals caps for Belgium, having won

his first at the age seventeen. His tally at May 2013 stood at fifty-five (four goals). He had the pleasure of scoring the winning goal in the Manchester derby at the Etihad Stadium in April 2012.

L

LAKE, Paul Andrew (Midfield)

Apps/goals: 134/11 Born: Denton, Manchester, 28/10/1968

Career: St Thomas More School/Denton, Blue Star FC, CITY (July 1985–May 1996); qualified as a physiotherapist at Salford University; subsequently physio/trainer at Altrincham, Burnley, Oldham Athletic, Macclesfield Town & Bolton Wanderers; now runs his own physiotherapist practice in Greater Manchester.

Details: Spotted by City scout and ex-player Ken Barnes, Paul Lake gained an FA Youth Cup winner's medal in his first season at Maine Road and over the next three campaigns was a first-team regular, making 125 appearances, actually donning nine different numbered shirts in 1988/89. Playing against Leicester in March 1989, he swallowed his tongue and was grateful for the timely intervention of trainer Roy Bailey.

Six months later he suffered a cruciate knee-ligament injury in a collision with Aston Villa striker Tony Cascarino. It took him two years to recover, but then, in his second 'return' game, he was carried off at Middlesbrough and sadly never played again, announcing his retirement at the age of twenty-seven. A year later, 21,262 attended his testimonial match.

Lake, who underwent fourteen operations as a City player, won one 'B' and five U21 caps for England. He was inducted into the Manchester City Hall of Fame in 2004, an apt show of appreciation for his years of loyal service to the club.

His brothers, Mike and Dave, had unsuccessful trials with City in 1985 and 1988 respectively.

LAMBIE, William Allan (Forward)

Apps/goals: 3/1 Born: Larkhall, Lanarkshire, 10/1/1873 Died: Glasgow, c. 1945

Career: Queen's Park, CITY (briefly, 1890), Queen's Park, CITY (September/December 1892), Queen's Park; retired injured, 1900.

Details: An amateur throughout his career, Bill Lambie, of burly build was an individualist 'fast and dashing', who did not militate against impeccable conduct on the field. He scored his only goal for City in a 4-1 League win over Walsall Town Swifts, but after further outings against Northwich Victoria and Small Heath he returned to Glasgow. Lambie, who won the Scottish Cup with Queen's Park in 1893, gained nine caps for Scotland, 1892–97. His brother, John, also played for Queen's Park and Scotland.

LAMPH, Thomas (Half-back)

Apps: 11 Born: Gateshead, 16/11/1892
Died: Leeds, 24/2/1926

Career: Pelaw United, Spennymoor United, Leeds City, CITY (£800, October 1919/March 1920), Derby County, Leeds United; retired through ill-health, 1921.

Details: One of the Leeds City players sold at auction, Tom Lamph represented the North Easter League against the Southern & District Leagues in his early days. He made only forty-four League appearances during his career, which effectively was disrupted by the First World War, he played his first game for City in a 4-2 win over Sheffield Wednesday eight days after signing.

LANGFORD, Leonard (Goalkeeper)

Apps: 125 Born: Sheffield, 30/5/1899
Died: Stockport, 26/12/1973

Career: Sheffield Boys, Sheffield City Schools, Attercliffe Victory, Rossington Colliery, Nottingham Forest, CITY (June 1930–June 1934), Manchester United; retired May 1937; served with the Coldstream Guards during the First World War; kept wicket in Lancashire League cricket, and was a champion boxer.

Details: Len Langford took over from Barber in the City goal and was outstanding on his debut, in a 3-0 win over Bolton in November 1930, and missed only three out of a possible eighty games during his first two years at Maine Road. However, he was at fault for Everton's first goal in the 1933 FA Cup final, dropping a high cross for Stein to score from close range. Dixie Dean then barged him and the ball into the net for Everton's second goal. He made only nineteen more appearances for City (replaced by Frank Swift) before joining United. Generally described as being a 'safe handler who commanded his area with authority' Langford made 263 League appearances. He won the Household Brigade middle-weight boxing title in 1921

LANGLEY, Kevin James (Midfield)

Apps: 9 Born: St Helens, 24/5/1964

Career: Wigan Athletic, Everton (£100,000), CITY (£150,000, March 1987/March 1988), Chester City (loan), Birmingham City, Wigan Athletic (£50,000), Halifax Town, Bangor City; retired 1996; Wigan Athletic (School of Excellence coach).

Details: Tall, elegant and hard-working, Kevin Langley's League career spanned fourteen years during which time he amassed over 400 club appearances. He played twice at Wembley in 1986 – for Wigan in the FRT final and Everton in the FA Charity Shield – and in 1995 won the League of Wales title with Bangor.

Perhaps a shade out of his depth in the First Division, the first of his nine top-flight outings for

City came just days after his move from Goodison Park – in a crushing 4-0 defeat at Leicester.

LAW, Denis (Inside-forward)
Apps/goals: 82/38 Born: Aberdeen, 24/2/1940

Career: Aberdeen Grammar & Powis Academy (now St Machar Academy), Huddersfield Town, CITY (British record £55,000, March 1960/July 1961), Torino/Italy (£110,000), Manchester United (£115,000), CITY (July 1973, retired August 1974); subsequently a BBC radio football commentator/summariser, later with Granada TV; Football Aid (Patron).

Details: Denis Law will grace any gallery of all-time great forwards. A superb entertainer and snapper-up of half-chances, he was brilliant in the air and scored some stunning goals during a wonderful career.

He top-scored for City in 1960/61 with twenty-nine goals and his tally did not include the six he netted in the abandoned FA Cup tie at Luton! He also became the first City player to find the net in three major competitions in the same season – League, FA Cup, League Cup.

The last goal of his career, in what proved to be his final game, was that 'infamous' eighty-first-minute back-heel winner for City at Old Trafford in April 1974 – although it was actually irrelevant since United were already doomed to the drop! A distraught Law was immediately substituted as United fans mounted a pitch invasion, causing the referee to abandon the game. Nevertheless, the score stood.

Voted European 'Footballer of the Year' in 1964, Law was a superb marksman whose total of thirty goals in fifty-five internationals for Scotland (1959–72) has only been equalled by Kenny Dalglish. He also won three U23 caps, played twice for the Football League, once for the Italian League, represented the Rest of the World v. England in 1963, won the FA Cup and two League titles during his eleven years with rivals United and followed up with a League Cup runner's-up medal with City in 1974.

As a fifteen-year-old, walking into Huddersfield's Leeds Road ground, wearing spectacles because of a slight squint, and weighing barely eight stones, no-one, not even his manager who signed him, Andy Beattie, seriously believed Law would become such a magnificent marksman. The Scot got better and better, season by season, and when he retired in 1974, his personal record stood at 333 goals in 655 first-class matches for clubs (four of them) and country.

In February 2010, Law was named as Patron of the UK based charity Football Aid, taking over from the late Sir Bobby Robson, and a year later featured on a set of Commemorative stamps issued by The Royal Mail to celebrate 150 years

of the Football Association along side former City manager Kevin Keegan, John Barnes, George Best and Sir Bobby Charlton.

LAWRENCE, Valentine (Half-back)
Apps: 22 Born: Arbroath, 1890

Career: Dundee Violet, Newcastle United (trial), Forfar Athletic, CITY (July 1911/May 1913), Oldham Athletic (£50), Leeds City, Darlington, Southend United, Abertillery; retired May 1925.

Details: Mainly a reserve with City, Val Lawrence made his debut against his future club, Oldham, in October 1911 when his natural ability and enthusiasm immediately caught the eye. However, he was overshadowed by Messrs Moffatt, Roberts and Wilson and wanting regular first-team football, chose to move to Boundary Park, but even then he was never able to gain a place.

LEE, Francis Henry (Forward)
Apps/goals: 330/148 Born: Westhoughton near Bolton, Lancs, 29/4/1944

Career: Lancashire Schools, Bolton Wanderers, CITY (£60,000, October 1967–August 1974), Derby County (£110,000); retired May 1976; became a millionaire via the paper business and also a successful racehorse trainer, gaining his National Hunt licence in 1984 and a Flat racing licence in 1987; CITY (club Chairman, February 1994–January 1998).

Details: Francis Lee was only sixteen when he made his League debut for Bolton (alongside Nat Lofthouse) in November 1960. Bubbly and diminutive, after leaving Burnden Park for City in 1967, he became a real 'real livewire' whether playing down the right flank or directly through the middle.

For his three clubs, he amassed a grand total of 622 appearances (500 in the League) and scored 284 goals, with roughly half of his appearances and goals coming with City.

At his peak, he was much-admired by England boss Alf Ramsey and between 1969 and 1972 gained twenty-seven full caps, netting ten goals. He also represented the United Kingdom in 1969 and the Football League.

An effervescent character, stocky, well-built, confident on the ball with a booming right-foot shot, he had a direct approach, gave defenders plenty to think about and won penalties by whatever means possible! He was once accused by Norman Hunter (Leeds United) of diving to earn a penalty in a League match in 1975, and it resulted in the two of them engaging in a notorious fist fight and a sending-off, followed by a four-week suspension.

His conversion rate from the spot was near perfect. Once awarded a penalty, he often found the net, although he did miss two for England! In fact, in 1971/72, Lee scored a record fifteen penalties for City (thirteen in the League) in a total of thirty-three goals in the League, thus becoming the first City player to score over thirty in a season for thirty-five years, since Peter Docherty bagged thirty-two in 1936/37.

Overall Lee fired home a record forty-six spot-kicks, hence his nickname of 'Lee One Pen.' He was City's top marksman on four occasions between 1968 and 1974, notched the club's first League Cup hat-trick *v.* Walsall in October 1973 and scored more goals in Europe than any other City player – ten.

During his seven years at Maine Road, Lee helped City win the First Division, FA Cup, European Cup Winner's Cup and League Cup. Unfortunately, he left 'under a cloud' after failing to win an improved contract. He went on to gain a second League championship medal with Derby.

After returning to Maine Road as Chairman in 1994, he came under heavy criticism when City faced their second relegation in three seasons. He once employed current comedian Peter Kay in his paper factory.

LEE, Frederick Stuart (Forward)
Apps/goals: 7/2 Born: Manchester, 11/2/1953

Career: Bolton Wanderers, Wrexham, Stockport County, CITY (£100,000, September 1979/March 1980), Portland Timbers, Kansas City Comets, Carolina Lightnin', Los Angeles Lazers (two spells), Tampa Bay Rowdies, St Louis Steamers, Kansas City Comets, Dallas Sidekicks; retired 1989; Seattle Storm (manager); FC Seattle YC (director).

Details: Stuart Lee netted fifty-three goals in 188 League games before joining City. Unfortunately, he never quite fitted in at Maine Road, and after six months moved into the NASL when he played both indoor and outdoor soccer for nine years, scoring 214 goals in 408 appearances for eight different clubs. Both his City goals came against two Albions, Brighton and West Bromwich.

LEIGH, Peter (Full-back)
Apps: 2 Born: Wythenshawe, 4/3/1939

Career: Stamford Lads, Altrincham (trial), CITY (March 1957–June 1961), Crewe Alexandra; retired 1972.

Details: Released by City after just two First Division outings (in place of Cliff Sear) against Bolton and Preston in April 1960, Peter Leigh went on to give Crewe tremendous service for eleven years, amassing 473 appearances, 430 in the Football League. Only Tommy Lowry (482) has more for the Gresty Road club. City played the 'Alex' in a testimonial match for Leigh in May 1967.

LEIVERS, William Ernest (Full-back)
Apps/goals: 281/4 Born: Bolsover, Derbyshire, 29/1/1932

Career: Clay Lane Sports Club, Chesterfield, CITY (£10,500, November 1953–July 1964), Doncaster Rovers player-manager); retired May 1966; Workington (manager), Cambridge United (manager), Chelmsford City (manager), Cambridge City (manager & general manager); now lives in St Austell, Cornwall.

Details: Bill Leivers began his professional career in February 1950. He moved to Manchester City FC at the age of twenty-one and made his debut against Preston in August 1954 – the match when manager Don Revie introduced his new tactical system which became known as the 'revie plan'. Unfortunately Leivers sustained an injury as City lost 5–0 and it was to be another five months before he made another senior appearance. Initially a centre-half, he established himself in City's first team during the 1955/56 season as a right-back, playing in the FA Cup final victory over Birmingham, his only major prize of his career. A committed defender, and occasional team captain, he broke his nose five times and his elbow and ankle once in ten years at Maine Road. He represented the FA in 1956 (*v.* the Army).

LEMAN, Dennis (Forward/midfield)
Apps/goals: 25/3 Born: Newcastle, 1/12/1954

Career: Newcastle Boys, CITY (July 1970–December 1976), Sheffield Wednesday (£8,500), Wrexham (loan), Scunthorpe United, Burton Albion, Cardiff City; retired 1984; became deputy administrator for the PFA.

Details: England schoolboy international Dennis Leman made twelve of his twenty-five appearances for City as a substitute, and never really established himself as a first-team regular. But after leaving Maine Road he upped his game with Sheffield Wednesday, for whom he scored ten goals in 116 outings, helping the Owls gain promotion from the Third Division in 1980.

LENNON, Neil Francis (Right-back)
Apps: 1 Born: Lurgan, 25/6/1971

Career: Belfast Boys, Lurgan Celtic, CITY (October 1987–July 1990), Crewe Alexandra (free), Leicester City (£750,000), Glasgow Celtic, Nottingham Forest, Wycombe Wanderers; retired April 2008; Celtic (coach/assistant-manager, then manager).

Details: Neil Lennon's only outing for City was in the 3-0 win at Birmingham in April 1988, when he was substituted by David White. After leaving Maine Road he developed into a fiery midfield dynamo, and went on to make 732 appearances at club level, including 188 for Crewe, 208 for Leicester and 304 for Celtic. He won the League Cup twice with Leicester and gained forty full caps for Northern Ireland, to go with those he gained earlier at youth, U21, U23 and 'B' team levels.

And so far as a Celtic player and manager, he has won the SPL six times, the Scottish Cup on five occasions and the League Cup twice.

When playing for his country, he was treated disgracefully by some sections of his own supporters during a World Cup qualifier against Cyprus in Belfast in 2000, due to his Catholic background and his association with Celtic. He showed great character to put those incidents behind him. In September 2008, Lennon was assaulted while in the west end of Glasgow. His attackers were subsequently charged, convicted and jailed for two years each. In January 2011, Lennon reached an out of court settlement with the Bank of Ireland after a company of which he was a company director defaulted on a 3.7 million Euro loan. Also in 2011, the Royal Mail intercepted packages containing bullets and a bomb device addressed to Lennon who also received death threats. In response to these threats, Scotland's First Minister, Alex Salmond, condemned those that 'use football as a pretext for their pathetic and dangerous prejudices' and UEFA President Michel Platini said he would fight violence and sectarianism.

Former Celtic Director Michael Kelly described the bombs and bullets as terrorism. Lennon was put under twenty-four hour protection for a short while. Later in the year, a Heart of Midlothian FC supporter was sentenced to eight months in prison. He was found guilty of a breach of the peace, after running into the technical area of the football pitch, and shouting and swearing at Lennon, during a match against Celtic. One who escaped from the City net? Most definitely.

LEONARD, Patrick (Outside-left)
Apps/goals: 17/5 Born: Paisley, Scotland, 1873
    Career: St Mirren, CITY (May 1897–May 1898), New Brompton, Thames Ironworks, Canning Town, CITY (May 1898–May 1900), Paisley Swifts; retired 1905.
    Details: In his initial spell with City, Pat Leonard played in fifteen of the first League games of the season, scoring in his second outing at Darwen (won 4-2). He then slipped into the reserves, following the arrival of George Dougal, whom he deputised for in one match when returning to Hyde Road, scoring in a 4-1 win at Bury.

LESCOTT, Joleon (Defender)
Apps/goals: 136/9 Born: Quinton, Birmingham, 16 August 1982
    Career: Four Dwellings High School/Birmingham, Wolverhampton Wanderers (apprentice, June 1998, professional, August 1999), Everton (£5 million, June 2006), Manchester City (£23 million, August 2009).
    Details: Joleon Lescott who made 235 appearances for Wolves and 142 for Everton before joining City

in 2009, has over the last four seasons proved sturdy, resolute and reliable at the heart of the defence, performing mainly alongside Vincent Kompany. He gives very little away and gained FA Cup and Premiership winner's medals in 2011 and 2012.

Capped twice by England at U21 level, his senior international debut followed in a 3-0 win over Estonia in October 2007. Injury ruled him out of contention for the 2010 World Cup finals but he was John Terry's back-four partner at Euro 2012, scoring England's first goal of the tournament against France. At the end of the 2012/13 season he had twenty-six full caps to his credit (one goal scored), but with so many other defenders vying for a place in the team, he may find it hard to that tally.

His brother, Aaron, played for Aston Villa, Sheffield Wednesday and Stockport, among others.

LESLIE, Alexander John (Centre-half)
Apps: 1 Born: Methill, Greenock, 1900
    Career: St Mirren, CITY (January 1923–July 1925), Tranmere Rovers, Crossley Brothers: retired 1931.
    Details: Always a reserve at Maine Road, Alex Leslie's only first-team appearance for City was against Tottenham Hotspur (away) in April 1924 when he was completely out of touch in a 4-1 defeat. He made fourteen League appearances for Tranmere.

LESTER, Michael John Anthony (Forward)
Apps: 4 Born: Manchester, 4/8/1954
    Career: Manchester Schools, Oldham Athletic, CITY (£50,000, November 1973–March 1977), Stockport County (loan), Washington Diplomats, Grimsby Town, Barnsley, Exeter City, Bradford City, Scunthorpe United, Hartlepool United (loan), Stockport County, Scarborough, Ludvika FK/Sweden, Blackpool (non-contract), Chorley; retired 1991.
    Details: Before becoming a professional footballer with Oldham in December 1972, Mike Lester was a noted amateur sprinter, clocking 10.5 seconds for the 100 yards. He joined City at the age of nineteen and made his debut in a 2-1 home defeat by Arsenal five days after moving from Boundary Park. He never really got a look in at Maine Road and after loan spell with Stockport, switched his duties to the NASL.

In a nomadic career, which began with cartilage trouble, Lester made 447 appearances with fourteen different clubs over a period of nineteen years.

LEWIS, William (Centre-forward)
Apps/goals: 13/4 Born: Bangor, 1864
Died: Manchester, 1935
    Career: Bangor Rovers, Bangor City, Everton, Bangor City, Crewe Alexandra, Chester, CITY (September 1896/September 1897), Chester;

retired 1898; later licensee of the Duke of York pub, Chester.

Details: Billy Lewis had already played for Wales when he appeared in Everton's first-ever Football League game *v.* Accrington on 8 September 1888. However, he never settled on Merseyside and returned to Bangor. Following spells with Crewe and Chester, he then tried his luck with City but after one season at Hyde Road, having scored in his first two games, he went back to Chester. He won twenty-seven caps overall (twelve goals scored) and, in fact held the record for most international appearances for the Principality until Billy Meredith overhauled him in 1908. Lewis gained seven caps while with Chester and this small total remained a club record for more than 100 years – until broken by the Trinidad & Tobagan international Angus Eve in April 2000. Lewis also represented the North Wales FA *v.* Liverpool in 1884 and played in two Test Matches on Wales' tour to Canada in 1891. One assessment of Lewis described him as being 'a speedy forward and very clever – does not use sufficient judgment.'

A stonemason by trade, and known as 'Billy Cae Top' he was a champion athlete at school.

LEYLAND, John (Half-back)
Apps: 3 Born: Northwich, 1889
Career: Witton Albion, CITY (May 1920–May 1923), Manchester North East.

Details: A reserve to Max Woosnam and Micky Hamill during his three seasons with City, Jack Leyland made his debut against Huddersfield in November 1920 and played his second and third games at the start of the following campaign against Aston Villa and Liverpool.

LIEVESLEY, Ernest Frederick (Forward)
Apps: 2 Born: Netherthorpe, 24/7/1899
Died: Staveley c. 1960
Career: Staveley, CITY (May 1919–June 1922), Southend United, Exeter City, Rotherham United.

Details: It took Fred Lievesley quite a while to get going! He made only six appearances for his first three League clubs but then did well with his fourth, banging in twenty-eight goals in 108 outings for Rotherham. His debut for City was against that season's champions, West Bromwich Albion in December 1919 when he deputised for Horace Barnes. Four other members of the Lievesley family also played football – cousins Harry for Doncaster (1934/35), Joe Lievesley for Sheffield United and Arsenal (1904–14) and Les for Doncaster, Manchester United, Chesterfield, Torquay and Crystal Palace (1929–39) and brother Wilf for Derby County, Manchester United, Exeter City, Wigan Borough and Cardiff City.

LILLIS, Mark Anthony (Forward)
Apps/goals: 51/15 Born: Manchester, 17/1/1960
Career: Manchester Boys, Lancashire County Youths, CITY (schoolboy forms, season 1976/77), Huddersfield Town, CITY (£150,000, June 1985/ August 1986), Derby County (£100,000), Aston Villa (£130,000), Scunthorpe United (£40,000), Stockport County, Witton Albion, Macclesfield Town; retired 1993; Huddersfield Town (coach), Scunthorpe United (assistant-manager), Halifax Town (manager), Derby County (coach), Northern Ireland (part-time coach), Stockport County (assistant-manager), Huddersfield Town (Football in the Community officer & Youth Coach).

Details: A useful player to have around, Mark Lillis always gave a good, honest account of himself and most defenders knew they had been in game after facing him. He made all his appearances for City in one season, missing only four matches. He scored in his second outing *v.* Leicester and, in fact, thirteen of his fifteen goals came in singles; his other two came in the FMC final defeat by Chelsea at Wembley. It was a surprise to some fans when he left to join Derby.

A star of Huddersfield's Third Division promotion winning team of 1982/83, Lillis netted sixty-three goals in 242 appearances in seven years with the Terriers. He also helped Aston Villa win the Second Division title in 1986/87.

LINACRE, William (Outside-right)
Apps/goals: 79/7 Born: Chesterfield,
10/8/1924 Died: Chesterfield, 16/1/2010
Career: Chesterfield; Second World War guest for Nottingham Forest & Southport; CITY (£2,000, October 1947/September 1949), Middlesbrough (£12,500), Goole Town, Hartlepool United, Mansfield Town.

Details: Lively with good skills and neat body swerve, Bill Linacre's career was dogged by injury. He broke his right leg twice with Chesterfield in the same season, fractured it again playing for Middlesbrough against City in 1950, suffered four twisted ankles, a dislocated shoulder and was knocked out twice! Yet he always bounced back, and would surely have gone on to greater things had he not be confined to hospital and the treatment room for lengthy periods. He made his City debut against Burnley soon after moving from Chesterfield and struck his first goal a month later at Bolton. It is understood that City offered Middlesbrough cash plus Linacre, but 'Boro turned down the deal and only money was involved.

Linacre, who had a bit of temper, getting himself sent off with Henry Cockburn in the 2-1 Manchester derby defeat in September 1949, scored twenty-one goals in 230 League appearances.

John Linacre (no relation) was on City's books in 1945/46.

LISTER, Herbert Francis (Forward)
*Apps: 2 Born: Manchester, 4/10/1939
Died: Manchester, 10/7/2007*

Career: Manchester Schools, CITY (December 1954–September 1960), Oldham Athletic (£10,000 plus Ken Branagan), Rochdale, Stockport County, Altrincham; retired injured, 1969; became a part-time taxi driver in Blackpool.

Details: One of Oldham's most prolific goalscorers ever, Bert Lister netted ninety-five goals in 152 games for the Latics in less than five years, two of his most notable achievements being his double hat-trick (six goals) against Southport on Boxing Day 1962 and a goal after just ten seconds from the kick-off against Chesterfield in April 1963. All this after he had been 'given away' by City for whom he made just two League starts, both in the Black Country, in a 2-0 defeat at Wolves in October 1958 and a 3-0 loss at WBA in March 1959.

LITTLE, Roy (Left-back)
Apps/goals: 168/4 Born: Manchester, 1/6/1931

Career: Greenwood Victoria, CITY (August 1949–October 1958), Brighton & Hove Albion, Crystal Palace, Dover Athletic (player-manager), Christchurch City; retired 1968; thereafter worked for twenty-five years at the University of Manchester Sports Centre, Wythenshawe; a university football competition is named in his honour.

Details: Roy Little was a fine defender, sure-footed, a good marker and keen tackler. He played for City in successive FA Cup finals, gaining a winner's medal the second *v.* Birmingham in 1956. After his League debut at Liverpool in 1953, he established himself as Ken Branagan's full-back partner the following season, when he scored his first League goals, at Huddersfield (1-1) and at home to Sheffield Wednesday (won 3-2). He retained his position until Cliff Sear took over in 1957.

LITTLE, Thomas (Outside-left)
Apps/goals: 16/5 Born: Dumfries, 20/4/1872

Career: Derby County, CITY (June-October 1894), Baltimore Orioles/USA, CITY (November 1894-June 1896), Ashton North End, Wellingborough, Luton Town, Swindon Town, Barnsley, Dumfries; retired 1905.

Details: Along with three of his City colleagues – Archie Ferguson, Mitch Calvey and Alec Wallace – Tommy Little move to the USA and was the only one to return to the club. He netted three goals in seven League games before leaving Hyde Road, including a strike on his debut (with Calvey) in a 4-2 defeat Bury in September 1894. He made only sixty-eight Football League appearances during his career.

LIVINGSTONE, George Turner (Inside-forward)
Apps/goals: 88/20 Born: Dumbarton, 5/5/1876 Died: Helensburgh, Dunbartonshire, 15/1/1950

Career: Sinclair Swifts/Dumbarton, Artizan Thistle/Dumbarton, Parkhead FC/Glasgow, Heart of Midlothian, Everton, Sunderland (£175), Glasgow Celtic (£250), Liverpool, CITY (May 1903–January 1907), Glasgow Rangers, Manchester United (later reserve team player-manager; retired 1918); Dumbarton (manager), Clydebank (manager), Glasgow Rangers (trainer), Bradford City (trainer); later ran his own plumbing/gas-fitting business in Helensburgh.

Details: Billy Meredith's canny right-wing partner at City, 'Geordie' Livingstone, gained an FA Cup winner's medal in 1904. In fact, it was his pass that set up Meredith for the only goal *v.* Bolton. Two years later he was one of the many players suspended and fined following the FA inquiry into illegal payments. When his ban was lifted he returned to Scotland and joined Rangers.

Before that, however, Livingstone had given City fans enormous pleasure with a combination of passing and shooting. A big man with a sunny disposition, he was the dressing room comedian.

Shortly after joining City's arch-rivals United in 1909, he scored twice on his debut for the Reds in the Manchester derby, being one of three ex-City players in the home line-up.

The first City player to represent Scotland (two caps gained), Livingstone was an international trialist in 1906, starred for the Scottish League against the Football League and Glasgow against Sheffield, and was a runner-up with Celtic in the 1902 Scottish Cup final. He made over 300 club appearances during his career.

LLOYD, Norman (Left-half)
Apps: 3 Born: Salford, 1912

Career: Manchester Central, CITY (May 1932–May 1935), New Brighton; retired during Second World War.

Details: A reserve with City for three seasons, Norman Lloyd made his three appearances towards the end of the 1933/34 season in place of Jimmy McLuckie.

LOGAN, Shaleum Narval (Defender)
Apps: 3 Born: Wythenshawe, 29/1/1988

Career: CITY (June 2004–June 2011), Grimsby Town (loan), Scunthorpe United (loan), Stockport County (loan), Tranmere Rovers (loan), Brentford.

Details: Shaleum Logan made his PL debut for City in a 2-0 away defeat at Portsmouth in February 2009, starting the game and playing the full ninety minutes. Eighteen months later he was a surprise inclusion in the club's 25-strong Premier League squad, making him City's eleventh Englishman and twelfth home-grown player in the list. In 2011, along with Marcel Eger, he joined Brentford, managed by former City star, Uwe Rosler.

Above right: Programme from City's 9-2 defeat at the Hawthorns in 1957.

Below left: A portrait of Mario Balotelli. (Good Times Creations)

Below right: Malcolm Allison, twice City's manager, 1971–73 and 1979–80.

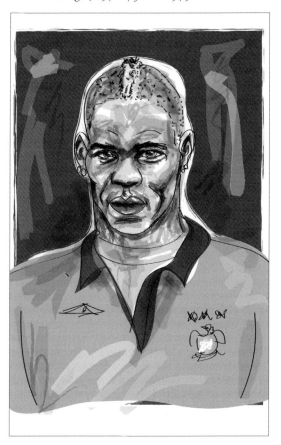

Above left: Jackie Bray.

Above middle: Matt Busby, future Manchester United manager.

Above right: Eric Brook.

Below left: A caricature of England midfielder Colin Bell.

Below middle: Samuel Cookson, who made over 300 appearances for City.

Below right: Middle right: Johnny Crossan, December 1963.

Above left: Samuel Cowan.

Above middle: Wyn Davies in Newcastle gear.

Above right: Wyn Davies wearing a Bolton top.

Below: Doherty hooks the ball over Arsenal's goalkeeper and into the net to help Manchester City win the 1938/37 championship.

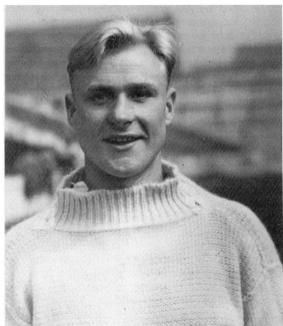

Above left: Peter Dobing.

Above right: Verdi Godwin, 1948.

Below: England goalkeeper Joe Hart.

Above left: George Hannah (in stripes).

Above right: City captain Vincent Kompany.

Below: Strong-kicking defender Joleon Lescott.

Left: A caricature of
Francis Lee.

Below left: James McMullan.

Below middle: Right-back
Jimmy Meadows, 1953.

Below right: Roy Paul.

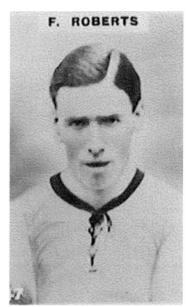

Above left: Christopher
Ross Pringle.

*Above middle and above
right:* Frank Roberts.

Right: A caricature of winger
Mike Summerbee.

Above left and above middle: Bert Trautmann.

Above right: Goalkeeper Frank Swift.

Below left: International goalkeeper Frank Swift jumping for the ball.

Below right: Frank Swift with his dog.

LOMAS, Stephen Martin (Midfield)
Apps/goals: 137/11 Born: Hanover, Germany, 18/1/1974

Career: CITY (May 1990–March 1997), West Ham United (£1.6 million), Queen's Park Rangers (free), Gillingham, St Neot's Town (player-manager); retired 2011; St Johnstone (manager).

Details: Steve Lomas was impressive in City's youth and second XIs before establishing himself in the first team. A midfielder with a 'lovely' touch, highly competitive and never afraid to shoot, he became a great clubman, who will often be remembered by the fans for his misfortune of scoring an own-goal on the last day of the 1995/96, which meant that City could only manage a 2–2 draw at home to Liverpool FC and were relegated from the Premier League on goal difference. That apart, he was often the driving force in centre-field for club and country, and before entering non-League football in 2008, drew up a superb record in senior football of twenty-six goals in 429 League and Cup appearances, his best set of 'stats' (thirteen goals in 226 outings) coming with West Ham, who he helped win the InterToto Cup in 1999. Lomas also gained forty-five caps for Northern Ireland, following those he collected at schoolboy, youth and 'B' team levels.

LOMAX, Geoffrey William (Full-back)
Apps: 28/1 Born: Droylsden, 6/7/1964

Career: Schoolboy football, CITY (July 1981–December 1985), Wolverhampton Wanderers (loan), Carlisle United, Rochdale; retired 1989; later Bolton Wanderers (Football in the Community officer).

Details: A capable full-back, able and willing, Geoff Lomax made 138 League appearances during his career, seventy with Rochdale. Reserve to Ray Ranson and then Andy May at Maine Road, he made his City debut in a 4-1 defeat at Southampton in March 1983, scoring his only goal in a 3-1 win at Huddersfield nine months later.

LOPES, Marcos Paulo Mesquita (Midfield)
Apps: 1/1 Born: Belém, Para State, Brazil, 28/12/1995

Career: Benfica, CITY (£790,000, June 2011).

Details: Marcos Lopes played for Benfica's youth team and represented Portugal ten times at intermediate level before joining City. He went on the club's pre-season tour and appeared in six out of seven friendly fixtures, but had to wait until January 2013 before making for his senior debut against Watford in a third-round FA Cup tie. Introduced as an eighty-eighth-minute substitute, he made an instant impact by netting the final goal in a 3–0 victory – thus becoming one of the youngest-ever City scorers in a competitive match.

LYALL, John (Goalkeeper)
Apps: 44 Born: Dundee, 16/4/1881
Died: Detroit, USA, 17/2/1944

Career: Jarrow, Sheffield Wednesday (£100), CITY (September 1909–April 1911), Dundee, Ayr United, Jarrow; First World War guest for Sheffield Wednesday; retired 1917; served in the Army, immigrated to Canada in 1920s.

Details: In 1902 while living in Jarrow, Jack Lyall was selected to play for England, but after declaring he was born north of the border, he was subsequently capped by Scotland in 1905 *v.* England, and later played in two international trials (1909 and 1910). With a long reach and excellent at dealing with high crosses and shots, he could kick long and straight, requiring but a modicum of space. He won the FA Cup and two League championships with Wednesday, for whom he made 296 appearances and after taking over from Walter Smith, helped City clinch the Second Division title in 1910.

LYON, William John (Left-half)
Apps: 6 Born: Clachnacuddin, 1887
Died: Scotland, 1959

Career: Walsall, Bristol Rovers, CITY (May 1903/March 1904), Preston North End; retired 1910.

Details: After failing to gain a place in City's first XI – due to the presence of Sam Ashworth – Bill Lyon left Hyde Road and immediately helped Preston win the Second Division title. He was suspended for a month in January 1910 for a 'high tackle' on Aston Villa's Harry Hampton ans was so upset he retired at the end of the season, having made 222 appearances for North End.

M

McADAMS, William John (Forward)
Apps/goals: 134/65 Born: Belfast, 20/1/1934

Career: Belfast Distillery, CITY (December 1953–September 1960), Bolton Wanderers (£15,000), Leeds United, Brentford, Queen's Park Rangers, Barrow; retired 1968.

Details: Billy McAdams netted a hat-trick in only his second senior game for City, in a 5-2 FA Cup win at Bradford in January 1954, ending that season with eleven goals. Dogged by injuries after that, he top-scored for the second XI in 1956/57, at a time when he was battling to win a regular place in the first team. He eventually had two good campaigns in the late 1950s, heading the scoring charts at senior level in 1959/60 with twenty-one goals. Capped fifteen times by Northern Ireland, McAdams hit 147 goals in 343 League appearances in a career which lasted fifteen years, 1953–68.

McALINDEN, Robert (Outside-left)
Apps: 1 Born: Salford, 22/5/1946

Career: Salford Boys, Aston Villa, CITY (March 1962–May 1965), Port Vale, Los Angeles Aztecs/ USA, Bournemouth, Toronto/Canada.

Details: Bob McAlinden made just one League appearance in three years with City – deputising for Dave Wagstaffe in a 3-2 home defeat by Preston in October 1963. He did much better in the NASL.

McBRIDE, James (Left-half)
Apps/goals: 75/2 Born: Renton, Scotland, 30/12/1873 Died: Dunbartonshire, c. 1950

Career: Renton Wanderers, Renton FC, Liverpool, CITY (November 1894 –September 1897), Ashton North End; retired 1898; later worked in a Glasgow shipyard.

Details: Jim McBride was involved in the 1891 litigation enquiry surrounding Renton FC, who had been expelled by the SFA for professionalism, before helping Liverpool win the Second Division title. Replacing Joe Nash, he showed plenty of endeavour during his three years with City, scoring his first goal in his second game, a 4-1 win over Woolwich Arsenal in December 1894.

McCABE, Arthur (Outside-left)
Apps: 1 Born: Sheffield, 1873

Career: Rotherham Town, Sheffield United, Rotherham Town, CITY (January/May 1896), Rochdale.

Details: Archie McCabe scored four goals in eighteen games for Rotherham before joining City. Unfortunately he never settled at Hyde Road and left after just four months, having played in one League match, a 3-0 defeat at Notts County.

McCARTHY, Michael (Defender)
Apps/goals: 163/3 Born: Barnsley, 7/2/1959

Career: Barnsley, CITY (December 1983–May 1987), Celtic, FC Lyon/France, Millwall (loan/ signed; retired 1992; appointed manager), Republic of Ireland (manager), Sunderland (manager), Wolverhampton Wanderers (manager), Ipswich Town (manager).

Details: A quick, skilful and commanding defender, tough and uncompromising, with an ungainly gait, Mick McCarthy had a big hand in Barnsley's rise from the Fourth, to the Third and into the Second Division between 1978 and 1981. Replacing Tommy Caton in City's back line, within five months he was voted 'Player of the Year' and in 1985 helped the Blues reach the top flight. He remained at Maine Road for two more seasons before joining Celtic, with whom he won two Scottish Cup winner's medals.

McCarthy, who had the pleasure of scoring for City in the first-ever televised 'live' Manchester derby in October 1986, amassed over 500 club appearances, 314 with Barnsley. He gained one U23 and fifty-seven full caps for the Republic of Ireland, captaining the side in the 1988 European Championships and 1990 World Cup finals, and also played three times for the Eire FA. One of only four former City players to have managed a national team, he was in charge of Eire from 1996 to 2002.

McCLELLAND, John Bonar (Outside-right)
Apps/goals: 8/1 Born: Bradford, 5/3/1935

Career: Manchester YMCA, CITY (September 1953–September 1958), Lincoln City (part exchange for George Hannah), Queen's Park Rangers (£14,000), Portsmouth (£10,000), Newport County; retired May 1969.

Details: A fast, clever winger who could cross a ball at pace, Jack McClelland scored 104 goals in 373 League appearances during his sixteen-year career, having his best seasons with Portsmouth (1962–67). He was reserve to Fionan Fagan, Billy Spurdle and Colin Barlow at Maine Road, managing just eight first-team appearances in five years. His only goal came in a 2-2 draw at Aston Villa in February 1957.

McCLOY, Phillip (Full-back)
Apps: 157 Born: Uddingston, Lanarkshire 15/4/1896 Died: Scotland, 1972

Career: Kilsyth Emmett, Mossend Swifts, Ballieston Juniors, Ayr United, CITY (£3,000, August 1925–August 1932), Cork City, Stade Rennais, Workington, Kidderminster Harriers; retired 1936.

Details: Phil McCloy had a memorable partnership at Ayr with 'Fermer Jock' Smith that culminated in their joint selection for the 1924 Scotland *v.* England international at Wembley. McCloy added a second cap to his tally a year later. A cool, calculating, fearless full-back who inspired confidence, he played in the 1926 FA Cup final and won the Second Division championship with City two years later. He made his City debut against Cardiff in August 1925, having his last game in the Manchester derby in February 1930.

McCONNELL, Thomas (Outside-left)
Apps: 2 Born: Manchester, 1874

Career: Moss End Swifts, CITY (July 1896/May 1897), Woolwich Arsenal.

Details: A one-season reserve, Tom McConnell was the fifth player used on the left-wing by City in the first eleven matches of 1896/97 when he made his debut in a 4-2 home win over Blackpool in early November. He failed to get a game with Arsenal.

McCORMACK, Murdoch (Outside-left)
App: 1 Born: Glasgow, 7/10/1920 Died: 1951

Career: Glasgow Rangers, CITY (April/July 1947), Blackpool, Crewe Alexandra; returned to Scotland, 1950.

Details: Murdock McCormack's only game for City came in a 3-1 defeat at WBA in May 1947 when he partnered George Smith on the left-wing. He made forty-three League appearances after leaving Maine Road.

McCOURT, Francis Joseph (Wing-half)
Apps: 61/4 Born: Portadown, 9/12/1925
Died: Ireland, 19/7/2009

Career: Shamrock Rovers, Bristol Rovers, Shamrock Rovers, Bristol Rovers, CITY (November 1950–June 1954), Colchester United; retired injured, 1956.

Details: After two spells in Ireland and two with Bristol Rovers, Frank McCourt spent just under four years at Maine Road. A tough-tackling defender, he played in the last sixteen League games of the 1950/51 season, had thirty-one outings the following term, thirteen more in 1952/53 but made only start in his last term, Roy Paul having bedded himself in at left-half. He won six caps for Northern Ireland as a City player.

McCOURT, James (Centre-half)
Apps: 4 Born: Bellshill near Glasgow,
8/9/1897 Died: Glasgow, c. 1968.

Career: Bedlay Juniors, Third Lanark, Sheffield United, CITY (August 1924/October 1925), Dykehead; retired 1930.

Details: Jim McCourt made over sixty appearances for Sheffield United before City signed him as half-back cover. With Jimmy Elwood absent, he played in the first three games of the 1924/25 season, making made his debut in the 2-0 win at Bury. His last outing came in a 3-2 victory at Preston in the November.

McCULLOUGH, Keillor (Half-back/forward)
Apps/goals: 18/1 Born: Larne, 1912

Career: Belfast Distillery, CITY (October 1935–March 1938), Northampton Town.

Details: A versatile Northern Ireland international, capped five times (three with City), Keillor McCullough occupied both wing-half and both inside-forward positions during his two-and-a-half years with City, scoring his only goal in a 3-0 League win over Sheffield Wednesday in November 1935. He played in thirty-eight League games for Northampton up to the Second World War.

McDONALD, Robert (Full-back)
Apps: 6 Born: Old Kilpatrick, Scotland,
26/10/1935

Career: Clydebank Schools, Vale of Leven, CITY (September 1956–August 1963), Bournemouth, Christchurch; retired injured, 1965; now living in Dorset.

Details: Initially a reserve, Bob McDonald got his chance at right-back when Barrie Betts was injured, but he failed to retain his place as City boss Les

McDowall chose to use Bobby Kennedy instead. He made his League debut against Nottingham Forest in October 1961 and his last game for City came in the Manchester derby in February 1962 when 50,000 fans saw United win 2-0 at Maine Road.

McDONALD, Robert Wood (Full-back/midfield)
Apps/goals: 112/16 Born: Aberdeen, 13/4/1955

Career: Aberdeen schoolboy football, King's Street Sports Club/Aberdeen, Aston Villa, Coventry City (£45,000), CITY (£270,000, October 1980–September 1983), Oxford United, Leeds United, Wolverhampton Wanderers (loan), VS Rugby, Burton Albion, Nuneaton Borough, Worcester City, Sutton Coldfield Town, Armitage, Redditch United; retired injured, May 1993; later employed by the Scottish Ambulance service as a TV rigger.

Details: Efficient, hard-working with a useful left-foot, Bobby McDonald had a fine career which saw him play in over 500 matches for six different League clubs, having his best spell with Coventry City. Capped by Scotland at schoolboy and youth team levels, he won the League Cup and gained promotion to the First Division with Aston Villa in 1975 and was one of John Bond's first signings for City, for whom he made his debut in a 2-1 win at Brighton in October 1980. He played in the 1981 FA Cup final defeat by Spurs and retained the left-back position for two more seasons.

Also a very capable stand-in goalkeeper, McDonald was brilliant for eighty-seven minutes against Watford in September 1982 after Joe Corrigan had gone off injured, helping City win 1-0. McDonald's father, Ralph, played for Aberdeen in the 1950s.

McDOWALL, Leslie John (Half-back)
Apps/goals: 126/8 Born: India, 25/10/1912
Died: Manchester, 18/8/1991

Career: Glenryan Thistle, Sunderland, CITY (£7,500, March 1938–June 1949), Wrexham (player-manager); retired May 1950; CITY (manager, June 1950–May 1963), Oldham Athletic (manager).

Details: Les McDowall's presence in the half-back line failed to prevent City dropping into the Second Division at the end of the 1937/38 campaign. The following season he was absent from only four League games as promotion was missed by just five points. He then made 114 appearances during the Second World War, before spending three more years at Maine Road, helping the team win the Second Division championship in 1947 while serving his last two campaigns mainly in the reserves.

The son of a Scottish missionary, McDowall was a shipyard draughtsman before becoming a victim of the '1930 slump'. He was spotted by a Sunderland scout while playing football with other unemployed men and quickly made inroads at Roker Park, prior to making a name for himself with City.

He was brought back to the club as manager to replace John Thomson. He stayed for thirteen years, during which time he signed some exciting players, Denis Law among them, and guided to City to two FA Cup finals, winning in 1956. He left following the team's relegation in 1963, replaced by George Poyser.

McDowall simply had an infectious enthusiasm for the game. He introduced the 'Revie Plan' and the 'M' Plan'.

McDOWELL, Arthur (Right-back)
Apps: 4 Born: Manchester, c. 1871
Career: CITY (July 1893–May 1895)
Details: A relatively unknown reserve, Arthur McDowell's four outings for City came at the end of the 1893/94 season, his first in a 3-1 win at Rotherham Town, his last in a 5-2 defeat at Walsall Town Swifts.

McGIVERN, Ryan (Left-back)
Apps/goals: 4/1 Born: Newry, County Down, 8/1/1990
Career: CITY (June 2006), Morecambe (loan), Leicester City (loan), Walsall (loan), Crystal Palace (loan), Bristol City (loan), Hibernian (loan).
Details: A product of the club's youth system, Ryan McGivern, discovered by former scout Willie McKeown, played in City's 2008 FA Youth Cup final win over Chelsea. He was named in the Premiership squad for the first time *v.* Fulham in April 2009, finally making his senior debut in a 5-0 win over Sunderland two years later, appearing as a seventieth-minute substitute for Dedryck Boyata. Capped by Northern Ireland twenty-three times between U16 to U23 levels, McGivern has now played in nineteen full internationals since 2008.

McGOLDRICK, Edward John (Midfield)
Apps: 45 Born: Islington, London, 30/4/1965
Career: Nuneaton Borough, Northampton Town, Crystal Palace, Arsenal (£1 million), CITY (£300,000, September 1996–May 1998), Stockport County (loan); retired June 1998.
Details: A constructive midfielder, Eddie McGoldrick was twenty-one when he entered League football with Northampton, but quickly made up for lost time by making 130 appearances for the Cobblers, helping them win the Fourth Division title in 1987. He then played a further 189 games for Palace, gaining a ZDSC winner's medal in 1991 before having fifty-seven outings with Arsenal and forty-five for City, for whom he had a fine 1986/87 season when playing alongside Georgi Kinkladze. Unfortunately, McGoldrick suffered with sciatica quite a lot and this problem

forced him into early retirement. He represented the Republic of Ireland in one 'B' and fifteen full internationals.

McGUIRE, Patrick (Full-back)
Apps: 15 Born: Manchester; 1895 Died: Killed in action, France, 15/10/1916
Career: Hurst FC, CITY (August 1912 until his death).
Details: A reserve to Eli Fletcher and Billy Henry, Pat McGuire deputised for both during his short time with City, making his League debut (in place of Fletcher) in a 2-1 defeat at Chelsea in March 1913. He was only twenty-one when he tragically lost his life on a French battlefield.

McILROY, Samuel Baxter, MBE (Midfield)
Apps/goals: 16/1 Born: East Belfast, 2/8/1954
Career: Ashfield School/Belfast, Manchester United, Stoke City (record £350,000), CITY (free, August 1985–March 1987), Orgryte/Sweden (loan), Bury, Modling/Norway, Admira Wacker (loan), Preston North End (player-coach), Northwich Victoria (player, then manager; retired as a player, 1992); Ashton United (manager), Macclesfield Town (manager), Northern Ireland (manager), Stockport County (manager), Morecambe (manager).
Details: The son of a Linfield footballer, Sammy McIlroy spent eleven years at Old Trafford (1971–82), being the last youth player signed by Matt Busby, therefore making him the last of the *Busby Babes*. Dubbed 'the next George Best', he was seventeen when he scored the first of his seventy goals for the Reds on his debut in a 3-3 draw in the Manchester derby in November 1971. He went on to make 418 senior appearances for City's rivals, who he helped win the Second Division and FA Cup. He did well at Stoke (144 outings) before spending almost two seasons at Maine Road, netting a debut goal *v.* Coventry City. Unfortunately, he struggled with injuries at Maine Road. He retired with a League record of seventy-four goals in 565 appearances. He also gained eighty-eight caps for Northern Ireland (five goals) having represented his country at schoolboy level when he was fourteen.

McLEOD, Edward Hughes (Forward)
Apps/goals: 4/2 Born: Glasgow, 5/2/1914 Died: 1988
Career: East Fife, CITY (November 1938–August 1940, Hibernian, Shrewsbury Town; served in the Army during the Second World War.
Details: Ted McLeod scored on his City debut in a 2-1 win over Southampton and, despite not being around for the first three months of the season, still finished up as joint top scorer with Jimmy Heale in City's the last Central League campaign before the Second World War.

McLEOD, John Simpson (Forward)
Apps/goals: 14/11 Born: Glasgow, 20/4/1912 Died: Glasgow, c. 1987

Career: Larne, CITY (December 1935–July 1937), Millwall.

Details: A reserve like his younger brother, Jock McLeod also scored on his City debut in a 5-1 defeat at WBA and was twice leading marksman for the second XI in 1935/36 and 1936/37. He netted twelve goals in twenty-seven League games for Millwall before the outbreak of the Second World War.

McLUCKIE, James Sime (Left-half)
Apps/goal. 38/1 Born: Stonehouse, Lanarkshire, 2/4/1908 Died: Edinburgh, 11/11/1986

Career: Hamilton Acciesy, Tranent Juniors, Hamilton Academical, CITY (February 1933/December 1934), Aston Villa (£6,500), Ipswich Town; Second World War guest for Clapton Orient, Hamilton Academical, Norwich City, Queen's Park Rangers, Southend United, Leyton Orient, Queen's Park Rangers; Clacton Town (player-manager/coach); retired June 1949.

Details: A brilliant ball artist and inspiring captain, Jimmy McLuckie was capped by Scotland against Wales in 1934 and during his career made well over 250 club appearances, being the first professional at Portman Road in 1936. He had a fine 1933/34 season with City, but alas, he missed the FA Cup final win over Portsmouth, Jackie Bray being preferred instead.

McMAHON, John (Full-back)
Apps/goals: 109/1 Born: Clyde, 1878 Died: Glasgow, 1933

Career: Clyde, Preston North End, CITY (record £450, December 1902–December 1906), Bury; retired injured, 1909.

Details: A steady, reliable defender, Jock McMahon took over from Orr as City's right-back and stayed there until April 1906, when he was injured playing against Arsenal. He scored his only goal for the Blues in a 4-0 League win over Middlesbrough in September 1905. He was a Scottish international trialist in 1903.

McMAHON, Stephen (Midfield)
Apps/goals: 98/1 Born: Halewood, Liverpool, 20/8/1961

Career: Everton, Aston Villa (£300,000), Liverpool (£350,000), CITY (£900,000, December 1991–November 1994), Swindon Town (player-manager), Blackpool (manager), Perth Glory/Australia; retired 2006; currently a football pundit for the Asia-based sports broadcaster ESPN Star Sport.

Details: Steve McMahon made his City debut two days after joining from Liverpool, but went off injured in a 2-1 win over Norwich. During his time at Maine Road, the midfielder was initially seen as someone who would help raise their game due to his aggression and quality, but unfortunately the quality of team around him was not the same as at Anfield. Niall Quinn pointed out in his autobiography that McMahon reminded him of Roy Keane in his intensity and will to win. At times he certainly injected some venom into City's midfield! A member of Liverpool's double-winning team of 1986, McMahon collected three championship and two FA Cup winner's medals with the Merseysiders, won six U21, two 'B' and 17 full caps for England (1988–90) and made over 500 League appearances during his career. In 1993, McMahon was featured in Vinnie Jones's infamous *Soccer's Hard Men* video in which Jones talks about his adoration and respect for other 'hard men'. McMahon's brother, John, has worked on the staff at Tranmere, Shrewsbury and Liverpool while his son, Steve junior, has played for Perth Glory, Blackpool and Kidderminster Harriers.

McMANAMAN, Stephen (Forward)
Apps: 44 Born: Kirkdale, Liverpool, 11/2/1972

Career: Bootle Boys, Liverpool, Real Madrid (free), CITY (free, August 2003– released, May 2005).

Details: In 2003, along with Claude Makélélé' and Fernando Hierro, Steve McManaman left Real Madrid and headed back to the Premier League. Initially reported to be joining Arsenal or Everton, he eventually decided to join long-time admirer Kevin Keegan at The City of Manchester Stadium, resulting in a reunion with several ex-colleagues including Robbie Fowler, Nicolas Ankelka, and later, David James, prompting the media to state that Keegan was 'reuniting the Spice Boys'.

McManaman made his City debut a month after signing, in a 4-1 win over Aston Villa, and quickly started to produce the goods as progress was made in the UEFA Cup, but by Christmas results had fallen, the team was struggling and McManaman got injured. Unfortunately, the former Real Madrid star was ultimately deemed a disappointment, and was increasingly vilified by the City fans, who actually jeered him off the pitch after a draw with Norwich, nicknaming him 'McMoneyman.' A combination of niggling injuries and the rise of Shaun Wright-Phillips saw him lose his preferred right midfield position and after two seasons of in-and-out performances, he never played again after Keegan's resignation in March 2005.

No doubt a class player on his day, McManaman won the FA Cup and League Cup with Liverpool for whom he scored sixty-six goals in 364 appearances. He helped Real win two Champions League finals and two La Liga titles to his collection and gained four youth, seven U21 and thirty-seven full caps for England. It was reported he earned £10,250 in four years at the Bernabeu in Madrid.

Off the field at City, McManaman and Fowler were caught up in a sex scandal that appeared in the *News of the World,* following a failed attempt by the pair to gain an injunction to prevent publication – costing them £50,000, in addition to making the case look like an invariable admission of guilt.

McMORRAN, Edward James (Forward)
Apps/goals: 36/12 Born: Larne, Northern Ireland, 2/9/1923 Died: Larne, 27/1/1984
Career: Larne School, Ballyclare, Larne Olympic, Belfast Celtic, CITY (£7,000, July 1947–January 1949), Leeds United, Barnsley (£10,000), Doncaster Rovers, Crewe Alexandra, Frickley Colliery; retired 1960; Dodsworth Miners' Welfare (coach).
Details: A very powerful forward, with a strong shot, Eddie McMorran did very well as a schoolboy, scored over 100 goals for Belfast Celtic, including sixty in 1945/46 when the Irish Cup was won, and represented the League of Ireland. He then started off brightly with City. Playing up front with Andrew Black and George Smith, he scored on his debut and ended his first season with ten goals. Unfortunately he lost his way after that, but despite leaving for Elland Road long before the 1948/49 season ended, McMorran still finished up as leading scorer for City's second XI. He later had decent spells with Barnsley (thirty-two goals in 104 League games) and with Doncaster (thirty-two in 126), and at the same time upped his total of full international caps to fifteen.

McMULLAN, James (Half-back)
Apps/goals: 242/12 Born: Denny, Stirlingshire, 26/3/1895 Died: Sheffield, 28/11/1964
Career: Denny Hibernian, Third Lanark, Partick Thistle, Maidstone United (player-manager), Partick Thistle, CITY (record £4,700, February 1926; retired May 1933); Oldham Athletic (manager), Aston Villa (manager), Notts County (manager), Sheffield Wednesday (secretary-manager); quit football, 1942.
Details: Perhaps the finest Scottish left-half of the 1920s, Jimmy McMullan was small and brainy, unsurpassed at 'along the turf distribution' and an inspirational captain for club and country, skippering his country (the 'Wembley Wizards') to a 5-1 win over England in 1928, the same year he played in an international trial and won the Second Division championship with City, when he netted four goals (including the winner at South Shield) in thirty-eight League appearances.

He won eight of his sixteen full caps with Partick Thistle and was once again a Cup final loser with City in 1933. McMullan also played in four

Victory internationals in 1919 and represented the Scottish League on four occasions.

McNAB, Neil (Midfield)
Apps/goals: 266/19 Born: Greenock, 4/6/1957
Career: Morton, Tottenham Hotspur, Bolton Wanderers, Brighton & Hove Albion (£250,000), Leeds United (loan), Portsmouth (loan), CITY (£35,000, July 1983–January 1990), Tranmere Rovers, Huddersfield Town (loan), Ayr United, Darlington, Derry City, Witton Albion; retired 1994; CITY (youth team coach, July 1994–May 1997), Portsmouth (coach), Exeter City (manager).
Details: A real bargain at £35,000, Neil McNab was arguably City's star of the eighties, being voted Player of the Year in both the 1986/87 and 1988/89 seasons. A skilful and very combative defensive midfielder, full of character, he twice inspired a relatively young team to promotion from the Second Division. A fine penalty-taker (ten converted), he was a credit to the club, and indeed to the others he served during a twenty-year career.

A Scottish schoolboy, youth and U21 international, his dedication and resilience resulted in 715 club matches (at various levels). He also won promotion with Tottenham and Tranmere and played in two Leyland DAF Cup finals for the latter, both at Wembley.

McNAUGHT, Kenneth (Defender)
Apps: 7 Born: Kirkcaldy, Fife, 17/1/1955
Career: Everton, Aston Villa (£200,000), West Bromwich Albion (£125,000), CITY (loan, December 1984/March 1985), Sheffield United; retired May 1986; Dunfermline Athletic (coach), Swansea City (assistant-manager), Vale of Earn/ Scotland (manager); manager of the professional golf shop at Gleneagles, Scotland.
Details: The recipient of youth and amateur caps for Scotland, Ken McNaught, commanding in the air, strong in the tackle, was the backbone of the Aston villa team that won the League title, European Cup and Super Cup in the early 1980s under the reign of former City manager, Ron Saunders. He had already made 375 club appearances before having seven more as a loanee at Maine Road, when he partnered Mick McCarthy in the back four. His father, Willie, played for Raith Rovers, Brechin City and Scotland.

McOUSTRA, William (Left-half)
Apps: 65/6 Born: Glasgow, Scotland, 1878 Died: Glasgow, 1953
Career: Ashfield, Celtic, CITY (£100, January 1902–October 1907), Blackpool, Stenhousemuir, Alloa Athletic; retired 1914; served on the Western front during the First World War; Celtic (groundstaff).

Details: Willie McOustra was initially an inside-left, fast, energetic, and always prepared to work hard for his team. However, his speed was also a problem inasmuch as he had the tendency to over-run the ball. After a dip in form, he was sold to City with Jimmy Drummond for an 'enormous price.' Eventually converted into a half-back at Hyde Road, McOustra was outstanding in 1902/03 when City won the Second Division championship.

MacRAE, Keith (Goalkeeper)
Apps: 72 Born: Glasgow, 5/2/1951
   Career: Motherwell, CITY (£100,000, October 1973–March 1981), Portland Timbers, Leeds United; retired 1983.
   Details: Keith MacRae arrived at Maine Road with a glowing reputation. The flame-haired stopper was a firm favourite at Motherwell, and was voted Player of the Year in 1969/70, the season he played right-back in a SLC game. He made his City debut in a 2-1 win at Sheffield United just after signing, replacing the out of form Joe Corrigan. MacRae kept eight clean sheets in the last twenty-five League games of 1973/74. He then over the next seven years contested the number one spot with 'Big Joe', although, incredibly, he made only four League appearances between November 1975 until his departure in March 1981. Interestingly, during this time, he took a part-time job as a journalist for the *Manchester Evening News*. He averaged just nine outings per year with City.

McREDDIE, Walter William (Forward)
Apps/goals: 31/12 Born: Lochee, Scotland, 1871 Died: Glasgow, 1939
   Career: Lochee Harp, Dundee Harp, Stoke, Middlesbrough Ironopolis, Stoke, CITY (October 1894/December 1895), Bolton Wanderers, Glasgow Celtic; retired injured, August 1896.
   Details: Wally McReddie was a clever forward but unfortunately his career was plagued by injury. He made less than 100 club appearances in total, a third of them with City, for whom he made his debut in a 3-1 win at Notts County, scored his first goal a fortnight later in a 4-3 victory over Newcastle and played his last game in a 1-1 draw with Burton Swifts in November 1895, being replaced in the front line by Hugh Morris. He also bagged four goals in City's record League win, 11-3 at Lincoln in March 1895.

McTAVISH, John Robert (Half-back)
Apps: 96 Born: Glasgow, 2/2/1932
   Career: Dalry Thistle, CITY (June 1952–November 1960), St Mirren.
   Details: Jock McTavish scored an own-goal in League games *v.* West Ham, WBA and Newcastle in November 1959, all past the unfortunate Bert Trautmann. Nevertheless, he was a useful defender who played alongside Dave Ewing during the second half of the 1953/54 season. Thereafter, regarded as a reliable reserve, he had his best run in the first team between February 1959 and April 1960.

McVICKERS, John (Right-back)
Apps: 31 Born: Edgbaston, Birmingham, 1870 Died: c. 1940
   Career: Birmingham St George's, Accrington, CITY (March 1892–May 1894), Macclesfield.
   Details: John McVickers played in City's first-ever game in the Football League *v.* Bootle in September 1892, partnering Davie Robson at full-back. When fit, he held his position until December 1893.

McWHINNIE, William John (Inside-forward)
Apps/goals: 13/4 Born: Ayrshire, Scotland, 1865
   Career: Ayr United, CITY (May 1890–May 1892), Walsall Town Swifts.
   Details: Signed with fellow Scots Bill Douglas, Davie Robson and Bill Campbell, Jock McWhinnie scored twice in City's first-ever FA Cup tie – a 12-0 qualifying victory over Liverpool Stanley in October 1890. He also played in eleven Football Alliance games for the Blues.

MACKEN, Jonathan Paul (Striker)
Apps/goals: 59/12 Born: Blackley, Manchester, 7/9/1977
   Career: Manchester United, Preston North End (£250,000), CITY (£4 million, March 2002–June 2005), Crystal Palace (£1.1 million), Ipswich Town (loan), Derby County (free), Barnsley (loan/signed for £100,000), Walsall, Northwich Victoria, Stockport County.
   Details: Jon Macken scored a dramatic late goal to earn City (3-0 down) a 4-3 win over Bournemouth in May 1989. Unfortunately, injuries and a plethora of striking options limited the number of starts he made for City.
   Although capped by England at youth team level, Macken played for the Republic of Ireland against Bulgaria in 2005. He helped Preston win the Division Two title in 2000 and reached the milestone of 500 club appearances in 2012/13.

MACKENZIE, Stephen (Midfield)
Apps/goals: 76/10 Born: Romford, Essex, 23/11/1961
   Career: Havering & Essex Schools, Byron Red Star/Romford, Crystal Palace, CITY (£250,000, July 1979–July 1981), West Bromwich Albion (£650,000), Charlton Athletic (£200,000), Sheffield Wednesday, Shrewsbury Town, Willenhall Town, Bromsgrove Rovers, Stafford Rangers, Atherstone Town (player-coach, then assistant manager), Pelsall Villa (player-manager), Gresley Rovers (player-coach), West

Bromwich Albion (Academy coach), later Press Association/PF, working on betting-related match commentary.

Details: Signed without playing a League game for Palace, Steve Mackenzie was a fine footballer, strong and hard-working with a powerful shot. In 1981, he scored one of the best FA Cup final goals ever, for City against Tottenham, and another fine strike that very same season won the Manchester derby. He made fifty-three of his senior appearances for the club in 1980/81.

By coincidence, Mackenzie made his WBA debut against City and during his time at The Hawthorns he played with David Cross, John Deehan, Tony Grealish, Robert Hopkins, Ken McNaught, Gary Owen and Imre Varadi, all of whom were associated with City at some time or another, while one of his managers was Ron Saunders.

'Macca' won the FA Youth Cup with Palace, gained fifteen youth and three U21 caps, and also played once for the England 'B' team.

MAICON, Douglas Sisenando (Wing-back)
Apps: 13 Born: Novo Hamburgo, Brazil, 26/7/1981
Career: Grëmo, Criciúma, Cruzeiro, AS Monaco, Inter Milan, CITY (August 2012).

Details: Right-wing back Maicon found it hard to get into City's first team and made only thirteen appearances in his first season at The Etihad Stadium. Highly skilful, strong and resilient, he has powered down the flank in over 450 club and international matches since making his debut in senior football for Cruzeiro in 2001. He won four trophies with Cruzeiro, collected four Serie 'A', two Coppa Italia, three Supercoppa Italia, the Champions' League and the FIFA Club World Cup winner's medals with Milan and helped Brazil win the FIFA Confederations Cup and the Copa America twice, while also gaining sixty-six full and four U21 caps on the international scene.

MALEY, William Patrick (Half-back)
Apps: 1 Born: Newry Barracks, County Down, Northern Ireland, 25/4/1868 Died: Glasgow, 2/4/1958
Career: Cathcart Hazelbank Juniors, Third Lanark, Celtic (player, match secretary, player-secretary), CITY (loan, February 1896), Celtic (player-secretary, then retired May 1897; appointed full-time secretary-manager); also President of the Scottish League.

Details: A strong personality, Willie Maley was largely responsible for building Celtic's greatness and the best known member of a famous soccer dynasty. He was appointed secretary-manager of the Glasgow club at the age of thirty-one and held his position for almost forty-three years.

He built teams to win with spirit, passion and panache, although his time in office ended in a less than happy fashion. With Celtic sitting at the bottom of the table in February 1940, Maley announced his retirement after a meeting with the board of directors. By far the longest serving manager in Celtic's history, he won sixteen Scottish Premier League titles, fourteen Scottish Cup, fourteen Glasgow and nineteen Glasgow Charity Cups. A strict disciplinarian, he described his fifty-three-year association with the Bhoys as being a 'labour of love'. Maley, whose father Tom was a soldier in the British Army, moved to Scotland with his family as a youngster and at school was a fine athlete, winning the 100 yards and half-mile races. He eventually took up soccer and signed for Celtic in 1887. A big man, strong and dependable, never flurried, he made ninety-six appearances for the Bhoys and, out of the blue, made one appearance for City in a Football League Second Division match against Loughborough FC in February 1896, deputising for Jim McBride in a 5-1 win.

Having spent a considerable amount of his childhood in Scotland, Maley gained two caps for his adopted country, playing against the English National team and ironically the Irish national football team, in 1893. He also represented the Scottish XI League. His brother Tom also played football, and was of course manager of City from 1902–06. Another brother, Alex, managed Clydebank, Hibernian and Crystal Palace in the 1920s, while Walfrid Maley (a relative), was a priest in a Glasgow church, and it was he who was solely responsible for the birth of Celtic football club – admitting he knew nothing about the practical side of the game!

MANN, Arthur Fraser (Full-back)
Apps: 44 Born: Falkirk, 23/1/1948 Died: Birmingham, 3/2/1999
Career: Denny High School, Lochore Welfare, Heart of Midlothian, CITY (record £85,000, November 1968–July 1972), Blackpool (loan), Notts County (£15,000), Shrewsbury Town (£30,000), Mansfield Town (£36,000), Boston United, Kettering Town, Boston United (player-caretaker-manager, player-manager); retired 1989; Grimsby Town (assistant-manager/coach), West Bromwich Albion (assistant-manager/coach).

Details: The most expensive full-back to come out of Scotland when he moved to Maine Road, Arthur Mann was very useful on the overlap and triggered several attacks; yet despite helping City win the League Cup in 1970, his first-team chances at the club were somewhat limited, which led to his transfer to Meadow Lane. He made 292 appearances for the Magpies in seven seasons. Mann was tragically killed in a fork-lift truck accident, aged fifty-one.

MANN, George William (Right-half)

Apps: 64/7 Born: Scotland, 1873

Career: East Stirlingshire, Blackburn Rovers, CITY (July 1894–August 1897), Bristol City.

Details: A reserve at Blackburn, George Mann was recruited by City to fill, what seemed at the time to be a problematic right-half position – seven different players had occupied that berth the previous season. Resilient and committed, he did well and had three decent campaigns at Hyde Road, scoring five of his seven goals in 1896/97, including two in the 4-1 home win over Darwen.

MANSFIELD, Ernest (Forward)

Apps: 1 Born: Manchester, 1887

Career: Northern Nomads, CITY (March/May 1909).

Details: A one match wonder, Ernie Mansfield's only appearance for City was in a 3-0 defeat at Middlesbrough, two days after joining the club.

MARGETSON, Martyn Walter (Goalkeeper)

Apps: 56 Born: West Neath, South Wales, 8/9/1971

Career: Junior football, CITY (July 1988–August 1998), Bristol Rovers (loan), Bolton Wanderers (loan), Luton Town loan), Southend United, Huddersfield Town, Cardiff City; retired 2008; engaged as goalkeeping coach by Cardiff City, Wales (under Gary Speed) and West Ham United; now runs his own property business in Cardiff.

Details: Martyn Margetson featured largely as understudy during a downturn in City's fortunes. His debut came as a substitute *v.* Torquay in a League Cup tie in October 1990, followed by his first start in May 1991 when he deputised for the suspended Tony Coton in a 1-0 defeat in the Manchester derby at Old Trafford, playing in the next game *v.* Sunderland. After failing to get a single outing between August 1993 and May 1995, he made just six appearances in the next five seasons, and was actually substituted at half-time after conceding three goals in forty-five minutes at Everton in May 1993. Two years later, he came off the bench as a striker in a League Cup tie against Wycombe, after both outfield 'subs' had already been used. He had his best spell with City in 1997/98, playing in thirty games. Unfortunately, in the penultimate match of that season against relegation rivals QPR on 25 April, he was penalised for picking up a back pass! From the resulting free-kick, taken by Kevin Gallen, ex-City star Mike Sheron scored (1-1). Later in the game, Margetson conceded an own-goal, headed in by Jamie Pollock and the points dropped in the 2-2 draw effectively cost City dearly, as they were relegated while QPR stayed up! Margetson played for Wales at schoolboy, youth, U21 (5) and 'B' team levels before gaining his only full cap *v.* Canada in 2004.

MARSDEN, Keith (Half-back/inside-left)

Apps/goals: 14/1 Born: Darley Dale, 10/4/1934 Died: South Africa, 1986

Career: Youlegreave BC, Chesterfield, CITY (July 1955–June 1959), Accrington Stanley; retired 1960; ran the Empress Cabaret Club, Stockport for several years.

Details: Keith Marsden was the 'centre-piece' of City's 'M Plan' formulated by manager Les McDowall in the mid-1950s. It proved a disaster, as the team suffered two humiliating defeats – 6-1 at Preston and 9-2 at WBA. Unfortunately, he never played for the club again. He netted just once for City, on his debut in a 2-1 defeat at Chelsea in October 1955, and scored fifteen goals in twenty-two League games for Chesterfield. He was killed in a car crash in South Africa, aged fifty-two.

MARSH, Rodney William (Forward)

Apps/goals: 152/47 Born: Hatfield, Herts, 11/10/1944

Career: Hackney Schools, Alexander Boys' Club, West Ham United, Fulham, Queen's Park Rangers (£15,000), Manchester City (£200,000, March 1972–January 1976), Cork Hibernians (loan), Tampa Bay Rowdies/USA (£45,000), Fulham, Tampa Bay Rowdies, New York United/USA (manager), Carolina Lightnin'/USA (manager), Tampa Bay Rowdies/USA (Indoor League; then Chief Executive); became a soccer pundit on TV.

Details: Rodney Marsh was signed by Malcolm Allison for a then club record £200,000. At the time, City were four points clear at the top of the table, but by the end of the season had slipped to fourth. Marsh himself has since claimed that it was he who cost the club the League title that year, believing his style simply did not suit that of the team. He nevertheless became one of City's star players, top-scoring with nineteen goals in 1972/73 when he also became the first player to net in four different competitions in the same season. Often dazzling the crowd with his skills, his superb goal against his former club, QPR, in September 1974 is regarded as one of the best-ever seen at Maine Road. He left Maine Road after disagreements with new manager Tony Book.

A Third Division championship winner and League Cup final victor in 1967 with QPR, Marsh collected a runner's-up prize in the 1974 League Cup final when City lost to Wolves.

He made his England debut as a substitute for Francis Lee, in the 1-1 draw with Switzerland at Wembley in 1971. Sir Alf Ramsey responding to the crowd chants of 'Rod-Nee, Rod-Nee.'

Marsh went on to appear in eight more internationals, scoring one goal, in a 3-0 win over Wales in May 1972, before falling out with Sir Alf!

Also capped twice at U23 level, Marsh never quite fulfilled his potential, yet still netted 270 goals in 606 appearances at club level, 134 of his goals coming in 242 appearances for QPR. He played alongside George Best at Fulham in 1976.

MARSHALL, Robert Samuel (Half-back/inside-left)
Apps/goals: 356/80 Born: Hucknall, Notts, 3/4/1903 Died: Chesterfield, 27/10/1966

Career: Hucknall Olympic, Sunderland, CITY (March 1928–March 1939), Stockport County (player-manager); retired during the Second World War; became a publican in Chesterfield.

Details: As an inside-forward, Bobby Marshall possessed exquisite ball control and was a regular marksman at Sunderland, for whom he scored sixty-eight times in 198 League matches, including a hat-trick in successive matches in 1927. He continued to find the net with City, having his best season in 1929/30 when he bagged twenty-one goals, five of them coming in an 11-1 FA Cup win over Swindon.

Marshall replaced the injured Fred Tilson in the 1933 FA Cup final defeat by Everton but returned to Wembley twelve months later and played his part in the 1-0 victory over Portsmouth. Known as 'Sunny' he switched to centre-half on the departure of Sam Cowan and collected a League championship winner's medal in 1937. He received what was then a record £650 from his testimonial in 1934.

MASON, Gary Ronald (Midfield)
Apps/goals: 24/1 Born: Edinburgh, 15/10/1979

Career: CITY (June 1996–December 2000), Hartlepool United (loan), Dunfermline Athletic, St Mirren, Dunfermline Athletic; retired July 2012.

Details: Gary Mason looked the 'fittest player on the pitch' when making his League debut in a 3-0 win over Blackpool in August 1998. He produced some fine displays after that, producing a brilliant performance on a soggy pitch at Wigan. However, he was held back during the second of the campaign and after a loan spell with Hartlepool was, perhaps surprisingly, released by manager Joe Royle halfway through 2000/01. A Scottish schoolboy international, he gained one U21 cap as a substitute *v.* Lithuania and made over 300 appearances in two spells with Dunfermline.

MAUGE, Ronald Charlton (Midfield)
Apps: 1 Born: Islington, London, 10/3/1969

Career: Charlton Athletic, Fulham, Bury (£40,000), CITY (loan, September/November 1991), Plymouth Argyle (£40,000), Bristol Rovers, St Albans City, Aldershot Town, Whitton United (player-manager); retired 2007.

Details: Ronnie Mauge made over 400 appearances at senior level and gained eight caps for Trinidad and Tobago. However, he broke his leg in a Gold Cup match against Mexico in February 2000, which set him back when he was in good form. His solitary outing for City came in 3-2 FMC defeat at Sheffield Wednesday.

MAY, Andrew Michael Peter (Midfield)
Apps/goals: 174/8 Born: Collyhurst, 26/2/1964

Career: Schoolboy football, CITY (May 1980–July 1987), Huddersfield Town, Bolton Wanderers (loan), Bristol City, Millwall, Larne (loan), Welling United.

Details: Nurtured through the youth system, Andy May was seventeen when he made his League debut for City at Ipswich in April 1981. He played in fourteen first-class matches over the next two years before having an ever-present campaign in 1983/84, following up with appearances tallies of 44 and 49. After playing in half of the fixtures in 1986/87, he moved to Huddersfield, and six months later was in the Huddersfield team that got clattered 10-1 by City, May scoring a late consolation penalty for the Terriers.

Capped once by England at U21 level, he made 481 League and Cup appearances before moving into non-League football in 1995.

MAZZARELLI, Giuseppe (Defender)
Apps: 2 Born: Uster, Switzerland, 14/8/1972

Career: FC Zurich, CITY (loan, March/May 1996), Grasshoppers, St Gallen, Bari, Baden.

Details: After impressing in a handful of second XI games, tall, rugged defender Giuseppe Mazzarelli made two substitute appearances for City in successive away League games against London clubs, Chelsea and West Ham in March 1996, before returning to Zurich. He won thirteen caps for Switzerland between 1994 and 2002.

MEADOWS, James (Full-back)
Apps/goals: 141/31 Born: Bolton, 21/7/1931 Died: Didsbury, Manchester, 11/1/1994

Career: Bolton YMCA, Southport, CITY (March 1951, retired injured, October 1957; trainer, June 1959, trainer-coach, August 1960–April 1965); Stockport County (trainer-coach, then manager), Bury (assistant-manager), Blackpool (trainer, acting manager, assistant-manager), Bolton Wanderers (manager), Southport (manager), Stockport County (manager), Blackpool (caretaker-manager); later Kuwait Sporting Club (assistant-manager/coach); GIF Sundsvall/Sweden; quit football, 1979.

Details: A centre-forward at school and an outside-right with Southport and initially with City, Jimmy Meadows developed into an international right-back who was capped by England in a 7-2 win over Scotland in 1955. Meadows who also played for an FA XI and the Football League, had two excellent seasons on the wing with City, supplying crosses for the likes of Westcott and Smith. His best scoring campaign came in 1952/53 with ten goals. In 1953/54 he led the attack before taking the number 2 shirt off Branagan, but unfortunately went off injured in the twenty-first minute of the 1955 FA Cup final defeat by Newcastle. He missed the whole of the next two seasons and retired at the age of twenty-six. As a manager, Meadows guided both Stockport (1967) and Southport (1973) to the Fourth Division title. A crowd of 38,000 attended Meadows' testimonial match in April 1958 when City played a Great Britain XI.

MEARS, Tyrone (Full-back)
Apps: 1 Born: Chadderton, Oldham, 18/2/1983
Career: CITY (May 1999–July 2002), Preston North End (£175,000), West Ham United (£1.9 million), Derby County (loan/signed, £1.1 million), Olympique Marseille (loan), Burnley (£600,000), Bolton Wanderers (£3 million with Chris Eagles).

Details: After making just one senior outing for City, as an eighty-fourth-minute substitute for Stuart Pearce against Nottingham Forest in March 2002, Tyrone Mears has gone on to make over 250 appearances for six other clubs, having his best spell with Burnley. He scored for Marseille in a UEFA Cup game against Ajax. Of Sierra Leonean descent, Mears, despite being ineligible to do so, played for Jamaica against Nigeria in 2009.

MEE, Benjamin Thomas (Defender)
Apps: 1 Born: Sale, Cheshire, 21/9/1989
Career: CITY (May 2006–January 2012), Leicester City (loan), Burnley (loan/signed).

Details: After captaining City's Academy side to FA Youth Cup glory in 2008, Ben Mee made his only senior appearance for the club in a League Cup tie against WBA in September 2010, lining up alongside Javan Vidal and John Guidetti. Six City's starters in that game were aged twenty-one or younger. Capped by England eight times at U19 and U20 levels, Mee has since appeared in two U21 internationals. He played under Sven-Göran Eriksson at Leicester.

MEEHAN, Peter (Full-back)
Apps: 6 Born: Broxburn, Scotland, 28/2/1872 Died: 1915
Career: Broxburn Shamrock, Hibernian, Sunderland, Glasgow Celtic, Everton, Southampton (record £200), CITY (£100, September 1900/May 1901), Barrow, Clyde, Broxburn Athletic; retired 1905.

Details: Originally employed in the Linlithgowshire coal mines, well-built right-back Peter Meehan helped Southampton win the Southern League title for the third time and also played in the 1900 FA Cup final before joining City. In his only season at Hyde Road he partnered Di Jones in each of his six League games.

MEGSON, Gary John (Midfield)
Apps/goals: 97/2 Born: Manchester, 2/5/1959
Career: Frampton Rangers, Parkway Juniors, Mangotsfield United, Plymouth Argyle, Everton (loan/signed, £250,000), Sheffield Wednesday (£130,000), Nottingham Forest (£170,000), Newcastle United (£110,000), Sheffield Wednesday (loan/signed, £65,000), CITY (£250,000, January 1989–July 1992), Norwich City (player/assistant-manager), Lincoln City, Shrewsbury Town; retired October 1995; Bradford City (assistant-manager/coach), Norwich City (manager), Blackpool (manager), Stockport County manager), Stoke City (manager), West Bromwich Albion (manager), Nottingham Forest (manager), Leicester City manager), Bolton Wanderers (manager), Sheffield Wednesday (manager), Blackburn Rovers (manager for twenty-eight minutes, 2013).

Details: Hard-working and aggressive, Gary Megson had an excellent career, which spanned eighteen years, during which time he scored fifty goals in 588 club appearances (499 in the Football League). He made a scoring debut for City against Oldham Athletic soon after arriving at Maine Road and played his part in clinching promotion that season. Absent for the first half of the 1989/90 campaign, he returned in mid-December against his former club, Everton, and went on to make almost 100 appearances for the Blues before switching to Carrow Road.

Megson, whose father, Don was a full-back with Sheffield Wednesday, was Everton's first-ever loan signing (1979) and played in three losing FA Cup semi-finals: 1980, 1983 and 1986. As a manager, he twice took WBA into the Premiership (2002 and 2004) and up to 2013 had been in charge in 648 matches.

MELLOR, Ian (Forward)
Apps/goals: 50/10 Born: Sale, Cheshire, 19/2/1950
Career: Wythenshawe Schools, CITY (November 1967–March 1973), Norwich City (£65,000), Brighton & Hove Albion, Chester City, Sheffield Wednesday, Bradford City; retired May 1984; was an executive with the PFA for many years; also worked for Puma and Gola sportswear companies.

Details: Nicknamed 'Spider', Ian Mellor spent five-and-a-half years at Maine Road, having his best season in 1971/72 when he had twenty-three outings, scoring three goals, including the winner against Liverpool (1-0).

His career spanned almost seventeen years, during which time he amassed over 350 club appearances, having his best spell with Brighton (1974–78). His father Neil played for Preston.

MELROSE, James Millsop (Forward)
Apps/goals: 42/11 Born: Glasgow, 7/10/1958

Career: Eastercraigs FC, Partick Thistle, Leicester City (£250,000), Coventry City (player-exchange), Celtic (£100,000), Wolverhampton Wanderers (loan), CITY (£40,000, November 1984–March 1986), Charlton Athletic (£45,000), Leeds United (£50,000), Shrewsbury Town (loan/signed, £50,000), Macclesfield Town, Curzon Athletic; retired May 1991; later worked in advertising and printing.

Details: 'Carrot top' Jim Melrose scored 131 goals in 486 club appearances. He made his City debut as a substitute against Birmingham soon after signing and during December 1984, netted in five consecutive League games, including a strike against his future club Charlton.

He gained Scottish Cup and League Cup runner's-up medals with Celtic, played for Charlton in the 1987 FMC final at Wembley, won eight U21 caps for Scotland and twice represented the Scottish League.

In 1988, Melrose fractured his cheek-bone in a clash with Swindon's Chris Kamara. At Shrewsbury Magistrates Court, Kamara was found guilty of assault and fined £1,200 (plus costs) and made to pay Melrose £250.

MEREDITH, William Henry (Outside-right)
Apps/goals: 394/151 Born: Black Park, Chirk near Wrexham, 30/7/1874 Died: Withington, Manchester, 19/4/1958

Career: Black Park FC, Chirk, Wrexham, Northwich Victoria, CITY (October 1894–May 1906); Manchester United, Port Vale (First World War guest), CITY (July 1921, player-coach, retired April 1924); Manchester Central (coach); was also a partner in the sports outfitters, Pilling and Briggs.

Details: Considered one of the game's early superstars, wing-wizard Billy Meredith made his senior debut with Chirk in 1890 and played his last competitive game, for City, in 1924. Banned for eighteen months for bribing Aston Villa defender Alex Leake with £10 to lose a match, he missed the whole of the 1905/06 season, yet played regularly during the First World War, and taking everything into account, stayed in the game for thirty-three years.

The youngest of ten children, Meredith won his first medal at the age of ten at dribbling while being coached at school by Mr T. E. Thomas, who was a firm believer in 'keeping the ball on the ground.' Meredith never forgot that advice.

As a youngster, he worked down the pit as a pony driver, 'unhooking' tubs and 'hutching' with no real intention of becoming a footballer. In fact, he hinted that he wanted to be an engineer like his father and brother Elias. However, at the age of sixteen he was recruited by Chirk and, after making good progress, played in the Welsh Combination with Wrexham before teaming up with City – this, after Bolton Wanderers' secretary John Bentley had 'shilly-shallied' about signing him, following a request by future City star Di Jones, a friend of Meredith's who was already playing for Bolton, who simply knew that his pal would become a class performer.

He made his City debut against Newcastle in November 1894 and it was quite a coincidence that he should play his last game of football at the age of forty-nine years and 245 days for City against the same opponents in the 1924 FA Cup semi-final.

In a wonderful career, Meredith scored 218 goals in 872 club/international matches, with 186 of his goals coming in 726 appearances for City and United alone. An ever-present in City's ranks four times, he captained the Blues to their first major trophy, a 1-0 FA Cup final victory over Bolton in 1904 when he drove home the all-important goal. He twice won the League title with rivals United, 1908 and 1910, collected a second Cup winner's medal in 1909 and was a victor in two FA Charity Shield matches. He also netted nine hat-tricks for City and a crowd of 15,000 attended his benefit match in 1925.

He gained twenty-two of his forty-eight Welsh caps while at Hyde Road and netted eleven international goals in total. He also played for Denbighshire against Mid Wales. A natural rebel, he helped form the Players' Union (the forerunner to the current PFA) and in 1909, was declared bankrupt after failing as a businessman with Pilling & Briggs. Meredith, nicknamed 'old skinny', always played with a toothpick in his hand, and was described by one reporter as being '…like the brook, he dribbles on forever.' Oh, yes, he could certainly do that – he loved it. His brother, Sam, played for Stoke while Charlie Roberts (ex Manchester United) was his brother-in-law. In 2007, Meredith was inducted into the Football Hall of Fame. There is also a road in Manchester called Billy Meredith Close.

METTOMO, Lucien (Defender)
Apps/goals: 31/1 Born: Douala, Cameroon, 19/4/1977

Career: Tonnerre Yaounde, St Etienne, CITY (£1.5 million, October 2001–March 2003), FC

Kaiserslautern, Kaysem Ereiyesspor, Luzern, Southampton, Veira FC.

Details: A Kevin Keegan signing, Lucien Mettomo, 6 feet tall, made his City debut as a substitute in a 6–0 League Cup win over Birmingham City, but endured a rather frustrating second year at the club, rarely featuring in the first team due to the signing of Sylvain Distin. He scored his only goal against Bradford City in his first season and helped the Blues win the First Division title in 2002. He won twenty-nine caps for Cameroon (1997–2004), playing in the 2002 and 2004 World Cups.

MIDDLETON, Harold (Defender)
Apps/goals: 41/4 Born: Ashbourne, Derbyshire, 1869
Career: Derby Junction, CITY (March 1892–February 1894), Loughborough Town.
Details: Stocky and resourceful, Harry Middleton made his debut for City at left-back in an Alliance game against Walsall Town Swifts a week after joining. In 1892/93 he was the club's regular right-half, missing just one game and scoring two goals. He also played at right-back and inside-right.

MIKE, Adrian Roosevelt (Forward)
Apps/goals: 19/2 Born: Manchester, 16/11/1973
Career: Junior football, CITY (July 1990–August 1995), Bury (loan), Linkoping (loan), Stockport County (£60,000), Hartlepool United (loan), Doncaster Rovers (loan/signed), Leek Town, Hednesford Town, Southport, Northwich Victoria, Stalybridge Celtic, Lincoln City, Gainsborough Trinity (loan), Cliftonville/Ireland, Droylsden, Mossley, Leek Town; retired 2004; now a personal fitness trainer.
Details: An England schoolboy and youth international, and City's Young Player of the Year in 1991, Adie Mike came through the junior ranks to make his senior debut against Notts County in April 1992, scoring his first goal in the next match against Oldham. He also played in three Premiership games before transferring to Stockport. Injuries let him down badly and during his career Mike made 199 FL appearances and 125 at non-League level.

MIKE, Leon (Forward)
Apps: 2 Born: Manchester, 4/9/1981
Career: CITY (July 1997–February 2002), Oxford United (loan), Halifax Town (loan), Aberdeen, Mossley, FC United; retired 2006; began a Law Degree at Liverpool college in 2007.
Details: Leon Mike had his first taste of League football on loan at Oxford in 2000/01. The following season he was part of a group of youngsters selected to train with City's senior squad, and after scoring a hat-trick in a second XI game in the November, he made his debut as a

first-half substitute for the injured Shaun Goater at Portsmouth, making his only start for the club in the match against Rotherham. He later made thirty-three SPL appearances for Aberdeen.

MILARVIE, Robert (Outside-left)
Apps/goals: 73/14 Born: Pollockshields, 8/4/1864 Died: Gorton, 30/11/1912
Career: Pollockshields, Hibernian, Stoke, Derby County, Burslem Port Vale, Derby County, Newton Heath, CITY (May 1891–retired May 1896).
Details: A direct winger, Bob Milarvie appeared for Stoke in the inaugural season of League football, starred in City's first-ever League game against Bootle in September 1892, and was the first player to serve both major clubs in the Potteries and also in Manchester. He scored twenty-six goals in 120 club appearances during his career, having his best spell by far with City. The FA censored Port Vale for fielding Milarvie after he had rejoined Derby in 1889.

MILLER, Ishmail Anthony (Striker)
Apps: 20 Born: Moston, Manchester, 5/3/1987
Career: CITY (July 2003–August 2007), West Bromwich Albion (loan/signed, £1.2 million), Queen's Park Rangers (loan), Nottingham Forest, Middlesbrough (loan).
Details: An attacking midfielder before becoming an out-and-out striker, Ishmail Miller, 6 feet 3 inches tall, fourteen stone in weight, impressed in City's second XI, before making his Premiership debut as a substitute against Wigan in March 2006. He top-scored for the reserves that season and featured regularly in manager Stuart Pearce's plans during 2006/07, making his first senior start in a 2–0 victory over West Ham. Unfortunately, he failed to establish himself in the team, nor could he score goals, and eventually moved to WBA. He helped the Baggies gain promotion from the Championship in his first season at The Hawthorns and did likewise with QPR in 2011.

MILLAR, James (Half-back)
Apps: 4 Born: Bolton, 1870
Career: Bolton Wanderers, CITY (March–May 1896), Bolton Wanderers.
Details: Recruited on a short-term basis, Jim Miller played in two League games (v. Newcastle & Notts County) and two Test Matches (v. Small Heath) before returning to Bolton.

MILLER, John (Inside-right)
Apps/goals: 8/2 Born: Edinburgh, 5/5/1878 Died: Johannesburg, c. 1945
Career: Hamilton Academical, CITY (August 1902–October 1903); emigrated to South Africa.
Details: Jack Miller partnered Billy Meredith on the right-wing in all of his eight League outings for

City, scoring in the 1-1 draw at Burnley and a 3-0 win over Gainsborough Trinity. After losing his place to Jimmy Bannister and being overlooked for a year, he chose to leave the UK.

MILLS, Daniel John (Right-back)
Apps: 54/1 Born: Norwich, 18/5/1977

Career: Norfolk Schools, Norwich City, Charlton Athletic (£350,000), Leeds United (£4.37 million), Middlesbrough (loan), CITY (free, June 2004), Hull City (loan), Charlton Athletic (loan), Derby County (loan); retired August 2009; became a TV soccer pundit.

Details: As a teenager, right-back Danny Mills made the strange admission that he disliked football and would never watch it once he stopped playing! Despite his odd attitude, he made 387 appearances for his seven clubs (six goals), won the League Cup with Middlesbrough and collected three Youth, one 'B', fourteen U21 and nineteen full caps for England, playing every minute of the 2002 World Cup campaign.

He made his City debut on the opening in August 2004, a 1-1 draw with Fulham, started the majority of matches that season, but was dropped in March 2005 by new manager Stuart Pearce. He regained his place seven months later and scored his only goal for City with a cracking 25-yard drive against Everton. However, a month later, he sustained a shin injury that resulted in a fifteen-game absence. The injury coincided with the emergence of Micah Richards and after that he struggled to get into the first team. Three loans spells with different clubs, followed before his contract expired, announcing his retirement on air on *BBC Five Live* soon afterwards.

Keeping himself fit, Mills ran in the 2010 Brighton marathon in a time of two hours forty-three minutes.

MILLS, Lee Rowan (Striker)
Apps: 3 Born: Mexborough, 10/7/1970

Career: Stocksbridge Park Steels FC, Wolverhampton Wanderers, Derby County (£400,000), Port Vale (£200,000), Bradford City (£1 million), CITY (loan, March/April 2000), Portsmouth (£1m), Coventry City (free), Stoke City (loan/signed), Telford United, Hereford United; retired 2005; Bridgnorth Town (manager).

Details: Following his debut against Barnsley, Lee Mills made little impact after being asked to play wide on the wing by manager Joe Royle, although he did set up Paul Dickov's late winner against Bolton with Premiership football beckoning. Mills scored 125 goals in over 400 career appearances, helping Hereford reach the Conference play-offs before retiring.

MILLS, Matthew Claude (Defender)
Apps: 2 Born: Swindon, 14/7/1986

Career: Southampton, Coventry City (loan), Bournemouth (loan), CITY (£750,000, January 2006/August 2007), Colchester United (loan), Doncaster Rovers (loan/signed), Reading, Leicester City, Bolton Wanderers.

Details: After winning nine caps for England at U18 and U19 levels, strapping central defender Matt Mills joined City, linking up with reserve manager Steve Wigley, with whom he had worked at Southampton's Academy. Displaying confidence, he played well in the second XI but managed only two Premiership outings; his first as a substitute at Chelsea, before transferring to Reading whom he captained in the Championship play-off final of 2011, scoring in the defeat by Swansea at Wembley.

MILNE, John (Utility)
Apps/goals: 37/8 Born: Farnworth, Bolton, 1862

Career: Bolton Wanderers, CITY (July 1890–May 1894).

Details: Jack Milne set up three of City's twelve goals in their first victory in the FA Cup *v.* Liverpool Stanley in October 1890. He scored five times himself in eighteen Football Alliance games in 1891/82 and made eight appearances in City's first season in Division Two. During his time with the Blues, he occupied all three half-back and the five forward positions, such was his versatility. He played in all twenty-two games for Bolton in the first season of League football.

MILNER, James Philip (Wide-midfield)
Apps/goals: 114/8 Born: Wortley, Leeds, 4/1/1986

Career: Rawden FC, Leeds United, Swindon Town (loan), Newcastle United (£3.6 million), Aston Villa (loan/signed for £12 million), Manchester City (£13 million, plus Stephen Ireland, August 2010).

Details: An all-purpose footballer, with good pace and a fair bit of skill, James Milner is able, and willing, to play at full-back, in the centre of midfield, out on the flanks and even through the middle. A real workhorse, he represented England at U15, U17, U19, U20 and U21 levels (scoring nine goals in a record forty-six appearances in the latter category) before winning his first full cap in August 2009, coming on as a second-half substitute in the friendly against Holland. He subsequently played in the 2010 World Cup finals, in all of the Euro 2012 Championship matches and was in Roy Hodgson's squad for the 2014 World Cup. He ended 2012/13 with thirty-eight senior caps to his name (one goal).

Joining City in a deal that took Stephen Ireland to Villa Park (both players being rated at £13 million each), he has so far had three solid seasons at the club, making well over 100 appearances and gaining FA Cup and Premiership winner's medals in 2011 and 2012.

At May 2013, Milner had played in almost 450 club games and when he netted for Leeds against Sunderland on Boxing Day 2002, he became, at that time, the Premiership's youngest-ever goalscorer at sixteen years, 356 days.

MILSOM, John (Forward)
Apps/goals: 34/22 Born: Bedminster, 22/7/1907 Died: Ashton, 20/4/1977

Career: Hopewell House Mission/Bristol, Exeter City (trial), Bristol Rovers, Kettering Town, Rochdale, Bolton Wanderers (£1,750), CITY (£4,000, February 1938; retired May 1943); Second World War guest for Bristol City and Fulham.

Details: Jack Milsom scored seven goals in two days against Tranmere in December 1938 – four in a record 9-3 away win on Boxing Day and a hat-trick in a 5-2 home victory twenty-four hours later. Playing between Alec Herd and Peter Doherty, he was terrific during the first half of that season before an injury let in Jimmy Heale.

Discarded by Kettering (as a crock), he was Bolton's leading scorer six seasons running from 1931 to 1937, banging in 153 goals in 255 appearances during his nine years at Burnden Park, helping the Trotters win promotion in 1935. Five years earlier, in October 1930, he fractured his right leg in a Lancashire Cup tie against his future club, City!

MIMMS, Robert Andrew (Goalkeeper)
Apps: 3 Born: York, 12/10/1963

Career: Halifax Town, Rotherham United, Everton (£150,000), Notts County (loan), Sunderland (loan), Blackburn Rovers (loan), CITY (loan, September–October 1987), Tottenham Hotspur (£325,000), Aberdeen (loan), Blackburn Rovers, Crystal Palace, Preston North End, Rotherham United, York City (player-coach), Mansfield Town (player-coach); retired May 2002; Wolverhampton Wanderers (goalkeeping coach), Blackburn Rovers (goalkeeping coach).

Details: Bobby Mimms, who made his debut for Everton against City in October 1985, was loaned out from Goodison Park to Maine Road two years later and played in successive League games for City against Leeds, Hull City and Leicester when Eric Nixon was sidelined. During his twenty-year career, he made a total of 507 appearances with thirteen clubs, played under fifteen different managers, gained three England U21 caps, and won the First Division with Everton in 1987 and the Premiership with Blackburn in 1995.

MITCHELL, James Frederick (Goalkeeper)
Apps: 109 Born: Manchester, 18/11/1897 Died: Manchester, 30/5/1975

Career: Arnold Grammar School/Blackpool, Manchester University, Blackpool, Northern Nomads, Preston North End, CITY (May 1922–October 1926), Leicester City; retired May 1927; was a schoolteacher at Arnold GS; later secretary of Stead & Simpson Sports Club; competed in the high jump at the 1920 Olympic Games.

Details: The son of a champion billiards player, Fred Mitchell's impressive start to his League career was halted by the First World War. A hefty goalkeeper who used his feet more than his hands, he was the first footballer to play in a League game, an FA Cup final and also a full international for England, wearing spectacles. His last game for Preston was, in fact, the 1922 Cup final defeat by Huddersfield. He then served City for over four years, sharing the duties initially with Jimmy Goodchild before going on to make over 100 appearances, up to December 1925 when Goodchild reclaimed his first-team place.

Gaining his only cap in 1924 against Ireland, Mitchell also appeared in six amateur internationals, two as a City player. Unfortunately, he missed several games because of his duties as a schoolteacher.

MOFFATT, James (Half-back)
Apps: 22/4 Born: Paisley 1875 Died: Glasgow, c. 1954.

Career: Bo'ness, Aberdeen, Bo'ness, Paisley St Mirren, Chatham, Gravesend United, Walsall, Tottenham Hotspur, St Mirren, CITY (December 1902–May 1906), Kilmarnock, Watford, Aberdeen; retired 1912.

Details: During a varied career spanning some twenty years, Jimmy Moffatt ventured here, there and everywhere. A hard tackling defender, he had his best spells with Walsall (1899/1900) and City, making his debut for the Blues against Doncaster Rovers on New Year's Day 1903 and scoring in his final game, a shattering 6-1 defeat at Middlesbrough in April 1906. He is the brother of Bobby Moffatt (below).

MOFFATT, Robert (Half-back)
Apps: 163/7 Born: Dumfries, 1872 Died: Kilmarnock, c. 1938

Career: St Mirren, CITY (August 1895–April 1903; then reserve team player-coach; retired as a player, May 1907); Kilmarnock (coach).

Details: The mustachioed Bobby Moffatt was the 'feeder-in-chief' for right-winger Billy Meredith. After long period of reserve team football, he established himself in the first XI in 1897 and over the next five years produced some manful performances, his skill and endurance making him a stand-out figure. He made his City debut at Crewe in October 1895 and played his last game against Doncaster in January 1903. The Moffatt brothers, albeit in different roles, were at Kilmarnock together in 1907/08.

MOONEY, Felix (Inside-left/centre-forward)
Apps/goals: 9/4 Born: Liverpool, c. 1870
Died: Staffordshire, after 1920.
    Career: Bootle, CITY (November 1892–June 1895), Bury, Walsall.
    Details: Felix Mooney, although regarded as a reserve, certainly came up trumps when called into the first team, scoring four goals in nine starts during the second half of the 1892/93 season. Unfortunately he never figured after that due to the presence of so many other preferred forwards – over twenty of them!

MORGAN, Hugh (Forward)
Apps: 15/2 Born: Lanarkshire, c. 1878
    Career: Harthill Thistle, Airdrieonians, Sunderland, Bolton Wanderers (£200), Newton Heath, CITY (July 1901/May 1902), Accrington Stanley, Blackpool; retired 1910.
    Details: A fair-haired, energetic forward, small and skilful, Hugh Morris helped Sunderland finish second in the First Division in 1898 and suffered relegation from the top flight with Bolton before suffering a similar fate with City in 1902, when he played in a third of the League games, scoring once, in a 3-1 win over Nottingham Forest. His other goal came in a 4-2 FA Cup win over Preston. In a career of many peaks and troughs, Morris netted thirty-seven goals in 144 League appearances.

MORLEY, David Thomas (Defender)
Apps: 3 Born: St Helens, 25/9/1977
    Career: CITY (July 1994–August 1998), Ayr United (loan), Southend United, Carlisle United (loan/signed), Oxford United (loan/signed), Doncaster Rovers, Macclesfield Town, Hyde United, Bangor City.
    Details: A commanding defender (6 feet 2 inches tall), Dave Morley made 20 starts for City's second XI in 1996/97 before breaking into the first team the following season, scoring on his debut against Bury in September 1997. Two substitute outings followed before his departure to Southend. He made over 100 appearances for Macclesfield (2005–07).

MORLEY, Trevor William (Forward)
Apps/goals: 82/21 Born: Nottingham, 20/3/1961
    Career: Corby Town, Nuneaton Borough, Northampton Town (£20,000), CITY (£175,000, player-exchange deal involving Tony Adcock, January 1988/December 1989), West Ham United (£500,000), FC Brann Bergen/Norway (loan, three spells), Reading, Sogndal/Norway; retired 1998; Arsenal (scout in Norway), Bergen Sparta/Norway (manager); lives in Norway, works as a TV soccer pundit.
    Details: Trevor Morley's equalising goal for City at Bradford on the final day of the 1988/89

season clinched automatic promotion from the Second Division. Having made his debut at home to Aston Villa four months earlier, he played very well alongside David White, Imre Varadi and Paul Simpson and continued to produce the goods the following season when Paul Moulden joined the attack. He left Maine Road shortly after new manager Howard Kendall had taken over from Mel Machin. In an excellent career, Morley netted 174 goals in 517 appearances for his four Football League clubs, and gained six semi-international caps for England before joining Northampton, whose manager was Graham Carr, father of TV comedian Alan Carr.

MORRIS, Hugh (Forward)
Apps/goals: 73/31 Born: Chirk, 1872
Died: Chirk, 20/9/1897
    Career: Chirk, CITY (March 1891–December 1893), Sheffield United, CITY (November 1895/May 1896), Grimsby Town, Millwall Athletic (until his death).
    Details: An industrious forward, 5 feet 6 inches tall, a writer dubbed Hugh Morris as 'an exceedingly clever player', while another wrote 'inclined to pass to and fro when a well aimed shot was needed.' Capped three times by Wales (once with each of his League clubs), he scored twice in City's first-ever League game, a 7-0 home win over Bootle in September 1892. The previous season he bagged a goal in City's first Alliance match, also against Bootle. He actually finished up as City's top marksman in 1893/94 despite leaving the club halfway through the campaign. Sadly, Morris died from tuberculosis just after signing for Millwall.

MORRIS, Hugh (Outside-right)
Apps: 61 Born: Giffnock, Renfrewshire,
19/11/1900 Died: c. 1965
    Career: Hardgate BC, Clyde, CITY (August 1922–July 1924), Nottingham Forest, Notts County, Southend United, Newport County; retired 1931.
    Details: Hugh Morris partnered Frank Roberts on City's right-wing for the majority of the 1922/23 season and Roberts and Jack Warner in the next campaign. Quick over the ground, surprisingly he never scored for City and only netted once for Forest, having his best spell with Southend – fourteen goals in 117 League games.

MORRISON, Andrew Charles (Defender)
Apps/goals: 48/5 Born: Inverness, 30/7/1970
    Career: Kinlochbervie BC, Plymouth Argyle, Blackburn Rovers, Blackpool, Huddersfield Town, CITY (£80,000, October 1998–May 2002), Blackpool (loan), Crystal Palace (loan), Sheffield United (loan), Bury (trial); retired June 2002; Worcester City (assistant-manager/

coach), Northwich Victoria (coach), Airbus UK Broughton (assistant-manager/coach).

Details: Powerful centre-back Andy Morrison brought some organisation and solidity to City's defence. But his conduct on the field led to numerous yellow cards, plus a few red (one for spitting at Wimbledon's Carl Cort in 1999) and lengthy suspensions. In fact, he was dismissed in a Division One game *v.* Fulham for sticking out his tongue at Stan Collymore, and during an FA Cup tie against Liverpool was cautioned by a police officer after squirting water at opposition fans.

Morrison made twenty-eight appearances in his first season at Maine Road and aptly with his 'fearsome' reputation, scored on his Halloween debut *v.* Colchester (won 2-1), but injuries were to affect him badly as time wore on and in fact he was also in line for an international call from Scotland manager Craig Brown but suffered serious knee damage which persisted and eventually resulted in early retirement.

Regarded as something of a cult hero among City supporters, he captained the team to victory in the 2000 Division Two play-off final over Gillingham at Wembley and the club's official magazine voted him as City's third best skipper ever, behind Tony Book and Roy Paul. His club career realised 310 appearances, 133 coming with Plymouth.

In August 2006, Morrison pleaded guilty to four charges of fraud concerning income support, jobseeker's allowance, and council tax benefits, dating from August 2003 to July 2005 that amounted to £6,500. He failed to inform the authorities that he had £58,000 in his bank account while claiming benefits. He was ordered to pay £95 costs and carry out a fifty-hour community punishment order.

MOULDEN, Paul Anthony (Striker)
Apps/goals: 78/26 Born: Farnworth, Bolton, 6/9/1967
Career: Bolton Lads' Club, CITY (June 1984–June 1989), Bournemouth (£160,000), Oldham Athletic (£225,000), Brighton & Hove Albion (loan), Birmingham City (£150,000), Huddersfield Town, Rochdale, Accrington Stanley, Bacup Borough; retired May 1999; Bolton Lads' Boys Club (coach), CITY (Academy coach, mid-2000s).

Details: As a teenager, Paul Moulden was highly-rated, a star of the future, after netting 289 goals in just forty matches in 1981/82 when playing for the Bolton Lads' Club. This terrific feat earned him a place in the Guinness Book of Records. He continued to find the net for City, bagging twelve goals in thirteen FA Youth Cup games in 1985/86, collecting a winner's medal for his efforts. He was then leading marksman for the first team in 1988/89 with seventeen goals, his best season in term of goals scored and appearances made (forty-

two). His League career bought him forty-six goals in 183 outings.

His father, Tony Moulden, played for Bury, Rochdale, Peterborough and Notts County.

MPENSA, Eka Basunga Lokonda (Striker)
Apps/goals: 11/3 Born: Zelik, Belgium, 4/7/1978
Career: LC Mesvins, KV Kortrijk, Racing Excelsior Mouscron, Standard Liege, Schalke 04, Standard Liege, Hamburger SV, Al-Rayyan/Qatar, CITY (loan/signed, February 2007/July 2008), Plymouth Argyle, Sion, Neftchi Baku.

Details: Signed after playing and scoring in a specially arranged match at Eastlands, 'Emile' Mpenza told Belgian radio station Bel-RTL ,'I make this move as revenge, with respect to all those who criticised my decision to play in Qatar'. Initially on loan, he made his City debut against Wigan Athletic as a half-time substitute for Georgios Samaras and was arguably City's best player. He scored his first Premiership goal in the 2–0 win over Middlesbrough a month after joining. However, facing competition from Roland Bianchi, Valeri Bojinov, Geovanni Deiberson Maurício and Elano, all signed by new manager Sven-Göran Eriksson in summer 2007, Mpenza did not score again after September, and was released at the end of the season. Capped seventeen times by Belgium at U18-21 levels, he scored nineteen goals in fifty-seven full internationals between 1997 and 2009.

MULHEARN, Kenneth John (Goalkeeper)
Apps: 62 Born: Liverpool, 16/10/1945
Career: Stockport County, CITY (September 1967–March 1971), Shrewsbury Town, Crewe Alexandra; retired 1983; later ran a pub in Shrewsbury.

Details: Two days after Ken Mulhearn joined City, first choice goalkeeper Harry Dowd sustained an injury, and as result, Mulhearn made his debut in front of 63,000 fans in the Manchester derby. He kept his place for the remainder of the season, gaining a League championship medal. He started the following campaign as first choice, but was dropped by manager Malcolm Allison following after a 'poor show' in the European Cup game against Fenerbahçe. Demoted to third choice behind Dowd and Joe Corrigan, he returned to the first team off and on during the 1969/70 season, but after Corrigan had cemented himself between the posts, he eventually switched his allegiance to Shrewsbury. He made 608 League appearances overall, 370 for Crewe.

MULLIGAN, James Alphonso (Left-back)
Apps: 3 Born: Belfast, 27/4/1895
Died: Manchester, 1960
Career: St Patrick's College, Bessbrook Strollers, St David's Swifts, Belfast Celtic, CITY (November

1920–September 1923), Southport, Manchester North End, Manchester Central; retired 1930.

Details: Reserve Jimmy Mulligan made two of his three appearances for City against Burnley and Newcastle in April 1922 when he deputised for Eli Fletcher. His third game followed against Oldham eight months later.

MUNDY, Harold James (Forward)

Apps: 3 Born: Wythenshawe, 2/9/1948

Career: Ashland Rovers, CITY (August 1966–June 1971), Bangor City.

Details: Reserve to several quality goalscorers during his five seasons at Maine Road, Jim Mundy made his City debut as a substitute at Leeds in April 1969, started against Newcastle a month later and made his third and final appearance *v.* Wolves in October 1969.

MUNN, Stuart (Half-back)

Apps: 20 Born: Glasgow, 22/8/1873

Career: Maryhill, Third Lanark, Burnley, Grimsby Town, CITY (November 1897–May 1901), Watford; returned to Scotland.

Details: A very serviceable, hard-working Scot, good in the tackle, Stuart Munn had his best spell with City at the end of the 1897/98 season, making eight appearances while occupying both wing-half positions.

MUNRO, James Francis (Forward)

Apps: 25/4 Born: Garmouth, Scotland, 25/3/1926 Died: c. 2000

Career: West End FC, Elgin City; Second World War guest for Aberdeen and Dunfermline Athletic; Waterford United, CITY (November 1947–March 1950), Oldham Athletic (£5,750), Lincoln City, Bury, Weymouth, Poole Town; Elgin City (player-coach); retired 1963; later worked for a brewery and spent seventeen years with the Post Office.

Details: A small but gifted footballer, two-footed and a clever dribbler, Jimmy Munro failed to score in his first seven outings for City, but after a very quiet second season, he earned his wages with three goals in seventeen appearances in 1949/50, including one in the Manchester derby in September.

Munro occupied all five forward positions during his career that saw him net almost seventy goals in 375 club appearances (fifty-six in 346 League games).

MURPHY, William (Forward)

Apps: 220/31 Born: St Helens, 23/3/1895 Died: Liverpool, 7/1/1962

Career: Peasley Cross Juniors, Alexandra Victoria, Liverpool (trial), CITY (February 1918–August 1926), Southampton (£350), Oldham Athletic (£100), Tranmere Rovers, Ellesmere Port;

Second World War guest for Grimsby Town; retired 1942.

Details: 'Spud' Murphy was a fast-raiding, tricky outside-left ('quick, cute and clever' wrote one scribe). He also had plenty of added stamina and ,when the opportunity arose, could let rip with a thumping good shot. A brilliant cross-country runner, he took up football when his athletics club disbanded, and shortly before the outbreak of the First World War he joined Alexandra Victoria, switching to City in 1918, to start a seven-year association with the club. After twenty-three wartime appearances, he made his League debut against Bolton in September 1919 and missed only six games that season. In fact, from his debut day until the end of February 1923, he missed only four competitive matches of a possible 159, having his best scoring spell in 1921/22. He retained his wing position until February 1924, and although a few injuries interrupted his routine after that, he went marching on before transferring to Southampton, having been replaced by George Hicks.

Murphy was reputed to be so fast that he was in great demand by pigeon fanciers for conveying the time of arrival of birds to headquarters!

MURRAY, Hugh (Outside-left)

Apps: 1 Born: Drybridge, 5/8/1936

Career: Dalry Thistle, CITY (April 1954–June 1960), Altrincham.

Details: A permanent reserve at Maine Road, Hugh Morris made his solitary League appearance for City in the 3-1 home win over Sheffield United in April 1956, when he stood in for Roy Clarke.

MURRAY, Colin James Robert (Centre-forward)

Apps/goals: 79/46 Born: Elvington, Kent, 11/10/1935 Died: Lichfield, 27/9/2008

Career: Eythorne BC, Wolverhampton Wanderers, CITY (£27,000, November 1963–May 1967), Walsall, Telford United; retired May 1971; ran a grocery business in Tamworth for twenty-four years; also worked for a contract car firm.

Details: Jimmy Murray and his strike-partner Derek Kevan netted a combined total of ninety-one goals in two seasons for City (1963–65). A scoring machine, he had previously bagged 166 goals in 299 appearances for Wolves, with whom he won two League championships and the FA Cup. He also notched a double hat-trick (six goals) in a reserve game against Chesterfield in 1961 and gained two England U23 caps as a 'Wolf.' Signed by manager George Poyser, who first spotted him while scouting for the Molineux club in the early 1950s, Murray was two-footed, quick over 20–30 yards and, given the chance, could use his head as well. He scored on his City debut at Southampton, and in fact struck thirteen goals in his first eight outings, including hat-tricks in 6-1 and 8-1 wins over Rotherham and Scunthorpe in the space of five days either side of Christmas. After two relatively quiet campaigns, he moved back to the Midlands and joined Walsall, later playing in two FA Trophy finals at Wembley with Telford. He died from prostate cancer.

MURRAY, William Joseph (Half-back/forward)
Apps/goals: 24/1 Born: Burnley, 26/1/1922 Died: 1992
    Career: Arbroath, CITY (January 1947–August 1950), Macclesfield Town.
    Details: Part of a large post Second World War squad initially assembled by manager Wilf Wild and added to by Sam Cowan, Bill Murray made his City debut in a 0-0 draw with Luton in April 1947, taking over from Alec Herd at inside-right. The following season he had a few games at right-half, failed to appear in 1948/49 and ended with thirteen outings in 1949/50, the majority at left-half in place of Albert Emptage.

MUSAMPA, Kizito (Wide midfield)
Apps: 45/4 Born: Kinshaha, DR Congo (formerly Zaire), 20/7/1977
    Career: Jong Ajax, Ajax Amsterdam, Bordeaux, Malaga, Atletico Madrid, CITY (loan, January 2005/August 2006), Trabzonspor, AZ Alkmaar, FC Seoul, Willem II.
    Details: During his spell at City, 'Kiki' Musampa – dubbed 'Chris' and 'Christmas Hamper' by the fans – produced some enterprising displays on the left side of midfield during his extended loan spell at the club. Fast and strong, he loved to run at defenders and packed a pretty powerful shot in both feet, proving a real handful for opponents. Unfortunately, his form dipped after an excellent twelve months and after losing his place he duly returned to Spain. His first City goal came in the vital home win over Liverpool. He won one U20 and 22 U21 caps for the Netherlands.

MWARUWARI, Benjani (Striker)
Apps/goals: 31/7 Born: Bulawayo, Zimbabwe, 13/8/1978
    Career: Air Zimbabwe Jets, Jomo Cosmos, Grasshopper/Switzerland, Auxerre, Portsmouth, CITY (£8 million, February 2008–August 2010), Sunderland (loan), Blackburn Rovers, Portsmouth.
    Details: Zimbabwean international Benjani, capped thirty-one times, was initially paid £50,000-a-week by City after being signed by Mark Hughes. He quickly earned hero status by scoring the winner against rivals United in the Manchester derby, having earlier netted his first goal for the Blues against his former club Portsmouth. The keen, aggressive striker was sidelined with a tedious thigh strain for the first part of 2008/09 and was ruled out again with a similar injury later

in the campaign. Eventually squeezed out of the team by the presence of Adebayor, Tévez and Santa Cruz, he was given another chance to establish his credentials by Roberto Mancini, but in the end made a reluctant departure to Blackburn.

N

NASH, Carlo James (Goalkeeper)
Apps: 41 Born: Bolton, 13/9/1973
    Career: Moss Bank, Manchester United (Academy), Rossendale, Clitheroe, Crystal Palace (£35,000), Stockport County, Wolverhampton Wanderers (loan), CITY (£100,000, January 2001–August 2003), Middlesbrough (£150,000), Preston North End(£175,000), Wigan athletic (loan/signed), Stoke City (loan), Everton, Stoke City.
    Details: Carlo Nash had a nightmare debut for City – conceding four goals in the first thirty-five minutes against Arsenal at Highbury in April 2001. Blamed not, he kept his place in the side, produced some excellent performances, especially against Manchester United, and quickly won over the fans; but alas his efforts were not enough to keep City in the top flight. A giant at 6 feet 5 inches, Nash then helped the Blues quickly regain top-flight status as Division One champions in 2002 before losing his place to Peter Schmeichel.

NASH, Joseph (Half-back)
Apps/goals: 17/1 Born: Uxbridge, 1870
    Career: Uxbridge, Burnley, Nelson, CITY (June 1894/May 1895).
    Details: Having failed to make inroads with Burnley and Nelson, Joe Nash did reasonably with City, playing in seventeen of the thirty League games during his only season with the club. He made his debut against Bury and scored his only goal in a 6-1 home win over Walsall Town Swifts in October.

NASRI, Samir (Midfield)
Apps/goals: 83/11 Born: Marseille, 26/6/1987
    Career: Pennes Mirabeau, Olympic Marseille, Arsenal (£13.5 million), CITY (£25 million, August 2011).
    Details: Primarily an attacking midfielder or midfielder, although he has also been deployed in the centre midfield, Samir Nasri has wonderful technical ability, creativity, pace, and the ability to read the game. Of Algerian cultural heritage, he has been described as a player whose 'vision and imagination make him an unpredictable opponent' ,while his playing style, ability and cultural background have drawn comparisons to French legend Zinedine Zidane. He joined City having scored twelve goals in 166 games for Marseille and twenty-seven in 125 outings for Arsenal. He made three goals on his debut

in a 5-1 win at Tottenham, and went on to play a key role as City went on to win the Premiership title. Capped by France fifty times at U16–U21 levels, he has now scored four times in thirty-five full internationals, representing his country in both Euro 2008 and Euro 2012. He also won the InterToto Cup with Marseille in 2005.

NASTASIĆ, Matija (Defender)
Apps: 30 Born: Valjevo, Serbia (FR Yugoslavia), 28/3/1993
   Career: Partizan Belgrade, FK Teleoptik Zemun, Fiorentina, CITY (June 2012).
   Details: After signing a five-year contract, Matija Nastasić made his debut for City in mid-September, in a Champions League away game against Real Madrid in the Santiago Bernabéu stadium, following up with his premier league baptism eleven days later at Fulham FC. After his fairly ominous start, he cemented his place in the starting XI and his form won him the club's Player of the Month Award for November. Now a huge favourite with the fans, he pushed Joleon Lescott out of the team as he bedded in nicely alongside Vincent Kompany. Nastasić won a total of thirty-six caps at U17, U19 and U21 levels and by May 2013 had played in nine full internationals for Serbia.

NAYLOR, James (Half-back)
Apps: 1 Born: High Crompton, Lancs, 2/3/1901 Died: Shaw, near Oldham, 31/8/1983
   Career: Shawside, Oldham Athletic, Huddersfield Town (£3,750), Newcastle United (£4,000), CITY (£500, October 1932/February 1933), Oldham Athletic (loan), Macclesfield Town, Nelson, Wigan Athletic; retired 1939.
   Details: In his prime, Jimmy Naylor operated mainly down the right side of midfield, but was also very efficient on the opposite flank. Blessed with clever footwork, he was a fine passer of the ball and could read the game well. He was past his best when he joined City, for whom he played just once, in a League game at Middlesbrough in January 1933. He made 249 appearances for Oldham early in his career, was on the fringe of an England cap after a successful trial in 1929, played in the 1930 FA Cup final for Huddersfield, but did very little at Newcastle.

NEGOUAI, Christian (Midfield)
Apps/goals: 10/2 Born: Fort de France, Martinique, 20/1/1975
   Career: Vaux-en-Velin/France, Lyon, UR Namur, RSC Charleroi/Belgium, CITY (£1.5 million, November 2001–July 2005), Coventry City (loan), Standard Liege, Aalesund, FC Brussels.
   Details: A towering midfielder, 6 feet 4 inches tall, Christian Negouai was unable to force his way into City's first team and was sent off (for two yellow cards) in his first season with the club, against Blackburn in the League Cup. He later suffered the same fate in the Premiership game at Everton on Boxing Day, 2004. His first City goal was scored in the UEFA Cup *v.* The New Saints in 2003. He did much better in the reserves as a striker!

NEILSON, Richard (Half-back)
Apps/goals: 20/1 Born: Blackhall, Durham, 1/4/1916 Died: Manchester, 14/12/2005
   Career: Easington Juniors, Blackhall Colliery Welfare, Dawdon Colliery, CITY (September 1935–May 1947); Second World War guest for Rochdale and Stockport County; Droylsden; retired May 1950.

NELSON, John Harold (Outside-right)
Apps: 8 Born: Manchester, 1888
   Career: CITY (January 1911–May 1912); did not play after the First World War.
   Details: Jack Nelson had a short career, spending a season-and-a-half with City. Deputising for George Stewart on eight occasions, he made his debut in a 2-2 draw at Sheffield United in February 1911 and played his last game *v.* Bristol City at home ten weeks later.

NEWTON, William Alfred Andrew (Full-back)
Apps: 2 Born: Romiley, Cheshire, 24/3/1896
   Career: Romiley St Chad's, Park Albion, Marple Amateurs, Newton Heath, Hyde United, Droylsden, First World War guest for Burnley, CITY (February 1916–June 1920), Port Vale (First World War guest/signed), Southend United, Accrington Stanley, Hyde United, Ashton National; retired 1931.
   Details: Andie Newton made thirteen appearances for City during the First World War, before playing in two League games at left-back in place of Eli Fletcher in successive away games at Oldham and Sheffield United in September 1919.

NICHOLLS, James Henry (Goalkeeper)
Apps: 16 Born: Bilston, 24/9/1908 Died: Dudley, 20/8/1984
   Career: Moxley Road School, Darlaston, Cradley Heath, Sunbeam Motors, Bloxwich Strollers, Bilston Borough, Blackpool, CITY (May 1932–May 1934), Brentford, Port Vale; Second World War guest for Doncaster Rovers; retired injured, 1942.
   Details: Standing 6 feet 3 inches tall, Jim Nicholls, deputising for Len Langford, made his City debut at Everton in September 1932, having twelve outings in succession (five wins, six defeats and one draw). He conceded eight goals in his last game against Wolves at Molineux in December 1933, and made only forty League appearances in total before a knee injury ended his career.

NIELSEN, Gunnar (Goalkeeper)
Apps: 1 Born: Torshavn, Faroe Islands, 7/10/1986
Career: HB Torshavn, BK Frem/Denmark, Blackburn Rovers, Motherwell (loan), CITY (January 2009, released, December 2012), Wrexham (loan).

Details: Gunnar Nielsen joined City on a two-and-a-half-year contract but played on loan for Wrexham before making his Premiership debut in April 2010, as a seventy-sixth-minute substitute for injured the Shay Given in a 0-0 draw with Arsenal – thus becoming the first Faroese footballer to play in the Premier League. He's so far won ten U21 and eleven full caps for his country.

NIMELY-TCHUIMENI, Alex (Striker)
Apps: 2 Born: Monrovia, Liberia, 11/5/1991
Career: Barrack YC, Mighty Barrolle, Cotonsport Garoua/Cameroon, CITY (May 2007), Middlesbrough (loan), Coventry City (loan), Crystal Palace (loan).

Details: A product of City's Academy, Alex Nimely made his Premiership debut as a substitute against Burnley in April 2010. He played for Liberia's youth team before making three U20 appearances for England.

NIXON, Eric Walter (Goalkeeper)
Apps: 84 Born: Harpurley, 4/10/1962
Career: Curzon Ashton, CITY (£1,000, October 1983–July 1988), Wolverhampton Wanderers (loan), Bradford City (loan), Southampton (loan), Carlisle United (loan), Tranmere Rovers (loan/signed, £60,000), Reading (loan), Blackpool (loan), Bradford City (loan), Stockport County (£100,000), Wigan Athletic (loan/signed), Tranmere Rovers (player-coach), Kidderminster Harriers (loan), Sheffield Wednesday (player-coach), retired May 2005, aged forty-two.

Details: A soccer nomad, Eric Nixon was sent out on loan five times as a City player and between August 1986 and January 1987, played in all four Divisions of the Football League – with Wolves (Div. 4), Bradford City (2), Southampton (1) and Carlisle (3). His best season at Maine Road was in 1985/86, making forty-one starts, including his League debut against West Ham in September. He made thirty-eight appearances in 1987/88, missing two games after being was sent-off in a 3-1 defeat by Crystal Palace in December.

During his twenty-two-year career, Nixon accumulated 658 club appearances (446 for Tranmere). A great practical joker, he helped the Birkenhead club win the Leyland DAF Cup at Wembley in 1990.

NORGROVE, Frank (Full-back)
Apps/goals: 98/1 Born: Hyde, 1880
Career: Glossop, CITY (April 1904–May 1912); did not play after the First World War.

Details: A well-proportioned, hard-tackling left-back, Frank Norgrove became a regular in City's first team in 1906, taking over from Charlie Burgess. He did well before losing his place to Bert Jackson halfway through the following season. Thereafter, he had brief spells of League action before leaving.

O

OAKES, Alan Arthur (Wing-half)
Apps/goals: 680/34 Born: Winsford, Cheshire, 7/9/1942
Career: Mid-Cheshire Boys, CITY (April 1958–July 1976), Chester (£15,000, player-manager), Altrincham; retired 1982; Port Vale (coach, played one game).

Details: Alan Oakes holds three records for City – most appearances in all competitions (680), most League appearances (564) and the most senior Cup appearances (104). He missed only thirty League games in ten years (1962–72), but was surprisingly never an ever-present. One of the club's longest-serving players, being engaged at Maine Road for eighteen years, he was one of the most consistent performers in the team during the heady days from 1965 to 1976, driving his players forward as the Second Division title, the League Championship, the FA Cup, the European Cup Winner's Cup and two League Cups all found their way into the Maine Road boardroom. A quiet, unassuming sort of player, he was brilliant at times and it was a pity that he didn't win an England cap; his only representative call was to play for the Football League against the Scottish League in 1969.

'Mr Dependable', he made his League debut (in Ken Barnes' absence) v. Chelsea in November 1959, scored his first City goal in a 3-1 home win over WBA in February 1962 and in 1969/70 played in fifty-nine out of a possible sixty-two competitive matches. After retiring, he was employed on a part-time basis by Port Vale and in an emergency, was called up to play in the 77th League game of his career against Plymouth in 1983, at the age of forty-one years, sixty days. Only seven players have appeared in more Football League games than Oakes: Peter Shilton, Tony Ford, ex-City star Tommy Hutchison, Graham Alexander, Terry Paine, Neil Redfearn and Robbie James. Oakes was a top player and a top man. His cousin is Glyn Pardoe (ex-City), his son Michael kept goal for Aston Villa, Wolves and Cardiff, while his nephew Chris Blackburn played for Chester, Morecambe and Wrexham.

OAKES, John (Forward)
Apps: 79/9 Born: Hamilton, 6/12/1919
Died: after 1965
Career: Wolverhampton Wanderers, Queen of the South, Huddersfield Town, Queen of

the South, Blackburn Rovers; Second World War guest for Brentford, Hartlepool United, Middlesbrough, Millwall and Stoke City; CITY (June 1948–July 1951), Queen of the South (free; retired 1960, aged forty; trainer for three years).

Details: Jackie Oakes made thirty-five League appearances for Blackburn during the first two post-war seasons. Replacing Bill Linacre on City's right-wing, he did very well before being asked to occupy both flanks in 1949/50 and then, having battled to retain his place, Jimmy Meadows came along and took over in March 1952. Oakes scored fifty-seven goals in 457 appearances in his three spells with Queen of the South. He was signed by Major Frank Buckley for Wolves, but never got a game during his time at Molineux.

OAKES, Thomas (Outside-right)
Apps: 1 Born: Manchester, 6/2/1922 Died: 1993
  Career: Manchester United (amateur), CITY (April 1947/May 1948), Goslings FC; retired 1954.
  Details: A reserve at Maine Road, Tom Oakes made his only appearance for City in place of Matt Dunkley in a 3-1 Second Division defeat by WBA in May 1947.

O'BRIEN, Joseph (Forward)
Apps: 2 Born: Manchester, 1870
  Career: CITY (September/November 1893), Walsall Town Swifts.
  Details: A short-term signing, Joe O'Brien played inside-left in League defeats at Middlesbrough and at home to Small Heath in September 1893, at a time when forwards were being used ten a penny!

OGDEN, Trevor (Forward)
Apps/goals: 9/3 Born: Culcheth, Cheshire, 12/6/1945
  Career: Golborne BC, CITY (October 1963–May 1965), Doncaster Rovers.
  Details: Trevor Ogden top-scored for City's second XI in 1964/65, but found it hard to get into the first team, although he did find the net on his League debut at home to Bolton (lost 4-2) when deputising for Jimmy Murray. His other two goals came in the 4-3 home victory over Preston in March 1965.

OGLEY, Alan (Goalkeeper)
Apps: 57 Born: Barnsley, 4/2/1946
  Career: Barnsley, CITY (July 1963–September 1967), Stockport County (exchange deal involving Ken Mulhearn), Darlington; retired 1977; became a haulage contractor in Barnsley.
  Details: An England schoolboy international at both football and cricket, Alan Ogley, brave and agile, was initially reserve to Harry Dowd and made only seven League appearances in his first season with City, conceding four goals on

his debut at Charlton. He played in half of the games in 1964/65, was second fiddle again in the Second Division championship-winning season and virtually likewise in 1966/67, eventually being swapped for Ken Mulhearn. He became something of a legend at Stockport, making 269 appearances.

After playing for City in a 1-0 defeat at Southampton in October 1964, Ogley received over 300 letters from Saints' supporters praising his performance, one saying 'It was the finest display of goalkeeping ever seen on an English pitch'.

OLDFIELD, David Charles (Forward)
Apps/goals: 30/9 Born: Perth, Australia, 30/5/1968
  Career: Stoke Goldington, Luton Town, CITY (£650,000, player/exchange for Wayne Clarke, March 1989/January 1990), Leicester City, Millwall (loan), Luton Town, Stoke City, Peterborough United, Oxford United, Stafford Rangers, Tamworth, Brackley Town (player-manager), Peterborough United (coach/caretaker-manager); West Bromwich Albion (Youth Development Officer).
  Details: After choosing City ahead of West Ham, David Oldfield formed part of the squad that gained promotion to the First Division in 19889. Although he stayed at Maine Road for less than a year, he is fondly remembered for his two goals in the Manchester Derby in September 1989 when City triumphed 5-1. He left the club five weeks after the manager who signed him, Mel Machin was sacked and replaced by Howard Kendall. During his senior career, Oldfield scored ninety-four goals in 654 appearances, helped Leicester reach the Premiership in 1994 and gained one England U21.

O'NEILL, Martin Hugh Michael, OBE (Midfield)
Apps: 16 Born: Kilrea near Coleraine, Northern Ireland, 1/3/1952
  Career: St Columb's College (Gaelic football), St Malachy's College (Gaelic football), Rosario FC/Belfast, Derry City, Distillery, Nottingham Forest (£25,000), Norwich City (£250,000), CITY (£275,000, June 1981/January 1982), Norwich City (£150,000), Notts County, Chesterfield, Fulham; retired 1987; Grantham (manager), Shepshed Charterhouse (manager), Wycombe Wanderers (manager), Norwich City (manager), Leicester City manager), Celtic (manager), Aston Villa (manager), Sunderland (manager).
  Details: Martin O'Neill has had a wonderful career in football. As a player, he scored 130 goals in 705 club appearances (netting eighty-five times in 532 League games). He won the Irish Cup in 1971 (aged nineteen), the European Cup twice, the League Cup twice, the First Division

championship, Super Cup, Anglo-Scottish Cup and FA Charity Shield with Nottingham Forest, and gained sixty-four caps for Northern Ireland (six goals), skippering his country at the 1982 World Cup finals. And as a manager, starting in earnest with Wycombe in 1990, he guided the Chairboys into the Football League (1993), won the FA Trophy twice and promotion to Division Two. He was a winner in two League Cup finals with Leicester, as well as claiming promotion to the Premiership in 1996, and with Celtic he won three SPL titles, the Scottish Cup three times and the League Cup once, completing the treble in 2001. He also saw the Bhoys lose to Porto in the 2003 UEFA Cup final. As a senior club manager, he has now been in charge for more than 900 matches.

Despite a clash of personalities with his boss at Nottingham Forest, Brian Clough (who dropped him for the 1979 European Cup final), O'Neill played his best football at The City Ground, netting sixty-two goals in 371 appearances in ten years. He loved to drive forward from midfield, bringing both wingers into the game whenever he could. Unfortunately, he was 'past his sell by date' when he joined City, but still gave a good account of himself during the first half of the 1981/82 season when he played alongside his former Forest teammates Trevor Francis and Asa Hartford. He was awarded the OBE in 1982 (for services to football).

ONUOHA, Chinedum (Full-back)
Apps/goals: 116/3 Born: Warri, Nigeria, 12/11/1986

Career: Nelson Primary and Hulme Grammar Schools, Xaverian College/Manchester, CITY (June 2002–January 2012), Sunderland (loan), Queen's Park Rangers (£3 million).

Details: 'Nedum' Onuoha, the son of a doctor, played regularly for City's reserves in 2003/04 before making his senior debut against Arsenal in a League Cup tie in October 2004 at the age of seventeen, starring in his first Premiership game against Norwich soon afterwards. Though his natural position is centre-half, manager Kevin Keegan used him at right-back with the intention of improving his passing ability, although he blotted his copybook when he was sent off in a League Cup match with Doncaster which lost on penalties! He made eighteen appearances in his debut season, but suffered a series of injuries seriously disrupted his progress over the next two years. He captained City to a 2-1 League Cup victory over Bristol City in 2007 and scored his first goal for the club in the home PL game *v.* Spurs in March 2008 in a 2-1 win. More injuries followed, and coupled with the influx of new players, he was eventually transferred to QPR. Onuoha – who was sidelined for fifteen weeks as a City player – gained twenty-one England U21 caps.

ORR, William (Right-back)
Apps: 41 Born: Ayr, Scotland, 1875
Died: Hertfordshire, 1912

Career: Ayr Parkhouse, Glossop North End, CITY (July 1901–May 1904), Fulham, Glossop, Watford (until his death).

Details: Hard and resilient, Willie Orr partnered Di Jones in twelve League games in his first season with City and fellow Scot Bob Davidson in his second, before losing his place to Jock McMahon. He made exactly 100 League appearances in his two spells with Glossop. He was only thirty-seven when he died.

ØSTENSTAD, Egil John (Striker)
Apps: 4 Born: Haugesun, Norway, 2/1/1972

Career: Torvastad IL, Viking IL/Stavanger, Southampton (£800,000), Blackburn Rovers, CITY (loan, February/May 2001), Rangers, Viking IL; retired May 2005.

Details: After scoring thirty-three goals in 109 games for Saints, Egil Østenstad became something of a fringe player at Ewood Park, hence his loan spell with City, recruited by Joe Royle to boost his strike force. He made his debut against Spurs, but failed to complete ninety minutes during his spell at Maine Road. Retiring at the age of thirty-three, he scored 128 goals in 396 club appearances (121 in 371 at League level) and collected five youth, twenty-seven U21 and eighteen full caps for Norway.

OWEN, Gary Alfred (Midfield)
Apps/goals: 124/23 Born: St Helens, 7/7/1958

Career: St Aidan's School/St Helens, Eccleston YC, Warrington & District Boys, Manchester Boys, CITY (August 1974–May 1979), West Bromwich Albion (£465,000), Panionios/Greece (£25,000), Sheffield Wednesday, Apoel Nicosia; retired injured, May 1990; became an art dealer (Gary Owen Fine Art) in North Staffs; worked for Century FM (Manchester); journalist for Manchester Evening News; CITY (part-time coach, School of Excellence).

Details: Gary Owen turned professional in 1975/6 and made his City debut against Wolverhampton Wanderers in March 1976, and scored his first goal in his fifth League game against West Ham in October of the same year. A fine passer of the ball, he linked up well with Asa Hartford and Colin Bell in City's midfield before being sold, as part of manager Malcolm Allison's clear-out, to WBA despite being a strong fans' favourite. Two months later his buddy, Peter Barnes, followed him to The Hawthorns. At Albion, he was a regular and became the club's penalty-kick taker before suffering a fractured shin, followed by a broken ankle and also meningitis, all in 1984/5! Never the same player again, he lost his place in the side and when the Baggies were relegated in 1986, he moved to Greece. Owen was capped four times by England as a youth player, on eight occasions by the 'B' team, a then record twenty-two times at U21 level and represented the Football League. He also scored ten penalties for City.

OWEN, Robert (Forward)
Apps/goals: 27/6 Born: Farnworth, Bolton, 17/10/1947
   Career: Bury, CITY (July 1968–June 1970), Swansea City (loan), Carlisle United, Northampton Town loan), Workington (loan), Bury loan), Doncaster Rovers.
   Details: Bobby Owen was City's leading scorer in Central League football in 1969/70, having done well in the first team the previous season when he made his debut in front of 51,236 spectators at Liverpool and netted his first two League goals for the club in a 4-2 home win over Chelsea in the January. After leaving Maine Road he had an excellent spell with Carlisle, bagging fifty-one goals in 204 League appearances.

OWEN, William (Centre-forward)
Apps: 10/3 Born: Llanfairfechan, Wales, 30/6/1914 Died: Devon, 1976
   Career: Northwich Victoria, CITY (June 1934–March 1936), Tranmere Rovers, Newport County; Second World War guest for Everton; Exeter City, Barry Town, Dartmouth United.
   Details: After leaving City, Billy Owen accumulated over 100 appearances for his next three clubs before joining Barry Town in 1947. Strong and mobile, he was reserve to Fred Tilson and made his League debut in a 4-1 defeat at Blackburn in October 1935, netting his first goal a fortnight later in a 2-1 home win over Brentford.

OXFORD, Kenneth (Goalkeeper)
Apps: 1 Born: Oldham, 14/11/1929 Died: Nottingham, 6/8/1993
   Career: Ardwick LC, CITY (May 1946–December 1948), Derby County (trial), Chesterfield, Norwich City, Derby County (£4,000), Doncaster Rovers, Port Vale, Boston United (player, reserve team player-coach), Boston FC (player/caretaker-manager; retired May 1969; then manager, later general manager); also worked for a security firm.
   Details: Third choice behind the great Frank Swift and Alec Thurlow at Maine Road, Ken Oxford made his only appearance for City in April 1948, keeping a clean sheet in a 0-0 draw with the champions Arsenal. After leaving the club, his career took off – making 162 appearances for Derby and 136 for Norwich.

P

PALMER, Roger Neil (Midfield/forward)
Apps/goals: 41/11 Born: Manchester, 30/1/1959
   Career: Manchester Boys, CITY (May 1975–November 1980), Oldham Athletic (£70,000); retired 1994; now lives in Sale, Cheshire.
   Details: An undemonstrative player, and a quiet and modest man off the field, Roger Palmer made his debut for City at Middlesbrough in December 1977. Later that season, he netted twice in a 2-2 draw at Newcastle and struck again forty-eight hours later in a 2-1 win over FA Cup finalists Ipswich. The following season was his best with City – six goals in twenty-one outings.
   A consistent performer throughout his career, Palmer made 112 consecutive appearances for Oldham between December 1981 and September 1984. He played in a League Cup final and two FA Cup semi-finals for the Latics as the Boundary Park club's all-time leading scorer with 141 goals in 461 League matches.

PANTER, Derek (Forward)
Apps: 2 Born: Blackpool, 22/11/1943
   Career: Chorlton Lads' Club, West Bromwich Albion (amateur), CITY (October 1960–May 1964), Torquay United, Southport.
   Details: With Jimmy Murray and Derek Kevan absent, Derek Panter partnered Paul Aimson up front when making his City debut in a 2-0 first leg League Cup semi-final defeat at Stoke in January 1964. Two weeks later he made his League bow in a 2-1 loss at Northampton.

PANTILIMON, Costel Fane (Goalkeeper)
Apps: 11 Born: Bacău, Romania, 11/2/1987
   Career: Aerostar Bacău, Politehnica Timisoara, CITY (loan, August/December 2011; signed for £3 million, January 2012).
   Details: Signed as cover for Joe Hart, following the departure of Shay Given, Costel Pantilimon had four outings in his first season with City, making his debut in the 1-0 League Cup victory over holders Birmingham City and following up with a second outing in a 5-2 win against Wolves in the next round. Then, after playing well and saving a Wayne Rooney penalty (but not the follow up) in the third-round FA Cup defeat by rivals United, he made his third League Cup start, helping City reach the semi-finals by beating Arsenal 1-0 at the Emirates Stadium and being named 'Man of the Match' for two stunning first-half saves. He played in every round of City's 2013 FA Cup run, but was left out for the final. He has so far gained five U17, three U19, twelve U21 and sixteen full caps for Romania.

PARDOE, Glyn (Full-back/midfield)
Apps/goals: 380/22 Born: Winsford, 1/6/1946

Career: Mid-Cheshire Boys, CITY (July 1961; retired April 1976; later club coach).

Details: City's youngest-ever player, Glyn Pardoe made his League debut at the age of fifteen years and 314 days against Birmingham City at Maine Road in April 1962. The club's first named League substitute *v.* Middlesbrough in August 1985 (unused), he established himself in the first team during the course of the season and missed only eleven League games in the next five years, going on to play in 305 at this level, helping City win the Second Division title (1966), the League championship (1968), the FA Cup 1969), the League Cup (1970) and the European Cup-winner's Cup (1971). He scored City's extra-time winner against WBA in the League Cup final, but nine months later suffered a broken leg in the Manchester derby at Old Trafford that kept him out of first team for almost two years. He returned, had a decent 1973/74 campaign, but never reached the standard he had set before his injury. An England schoolboy international, Pardoe won four caps at U23 level and played for City in every position except goalkeeper and centre-half.

PARK, Terence Charles (Forward)
Apps: 2 Born: Liverpool, 7/2/1957

Career: Wolverhampton Wanderers, Blackpool, Stockport County, Minnesota Kicks, Stockport County, CITY (loan, January/May 1983), Bury; ran a post office, later joined a Liverpool haulage company.

Details: Terry Park, with over 150 club appearances under his belt, was called into action twice by City, as a second-half substitute in successive League defeats at Coventry (4-0) and at home to Notts County (1-0).

PARLANE, Derek James (Striker)
Apps/goals: 52/23 Born: Helensburgh, Dunbartonshire, 5/5/1953

Career: Queen's Park, Glasgow Rangers, Leeds United (£160,000), Bulova/Hong Kong (loan), CITY (free, July 1983–January 1985), Swansea City, North Shore/Hong Kong, Racing Jette/Belgium, Rochdale, Airdrieonians, Macclesfield Town, Curzon Ashton; retired 1990; worked as a sportswear agent; now lives at Lytham St Anne's.

Details: Brave and resolute, strong on the ground and in the air, Derek Parlane – who replaced David Cross as leader of City's attack – was leading marksman in 1983/84 with nineteen goals, scoring on his debut at Crystal Palace and bagging a hat-trick in a 6-0 win over Blackburn. A Scottish international with one U21, five U23 and 12 senior caps, as well as two appearances for the Scottish League to his name, he scored on his debut for Rangers in the European Cup Winner's Cup semi-final against Bayern Munich and while at Ibrox, he gained two League, three Scottish Cup and two League Cup winner's medals in the space for four years (1975–79). He notched 111 goals in 300 appearances for the 'Gers and during his career (at home and abroad) he hit 188 goals in 595 club and international matches.

PATTERSON, John William (Forward)
Apps: 1 Born: Scotland, 1872

Career: Hibernian, CITY (June 1896–May 1899), Stockport County.

Details: Bill Patterson's only first-team appearance was against Arsenal in September 1896. He top-scored for the second XI in 1898/99 before going on to net four times in thirty-six games for Stockport.

N.B. Some references say another Patterson played for City in 1898/99.

PAUL, Roy (Wing-half)
Apps/goals: 294/9 Born: Gelli Pentre, Rhondda, 18/4/1920 Died: Treorchy, Wales, 21/5/2002.

Career: Tona BC, Ton Pentre, Swansea Town; Second World War guest for Bristol City and Cardiff City; CITY (record £25,000, July 1950–July 1957), Worcester City (player-manager), Brecon Corinthians, Garw Athletic (player-manager) retired 1962; became a lorry driver, living in Geill, Rhondda.

Details: Although Roy Paul appeared in several outfield positions, he was at his best as a left-half, here his natural leadership, strong tackling and accurate distribution made him a key figure in the City team.

As a coalminer, he used to kick a tin can around the street as a young lad, knowing that one day he would become a quality footballer! Indeed, in the 1950s he was appointed captain of City and after helping the team gain promotion. He then emulated Billy Meredith's feat by skippering the Blues in two FA Cup finals, losing to Newcastle in 1955, but then lifting the trophy and gaining a winner's medal when Birmingham were defeated 3-1 a year later. Capped thirty-three times by Wales (1949–56), he made 160 League appearances for Swansea with whom he won the Third Division (S) title (1949) and Welsh Cup (1950).

In the summer of 1949, ex-Marine Paul, who served in India as a PT instructor in the Second World War, was approached by the mega-rich Millionaires club of Bogota – and, with a handful of other League club players, including England international Neil Franklin, flew to Colombia to talk with officials, but turned down the offer. He was fortunate to escape with a £250 fine – others weren't so lucky and were banned by the FA.

PAYNE, John Frederick (Forward)
Apps/goals: 4/1 Born: Southall, Middlesex, 3/6/1906 Died: 1981

Career: Botwell Mission, Lyons Athletic, Southall, West Ham United, Brentford, CITY (January 1931–May 1934), Brighton & Hove Albion, Millwall Athletic, Yeovil & Petters United; retired during the Second World War.

Details: A winger with good pace, Jack Payne was reserve to Ernie Toseland during his time with City. He scored on his debut in a 5-1 win over Birmingham in March 1932 and actually played his last two games on the left-wing in place of Eric Brook. He had best years with Brentford, netting eighteen goals in fifty-two League games.

PEACOCK, Lee Anthony (Forward)
Apps: 10 Born: Paisley, 9/10/1976

Career: Carlisle United, Mansfield Town (£90,000), CITY (£500,000, November 1999/ August 2000), Bristol City (£600,000), Sheffield Wednesday, Swindon Town, Grimsby Town, Havant & Waterlooville, Eastleigh; retired May 2012.

Details: Covering for Shaun Goater, Paul Dickov and company, tall striker Lee Peacock made just five starts and five substitute appearances for City before leaving for Ashton Gate.

Capped by Scotland at Youth and U21 levels, he won the AWS and the LDV Trophy with Carlisle and helped Wednesday beat Colchester in the 2005 Play-off final at Wembley. In a fine career, at senior level, he scored 139 goals in 595 club appearances.

PEARCE, Stuart (Left-back)
Apps/goals: 43/3 Born: Hammersmith, London, 24/4/1962

Career: Fryent Primary School; Kingsbury School; Claremond High-School; Queen's Park Rangers (trial); Hull City (trial); Wealdstone, Coventry City (£25,000), Nottingham Forest (£450,000; later player-manager and caretaker-manager); Newcastle United (free), West Ham United (free), CITY (free, July 2001, retired May 2002; appointed coach, then manager, March 2005–May 2007); England U21 manager-coach; also acted as England senior team coach (briefly); Great Britain Olympic Games football team manager (2012).

Details: Stuart Pearce was Kevin Keegan's first signing for City. Installed immediately as captain, he brought experience and leadership qualities to the club and any doubts regarding his fitness were quickly dispelled when he made forty-three appearances, bringing a wonderful career to a close by lifting the First Division trophy.

A fierce-tackling left-back, a real lion-hearted defender – nicknamed 'psycho' – he wasn't afraid to put his head on the block after doing something wrong! Remember that penalty miss against the Germans in the World Cup semi-final shoot-out in Turin in July 1990 when England lost 4-3? It took him months to get over that agony ... but he was first in line to take the next spot-kick! He actually missed from the spot in his last ever League game, for City against Portsmouth in April 2002. If he'd scored it would have been his hundredth career goal.

The oldest outfield player ever to appear for England in the European Championships, Pearce was thirty-four years and sixty-three days old when he lined up against Germany at Wembley in June 1996. The 999th player to represent England at senior level, he gained seventy-eight full caps (five goals) and one at U21 level.

Only two full-backs – Kenny Sansom (eighty-six) and Ashley Cole (100-plus) – have made more appearances for England than Pearce.

A top player and a top man, Pearce made 942 appearances at club level (570 in the FL/Premiership) and netted 119 goals – the most by a full-back ever! If his England outings are added to his tally, then his career realised well over 1,000 games.

PEARSON, Frank (Centre-forward)
Apps/goals: 8/2 Born: Manchester, 18/5/1884 Died: Manchester, 1949.

Career: Preston North End, CITY (June 1903–October 1905), Chelsea (£250), Hull City, Luton Town, Rochdale, Eccles Borough; retired April 1911.

Details: After doing well at Preston (twenty goals in thirty-five games) Frank Pearson didn't quite fit the bill at City, despite scoring on his debut *v.* Notts County (September 1903) and netting again in last outing at Wolves (April 1905). He had all the physical requirements for a striker and was, in fact, Chelsea's first real centre-forward (eighteen goals in thirty appearances), but didn't do too well after leaving the Bridge.

PEARSON, Harry (Forward)
Apps: 1 Born: Stockport, 9/2/1899

Career: Bredbury FC, CITY (March 1921–May 1923).

Details: Another one-match wonder, Harry Pearson's only appearance in senior football came in City's 1-0 defeat at Sheffield United on April Fool's Day, 1922, when he deputised for Tom Johnson.

PENNINGTON, James (Outside-right)
Apps: 1 Born: Golborne, 26/4/1939

Career: Schoolboy football, CITY (December 1955–March 1961), Crewe Alexandra, Grimsby Town, Oldham Athletic, Rochdale.

Details: Yet another one-match performer for City, Jim Pennington's only game for the Blues was on the right-wing in place of Fionan Fagan, in a 2-1 defeat at Blackburn in April 1959. Short and stocky, he later scored eight goals in eighty-nine League outings for Grimsby and made over 170 club appearances during his career.

PERCIVAL, John (Half-back)
Apps/goals: 174/8 Born: Low Patrington, East Yorkshire, 16/5/1913 Died: 1979

Career: Durham City, CITY (October 1932–May 1947); Second World War guest for Oldham Athletic and Stockport County; Bournemouth; retired 1950.

Details: A loyal servant to City for fifteen years, either side of Second World War, Jack Percival covered for Matt Busby during his first three years at Maine Road, finally securing a place in the team in December 1936. An ever-present and key player the following season when City won the League championship, he continued to play right up to Second World War, having a further sixteen outings after the hostilities before joining Bournemouth. Joe Fagan eventually took over his position on a permanent basis in January 1947, but made enough appearances (sixteen) to collect a Second Division championship winner's medal.

PERCIVAL, Peter (Outside-right)
Apps: 2 Born: Reddish, 23/2/1911 Died: 1960

Career: Ashton National, CITY (December 1931–May 1935), Sheffield Wednesday, Chester; retired 1940.

Details: No relation to Jack (above), Peter Percival had a very 'quiet' career, as a reserve! His two outings for City (in four years) were against Leeds and Aston Villa in February/March 1934, replacing Ernie Toseland. He failed to make a single appearance for Wednesday and played just twice for Chester.

PETROV, Martin Petryov (Forward)
Apps/goals: 72/12 Born: Vratsa, Bulgaria, 15/1/1979

Career: Botev Vratsa, CSKA Sofia, Servette/Switzerland, VfL Wolfsburg/Germany, Atletico Madrid (£8.5 million), CITY (£4.7 million, July 2007–June 2010), Bolton Wanderers, Espanyol/Spain.

Details: Although Martin Petrov had big reputation on the European stage, he was a relatively unknown talent to the Premier League, yet made an excellent start with City, starring on his debut in a 2-0 win at West Ham. Favouring the left flank, he wreaked havoc in many defences during his first season when he scored five goals in thirty-eight appearances, although he was sent off against Everton for kicking Leon Osman.

A knee injury and loss of form restricted him to just fourteen outings in 2008/09 and following the influx of new players, including Carlos Tévez and Emmanuel Adebayor, Petrov was linked with a move to Tottenham Hotspur, but nothing materialised. After the sacking of manager Mark Hughes and the arrival of Roberto Mancini, Petrov was frequently moved in and out of the starting

eleven and in April 2010, he announced that his season was over due to his dodgy knee. He left the club, along with Benjani Mwaruwari, Karl Moore and Sylvinho, but stayed in the Premiership with Bolton. At 2013, Petrov had scored nineteen goals in ninety full internationals for Bulgaria.

PHELAN, Terry Michael (Left-back)
Apps/goals: 122/3 Born: Manchester, 16/3/1967

Career: Cathedral High School/Manchester, Salford and Great Manchester Schools, CITY (associate schoolboy, season 1982/83), Leeds United, Swansea City, Wimbledon (£100,000), CITY (joint record £2.5 million, August 1992–November 1995), Chelsea (£900,000), Everton (£850,000), Crystal Palace (loan), Fulham, Sheffield United, Charleston Battery/USA, Otago United/New Zealand (player-coach).

Details: An FA Cup winner with the 'Wombles of Wimbledon' in 1988, Terry Phelan had already made 274 club appearances before joining City. He had an excellent first season at Maine Road, missing only five games, followed up in 1993/94 with another thirty-six starts and added thirty-one outings to his tally in 1994/95, when his battling qualities went a long way in the successful fight to avoid relegation. A surprise signing by Chelsea, he extended his career in League football to 2001, moving to South Carolina having amassed 472 club appearances, as well as winning four youth, one 'B', one 21, one U23 and forty-one full international caps for the Republic of Ireland.

PHILLIPS, David Owen (Midfield)
Apps/goals: 99/16 Born: Wegberg, West Germany, 29/7/1963

Career: Plymouth Argyle, CITY (July 1984–May 1986), Coventry City (£150,000), Norwich City £550,000), Nottingham Forest, Huddersfield Town, Lincoln City, Stevenage Borough; retired 2003.

Details: Born in Germany where his father was stationed with the RAF, David Phillips played as a full-back, wing-half, in midfield and as a forward during his twenty-year career which produced some terrific figures: seventy-one goals in 738 club appearances. He also won four youth, four U21 and sixty-two senior full caps for Wales.

Confident on the ball, he packed a powerful shot, could deliver the inch-perfect cross, high or low, and was also a dead-ball specialist. While with City, he featured several times on the BBC's *Match of the Day* programme as a 'goal of the month' nominee for scoring some quite spectacular long-range beauties. So consistent and reliable, he missed only four games out of a possible 103 during his time at Maine Road, being an ever-present in his first season as City gained promotion with a 5-1 last-match win over Charlton when he was outstanding, scoring twice and having a hand in two other goals.

An FA Cup winner in 1987 with Coventry when he played alongside another ex-City player, Dave Bennett, Phillips was a superb clubman who gave 100 per cent each and every time he took to the field. Ankle injury eventually caught up with him at the age of forty.

PHILLIPS, Ernest (Full-back)
Apps: 82 Born: North Shields, 29/11/1923
Died: York, 10/1/2004
Career: South Shields, Ashington, CITY (£1,650, May 1947–November 1951), Hull City (£12,000, part-exchange with Don Revie), York City (£1,750), Ashington; retired 1960.

Details: Very classy, neat in style and effective without undue aggression, Ernie Phillips spent virtually two seasons in City's second XI before taking over at right-back in October 1949, retaining his position until Ken Branagan replaced him years later. He captained York on their charge towards the FA Cup semi-finals in 1955.

PHILLIPS, John Richard (Goalkeeper)
Apps: 1 Born: Weston Rhyn, 1901
Career: Chirk, CITY (March 1925, retired injured, May 1927); returned briefly with Oswestry Town.

Details: A knee injury ended Jack Phillips' League career after just one League appearance for City, in a 4-1 defeat at West Bromwich Albion in September 1925.

PHILLIPS, Martin John (Winger)
Apps: 16 Born: Exeter, 13/3/1976
Career: Schoolboy football, Exeter City, CITY (£500, November 1995–August 1998), Scunthorpe United (loan), Exeter City loan), Portsmouth, Bristol Rovers (loan), Plymouth Argyle (£25,000), Torquay United; retired May 2007; Plymouth Argyle (School of Excellence), Exeter City (Football in the Community officer); FA Tesco Skills coach (Somerset).

Details: Martin Phillips was signed by manager Alan Ball three times – for Exeter, City and Portsmouth. Noted for his skill on the ball, he could deliver the 'perfect' cross, but at times was over-elaborate with his trickery. He made sixty-five appearances for Exeter before joining City. Agonisingly, he sat on the bench several times, wearing his tracksuit top at Maine Road and, in fact, thirteen of his sixteen outings for City came as a substitute. He went on to play over 130 games for Plymouth, helping the Pilgrims win the Third Division title in 2000. A troublesome back injury forced Phillips into early retirement.

PHOENIX, Ronald James (Wing-half)
Apps/goals: 55/2 Born: Stretford, Manchester, 30/6/1925
Career: Humphrey Park FC, CITY (March 1950–June 1960), Rochdale.

Details: Ron Phoenix was almost twenty-five when he joined City, but staying loyal to the club he remained at Maine Road for ten years. He made his League debut at Arsenal in January 1952, but owing to the form of Ken Barnes, Roy Warhurst and others, had to wait until 1958/59 before having his best season in terms of appearances, making eighteen starts. He never got a first-team call-up between February 1953 and September 1955.

PICKFORD, Ernest (Forward)
Apps/goals: 8/3 Born: Manchester, c. 1871
Career: CITY (September 1893/May 1894)

Details: Six of Ernie Pickford's eight appearances for City came on the right-wing as partner to Alf Bennett. He scored two of his goals in a 3-2 win over Rotherham Town on Boxing Day 1893. He left the club at the end of the season, with Billy Meredith ready to move in!

PIZARRO, David Marcelo Cortés (Midfield)
Apps/goals: 6/1 Born: Valparaiso, Chile, 11/9/1979
Career: Santiago Wanderers, Udinese, Union de Chile (loan), Inter Milan, AS Roma, CITY (loan, January/May 2012), Fiorentina (loan).

Details: Roberto Mancini, who had previously managed David Pizarro at Inter Milan, signed the central midfielder as experienced back-up for the second half of 2011/12. 'He's a big player,' said Mancini, enigmatically.

Making his Premiership debut as a ninetieth-minute substitute for Adam Johnson in a 3-0 win over Fulham, thus becoming the first Chilean to play for the club; soon afterwards he came off the bench to score in a second leg 4-0 victory over FC Porto in the Europa League. Capped thirty-six times by his country, Pizarro won the Super Coppa twice and the Coppa Italia three times during his time with Inter and Roma, and by 2013 had made 354 appearances in Italian football.

PLATT, James (Centre-forward)
Apps: 1 Born: Chadderton, 1874
Career: CITY (May 1896/April 1897)

Details: A local player, Jim Platt's only League game appearance came at Gainsborough Trinity in September 1896. He was one of six different 'centre-forwards' used by City that season.

PLENDERLEITH, John Boyd (Defender)
Apps: 47 Born: Bellshill, Lanarkshire, 6/10/1937
Career: Ferndale Athletic/Brigton, Armadale Thistle, Hibernian, Armadale Thistle (loan), CITY

(£17,500, July 1960–September 1963), Cape Town City/South Africa, Queen of the South, Cape Town City, Bloemfontein City, Hellenic; returned to Scotland (1967); was a joiner by trade.

Details: Jackie Plenderleith, who made his debut for Hibs at the age of seventeen, employed orthodox pivotal tactics, refusing to be drawn out of position while defending with passion and commitment. Signed as cover for Dave Ewing (and John McTavish) he went straight into City's League side and made forty-one appearances in his first season before Ewing returned, and with Bill Leivers also being used at centre-half, Plenderleith hardly figured after that. Capped by Scotland against Northern Ireland in 1961, he also played in four youth and five U23 internationals.

POINTON, Neil Geoffrey (Left-back)
Apps/goals: 90/2 Born: Church Warsop, Mansfield, 28/11/1964

Career: Scunthorpe United, Everton (£75,000), CITY (£300,000 plus Andy Hinchcliffe, July 1990–August 1992), Oldham Athletic, Heart of Midlothian, Walsall, Chesterfield, Hednesford Town (player-manager), Retford Town (player-coach), Mossley (player-coach); retired 2003; Bolton Wanderers (Academy coach).

Details: Neil Pointon rejoined Howard Kendall at City and had two fine seasons at Maine Road as a first-team regular before teaming up with Joe Royle at Oldham. Replacing Andy Hinchcliffe at left-back, he missed very few games and his two goals came in League wins over Aston Villa in September 1990 and West Ham in April 1992. Quick in recovery, with good ball control, he amassed 691 senior club appearances, playing in the two FA Cup semi-finals for Oldham *v.* Manchester United in 1994, scoring in the first game. He won the League title with Everton in 1987.

POLLOCK, Jamie (Midfielder)
Apps/goals: 70/5 Born: Stockton-on-Tees, 16/3/1974

Career: Middlesbrough, CA Osasuna/Spain, Bolton Wanderers (£1.5 million), CITY (£1 million, March 1998–August 2000), Crystal Palace (£750,000), Birmingham City (loan), Spennymoor United (player-manager), Nunthorpe Juniors (coach).

Details: After making 193 appearances for Middlesbrough, failing to impress in Spain and having fifty-five outings for Bolton, Jamie Pollock played in a struggling City team. In fact, he had the misfortune to concede an own-goal that condemned City to relegation to the third tier for the first time, while keeping QPR in Division One. As a result, a group of Rangers' fans thanked him by voting him the 'most influential man of the past 2,000 years' in an internet poll. Jesus came second,

apparently! Capped by England at Youth and U21 levels, he helped both Middlesbrough (1995) and Bolton (1997).

PORTEOUS, Thomas Stoddard (Right-back)
Apps: 5 Born: Newcastle, 12/12/1864
Died: Sunderland, 23/2/1919

Career: Heart of Midlothian, Kilmarnock, Sunderland, Rotherham Town, CITY (January/March 1896), Rotherham Town; retired May 1896.

Details: Tom Porteous played for England against Wales in March 1891 – the first international to be staged in Sunderland. Twice a League championship winner with Sunderland (1892 and 1893) he played with 'proficiency and great steadiness' during a varied career, and in his short sell with City, partnered Davie Robson in all of his five League games.

POWELL, Ronald William Herbert (Goalkeeper)
Apps: 13 Born: Knighton, 2/12/1929
Died: Chesterfield, 1992

Career: Knighton Town, CITY (November 1948–June 1952), Chesterfield; retired December 1964.

Details: Owing to Alec Thurlow's illness, Ron Powell deputised for Frank Swift in twelve League games between August and November 1949. He did well at times, despite conceding four goals at Newcastle and Liverpool and five in an FA Cup tie at Derby in January 1950. He remained at Maine Road for two more seasons and after leaving, appeared in 508 games for Chesterfield, 471 in the Football League, in twelve years at Saltergate. In 1958, a certain Gordon Banks ended his record of 284 consecutive League games for the 'Spire-ites'.

Powell quit football at the age of thirty-five, following a car crash that killed his teammate Ralph Hunt and also injured colleagues Doug Wragg and Peter Stringfellow.

POWER, Paul Christopher (Midfield)
Apps/goals: 447/36 Born: Openshaw, Manchester, 30/10/1953

Career: Manchester Boys, Leeds Polytechnic, CITY (August 1973–June 1986); Everton (£65,000; retired May 1988; appointed coach); later community officer and coaching secretary for the PFA.

Details: Manager Tony Book handed Paul Power his League debut in August 1975, away to Aston Villa. He made twenty-four appearances that season and from then on, injuries apart, he played a vital part in City's fortunes over the next ten years, mainly as a left-sided midfielder, while having a few outings at left-back.

His brilliant extra-time goal, from a curling free-kick against Ipswich at Villa Park, booked City a place in the hundredth FA Cup final with Spurs in 1981 – but for all his efforts as captain, the

Londoners won the trophy after a relay. He then returned to Wembley five years later and lost again as Chelsea won the FMC final.

Power, who won an England 'B' cap (*v.* Spain in 1981) experienced relegation and enjoyed promotion with City, but after leaving gained his first major prize, a League championship winner's medal with Everton under manager Hoard Kendall.

PRINGLE, Christopher Ross (Half-back)
Apps/goals: 216/1 Born: Barrhead, Renfrewshire, 18/10/1894 Died: Glasgow, after 1945.

Career: Nitshill BC, Maryhill, St Mirren, CITY (June 1922–June 1928), Manchester Central, Bradford Park Avenue, Lincoln City, Stockport County; retired February 1933; FC Zurich/ Switzerland coach), Hurst FC (player-coach), Waterford/Ireland (trainer-coach), St Mirren (trainer).

Details: An unsung hero at Maine Road for six years Chris Pringle, only 5 feet 9 inches tall, was, nevertheless, a good, honest footballer, totally committed – one write-up said he was 'gritty, bustling and strong-tackling.' Between August 1922, when he made his debut against Sheffield United, and March 1928 when he played his last game *v.* Clapton Orient he missed only forty-nine competitive games, basically through injury. An ever-present once, his only goal helped beat Oldham 2-1 in September 1926. An FA Cup finalist in 1926, he helped City win the Second Division championship in 1928 and Lincoln clinch the Third Division (N) title in 1932. He gained one full cap for his country *v.* Wales in 1921, represented the Scottish League, captained each of his major clubs and was Billy Meredith's son-in-law.

PRIOR, Spencer Justin (Defender)
Apps: 37/4 Born: Southend-on-Sea, 22/4/1971

Career: Southend United, Norwich City (£200,000), Leicester City £600,000), Derby County, CITY (£500,000, March 2000/July 2001), Cardiff City (£700,000), Southend United (free), Newcastle Jets/Australia, Manly United/ Australia; retired 2009; Sydney Grammar School (coach), Mosnam FC (coach); also soccer analyst for Fox Sports TV (Australia).

Details: A number of clubs showed an interest in 6-foot-3-inch defender Spencer Prior before City signed him shortly before the transfer deadline of 2000. Recruited to replace the injured Andy Morrison, and as there were only two able-bodied central defenders available at the time (Gerard Wiekens and Richard Jobson), his impact was immediate. His goals earned City numerous victories, resulting in ultimate promotion. However, once in the Premiership, Prior's opportunities became limited as manager Joe Royle introduced several new faces and the return of Morrison. Prior

amassed 609 appearances with his six English clubs, won the League Cup with Leicester (1997) and the Division Two play-off final (2002) and the Welsh Premier Cup (2003) with Cardiff.

PRITCHARD, Harvey John (Forward)
Apps: 25/5 Born: Meridan, Warwickshire, 30/1/1913 Died: c. before 2000.

Career: Exhall Colliery, Coventry City, Crystal Palace, CITY (March 1938–February 1947), Southend United; retired 1952; served in the Army during the Second World War.

Details: A decent enough winger with good footwork, Jack Pritchard made all his senior appearances for City before the Second World War. He deputised for Ernie Toseland on nine occasions at the end of the 1937/38 season, scoring the winning goal on his home debut *v.* Chelsea (1-0) and also finding the net in a 5-3 victory over Charlton.

He played on the opposite flank eight times in place of Eric Brook the following season before making forty-eight appearances during the hostilities.

Q

QUIGLEY, Michael Anthony Joseph (Midfield)
Apps: 13 Born: Manchester, 2/10/1970

Career: Schoolboy football, CITY (June 1987/July 1995), Wrexham (loan), Hull City, Altrincham.

Details: Michael Quigley did well in City's YTS and second XI teams, but struggled to get much first-team action, making just thirteen appearances in total, nine as a substitute. Nicknamed 'Quigs', he made his senior debut in a 3-2 FMC defeat at Sheffield Wednesday in October 1991, before earning his first start in a 2-1 home League reverse against the same opposition in February 1993. A knee injury affected him later in his career.

QUINN, Niall John, MBE (Striker)
Apps/goals: 244/78 Born: Perrystown, Dublin, 6/10/1966

Career: Robert Emmets GAC (gaelic football), Dublin GAA (football & hurling), Manortown United, Fulham (trial), Arsenal, CITY (£800,000, March 1990–August 1996), Sunderland (£1.3 million; retired November 2001; later coach, Director of International Development, manager and chairman); named patron of the Sir Bobby Robson Foundation in 2010; now owns his own satellite company, Q Sat.

Details: Signed by Howard Kendall, 6-foot 4-inch striker Quinn helped City ensure top-flight status and followed up by becoming joint top scorer in 1990/91 with twenty-two goals, while finishing joint top with Mike Sheron in 1993/94 with just six, the fewest in a single campaign in the club's history. Tall and difficult to contain in aerial battles, Quinn scored some wonderful goals with both head and feet, forming a fine partnership David White, netting 114 goals together in four seasons, including what is believed to be the fastest-ever by a City player – just thirty seconds into the League game *v.* Bolton in March 1996. Quinn wasn't a bad goalkeeper either. He scored a penalty and then, after taking over from Tony Coton (sent-off) he saved one, from Dean Saunders in a 2-1 win over Derby in April 1991.

Although a knee injury sidelined him for a fair chunk of the 1993/94 season, he was fit enough to play for his country in the World Cup in the USA, having appeared in Italia 1990 four years earlier.

The subsequent decline in City's fortunes, which resulted in relegation, triggered Quinn's departure from Maine Road, seeing him team-up with Peter Reid at Sunderland. During his career, Quinn scored 167 goals in 558 club games and twenty-one in ninety-two internationals for The Republic of Ireland, who he also represented at Youth, U21, U23 and 'B' team levels as well as playing twice for the Eire FA. He won the League Cup with Arsenal (1987) and the First Division title with Sunderland (1999). In May 2002 he donated the proceeds of his testimonial (over £1 million) to children's charities. Awarded an honorary MBE, his book, *Niall Quinn – The Autobiography*, was published in 2002.

R

RACE, Harold Henry (Forward)
Apps/goals: 11/3 Born: Evenwood, County Durham, 7/1/1906 Died: Killed in action, France, 1941
    Career: Raby United/Durham, Liverpool, CITY (£3,000, August 1930–June 1933), Nottingham Forest, Shrewsbury Town, Hartlepool United; served with the Army until his death.
    Details: A hard-working inside-forward, Harry Race was the brains behind the attacks at Liverpool and Nottingham Forest, but failed to get to grips with the situation at Maine Road. Goalless in his first three outings for City, he netted a beauty in his fourth game, a 4-2 win over Middlesbrough in November 1930. Two years later he scored two fine goals in a 5-2 victory at Sheffield United. He won the Welsh Cup with Shrewsbury in 1938.

RAMSEY, John David (Left-half)
Apps: 1 Born: Scotland, 1888 Died: after 1945
    Career: Wishaw FC, CITY (March 1909/May 1910); returned to Scotland.
    Details: Perhaps out of his depth in English League football, Davie Ramsey's only game for City was in a 1-0 defeat at Bury in April 1909.

RANKIN, Bruce (Forward)
Apps: 2 Born: Glasgow, 21/7/1880
Died: Liverpool, 1946
    Career: Walton Council & St Bernard's schools/ Liverpool, White Star Wanderers, Kirkdale FC, Tranmere Rovers (trial), Everton, West Bromwich Albion (£500), CITY (£500, February/May 1907), Luton Town, Egremont Social club, Wirrall FC, Wrexham; retired May 1912; later worked at Liverpool docks.
    Details: An easy-moving, graceful winger, clever on the ball with a powerful shot, Bruce Rankin's stay with City was all too brief, his two appearances in February 1907 coming in away games at Preston (won 3-1) and Aston Villa (lost 4-1). Rankin represented The North *v.* The South in an international trial in 1903 and won the Welsh Cup with Wrexham in 1909. He left WBA in a 'huff' after being suspended for disciplinary reasons.

RANSON, Raymond (Right-back)
Apps/goals: 235/1 Born: St Helens, 12/6/1960
    Career: Schoolboy football, CITY (July 1976– November 1984), Birmingham City, Newcastle United, CITY (loan, January/May 1993), Reading; retired injured, 1995; worked for Benfield Gregg, Insurance Co. and became a wealthy businessman.
    Details: Ray Ranson made an impressive League debut in a 0-0 draw with Nottingham Forest in December 1978 and, following some more solid and workmanlike performances, gained a regular place in the City line-up the following season. He retained the right-back berth until Steve Lomax came along halfway through the 1983/84 campaign, moving to St Andrews a year later. Capped eleven times by England at U21 level, he was part of City's 1981 FA Cup final team. He was promoted and relegated into and out of the First Division with Birmingham and after returning to Maine Road, added seventeen appearances to his overall tally, eventually retiring with 445 League games under his belt. He then invested heavily in Benfield Gregg, an insurance company owned by the Chelsea director Matthew Harding and eventually sold his stake for several million pounds in 2002. He then started a venture funding football transfers on a sale and leaseback basis, including several deals with then Leeds United chairman, Peter Ridsdale.

In recent years, Ranson has twice headed a consortium in unsuccessful attempts to purchase Aston Villa (for £45 million) and in April 2007, put in an offer of what is believed to have been £90 million to buy Manchester City, pulling out of the proposed takeover after failing to come to an agreement with the then board. In October 2007, he attempted to take over Southampton on behalf of hedge fund company SISU before completing a deal to take over Coventry City in December 2007, just thirty minutes before the club was set to go into administration.

RAY, Richard (Full-back)
Apps/goals: 89/3 Born: Newcastle-under-Lyme, 4/2/1876 Died: Leeds, 28/12/1952
Career: Audley, Macclesfield, Burslem Port Vale, CITY (May 1896–May 1900), Macclesfield Town, CITY (September 1902/May 1903), Coventry City, Stockport County, Chesterfield Town, Leeds City, Huddersfield Town; retired 1919; Leeds United (manager/assistant-secretary), Doncaster Rovers (manager), Leeds United manager, again), Bradford City (manager), Millwall (chief scout).
Details: Dick Ray made over 250 appearances during his playing career, having his best years with City (first time round). Well-built and strong in the tackle, he was an ever-present in his first season at Hyde Road when he had three different full-back partners, Ditchfield, Harper and Read. A Second Division championship winner in 1899, he moved on once Di Jones and the aforementioned Read had bedded themselves in as the regular first-choice pairing.

RAZAK, Abdul (Midfield)
Apps: 10 Born: Boyake, Abidjan, Ivory Coast, 11/11/1992
Career: Crystal Palace, CITY (July, 2010), Portsmouth (loan), Brighton & Hove Albion (loan), Charlton Athletic (loan).
Details: Abdul Razak joined City's Elite Development Squad at the of seventeen and after some good displays in Manchester Senior Cup and second XI fixtures he was handed a surprise first-team debut as a substitute for David Silva in the final minutes of the Premier League game against West Bromwich Albion in February 2011 – the ninth youth player to graduate from Manchester City Reserves academy under manager Roberto Mancini in just over a year. The young Ivorian was shown a straight red card for a rash challenge in the fifty-first minute of the Premier Reserve League game against Bolton soon afterwards. Nevertheless, that showed commitment and he went on to make his first start, in September 2011, in 2011/12 Football League cup tie against Birmingham FC. Capped three times by his country at senior level, Razak was subsequently been loaned out to 'gain experience'.

READ, Thomas Herbert (Full-back)
Apps/goals: 119/2 Born: Manchester, 1871
Career: Stretford FC, CITY (August 1895–August 1902), Manchester United; retired injured, 1908.
Details: Mustachioed full-back Bert Read spent seven years with City before moving across 'town'

to join United. He severely injured his right knee playing against Small Heath/Birmingham in September 1901, which knocked him back considerably. He managed only one more outing for the club before departing. Prior to that, he had been a consistent performer, helping City win the Second Division title in 1899.

REDMOND, Stephen (Defender)
Apps/goals: 287/7 Born: Liverpool, 2/11/1967
Career: Liverpool Boys, CITY (July 1984–August 1992), Oldham Athletic (and Neil Pointon with Rick Holden joining City), Bury, Burscough, Leigh RMI; retired May 2004.
Details: A Liverpool supporter (even now), Steve Redmond, who chose City over his local club, made rapid progress at Maine Road and was in the first time by February 1986. He virtually stayed put for the next six years, producing some exquisite performances at home and away in all competitions. He appeared at Wembley in the FMC final at the age of eighteen, captained the youngsters to victory in the FA Youth Cup final and played for his country at U19 level.
Redmond's run of 134 consecutive League appearances between April 1987 and August 1990 included three ever-present campaigns, and as he got better he eventually replaced Kenny Clements as club captain (City's youngest-ever) while also lining up in fourteen U21 internationals, some as skipper. Voted 'Player of the Year' in 1988, he starred in City's promotion-winning team the following season and at the age of twenty-four, he was just thirteen games short of 300 when he left Maine Road for Boundary Park, with Neil Pointon, in 1992. He retired in 2004 with 727 club appearances to his name. Redmond's son, Danny, plays for Wigan Athletic.

REEVES, Kevin Peter (Striker)
Apps/goals: 158/39 Born: Burley, Hampshire, 20 October 1957
Career: Bournemouth, Norwich City (£50,000), CITY (£1.25 million, March 1980–July 1983), Burnley (£125,000; retired injured, June 1984; appointed coach); Swansea City (coach, Birmingham City (coach); Wrexham (assistant-manager/coach), Swansea City (assistant-manager/coach); Stoke City (scout), Swansea City (scout); Wigan Athletic (advisory coach).
Details: Kevin Reeves made his League debut in the mid-1970s for Bournemouth, but his League career lasted only eight years before a hip injury forced him to retire at the age of twenty-six, having netted over 150 goals in almost 400 appearances for his four clubs. Norwich's first £1 million sale (to City), he scored twice in his first nine League games with the Blues and then had an excellent first full season at Maine Road, despite playing several different

strikers. He had the pleasure of netting a penalty in the FA Cup final *v.* Spurs that went to a replay and was an ever-present in 1981/82 when he, Trevor Francis and Dennis Tueart bagged thirty-eight goals between them. After a lean season and a slight injury, he moved to Burnley. John Bond was his manager at each of his four clubs, while Reeves became coach under Bond at Turf Moor and St Andrew's.

The recipient of six U21, three 'B' and two full caps, Reeves made senior debut for England alongside Francis in a 2-0 European Championship qualifying victory over Bulgaria in 1979.

REGAN, Edward J. (Left-half)
Apps: 22 Born: Manchester, c. 1870
Career: CITY (May 1893/August 1894), Burslem Port Vale.
Details: Ted Regan spent one season with each of his two clubs. He made his City debut in the 1-0 home League defeat by Liverpool in September 1893 and although a left-half, he also played centre-forward (*v.* Newcastle), right-half and left-back.

REGAN, Robert Hunter (Outside-left)
Apps: 4 Born: Falkirk, 1912
Career: Linlithgow Rose, Partick Thistle, CITY (August 1936/July 1937), Dundee, Sheffield United.
Details: Reserve Bobby Regan, taking over from Eric Brook, who was switched to centre-forward, partnered Peter Doherty in four successive League games *v.* Stoke, Charlton, Derby and Wolves, in October 1936.

REID, Joseph Edmund (Half-back)
Apps/goals: 3/1 Born: Hebburn-on-Tyne, 30/6/1896 Died: 1936
Career: Hebburn Argyle, South Shields, CITY (November 1919/October 1920), Stockport County, Boston Town, Carlisle United, Newport County, Fulham; retired 1934.
Details: Although a half-back, Joe Reid's three games for City came in the forward-line, scoring on his debut *v.* Sunderland in December 1919. He went on to make 148 appearances in six seasons with Stockport, helping the Hatters win the Third Division (N) title.

REID, Nicholas Scott (Defender)
Apps/goals: 262/2 Born: Davyhulme, Manchester, 30/10/1960
Career: CITY (April 1977–May 1982), Seattle Sounders, CITY (October 1982–July 1987), Blackburn Rovers, Bristol City (loan), West Bromwich Albion, Wycombe Wanderers, Woking, Witton Albion, Bury (player-coach), Sligo Rovers (player-manager); retired 1999; later Burnley (assistant-physiotherapist).
Details: A competent, reliable right-sided defender who could pass a ball as good as any

midfielder, Nicky Reid had two separate five-year spells with City. He made his senior debut in March 1979 (*v.* Ipswich), played in the 1981 FA Cup final (both games), scored two winning League goals *v.* Portsmouth and Shrewsbury in 1984 and helped City regain top-flight status in 1985.

A scorer at Wembley, for WBA in their 1993 Division Two Play-off final win over Port Vale, during his long career Reid amassed over 550 club appearances, 209 for Blackburn, gaining a Premier League winner's medal in 1995. He also gained six England U21 caps.

REID, Peter (Midfield)
Apps/goals: 114/2 Born: Huyton, Lancs, 20/6/1956
Career: Huyton Boys, Bolton Wanderers, Everton (£60,000, later player-coach), Queen's Park Rangers, CITY (player-coach, December 1989, player-manager, November 1990–October 1993), Southampton, Notts County, Bury; Sunderland (manager); England U21 (manager), Leeds United (manager), Coventry City (manager), Thailand (national team manager/ coach); Stoke City (assistant-manager), Plymouth Argyle (manager); Kolkata Camelians FC/India (manager); also worked as a TV pundit.
Details: Hard-working midfielder Peter Reid broke his leg in 1979 and was out of action for over a year, but came back strongly and went on to have an excellent career, making 657 club appearances in major competitions (forty-one goals scored), helping Bolton win the Second Division title in 1978 and Everton the FA Cup in 1984, the League championship in 1985 and 1987 and the European Cup Winner's Cup, also in 1985, plus four FA Charity Shields. He won thirteen England caps (1985–88) and after replacing Bryan Robson (injured) he became the linchpin of the team in the 1986 World Cup finals, producing some excellent performances, but was one of the players left behind by Diego Maradona as he burst from inside his own half to score his second goal to add to his first he netted with his hand! Reid also played in six U21 internationals and was voted PFA 'Footballer of the Year' in 1985 when with Everton.

He had an excellent second half to the 1989/90 season with City, played in thirty League games the following term and thirty-one in 1991/92 before reducing his work-load during the initial Premiership campaign of 1992/93.

As a manager, he twice guided Sunderland into the Premiership and led Thailand to the T&T Championship in Vietnam. He replaced Paul Mariner as manager of Plymouth but was sacked after the Pilgrims suffered eight successive defeats at the start of 2011/12 and lay ninety-second in the 'League'. Kolkata Camelians bought Reid at auction for £128,000 ahead of the inaugural Indian Premier League season.

REKIK, Karim (Defender)
Apps: 3 Born: Haag, Netherlands, 2/12/1994
   Career: Scheveningen, Excelsior, CITY (July 2011), Portsmouth (loan), Blackburn Rovers (loan).
   Details: A very efficient defender, able to perform at centre-half or left-back, Karim Rekik represented his country in sixteen U17 and seven U19 internationals as a teenager and made his City in the Dublin Super Cup in pre-season just after signing. He then followed up with his first senior game v. Birmingham in a League Cup tie, substituting for Wayne Bridge in the last twelve minutes. He also made a late substitute appearance in the fourth round of the same competition away at Wolves. He was loaned out to gain experience.

REVIE, Donald George, OBE (Centre-forward)
*Apps/goals: 178/41 Born: Middlesbrough,
10/7/1927 Died: Edinburgh, 26/5/1989*
   Career: Archibald School, Newport Boys' Club/Middlesbrough, Middlesbrough Swifts, Leicester City, Hull City (£20,000), CITY (£13,000 plus Ernie Phillips, October 1951–November 1956), Sunderland (£23,000), Leeds United (£14,000, later player-manager, retired as a player, 1963, continued as manager to 1974); England (manager, 1974–77), UAE (manager-coach), Al-Nassr/Egypt (manager), Al-Ahly/Egypt (manager); Leeds United (consultant).
   Details: One of several big-money post-war signings, Don Revie was a regular in City's forward-line for four seasons and scored some excellent goals, while also converting ten penalties. He missed the 1949 FA Cup final (with Leicester) with a severe nose bleed, but played in the 1955 and 1956 FA Cup finals for City before transferring Sunderland. Unfortunately, older City fans will recall the 'Revie Plan' whereby manager Les McDowall used him as a deep-lying centre-forward. Unfortunately, the plan was dogged by controversy.
   Revie won six full caps for England, making his debut against Northern Ireland in 1954. He scored in a 7-2 win over Scotland in his second match. He also played for England 'B' and twice for a Football League XI, in a career that saw him amass almost 500 club appearances (474 in the Football League) and score just over 100 goals.
   FWA 'Footballer of the Year' in 1955, after retiring as a player, Revie managed a thoroughbred sort of team at Elland Road, steering Leeds to the Second Division championship (1964), two First Division titles (1969 and 1974), FA Cup glory (1972), a League Cup victory (1969), two Fairs Cup final successes (1968 and 1971) and numerous runner's-up prizes. However, he was unable to reproduce the success he had enjoyed at Leeds after taking over as manager of England, who failed to qualify for the 1976 European Championships, and were ready to miss out of the 1978 World Cup when Revie secretly negotiated a massively-paid coaching job in the UAE (believed to be worth £60,000-a-year) being bitterly criticised by the FA and the national press. Later suspended from British soccer and also banned for ten years from English football, he later won a High Court battle against the FA and was guaranteed an injunction quashing the ban. Awarded the OBE in 1970, Revie was struck down by motor neurone disease in 1987 and was confined to a wheelchair for the last two years of his life.

REYNA, Claudio (Midfield)
Apps/goals: 87/4 Born: Livingston, New Jersey, USA, 20/7/1973
   Career: St Benedict's PS, University of Virginia, Virginia Cavaliers, Bayer Leverkusen, VfL Wolfsburg (loan), Glasgow Rangers (£2 million), Sunderland (£4.5 million), CITY (£2.5 million, August 2003–January 2007), New York Red Bulls.
   Details: Claudio Reyna was already an experienced playmaker when Kevin Keegan signed him for City, Unfortunately, his time at Eastlands was frequently punctuated by injury, restricting him to thirty appearances in his first season, and causing him to miss six months of the 2004/05 campaign. In three-and-a-half seasons with the Blues, he made less than ninety appearances, yet was still very popular with the fans. Early in 2007, City boss Stuart Pearce agreed to terminate Reyna's contract for family reasons. During his lengthy career, he starred in 323 club matches (twenty-seven goals) and collected 111 caps for the USA (1994/2006). He won the Scottish Cup and SPL with Rangers and was named in the FIFA World Cup team for 2002.

RICHARDS, Micah Lincoln (Defender)
Apps/goals: 234/10 Born: Birmingham, 24/6/1988
   Career: CITY (July 2002).
   Details: Micah Richards became the youngest-ever England defender when, at the age of eighteen, he won his first full cap against Holland in November 2006. Signed as a fourteen-year-old, he bounded his way through City's Academy system, captained the youngsters to the FA Youth Cup final, was voted the club's Player of the Year and made his Premiership debut as a substitute at Arsenal in October 2005. Strong and forceful, with a terrific engine that enables him to pump and down the pitch with determination and commitment, he made over 150 appearances between 2005 and 2010, despite some niggling injuries. However, in recent years he has not been at his best, injuries

not helping matters, but being able to play at right-back, centre-half and in midfield, he is still a very important member of the senior squad. The recipient of fourteen U21 caps (being a regular in Stuart Pearce's team) he has also appeared in thirteen full internationals (one goal scored) and gained FA Cup and Premiership winner's medals in 2011 and 2012 respectively.

RIDDING, William (Forward)
Apps/goals: 9/4 Born: Heswall, Cheshire, 4/4/1911 Died: Heaton, Bolton, 20/9/1981
    Career: Heswall PSA, Tranmere Rovers, CITY (£3,000, March 1930/December 1931), Manchester United (£2,000, plus Billy Dale and Harry Rowley), Northampton Town, Tranmere Rovers, Oldham Athletic; retired injured, April 1936; Tranmere Rovers ('A' team coach, then manager/trainer), Bolton Wanderers (trainer, temporary manager, then secretary-manager); Lancashire CCC (physiotherapist).
    Details: Highly-rated as a seventeen-year-old – it was said he would become every bit as good as Dixie Dean or Pongo Waring – Bill Ridding's early promise was never fully realised, cartilage trouble blighting his career, forcing him to retire at the age of twenty-five. He scored for City in both home and away games *v.* Leeds United at the end of the 1929/30 season and against Sunderland (home) and Blackpool (away) during the next campaign. He later enjoyed a long and successful seventeen-year association with Bolton, seeing them win the FA Cup in 1958 and finding Francis Lee! A qualified physiotherapist and chiropodist, he was appointed trainer to the England squad at the 1950 World Cup in Brazil.

RIDLEY, John George (Right-back)
Apps: 185 Born: Bardon Mill, 19/1/1903 Died: Durham, after 1965
    Career: Mickley, South Shields, CITY (June 1927–June 1933), Reading, Queen's Park Rangers, North Shields; retired May 1937.
    Details: One of the smallest full-backs in the game, and a physical culturist, 'Micky' Ridley replaced Sam Cookson in City's line-up in 1927/28, holding his position until December 1931. A fine positional player, he made his League debut in a 1-0 win at South Shields in September 1927, going on to collect a Second Division championship winner's medal that season. Ridley made 402 League appearances during his seventeen-year professional career.

RIERA, Albert Ortega (Left-back)
Apps/goals: 19/1 Born: Manacor, Spain, 15/4/1982
    Career: RCD Mallorca, FC Girondis de Bordeaux, RCD Espanyol, CITY (loan, January/

May 2006), Liverpool (£8 million), Olympicos, Galatasaray.
    Details: Attacking left wing-back, Riera reached the milestone of 450 club and international appearances in 2013. After more than 100 appearances for Mallorca ('B' and senior levels) and over fifty for Bordeaux, he returned to Spain with Espanyol in 2005 but played only eight La Liga games, prompting a loan move to City where he was also unable to establish himself in the first team, despite scoring in a 3-0 win over Newcastle a month after joining. A scorer for Espanyol in their UEFA Cup final defeat by Sevilla in 2007, Riera won the Copa del Rey with each of his Spanish clubs, the Greek League with Olympiacos, completed the Turkish double with Galatasaray and gained eleven U18, fifteen U21 and sixteen full caps for Spain. He made forty appearances for Liverpool.

RIGBY, John (Defender)
Apps: 102 Born: Leigh, 29/7/1924 Died: 1997
    Career: Bryn Boys' Brigade, CITY (May 1946–March 1954), Peterborough United; retired 1960.
    Details: Jack Rigby was a good, solid centre-half who was a regular at the heart of City's defence from August 1950 until December 1952. A League debutant against Newcastle in May 1947, he took over the number '5' shirt from Joe Fagan and handed it to Dave Ewing two-and-a-half years later. After leaving Maine Road he made over 100 appearances for then Midland League club Peterborough.

RIMMER, Steven Anthony (Forward)
Apps: 1 Born: Liverpool, 23/5/1979
    Career: CITY (June 1995–July 1999), Doncaster Rovers (loan), Port Vale (free), Marine, Hyde United, Marine, Skelmersdale United; retired 2012; now a PE teacher at Parklands school, Chorley.
    Details: Steve Rimmer picked up a booking in his only game for City, in a 2-1 defeat by Mansfield Town in an Auto Windscreen Shield encounter in December 1997 that attracted the club's lowest-ever attendance, just 3,007. Two years later, on his debut for Port Vale (managed by ex-City boss Brian Horton) he was sent off on sixty-eight minutes for serious foul play against Barnsley. He made only three senior appearances in his career.

RITCHIE, Paul Simon (Defender)
Apps: 27 Born: Kirkcaldy, 21/8/1975
    Career: Links United, Heart of Midlothian, Bolton Wanderers, Glasgow Rangers (Bosman free), CITY (£500,000, August 2000–August 2003), Portsmouth (loan), Derby County (loan), Walsall (free), Dundee United, AC Amonia, Carolina Railhawks (retired 2009; became

assistant-manager); Vancouver Whitecaps (assistant-coach).

Details: Due to a groin injury, followed by a pelvic tweak late on, Paul Ritchie made only sixteen appearances for City in his first season at the club. These injuries troubled him again in 2001/02, when he was used nine times as substitute in eleven outings) and after a disastrous 2002/03 campaign when he was twice shipped out on loan, he left for Walsall for nothing, having cost half-a-million pounds three years earlier! He recovered sufficiently to make thirty-five appearances for Walsall before moving to Dundee.

Capped by Scotland as a schoolboy, Ritchie went on to play for his country in two 'B', seven U21 and seven full internationals and won the Scottish Cup with Rangers (1998). He retired in 2009 having amassed 325 club appearances.

ROBERTS, Charles Leslie (Inside-left)
Apps/goals: 8/2 Born: Halesowen,
28/2/1901 Died: 1980
Career: West Bromwich Albion (trial), Cradley St Luke's, Aston Villa, Redditch Town, Bristol Rovers, Chesterfield, Sheffield Wednesday, Merthyr Town, Bournemouth, Bolton Wanderers, Swindon Town, Brentford, CITY (January 1931/February 1932), Exeter City, Crystal Palace, Chester, Rotherham United, Scunthorpe & Lindsay United, New Brighton; retired 1939.

Details: Leslie Roberts served with sixteen different League clubs in twenty years and scored over 106 goals in 325 League and Cup appearances, having his best spell with Swindon (thirty-five goals in 119 outings between 1927–29). Unfortunately, after a pretty good start with City when he netted in his second and sixth games against Derby (won 4-3) and Grimsby (won 5-3), he played second fiddle thereafter to Fred Tilson before departing to Devon.

ROBERTS, Frank (Centre-forward)
Apps/goals: 237/130 Born: Sandbach, Cheshire,
3 April 1894 Died: Cheshire, 23 May 1961
Career: Sandbach Villa, Sandbach Ramblers, Crewe Alexandra, West Ham United, Bolton Wanderers, CITY (£3,400, October 1922–June 1929), Manchester Central, Horwich RMI; retired May 1932; became a licensee.

Details: City paid a big fee for opportunist centre-forward Frank Roberts; and it was worth it, as it went on to average more than a goal every two games during his near-seven year spell at Maine Road. Part of a deadly trio with Tom Johnson and Horace Barnes, together they notched 147 goals in three seasons between 1922–25. After Tommy Browell had replaced Barnes in the attack, he continued to find the back of the net, striking a five-timer in City's 11-4 FA Cup win over Crystal Palace in February 1926. He was leading marksman in 1924/25 (thirty-two goals) and again in 1925/26 (that season with thirty), the latter out of a team total of 120 as City suffered relegation and lost in the FA Cup final to Bolton. However, his twenty goals certainly went a long way in helping City win the Second Division championship in 1927/28.

Besides his excellent club form, Roberts also played in four internationals for England, making an impressive debut alongside Joe Bradford and Billy Walker in a 4-0 win over Belgium in December 1924 and scored twice in his second game, a 2-1 victory over Wales in late February 1925. He also represented the Football League and the FA and played in one international trial.

Roberts was suspended and transfer listed, and subsequently sold, by Bolton to City 'for taking over one of the principal hotels in that town'.

ROBERTSON, Douglas (Forward)
Apps/goals: 7/3 Born: Hyde, c. 1870
Career: CITY (October 1893/May 1894)
Details: An unknown reserve forward, Doug Robertson scored on his City debut in a 3-0 home win over Walsall Town Swifts in November 1893 and later netted in a 4-1 victory at Northwich Victoria.

ROBERTSON, George (Half-back/full-back)
Apps: 15 Born: Failsworth, 1905
Career: Ashton National, CITY (March 1927–August 1933), Southend United, Chesterfield; retired during the Second World War.

Details: Initially reserve to wing-halves Pringle and McMullan, George Robertson proved to be a fine club man during his six-and-a-half years at Maine Road who, after switching positions, made nine of his fifteen appearances at left-back in place of Bill Felton during the second half of the 1929/30 season.

ROBERTSON, James L. G. (Forward)
Apps/goals: 3/2 Born: Dundee, 23/7/1868
Died: Dundee, c. 1950.
Career: Dundee United, Notts County, Stoke, Ashton North End, CITY (February/May 1896), Dundee Wanderers; retired,1900.

Details: Jimmy Robertson who, despite some injury problems, did exceedingly well with Stoke, for whom he netted twenty-one goals in sixty-eight appearances, never settled at City, although his goals earned points off Burton Swifts (1-1) and Lincoln City (4-0) as the Second Division promotion race gathered momentum.

N.B. Some references list this player as Robinson.

(ROBINHO) De Souza Robson (Striker)
Apps/goals: 53/16 Born: São Vicente, Brazil,
25/1/1984

Career: Santos/Brazil, Real Madrid, CITY (British record £32.5 million, August 2008–August 2010), Santos (loan), AC Milan (£15 million).

Details: City manager Mark Hughes almost broke the 'bank' when he bought Robinho! The Brazilian star had been expected to join Chelsea, but as news of the takeover by ADUG broke, interest grew and Hughes swooped to complete the deal. Ironically, Robinho scored on his City debut against Chelsea and thereafter the goals continued to flow, his efforts against Portsmouth, his hat-trick against Stoke City and a sublime chip versus Arsenal, the pick of the bunch. However, an ankle injury suffered against the Gunners set him back somewhat. Thankfully, he returned and rounded off his first season in English football with special strikes against WBA, Everton and Blackburn to earn him the mantle as top scorer. Some player (in his day) Robinho unfortunately endured a nightmare in 2009/10, an ankle injury and loss of form restricting him to just twelve appearances, leaving Emmanuel Adebayor, Carlos Tévez and Craig Bellamy to do the business up front. When Roberto Mancini replaced Hughes halfway through the campaign, Robinho was given a chance by the Italian, but looked lame, and after scoring in his final game *v.* Scunthorpe, he was eventually loaned to his old club Santos before joining AC Milan.

Robinho hit seventy-one goals in 164 games for Santos (overall), thirty-five in 137 outings for Real Madrid and twenty-seven in 112 appearances for Milan (up to May 2013). He also notched three goals in eight U23 matches for Brazil while to date he's struck twenty-six times in ninety full internationals.

ROBINS, Mark Gordon (Forward)
Apps: 2 Born: Ashton-under-Lyne, 22/12/1969

Career: Manchester United, Norwich City (£800,000), Leicester City (£1 million), FC Copenhagen (loan), Reading (loan), CD Ourense, Panionios/Greece, CITY (free, March/August 1999), Walsall, Rotherham United, Bristol City, Sheffield Wednesday, Burton Albion; retired May 2007; Rotherham United (manager), Barnsley (manager), Coventry City (manager), Huddersfield Town (manager).

Details: As a player, Mark Robins had a wonderful career, scoring 139 goals in 459 senior appearances at club level as well as gaining six England U21 caps (seven goals). He won the FA Cup, European Cup Winner's Cup and Super Cup with Manchester United and the League Cup with Leicester. Unfortunately, he was not 100 per cent fit with City, his two appearances being as a substitute in League games against Preston and Lincoln.

ROBINSON, John James (Goalkeeper)
Apps: 2 Born: Blackburn, 23/4/1918 Died: 1993

Career: Sacred Heart FC, Accrington Stanley, CITY (April 1937–November 1946), Bury, Southend United; retired injured, 1948.

Details: Jack Robinson made sixteen League appearances for Accrington and one either side of Second World War for City, before adding a further eighteen to his tally with his last two clubs. Tall and well built, unfortunately he conceded six goals on his City debut (in place of Frank Swift) against his future club Bury in September 1938, and gave away two more against the same opposition eight years later before moving to Gigg Lane.

ROBINSON, Michael John (Forward)
Apps/goals: 35/9 Born: Leicester, 1/7/1958

Career: Blackpool Schools, Coventry City (schoolboy forms), Waterloo Wanderers/Blackpool, Dolphinstone FC/Blackpool, Preston North End, CITY (record £756,000, June 1979/July 1980), Brighton & Hove Albion (£400,000), Liverpool (£200,000), Queen's Park Rangers (£100,000), Osasuna/Spain; retired May 1990; President of Iberian Superleague/Spain (rugby); and has worked for Setanta Sports, Radio TV Española, Cadena SER's El Larguero and Canalplus; hosted the cult TV programme *El Día Después* for fourteen years and speaks fluent Spanish. He is now resident in Spain, with celebrity status.

Details: Aggressive and mobile, Mick Robinson was leading scorer in his only season at the club with just nine goals – the lowest tally by a City player since George Wynn also netted nine times in 1910/11. He went on to play in the 1983 FA Cup final for Brighton, helped Liverpool win the First Division title, League Cup and European Cup, collected a League Cup runner's-up medal with QPR and netted four goals in twenty-four internationals for the Republic of Ireland (1981–86). Robinson scored 101 goals in 364 career appearances (eighty-three in 328 League games).

ROBINSON, Peter (Half-back)
Apps: 2 Born: Manchester, 29/1/1922
Died: Manchester, 9/9/2000

Career: Urmston, CITY (October 1941–October 1947); Second World War guest for Aldershot and Queen's Park Rangers; Chesterfield (in exchange for Billy Linacre), Buxton Notts County, King's Lynn, Macclesfield Town (manager), Hyde United (manager), CITY (youth coach, 1960s), Preston North End (youth coach), CTY (scout, 1970s).

Details: Peter Robinson made 142 League appearances after leaving Maine Road, having been unable to establish himself in City's first XI following the Second World War. He was certainly one of the best wing-halves outside the First Division during the early 1950s.

ROBINSON, Richard Bernard (Forward)
Apps/goals: 4/2 Born: Manchester, 1870
   Career: CITY (May 1893/January 1894), Wolverhampton Wanderers, Blakenhall.
   Details: Local player Dick Robinson spent just eight months with City but made an impact by scoring in his first two League games – in a 4-2 defeat by Burslem Port Vale and a 6-1 win over Middlesbrough Ironopolis. He failed to make the first XI at Wolves.

ROBINSON, William Samuel (Half-back)
Apps: 1 Born: Prescot, 1880 Died: 1926
   Career: Prescot BC, Bolton Wanderers, CITY (February 1902–May 1905), Hull City, Bolton Wanderers; retired injured, 1911; Hull City (scout).
   Details: A reserve right-half with City for three years, Bill Robinson's only game was in a 4-0 win over Small heath in the penultimate League game of the 1903/04 season when he stood in for Sammy Frost. Later regarded as the undisputed regular pivot for Hull City, he missed only nine out of a possible 114 League games in three seasons with the Tigers.

ROBSON, David (Full-back)
Apps/goals: 114/1 Born: Scotland, 1869
Died: before 1945
   Career: Ayr United, CITY (May 1890–January 1894), Wolverhampton Wanderers, CITY (November 1894–May 1896), Millwall.
   Details: Davie Robson, a well-built, stocky defender, played alongside Haydock in City's first-ever FA Cup encounter which resulted in a 12-0 win over hapless Liverpool Stanley in October 1890. Making excellent progress, he then appeared in City's first game in the Football Alliance (*v*. Bootle) and followed up by making his League debut, also against Bootle, in September 1892. After a brief spell with Wolves (five games) he returned to City and took his appearance tally past the 100 mark. He later played sixty-three times for Millwall.

ROCASTLE, David Carlyle (Forward)
Apps/goals: 23/2 Born: Lewisham, London, 2/5/1967 Died: London, 31/3/2001
   Career: Roger Manwood's Boys' School, South London Schools, Arsenal, Leeds United (£2 million), CITY (£2 million, plus David White, December 1993/August 1994), Chelsea (£1.25 million), Norwich City (loan), Hull City (loan), Sabah FC/Malaysia; retired March 1999.
   Details: David 'Rocky' Rocastle, eighteen when he made his League debut for Arsenal, had an excellent career, scoring forty-one goals in 399 club

games. A wide player, physically strong with flair and a good technique, he was registered with City for barely eighteen months, his two goals coming in successive League games, in a 2-1 win over Swindon and a 1-1 draw at QPR. He also played in fourteen U21, two 'B' and fourteen full internationals for England. He won the League Cup and two First Division championships with the Gunners. In February 2001, Rocastle announced that he was suffering from non-Hodgkins lymphoma, an aggressive form of cancer that attacks the immune system. Despite lengthy chemotheraphy, his health deteriorated and sadly he died at the age of thirty-three. His son, Ryan, was Arsenal's mascot in their FA Cup final match against Liverpool. Arsenal has a youth team indoor training facility named after him as a tribute to his contributions to the club.

RODGER, Charles Colin (Forward/left-half)
Apps/goals: 20/7 Born: Ayr, 1911
Died: after 1960
   Career: Craigview Alpha, Ayr United, CITY (December 1935–March 1938), Northampton Town, Ipswich Town; retired during the Second World War.
   Details: A very accomplished utility player, Colin Rodger deputised for forwards Brook, Herd, Marshall and Tilson and wing-half Bray during his career with City. He made his debut at inside-left (No. 10) in a 2-1 home defeat by Huddersfield a month after signing, and scored his first two goals in a 4-1 home win over Everton in the championship-winning season of 1936/37.

RODGER, Simon Lee (Midfield)
Apps/goals: 8/1 Born: Shoreham-by-Sea, 3/10/1971
   Career: Bognor Regis Town, Crystal Palace (£1,000), CITY (loan, October 1996–October 2002), Stoke City (loan), Woking, Brighton & Hove Albion; retired 2004; now a licensed private hire chauffeur, married to QVC beauty expert, Alison Young.
   Details: Simon Rodger did wonderfully well with Crystal Palace for whom he made 328 appearances in twelve years, helping the Eagles win the First Division championship in 1994. Particularly useful in dead-ball situations, his loan spell with his brought him one goal – in a 2-1 League defeat at Portsmouth.

RODWELL, Jack Christian (Midfield)
Apps/goals: 15/2 Born: Southport, 11/3/1991
   Career: Everton, CITY (£12 million, August 2012).
   Details: A big-money capture from Everton, 6-foot 1-inch tall midfielder Jack Rodwell found it hard to get into City's first XI, injuries not helping him one iota! He made his debut just after arriving

at the club, in a 3-2 home win over Southampton FC played in a 2-2 draw at Liverpool FC and after being sidelined from October, made a successful return to action in January 2013 in a 1-0 FA Cup win at Stoke, and scored his first goals in a 3-2 home PL defeat by Norwich on the last day of the season. Capped by England thirty-eight times between U16 and U21 levels, he has three full caps to his credit, with more to come, he hopes! He joined Everton at the age of seven, and his transfer fee could rise to £17 million.

ROGERS, Joseph Henry (Left-half)
Apps/goals: 14/1 Born: Normanton, 1915 Died: before 2000
   Career: Oswestry Town, CITY (February 1935–May 1938), Chester, Shrewsbury Town; retired 1945.
   Details: Joe Rogers – reserve to Jackie Bray – made his first two League appearances for City in April 1936 and his next two in April 1936. He later had eight senior outings in a row (including two in the FA Cup) early in 1938 when he scored his only goal – in a 2-1 League win over Portsmouth.

ROSLER, Uwe (Forward)
Apps/goals: 177/64 Born: Altenburg, Germany, 15/11/1968
   Career: Traktor Starken, Chemie Leipzig, FC Lokomotiv Leipzig, FC Magdeburg, Dynamo Dresden loan), FC Nurnburg, CITY (trial, March 1994, signed for £375,000, May 1994–April 1998), FC Kaiserslautern, Tennis Borussia Berlin, Southampton, West Bromwich Albion (loan), SpVgg Unterhacking, Lillestroem; retired 2003; Lillestroem (manager); Viking FK (manager), Molde FK (manager), Brentford (manager).
   Details: City's top scorer three seasons running, 1994–97, netting fifty goals in total, Uwe Rosler's efforts even outshone his more illustrious countryman Jurgen Klinsmann. Nicknamed 'Der Bomber' and a huge favourite with the fans, he teamed up well with Walsh, Quinn and Kinkladze before giving way to Dickov and Goater. Capped six times by East Germany, his career yielded over 150 goals in more than 500 club appearances, including 106 in 394 games in the Football League. He has done well as manager of Brentford, taking the Bees to the 2013 FL1 play-off final (beaten by Yeovil).

ROSS, David (Inside-forward)
Apps/goals: 63/19 Born: Over Darwen, 8/1/1884 Died: 1947
   Career: Heywood United, Bury, Luton Town, Norwich City, CITY (record £1,200, February 1907–July 1912), Dundee; retired 1919.
   Details: Davie Ross, who made his League debut for Bury in 1903, was City's first four-figure signing. Strong and forceful with a powerful right-foot shot, he top-scored for Norwich in the Southern League in 1905/06 and had his best spell at Hyde Road in the 1908/09-relegation season when he netted five goals in twenty-three games. He then helped City win the Second Division at the first attempt, bagging six goals in eleven starts.

ROSS, James Daniel (Forward)
Apps/goals: 70/22 Born: Edinburgh, 28/3/1866 Died: Manchester, 12/6/1902
   Career: Edinburgh St Bernard's, Preston North End, Liverpool, Burnley, CITY (February 1899 until his death).
   Details: Jimmy Ross was said to be as 'clever as a monkey'; fast, brilliant on the ball, with a stunning right-foot shot. With a flamboyant Hercule Poirot-like moustache, he was certainly a star performer in the late 1880s/early 90s, scoring goals galore for Preston, with whom he won the League and FA Cup double in 1889 and a second League title a year later. Believed to be the first player to score seven times in an FA Cup tie, in Preston's 26-0 win over Hyde in 1887, he notched a double hat-trick against Reading soon afterwards and became the first footballer to bag a four-timer in a League game v. Stoke in 1889. Leading scorer for Preston on seven occasions in nine seasons, during his eleven years at Deepdale he struck 101 goals in 151 League and FA Cup appearances and 251 in 222 'other' games. Nicknamed the 'little demon', Ross hit forty goals in eighty-five outings for Liverpool and thirty-two in sixty-three for Burnley, helping the Clarets reach the top flight, before spending just over two seasons with City. Playing alongside Billy Meredith, he netted seven goals in his first nine outings, including one on his debut v. Walsall, fired in eleven more in 1899/1900 and added three more after that, playing his last game against his former club Preston in an FA Cup tie in January 1902.
   Surprisingly, or should that be amazingly, he was never capped by Scotland, and was just thirty-six when he died from what was described as 'acute skin disease'.

ROWAN, Alexander (Forward)
Apps/goals: 48/25 Born: Stirlingshire, 1869 Died: 1965
   Career: Albion Rovers, Nottingham Forest, Albion Rovers, Sheffield Wednesday, Burton Swifts, CITY (August 1894–May 1896); retired 1897; became a licensee.
   Details: 'Sandy' Rowan showed fine form in Scotland, failed to impress at Forest but was a 'class act' with Wednesday, striking twelve goals in thirty-four games. He gave City good service for two seasons, finishing second joint top scorer in 1894/95 when starring in attack alongside Meredith, Finnerhan, Sharples and McReddie.

ROWLEY, Henry Bowater (Forward)
*Apps/goals: 18/4 Born: Bilston, Staffs,
23/1/1904 Died: 19/12/1985*

Career: Southend United (trial), Shrewsbury Town, Manchester United (£100), CITY (exchanged for Bill Ridding, December 1931–February 1933), Oldham Athletic (loan/signed), Manchester United (£1,375), Burton Town (player-manager), Gillingham; retired during the Second World War.

Details: Harry Rowley scored thirty goals for Shrewsbury in 1927/28, and swiftly bridged the gap between non-League and First Division football by making an immediate impact with Manchester United. A powerful man, hard to knock off the ball, he left Old Trafford when the Reds were relegated, but failed to settle with City despite netting twice on his debut in a 5-2 win at Sunderland in January 1932. Then, after netting fourteen times in seventy-three outings for Oldham, he returned to United and hit nineteen goals in their Second Division title-winning season of 1935/36.

ROYLE, Joseph (Centre-forward)
Apps/goals: 126/32 Born: Liverpool, 8/4/1949

Career: Liverpool Schools, Everton, CITY (£200,000, December 1974–August 1980), Bristol City (loan), Norwich City (£60,000); retired injured, April 1982; Oldham Athletic (manager), Everton (manager), CITY (manager, February 1998–May 2001), Ipswich Town (manager), Oldham Athletic (manager).

Details: Striker Joe Royle, excellent in the air and pretty useful on the ground, made a slow start with City, netting only one goal in his first nineteen League games. But he was back on track in 1975/76, and besides his tally of twelve First Division goals, he also scored in every round of the League Cup up to the final that City won 2-1 v. Newcastle.

He made his League debut for Everton at the age of sixteen and held the record of being the youngest player to appear at senior level for Merseysiders until James Vaughan surpassed it by eleven days in April 2005.

He scored 119 goals in 270 appearances during his time at Goodison Park, gaining a League championship medal in 1970. After relegation battles with Bristol City (for whom he scored four goals on his debut v. Middlesbrough in November 1977) and Norwich, Royle retired having netted 152 goals in a total of 473 League games. He represented England at schoolboy, youth, U23 and senior levels, collecting the first of six full caps v. Malta in 1970. He also played for the Football League.

As an influential manager, Royle guided Oldham into the top flight of English football and to the 1990 League Cup final, won the FA Cup and Charity Shield with Everton and steered City to promotion in 2000. He was in charge of 1,096 matches as a manager, 608 with Oldham.

ROYLE, Stanley (Outside-right)
Apps: 1 Born: Manchester, 1896

Career: Heaton Chapel, CITY (July 1918–May 1922).

Details: An amateur throughout his career, Stan Royle's only senior game for City was against Sheffield United (away) in April 1922 when he occupied Billy Meredith's position on the right-wing.

RUDGE, James John (Outside-left)
*Apps: 2 Born: Hull, 25/10/1919
Died: Manchester, 13/12/1985*

Career: Fearons Tenure Athletic/Dublin, CITY (January 1938–March 1947), York City, Leeds United, Rotherham United, Scunthorpe United, Workington, Northwich Victoria, Stafford Rangers; retired 1955; CITY (matchday steward, late 1950s); served in the Durham Light Infantry during the Second World War; worked for Kelloggs/Manchester, serving as a union secretary for twenty-one years; also employed as a kitchen porter.

Details: Jack Rudge scored forty goals in 235 competitive games during his war-interrupted career. His two League starts for City came in successive weeks in November 1946 v. Nottingham Forest (a) and Southampton (h). He netted three goals in fourteen Second World War outings for City and helped Rotherham win the Third Division (N) title. His nephew Billy played for Birmingham, Bury, Grimsby, Rochdale and York City.

RUSHTON, Walter (Forward)
Apps/goals: 1/2 Born: Bolton, 1865

Career: Bolton Wanderers, CITY (May 1890–May 1892)

Details: Wally Rushton scored twice when City beat Liverpool Stanley 12-0 in the club's first-ever FA Cup match in October 1890. He was reserve for the Football Alliance and Second Division seasons that followed.

RUSSELL, Craig Stewart (Forward)
Apps/goals: 37/4 Born: South Shields, 4/2/1974

Career: Sunderland, CITY (£1m, plus Craig Russell, November 1997–April 2000), Tranmere Rovers (loan), Port Vale (loan), Darlington (loan), Oxford United (loan), St Johnstone (loan/signed), Carlisle United, Darlington; retired May 2005; Newcastle Falcons Rugby Club (physio), Newcastle United (physio), Sunderland (physio).

Details: After an indifferent first six months with City (one goal in twenty-six appearances) former England youth international Craig Russell scored twice in a 3-0 FA Cup win over Halifax in November 1998 in front of 11,108 fans, City's lowest home crowd since 1908. He was always struggling with his form at Maine Road, having earlier netted thirty-four goals in 174 outings for Sunderland, with whom he won a Second Division championship medal in 1996.

RUSSELL, David Kennedy (Centre-half)
Apps/goals: 19/3 Born: Beith, Ayrshire, 6/4/1864 Died: Edinburgh, 4/1/1918
Career: Shott Juniors, Stewart Cunningham FC, Broxburn, Heart of Midlothian, Preston North End, Nottingham Forest, Heart of Midlothian, CITY (July 1892/May 1893), Heart of Midlothian, Notts County, Heart of Midlothian, Celtic, Preston North End, Celtic, Broxburn; retired 1905.
Details: A huge man and a wonderful defender, with immaculate distribution skills and expert spoiling powers, Scottish international, capped six times, Davey Russell played in City's first-ever game in the Football League (*v.* Bootle) and had the misfortune of missing the club's first-ever penalty in this game. However, he made amends by scoring twice against Northwich Victoria in his second outing. He was even used as an emergency centre-forward against Grimsby before returning to Tynecastle.
One of the stars of Preston's double-winning team of 1888/89, he followed up with a second League championship medal in 1890 and also gained Scottish League and Cup winner's medals with both Celtic and Hearts, and helped Forest win the Football Alliance. Russell also represented the Scottish League and the East of Scotland FA.

RYAN, John Gilbert (Full-back/midfield)
Apps: 19 Born: Lewisham, 20/7/194
Career: Arsenal, Maidstone United, Fulham, Luton Town, Norwich City (£40,000), Seattle Sounders (£70,000), Sheffield United, CITY (January 1982/August 1983, player-coach), Stockport County (player-coach), Chester City (player-coach), Cambridge United (player-manager); retired 1984; Maidstone United (assistant-manager/coach), Sittingbourne (manager), Dover Athletic (manager), Dulwich Hamlet (manager; Dover Athletic manager); ran a transport/garage business in Maidstone, Kent; also FA School of Excellence (coach).
Details: John Ryan made 515 appearances in the Football League and over 600 in all competitions. A strong, attack-minded, right-sided player whose long passes at times were superb, he was thirty-four when he joined City but still produced some fine performances, one of his best coming in the Manchester derby draw at Old Trafford.

S

SADDINGTON, Harold (Utility)
Apps: 6 Born: Hulme, Manchester, 1870
Career: CITY (May 1893/April 1894).
Details: Versatile reserve Harry Saddington occupied four different positions (4, 7, 10 and 11) during his one season with City, making his League debut in a 1-0 home defeat by Liverpool.

SALT, George Oscar (Outside-left)
Apps: 1 Born: Cheadle, 1889
Career: CITY (January 1911–May 1913).
Details: Another reserve, George Salt's only League appearance of his career was for City against Bristol City in April 1911 when he deputised for Jimmy Conlin.

SAMARAS, Georgios (Striker)
Apps/goals: 65/12 Born: Heraklion, Greece, 21/2/1985
Career: OFI Crete, Heerenveen/Holland, CITY (£6 million, January 2006–July 2008), Celtic (loan/signed for £1 million).
Details: Giant 6-foot 4-inch striker Georgious Samaras' big-money move to City was a record for a Greek player, and at the time he stated he was 'excited about moving to England, because he saw them (City) as being the next stage in his development.' He made his Premiership debut a month after joining, as a sixty-fifth-minute substitute for Andy Cole in a 3-0 win over Newcastle and netted his first goal in the next home match *v.* Charlton, following up with two in sixty seconds in a 3-1 win over Sunderland. But then his form dipped, which prompted manager Stuart Pearce to publicly state that he (Samaras) would have to 'toughen up' if he wanted to be a success in the Premier League, and that his all-round game wasn't good enough. Some fans earlier had criticised Pearce for signing him in the first place!
Then, after Sven-Göran Eriksson had replaced Pearce, Samaras's form improved, and in 2006/07 he made forty-two appearances (twenty-two off the bench) but managed only six goals.
Nevertheless, the long-haired Greek international stuck it out and remained at the club until January 2008 when he joined Celtic on loan, signing permanently for the Glasgow club six months later at a huge loss! Over the last five years he has done well with the Bhoys, gaining three SPL, two Scottish Cup and a League Cup winner's medals, while taking his tally of full internationals caps to sixty-four (eight goals), having earlier played five times for his country's U21 team. At May 2013, Samaras had netted 105 goals in 387 club games.

SAMBROOK, Raymond (Forward)
Apps/goals: 67/13 Born: Wolverhampton, 31/5/1933

Career: Wednesfield, Coventry City, CITY (February 1958–June 1962), Doncaster Rovers, Crewe Alexandra; retired 1964.

Details: Injuries eventually caught up with Ray Sambrook, causing him to quit League football at the age of thirty-one. In his day he produced some good, honest performances for City, appearing in fifty-one out of a possible sixty-one first-class matches following his debut *v.* Nottingham in mid-January 1958. He was excellent at times in 1958/59 when partnering Joe Hayes on the left wing. He was replaced by Clive Colbridge at Maine Road.

SANTA CRUZ, Roque Luis Cantero (Striker)
Apps/goals: 22/4 Born: Asunción, Paraguay, 18/8/1981

Career: Olimpia, Bayern Munich (£5 million), Blackburn Rovers (£3.5 million), CITY (£17.5 million, June 2009; released June 2013), Blackburn Rovers (loan), Real Betis (loan), CF Malaga (loan).

Details: The tall Paraguayan striker had a frustrating first season with City with injuries, especially to his right knee, causing him all sorts of problems. Used mainly as a substitute by his two managers (Mark Hughes and then Roberto Mancini), Santa Cruz struggled to make the starting line-up and for his 'own good' was loaned out initially to Real Betis. Before joining City for a massive fee, he had netted thirty-five goals in 165 games for Bayern Munich and twenty-nine in seventy outings for Blackburn.

By May 2013, Santa Cruz had scored twenty-five times in ninety-two full internationals for his country, having earlier bagged six in thirteen U21 matches.

SAVAGE, John Alfred (Goalkeeper)
Apps: 31 Born: Bromley, Kent, 14/12/1929

Career: RAF football, Hull City, Halifax Town, CITY (£4,000, November 1953–January 1958), Walsall (£1,000), Wigan Athletic; retired 1964.

Details: Deputising for Trautmann, John Savage conceded fifteen goals (six at Preston and nine at WBA) in the space of four days in September 1957. The possessor of exceptional physical attributes in height (6 feet 3 inches) and weight (14 stone), he could get down quickly to low shots and deal with high crosses. It was the defenders in front of him that let him down! A goalscorer for Halifax in a League game (when injured and playing on the wing) he kept goal for the Southern Section against the Northern Section in the annual representative match as a Walsall player but was also sent off *v.* Swindon as a 'Saddler.'

SAVIĆ, Stefan (Defender)
Apps/goals: 20/1 Born: Mojkovac, Montenegro, 8/1/1991

Career: Brskvo, BSK Borcva, Partizan Belgrade, CITY (£6 million, July 2011–August 2012), Fiorentina/Italy (deal involving Matijo Nastasic).

Details: Granted a work permit by the Home office, Stefan Savić was the first Montenegrin to play for City, and, indeed, to feature in the Premiership. Initially signing a four-year contract, he left after just one season. After a solid debut in the FA Community Shield *v.* Manchester United at Wembley, he played his first Premiership game against Swansea and scored his first goal in a 4-0 victory at Blackburn; but for all his efforts, failed to gain a regular place in the starting line-up, being used mainly as a substitute. However, in January 2012, with Vincent Kompany suspended for four matches and Kolo Touré playing in the African Cup of Nations, he had an extended run in the first team in the left centre back position. He showed brief flashes of form during this time, but also looked nervous, resulting in frequent misplaced passes, clearances, and crucially conceded a penalty in a league cup defeat by Liverpool FC. When Kompany returned, it was back to the bench for Savić. His last game for City came in the 3-2 win over Sporting Lisbon in the Europa League in March. Surprisingly, he was one of the few City players to appear in all five competitions in 2011/12. He has represented Montenegro in three U17, seven U19, five U21 and twenty full internationals, playing against England in the 2014 World Cup qualifiers.

SCAPUZZI, Luca (Midfield)
Apps: 2 Born: Milan, 15/4/1991

Career: Olmi, AC Milan, Portogruaro, CITY (trial/signed, July 2011), Oldham Athletic (loan), Portsmouth (loan), AS Varese/Italy 1910 (loan).

Details: Scapuzzi scored as a substitute against a League of Ireland XI in the Dublin Super Cup while on trial with City's Elite Development Squad and was immediately signed on a three-year contract. In September 2011, he made his senior debut, also off the bench, in a League Cup tie *v.* Birmingham before starting against Wolves in the next round when his shot was a deflected home by opposing defender De Vries for an own-goal in a 5-2 win at Molineux. He was loaned out to 'gain experience.'

SCHMEICHEL, Kasper Peter (Goalkeeper)
Apps: 10 Born: Copenhagen, 5/11/1986

Career: CITY (June 2003–August 2009), Darlington (loan), Bury (loan, three spells), Falkirk (loan), Cardiff City (loan), Coventry City (loan), Notts County, Leeds United, Leicester City.

Details: Son of Peter (below), Schmeichel junior kept four clean sheets in his first seven Premiership games for City, and he also saved a penalty against Arsenal! But owing to the form of Andreas

Isaksson, he soon found himself back on the bench. He made seventy-three appearances as a loanee before joining Notts County (with whom he won the Division Two championship) and having represented Denmark in eight U19, one U20 and seventeen U21 internationals, he won his first full cap against Macedonia in February 2013.

SCHMEICHEL, Peter Boleslaw, MBE (Goalkeeper)
Apps: 31 Born: Gladsaxe, Denmark, 18/11/1963
Career: Høje-Gladsaxe, Gladsaxe-hero, Hvidovre IF, Brøndby IF, Manchester United, Sporting Club de Portugal, Aston Villa, CITY (July 2002, retired May 2003); Hvidovre IF (owner/director); BBC TV pundit; owned his own recording/music studio; host of TV3 quiz show *1-mod-100*.

Details: Schmeichel spent the last season of his illustrious career with City, going out on a high as he extended his 'unbeaten' record in Manchester derbies! Prior to joining the Blues, he had never been on the losing side in nine years when playing for United and in 2002/03 he helped City win at Maine Road and draw at Old Trafford.

Voted the 'World's Best Goalkeeper' in 1992 and 1993, he is, of course, best remembered for his time with Manchester United, who he captained to victory in the 1999 UEFA Champions League to complete The Treble, and also for leading Denmark to glory in UEFA Euro 1992.

With his intimidating physique (6 feet 3 inches tall and 16 stone in weight) he was a giant between the sticks. He had a specially made size XXXL jersey, donned a massive pair of gloves and wore size twelve boots. And really, he looked enormous to opposing forwards!

Having already played in 709 club matches and 129 internationals for Denmark (1987–2001), scoring eleven goals, including one for his country, Schmeichel looked as safe as ever and produced some outstanding performances, helping City win at Anfield. He retired at the end of the season after adding another thirty-one appearances to his career total. And he's the most capped player for the Denmark (1987–2001). The IFFHS ranked Schmeichel among the top ten goalkeepers of the twentieth century in 2000, while in 2001 poll held by Reuters, the majority of the 200,000 participants voted him as the best goalkeeper ever, ahead of Lev Yashin and Gordon Banks. Inducted into the English Football Hall of Fame in 2003, in recognition of his impact on the English game, a year later he was named as one of the '125 greatest living footballers' at the FIFA celebrations.

Schmeichel holds the record for the greatest clean sheets-to-games ratio in the Premier League with 42 per cent. Besides his treble-winning season with United, he also helped the Reds win four more Premiership titles, the FA Cup twice, the League Cup, European Super Cup and the Charity Shield on four occasions.

SCOTSON, James (Forward)
Apps/goals: 8/2 Born: Manchester, 1874
Career: CITY (May 1898–September 1903), Stockport County.

Details: Reserve to Drummond, Gillespie, Williams, Ross, McOustra and others, Jimmy Scotson scored twice in his fifth League game for City, in a 4-2 win over Aston Villa in April 1901.

SCOTT, Ian (Midfield)
Apps/goals: 34/4 Born: Radcliffe, 20/9/1967
Career: Bury Boys, CITY (June 1984–July 1989), Stoke City (£175,000), Crewe Alexandra (loan), Bury (loan/signed).

Details: A Schoolboy international (five caps), Ian Scott made thirty-one of his thirty-four appearances for City in 1987/88, scoring in three of his first six. He signed for Stoke at Manchester airport, after being met by manger Mick Mills. He didn't impress Crewe boss Dario Gradi!

SCOTT, Sidney (Centre-half)
Apps: 26 Born: Macclesfield, 11/2/1892
Died: after 1947
Career: Castle Primitives, Northwich Victoria, CITY (May 1913–June 1921); First World War guest for Tranmere Rovers; Norwich City, New Brighton, Stafford Rangers; retired 1924.

Details: A hardy player, Sid Scott lost his place to Max Woosnam in City's defence, and after winning the Cheshire County Cup with Tranmere, he sadly broke his leg on his debut for Norwich *v.* Luton.

SCULLY, Anthony Derek Thomas (Midfield/winger)
Apps: 9 Born: Dublin, 12/6/1976
Career: Crystal Palace, Bournemouth (loan), Cardiff City (loan), CITY (£80,000, August 1997/ March 1998), Stoke City (loan), Queen's Park Rangers (£155,000), Cambridge United, Southend United (loan), Peterborough United (loan), Dagenham & Redbridge, Barnet, Tamworth, Notts County.

Details: A Republic of Ireland international at schoolboy, youth, 'B', U21 and senior levels, gaining ten full caps in total, Tony Scully had a varied career, serving with thirteen different clubs while making just over 200 appearances. Eight of his outings for City came off the subs' bench.

SEAGRAVES, Mark (Defender)
Apps: 50 Born: Bootle, 22/10/1966
Career: Liverpool, Norwich City (loan), CITY (£100,000, September 1987–September 1990), Bolton Wanderers (£100,000), Swindon Town (£100,000), Barrow.

Details: An England youth international, Mark Seagraves failed to get a game with Liverpool and after a handful of appearances for Norwich, spent three seasons with City, occupying the right-back and right-half positions most of the time, having his best spell in the first team between March 1988 and January 1989, helping City gain promotion to the top flight in the latter campaign. He played in 195 games for Bolton and seventy-nine for Swindon, with whom he won the Division Two championship in 1996.

SEAMAN, David (Goalkeeper)
Apps: 26 Born: Rotherham, 19/9/1963
Career: Kimberworth Comprehensive School/ Rotherham, Leeds United, Peterborough United (£4,000), Birmingham City (£100,000), Queens Park Rangers (£225,000), Arsenal (£1.3 million), CITY (free, July 2003, retired January 2004); Arsenal (coaching staff).
Details: A commanding figure between the posts, England's second most-capped goalkeeper David Seaman, was brave, agile with a safe pair of hands, an expert at saving penalties who made very few mistakes, though his worst was against Brazil when he misjudged Ronaldinho's looping free-kick winner which knocked England out of the 2002 World Cup. Hoping to enjoy a swansong season, he took over from Peter Schmeichel in the City goal, but his career ended earlier than expected when he damaged his shoulder in a 4-2 defeat at Portsmouth.
Seaman played under seven different England managers, including two former City bosses, Kevin Keegan and Sven-Göran Eriksson; represented his country in one unofficial, six 'B', ten U21 and 75 full internationals; amassed 1,050 appearances for clubs and country, 712 in the Football League and Premiership alone; and in his 13 years with Arsenal, won the First Division championship, the Premiership twice, the FA Cup four times and the League Cup and European Cup Winner's Cup once. He has also appeared on the BBC TV shows *Strictly Come Dancing* and *Dancing on Ice* and received the OBE in 1997. Towards the end of his career, he signed his autograph 'safe hands.'

SEAR, Reginald Clifford (Full-back)
Apps/goals: 279/1 Born: Rhostyllen, 22/9/1936
Career: Oswestry Town, CITY (June 1955– April 1968); Chester (player-coach/manager/ assistant-manager); retired 1970; Wrexham (Youth Development Officer).
Details: Some say stylish full-back Cliff Sear should have played more times for Wales at senior level. As it was, he gained just one full and two U23 caps, mainly due to the form of Graham Williams. A former miner at Bershaw Colliery, he made his League debut on the last day of the 1956/57 season, in a 3-3 draw at Birmingham. He then bedded himself into the team at a difficult time in the club's history, adding stability to the defence and over the next seven years produced some outstanding performances. He subsequently joined former teammate Alan Oakes at Chester.

SHADWELL, William John (Left-half)
Apps: 2 Born: Bury, 1910 Died: Devon, after 1955
Career: Turton FC, CITY (May 1933–July 1936), Exeter City; retired injured, May 1946.
Details: Jack Shadwell spent three seasons in City's second XI, acting a cover for Jimmy McLuckie and Jackie Bray. His debut came in a 3-0 defeat at Huddersfield in March 1935. He went on to make ninety-one appearances for Exeter.

SHARP, Samuel (Half-back)
Apps/goals: 182/1 Born: Manchester, 1895
Career: Bolton Wanderers, CITY (April 1918– June 1929), Crewe Alexandra, Wigan Athletic; retired 1932.
Details: Sam Sharp established himself as City's regular right-half during the 1921/22 season, missed only one game the following term, was absent from eight in 1923/24 and starred in forty out of the scheduled forty-two League games in 1924/25 before losing his place to Cliff Coupland. A reserve thereafter, he was a City player for eleven years, and was described as being 'a good positional player, tireless, whole-hearted and a crisp tackler.' An FA representative in 1924, he was an England international trialist a year later.

SHARPLES, James (Forward)
*Apps/goals: 40/20 Born: Blackburn, 1874
Died: 1920*
Career: Rossendale, CITY (June 1894–May 1897), Wigan County, Swindon Town, Millwall Athletic.
Details: Able to play in any front-line position, Jim Sharples had an excellent first season at Hyde Road, finishing joint second top scorer with twelve goals, including a hat-trick in a 6-1 win over Walsall Town Swifts in October 1894. In fact, he netted seven goals in four games during that month, having started off by scoring in Gainsborough Trinity's first-ever League game (1-1 draw on 12 September).

SHAWCROSS, Francis David (Half-back)
Apps/goals: 55/2 Born: Stretford, Manchester, 3/7/1941
Career: Manchester Boys, CITY (July 1956– June 1965), Stockport County, Halifax Town.
Details: Although an accomplished half-back, David Shawcross was City's top Central League scorer in 1963/64. He made his senior debut at Arsenal in September 1958 and played his last

game against Derby County six years later. An England youth and U23 international, after leaving City he added a further 192 League appearances to his tally, 132 with Halifax.

SHELIA, Murtaz (Defender)
Apps/goals: 17/2 Born: Tbilisi, Georgia, 25/3/1969

Career: Amirani Ochamchire, Dinamo Tbilisi, 1 FC Saarbrucken, Dinamo Tbilisi, Spartak-Alania Vladikavkaz, CITY (£400,000, November 1997– January 2000), West Ham United (loan), Dinamo Tbilisi, Lokomotiv Tbilisi.

Details: Murtaz Shelia teamed up with his former Dinamo Tbilisi teammate Georgi Kinkladze at Maine Road and marked his debut with a goal at Birmingham City, though City lost the match 2-1. Six weeks later another Georgian, Kakhaber Tskhadadze, joined him in defence. But as the season reached its conclusion, injuries restricted Shelia's appearances. He scored his second goal against Nottingham Forest, but following the arrival of Andy Morrison and a series of knee and groin injuries, he returned for a third spell with Tbilisi. Shelia won twenty-nine caps for Georgia, 1994–98.

SHERON, Michael Nigel (Forward)
Apps/goals: 119/28 Born: Liverpool, 11/1/1972

Career: Schoolboy football, CITY (July 1988– August 1994), Bury (loan), Norwich City (£1 million), Stoke City (£450,000 plus Keith Scott), Queen's Park Rangers (£2.75 million), Barnsley (£1 million), Blackpool, Macclesfield Town, Shrewsbury Town.

Details: After progressing through the YTS ranks at Maine Road, and being named City's young Player of the Year in 1992, Mike Sheron developed into a very useful forward, with a 'purposeful approach, good pace and strong right-foot shot'. His best season with City was in 1992/93 (forty-five appearances, fourteen goals) and he was joint top scorer the following year with just six goals!

His career realised 768 appearances and 152 goals (with a League record of 688/26). He gained sixteen England U21 caps and was an AWS winner with Blackpool in 2004.

SHINTON, Robert Thomas (Forward)
Apps: 6 Born: West Bromwich, 6/1/1952

Career: West Bromwich Albion (trial), Lye Town, Walsall, Cambridge United (£22,000), Wrexham (£15,000), CITY (£300,000, June 1979/March 1980), Millwall (loan), Newcastle United (£175,000), Millwall (loan), Worcester City (player-manager), Weymouth; Willingham FC; retired 1988; became a glazier in Worcester.

Details: Long-haired, slightly-framed striker Bobby Shinton rose to prominence with Wrexham during the late 1970s, the club's historian writing 'he mesmerised the opposition at times'. He netted fifty-six goals in 175 appearances before lining up alongside several international stars at City, where he managed only six starts under manager Malcolm Allison who handed him his debut at Arsenal. He suffered a medial ligament injury while at Newcastle and never regained full fitness.

SHUKER, Christopher Alan (Forward)
Apps/goals: 6/1 Born: Huyton, Liverpool, 9/5/1982

Career: Everton, CITY (June 1998–March 2004), Macclesfield Town (loan), Walsall (loan), Rochdale (loan), Hartlepool United (loan), Barnsley, Tranmere Rovers, Morecambe, Port Vale.

Details: A nippy, right-sided player, just 5 feet 5 inches tall, Chris Shuker signed professional forms for City a year after leaving Everton's academy. Given his League baptism by Macclesfield, in March 2001, he broke into City's first team six months later, marking his debut with a sixty-fourth-minute goal after replacing Eyal Berkovic in a 4-2 League Cup win over Notts County. He later played cameo roles in 3-0 wins over Walsall and Barnsley, but managed only three appearances in City's promotion-winning season of 2001/02. Shuker was nearing his 400th club appearance as the 2012/13 season ended.

SHUTT, Carl Steven (Forward)
Apps: 6 Born: Sheffield, 10/10/1961

Career: Spalding United, Sheffield Wednesday, Bristol City, Leeds United, Birmingham City, CITY (loan, December 1993/January 1994), Bradford City, Darlington, Kettering Town (player/caretaker-manager and manager), Bradford Park Avenue (player-manager); retired 2006.

Details: Carl Shutt had scored over seventy goals in more than 250 club appearances before his brief loan spell at Maine Road. He stood in for David White when making his debut in a 2-0 defeat at Newcastle on New Year's Day 1994. He had earlier helped Leeds win the Second and First Division titles in 1990 and 1992 respectively.

SIBIERSKI, Antoine (Forward/midfield)
Apps/goals: 107/15 Born: Lille, France, 5/8/1974

Career: Lille, Auxerre, Nantes, Lens, Newcastle United, CITY (£700,000, August 2003–June 2007), Wigan Athletic, Norwich City (loan); retired May 2009; Racing Club de Lens (Sporting Director); also football agent.

Details: Antoine Sibierski scored on his City debut against Charlton, but after that spent quite sometime as a substitute, starting only twenty-two of the forty games he participated in during his first season. A regular in 2004/05, he had to fight for his place again the following season, being called off the bench fourteen times. In his day he was a gifted player with the ball at his feet, but looked 'average' with City. During a career in France and England, he scored eighty-five goals in 444 League games. He won the French Cup twice with Nantes (1999 and 2000) and gained 'B' and U21 caps for his country.

SIDDALL, Barry Alfred (Goalkeeper)
Apps: 6 Born: Ellesmere Port, 12/9/1954
Career: Bolton Wanderers, Sunderland, Darlington (loan), Port Vale, Blackpool (loan), Stoke City (£20,000), Tranmere Rovers (loan), CITY (loan, March/May 1986), Blackpool, Stockport County, Hartlepool United, West Bromwich Albion, Mossley, Carlisle United, Chester City, Northwich Victoria, Preston North End, Lincoln City (loan), Burnley, Birmingham City, Horwich RMI, Bury (loan); retired 1996; became a freelance goalkeeping coach, associated mainly with Burnley.

Details: Signed to replace the injured Eric Nixon, Barry Siddall conceded nine goals in his six League games with City as they battled to stay clear of the relegation zone. In a long career, which spanned almost twenty-five years, he served with twenty-one different clubs (seventeen in the Football League) and made over 700 appearances, having his best spells with Sunderland, Bolton and Blackpool, second time round. An England youth international, he helped Port Vale win the Fourth Division title in 1983.

SILKMAN, Barry (Midfield/forward)
Apps/goals: 21/3 Born: Stepney, London, 29/6/1952
Career: Barnet, Hereford United, Crystal Palace, Plymouth Argyle, Luton Town (loan), CITY (March 1979/July 1980), Brentford, Queen's Park Rangers, Leyton Orient, Southend United, Crewe Alexandra, Staines Town; retired 1988; became a successful greyhound trainer.

Details: A versatile player, Barry Silkman – with his curly black hair, gold earring and flamboyant approach – had a fine career, scoring thirty-one goals in 340 League games, covering thirteen years. Signed by Malcolm Allison who had been his boss at Plymouth, he made twenty appearances in succession for City, from his scoring debut at Ipswich in March 1979 until losing his place to £1.4 million signing Steve Daley in late September.

SILVA, David Josué Jimenéz (Midfield)
Apps/goals: 143/19 Born: Arguineguin, Spain, 8/1/1986
Career: UD San Fernando, Valencia, Eibar (loan), Celta Vigo (loan), CITY (£24 million, June 2010).

Details: A star performer for City from the word go, David Silva can create goals (sometimes out

of nothing) as well a score them, doing so from any angle with both feet and also his head! He made his debut in a 0-0 draw with Tottenham in August 2010, and since then, injuries apart, he has been generally outstanding, helping City win the FA Cup in 2011 and the Premiership and Community Shield double in 2012. Before entering the Premiership, he had appeared in more than 150 games in Spanish football, helping his country win the European Championship (2008) and the World Cup (2010). He then gained a second European Championship medal in 2012 while steadily building up his tally of full caps, which stood at seventy-five with twenty goals scored at May 2013. Earlier in his career Silva won the Copa del Rey with Valencia and represented his country fifty-four times at intermediate level (U16 to U21). In May 2011, Carlos Tévez lauded him (Silva) as the 'best signing City have made'.

SILVA, João Alves de Assis (Striker)
Apps/goals: 38/6 Born: São Paulo, Brazil, 20/3/1987
Career: Corinthians/Brazil, CSKA Moscow, CITY (record £18.5 million, September 2008–July 2011), Everton (loan, two spells), Galatasaray (loan), SC Internacional/Brazil, Atletico Mineiro/Brazil.

Details: In his first season with City, Brazilian international Jo scored once (v. Portsmouth) in nine Premiership games and twice in the UEFA Cup against Amonia Nicosia. Finding it difficult to establish himself in the team, he joined Everton on loan, returned to City, but then went back to Goodison Park for the whole of the 2009/10 season, with the option of a permanent move if he wished. However, after returning to Brazil without permission over the Christmas period, Everton manager David Moyes suspended him for a breach of conduct. Spell over, Jo returned to City, but was quickly off-loaded to Galatasaray. On his return to City, he netted in pre-season friendlies against Portland Timbers, New York Red Bulls, Borussia Dortmund and Valencia, in the Europa League win over Salzburg and also in the Football League cup tie at WBA. But after that he was in and out of the side up to his departure. In his day, Jo was a good striker who won seven U23 and seven full caps for Brazil (two goals), helped CSKA Moscow complete a domestic treble in 2006 and collect a football bronze medal at the 2008 Olympics and helped his country win the 2013 Confederations Cup.

SIMON, Frank Arthur (Half-back)
Apps: 1 Born: Manchester, 1869
Career: amateur football, CITY (July/November 1890).

Details: An amateur, Frank Simon played in City's first-ever FA Cup tie, a 12-0 win over Liverpool Stanley in October 1890.

SIMPSON, Albert (Forward)
Apps: 1 Born: Salford, 3/5/1899
   Career: CITY (May 1921–May 1923), Bournemouth, Peterborough & Fletton Athletic.
   Details: A reserve with City for two seasons, Bert Simpson's only first-team appearance came in a 3-1 League defeat at Birmingham in April 1922 when he deputised for Horace Barnes.

SIMPSON, Fitzroy (Midfield)
Apps/goals: 82/4 Born: Trowbridge, 26/2/1970
   Career: Swindon Town, CITY (£500,000, March 1992–August 1995), Bristol City (loan), Portsmouth (£200,000), Heart of Midlothian (£100,000), Walsall, Telford United.
   Details: A Jamaican international, capped thirty-nine times, Fitzroy Simpson proved a big asset in midfield, his late runs and overall commitment giving him important status within the squad. He made eleven successive appearances at the end of the 1991/92 season, scoring his first City goal in a 2-0 win over Notts County. He followed up with twenty-nine outings in the first Premiership campaign, fifteen in 1993/94 and sixteen in his final season at Maine Road. During an excellent first-class career Simpson bagged twenty-eight goals in 471 club appearances.

SIMPSON, Paul David (Forward)
Apps/goals: 155/24 Born: Carlisle, 26/7/1966
   Career: Cumbria Boys, CITY (July 1982–October 1988), Finn Harps (loan), Oxford United, Derby County, Sheffield United (loan), Wolverhampton Wanderers (loan/signed), Walsall (loan), Blackpool, Rochdale (player-manager), Carlisle United (player, caretaker-manager/player-manager); retired from playing 2005; Preston North End (manager), Shrewsbury Town (manager), Stockport County (manager), Northwich Victoria (manager).
   Details: Paul Simpson, quick and decisive, and useful in dead-ball situations, made his League debut for City as a sixteen-year-old against Coventry in October 1982, playing on the left side of midfield, his preferred position. He finally established himself in the first team in 1985/86 under manager Billy McNeill, scoring ten goals in fifty appearances as City escaped relegation by just four points. Released by Mel Machin, he took his career record to 179 goals in 804 senior appearances, winning promotion with City in 1985, Derby in 1996 and Blackpool in 2001, following up by helping the Seasiders win the Leyland DAF Trophy in 2002.
   An England youth international, Simpson was later capped five times at U21 level.

SINCLAIR, Graeme James (Defender)
Apps: 1 Born: Paisley, Scotland, 1/7/1957
   Career: Dumbarton, Celtic, CITY (loan, November/December 1984), Dumbarton (loan), St Mirren; retired injured, 1986.

   Details: Greame Sinclair spent just fourteen days with City, making one League appearance in the absence of Mick McCarthy, in a 2-2 home draw with Portsmouth, when he was substituted by Gordon Smith. He played well in 220 games for Dumbarton and twice represented the Scottish League (1978–80).

SINCLAIR, Scott Andrew (Forward)
Apps: 15 Born: Bath, Somerset, 25/3/1989
   Career: Ralph Allen School/Bath, Bath Arsenal, Bristol Rovers, Chelsea (£750,000), Plymouth Argyle (loan), Queen's Park Rangers (loan), Charlton Athletic (loan), Crystal Palace (loan), Birmingham City (loan), Wigan Athletic (loan), Swansea City, CITY (August 2012).
   Details: Scott Sinclair, a highly effective winger, signed by City on a four-year contract, made his debut for the Blues in September 2012, playing seventy-four minutes of a 1-1 draw at Stoke in the Premiership. Prior to his transfer to the Etihad Stadium, he had played for nine other League clubs, having loan spells with six of them between January 2007 and January 2010. An England schoolboy international, he has appeared nine times for his country between U16 and U21 levels and played in four games for team GB at the 2012 Olympics. Five years earlier, he was selected for an U19 game, but together with Andy Carroll and Ryan Bertrand, he was sent home after breaking a team curfew.

SINCLAIR, Trevor Lloyd (Forward)
Apps/goals: 98/6 Born: Dulwich, London, 2/3/1973
   Career: Blackpool, Queen's Park Rangers (£750,000), West Ham United (£2.7 million deal involving Iain Dowie & Keith Rowland), CITY (£2.5 million, July 2003–July 2007), Cardiff City (free); retired May 2008; now lives in Dubai, teaching football.
   Details: With pace and ability to beat defenders, Trevor Sinclair was a valuable presence in lending width to City down the left flank. He had an excellent first season at the club, claiming his first goal in the Manchester derby. Unfortunately, he struggled with an ankle injury in 2004/05 but returned fitter and stronger to go on and make almost 100 appearances for the club before joining Cardiff.
   During his senior playing career, Sinclair made 659 club appearances and scored eighty-three goals, having his best years with Blackpool and QPR and had the pleasure of netting the first goal at the CoSM for City against Total Network Solutions in the UEFA Cup in 2003. Meanwhile ,a brilliant bicycle kick strike for QPR against Barnsley in an FA Cup tie in 1997 was voted BBC Match of the Day's 'Goal of the Season'. Capped twelve times by England (four coming in the 2002

World Cup), he also played in one 'B' and thirteen U21 internationals and gained an FA Cup runner's-up medal with Cardiff in 2008.

SLATER, Percy (Full-back)
Apps: 23 Born: Adlington, 1879 Died: after 1945
Career: Blackburn Rovers, CITY (May 1900–May 1904), Bury, Oldham Athletic, Shaw FC; retired 1908.
Details: Capable cover for several players during his time with City, Percy Slater's best season was in 1901/02 when he made seventeen first-team appearances, eleven at left-back. He didn't play a single game for Blackburn or Oldham.

SMELT, Thomas (Centre-forward)
Apps: 2/1 Born: Rotherham, 5/11/1902
Died: Rotherham, 1980
Career: Mexborough Town, Chesterfield, Rotherham Town, Burnley, Wombwell, Accrington Stanley, Exeter City, Chesterfield, Morecambe, CITY (April 1927/May 1928), Oldham Athletic, Crewe Alexandra, Scunthorpe & Lindsay United, Rotherham United; retired injured, 1933; also played Lancashire League cricket for Crompton CC.
Details: *The Lancashire Daily Post Annual* stated that Tom Smelt was 'neat and clever in footwork, an opportunist and always a trier.' He was certainly that, netting seventy-five goals in 160 club appearances overall. Unfortunately, he failed to establish himself with City, despite scoring in his second game, a 4-1 defeat at Grimsby in November 1927, having made his debut the previous week *v.* Reading when Matt Barrass was moved back to left-half in place of Jimmy McMullan who was away on international duty.

SMITH, Frederick Edward (Centre-forward)
Apps/goals: 2/1 Born: Draycott, Derbyshire, 7/5/1926
Career: Spondon BC, Draycott, Derby County, Sheffield United, CITY (£6,000, May/September 1952), Grimsby Town (£3,750), Bradford City, Frickley Colliery; retired 1958.
Details: Ideally built for leading the attack, Fred Smith's lively play brought him a fair return in the way of goals. Head his best years with Sheffield United and Grimsby after finding it hard to get a game with City, for whom he scored on his debut in a 2-1 defeat at Stoke in August 1952.

SMITH, George Beacher (Forward)
Apps/goals: 179/80 Born: Fleetwood, 7/2/1921 Died: before 2000.
Career: Salford Adelphi BC (May 1938, retired May 1950); Second World War guest for Heart of Midlothian; Chesterfield (£5,000); retired 1958; Army service in South Africa during the war.

Details: George Smith shares City's joint scoring record for most goals in a game with a five-timer against Newport in June 1947. His total of thirty-eight in the League that season went a long way in bringing the Second Division championship to Maine Road. A gunshot wound sustained in wartime combat left Smith with a damaged hand, but this did not affect him one iota – his scoring exploits confirm that! Besides his outstanding record for City, he also netted over 100 goals (ninety-eight in the League) in 275 appearances for Chesterfield. He also had the pleasure of bagging home a four-timer when City won the FL (N) Manchester derby by 4-1 in April 1946.

SMITH, Gordon Duffield (Forward)
Apps/goals: 49/15 Born: Kilwinning, Ayrshire, 29/9/1954
Career: Kilmarnock, Glasgow Rangers (£65,000), Brighton & Hove Albion (record £440,000), Glasgow Rangers (loan), CITY (£35,000, March 1984–February 1986), Oldham Athletic (loan/signed for £5,000), Admira Wacker/Austria), FC Basil/Switzerland, Stirling Albion; retired 1989; became a financial consultant; football agent; contributed to a weekly newspaper; TV and radio pundit; Chief Executive of the Scottish FA (2007–10); Glasgow Rangers FC (director, 2011/12).
Details: Gordon Smith joined City, having scored over 100 goals in almost 400 appearances for his three previous clubs, gained one Scottish U21 cap and collected an FA Cup runner's-up medal, which should have been a winner's prize! With the scores level between Manchester United and his club, Brighton, in the 1983 final, Smith missed a sitter from inside the 6-yard area. United won the replay 4-0!
Tall, strong and willing, he made his debut for City in a 2-1 win over Cardiff shortly after moving to Maine Road and before the end of the season, struck his first goal, in a 3-1 home victory over Carlisle. The following term, he top-scored with fourteen goals as City finished third in Division Two to gain promotion. In fact, his sixth goal in a 2-0 win against his future club, Oldham, was his hundredth in League football. Years later he held a key position with the Scottish FA and also with Rangers before the Glasgow club went into administration.

SMITH, Henry E. (Right-back/right-half)
Apps: 18 Born: Darwen, 1870 Died: after 1915
Career: Blackburn Rovers, CITY (May 1894/May 1895), Stalybridge Celtic.
Details: Strong-tackling Harry Smith spent just the one season with City. He made his first ten appearances at right-back, being partnered by four different players, and his last eight at right-half in place of George Mann. He moved on when it was

revealed that Jack Harper would be joining City from Newtown.

SMITH, Jonathan Walter (Centre-forward)
Apps/goals: 20/7 Born: Derby, 1887

Career: Burton United, CITY (November 1909–March 1914), South Shields.

Details: A City reserve for four-and-a-half years, Jon Smith surprisingly scored six of his seven goals in sixteen matches in season 1910/11. Deputising most of the time for Irvine Thornley, he netted on his debut against Bristol City a week before Christmas, and later his strikes earned away points against Spurs, Liverpool, Sheffield United and Oldham while another goal helped beat Stoke in an FA Cup tie.

SMITH, Robert (Left-half)
Apps: 6 Born: Walkden, 1896 Died: Devon, c. 1968

Career: Walkden FC, CITY (September 1920–May 1924), Pontypridd, Plymouth Argyle, Torquay United; retired 1932.

Details: Bob Smith, one of several City reserves who hardly figured in the first team during the five years following the First World War, chose to stay at Hyde Road for perhaps longer than expected, making his six appearances in 1923/24, the last four as a replacement for Chris Pringle. He did a lot better with his two Devon clubs, especially Torquay, for whom he played 147 times.

SMITH, Walter Ernest (Goalkeeper)
Apps: 264 Born: Leicester, 25/3/1884

Career: Leicester Imperial, Leicester Fosse, CITY (£600, July 1906–October 1920); First World War guest for Fulham, Leicester Fosse; Port Vale.

Details: Although only 5 feet 7 inches tall, Walter Smith was a hefty but agile goalkeeper who was rated one of the best in the Second Division when he joined City. He had three good seasons at Hyde Road, before losing his place to John Lyall for the Second Division championship-winning campaign of 1909/10. However, he bounced back the following year, but was then pushed for supremacy between the posts by Jimmy Goodchild. He hung there, produced some fine performances and was rewarded with a £1,000 cheque from his benefit match *v.* Blackburn Rovers in 1911. Smith played for an England XI against a Scottish XI in 1914 and for the Football League *v.* the Scottish League in 1915.

On 23 October 1920, Smith was arrested on a charge of assaulting Barbara Lally, a chambermaid at The Regent Hotel where the Port Vale team had spent the night, ahead of a League game at South Shields. Released on bail, Smith played in the game, watched by a policeman in the crowd! At his trial a month later, he was found not guilty.

SMITH, William (Inside-forward)
Apps/goals: 57/22 Born: Cheadle, 1876

Career: Stockport County (May 1897–August 1900), Stockport County.

Details: After failing to break into Stockport's first team, Billy Smith tried his luck with City and in his first season, mainly as Billy Meredith's right-wing partner, he scored twelve goals, eight coming in four games during September 1897, including a hat-trick in a 4-1 home win over Woolwich Arsenal. Strong and combative, Smith played well at times and in a 9-0 last-day win over Burton Swifts, he set up four goals and netted two himself. He played in the first twenty-five League games of 1898/99 (eight goals scored), before losing his place to Jimmy Ross. Although finishing as top scorer for City's second XI in 1899/1900, he was unable to get back into the team and duly returned to Stockport for one more season.

SMITH, William (Half-back)
Apps/goals: 154/8 Born: Buxton, 1873

Career: Buxton Lime Firms, Buxton, CITY (April 1897–May 1902).

Details: A very solid, tough-tackling centre-half who gave nothing away, 'Buxton' Smith took over from Billy Holmes at the heart of City's defence and missed only two League games in his first season; was an ever-present in 1898/99, when the Second Division title was won; and again the following season before missing only two games in 1900/01. Eventually replaced by Tom Hynds, Smith was certainly a star performer for the Blues for five years and he played for an England XI against a German XI in 1901.

SOMMEIL, David (Defender)
Apps/goals: 58/5 Born: Pointe-a-Pitre, Guadalupe, 10/8/1974

Career: Saint-Lo, Caen, Rennes, Bordeaux, CITY (£3.5 million, January 2003–June 2006), Olympique Marseille (loan), Sheffield United, Valenciennes/France.

Details: David Sommeil scored City's first League goal at the CoMS – a dramatic eighty-ninth-minute equaliser to earn a 1-1 draw with Portsmouth in August 2003. Signed on a three-and-a-half-year contract, despite an initial run of first-team games, he lost his place early in 2004 and played very little over the next two seasons. Exchanged on loan with Daniel Van Buyten, he returned to City for the start of the 2004/05 season, but was dogged by injuries and managed only two appearances that season followed by sixteen in 2005/06, partly due to a fractured cheek bone, forcing him to wear a protective mask on his return, and a three match ban for a challenge on Spurs' player Lee Young-Pym. Out of contract, and with less than sixty games behind him, he was one of ten players released by City in June 2006. Capped once by France's 'B' team, he has now played in twenty-three full internationals for Guadalupe.

SOWDEN, William (Centre-forward)
Apps/goals: 11/2 Born: Manchester, 8/12/1930 Died: Stockport, 13/11/2010
   Career: Greenwood Victoria, CITY (April 1949–November 1954), Chesterfield; Macclesfield Town (player-coach); retired 1962.
   Details: Billy Sowden was top scorer for City's second XI in 1952/53 – this after netting twice in his second League game *v.* Tottenham Hotspur at the start of that season when deputising for Johnny Williamson. He later netted sixty-two goals in 104 games for Chesterfield, including thirty-three in 1955/56.

SPITTLE, Arthur (Forward)
Apps/goals: 1/1 Born: Manchester, 1891 Died: Manchester, c. 1963
   Career: CITY (September 1893/April 1894).
   Details: A City reserve for one season, Arthur Spittle scored in the only League game of his career, in a 2-1 defeat at Crewe in April 1894.

SPOTTISWOODE, Joseph Dominic (Outside-left)
Apps: Born: Carlisle, 11/7/1894 Died: London, c. 1970
   Career: Carlisle United, CITY (September 1913/March 1914), Bury, Chelsea, Swansea Town, Queen's Park Rangers; retired 1926.
   Details: Joe Spottiswoode was unable to make headway with any of his first four clubs, but came good with Swansea, for whom he scored nine goals in 159 League appearances. Four of his six outings for City came either side of Christmas 1913 when he deputised for Billy Wallace. His brother Bob also played for Carlisle and QPR.

SPROSTON, Bert (Full-back)
Apps/goals: 131/5 Born: Elworth, Sandbach, Cheshire, 22/6/1915 Died: Bolton, 27/1/2000
   Career: Sandbach Ramblers, Huddersfield Town (trial), Leeds United, Tottenham Hotspur (£9,500), CITY (£9,500, November 1938–August 1950); Second World War guest for Aldershot, Millwall, Port Vale and Wrexham; Ashton United, retired May 1951; Bolton Wanderers (trainer, later club scout and team attendant to 1984).
   Details: Bert Sproston was a very efficient, hard-working, strong-willed right-back, especially quick in recovery and a player who gave 110 per cent every time he took the field and helped City win the Second Division championship in 1947. He formed a wonderful full-back partnership with Eric Westwood which commenced in November 1938 and effectively ended in May 1949. He scored his first two goals for City against his former club,

Spurs, in a 3-2 League win at White Hart Lane in March 1939. During the Second World War, he had a further seventy-four outings with City.
   Sproston, who made almost 300 first-class appearances during his club career, including 140 for Leeds, won eleven England caps, the first at the age of twenty-one in a *v.* Wales in 1936, played in two Wartime internationals when on leave from in the Army and represented the FA against Belgium in 1945.

SPURDLE, William (Wing-half/forward)
Apps/goals: 172/33 Born: St Peter Port, Guernsey, 28/1/1926 Died: St Peter Port, 16/6/2011
   Career: Oldham Athletic, CITY (January 1950–November 1956), Port Vale (£4,000), Oldham Athletic (£1,000); retired May 1963.
   Details: The first Channel Islander to play in an FA Cup final – for City against Newcastle in 1955 – Bill Spurdle missed the victory over Birmingham twelve months later due to boils (replaced by Don Revie). Making his debut in 1951, he had his best season at Maine Road in 1955/56, making forty-two appearances and scoring nine goals, four in successive matches in December when partnering Joe Hayes on the right-wing. He moved to Vale Park once Fionan Fagan had settled into the front line. Ever-reliable, Spurdle made over 400 appearances during his career, 220 for Oldham. He lined up in six different positions for City.

STEEL, Alexander (Half-back)
Apps/goals: 32/1 Born: Newmilns, Scotland, 25/7/1886 Died: c. 1954
   Career: Newmilns, Ayr United, CITY (January 1906–August 1908), Tottenham Hotspur, Kilmarnock, Southend United, Gillingham; retired 1921.
   Details: Only nineteen when he joined City, rough and ready Alex Steel made his first four appearances for City at the end of the 1905/06 season and was a regular for most of the following term when he scored his only goal – in a 3-1 home win over Everton on Boxing Day. Steele and his two brothers Danny and Bobby were at Spurs together, 1908–11.

STEELE, Frederick (Utility)
Apps/goals: 18/1 Born: Manchester area, c. 1869
   Career: CITY (October 1892–May 1894)
   Details: A versatile reserve for virtually two seasons, Fred Steele occupied three different positions in his first three games – right-back, centre-half and centre-forward. Then, in an emergency, he deputised between the posts for Bill Douglas in the League game against Walsall Town Swifts in November 1893, keeping a clean sheet in a 3-0 win. He had netted his only goal in an 8-1 win over Burslem Port Vale in a month earlier.

STENSON, James (Defender)
Apps: 2 Born: Manchester, 1870
Career: CITY (September 1893/May 1894)
Details: One of thirty-five players utilised in 1893/94, Jim Stenson was City's right-back in a 6-0 walloping at Lincoln and left-half in the 5-2 defeat at Walsall Town Swifts three weeks later.

STEPANOVIĆ, Dragoslav (Defender)
Apps: 19 Born: Rekovac, Serbia (FPR Yugoslavia), 30/8/1948
Career: FK Mladi Proleter, OFK Belgrade, Red Star Belgrade, Eintracht Frankfurt, Wormatia Worms, CITY (£140,000, July 1979–May 1981), Wormatia Words; retired 1982; then manager/coach of FV Progress Frankfurt, FV Frankfurt, Riot-Weiss Frankfurt, Eintracht Trier, Eintracht Frankfurt, Bayer O4 Leverkusen, Athletic Bilbao, Eintracht Frankfurt, AEK Athens, VfB Leipzig, Stuttgart Kickers, FC Kickers Offenbach, Rot-Weiss Oberhausen, Shenyang Jinde, El Zamalek, Cukaricki, FK Vojvodina, FK Laktsi.
Details: Malcolm Allison hoped that Dragoslav Stepanović, a Yugoslavian international, capped thirty-four times between 1970 and 1976, and with League appearances under his belt (201 for OFK Belgrade) would be the man to slip into the left side of City's defence. He did well initially, but then injuries started to creep in and after that failed to get into the team; and when he was given an outing he had an absolute 'nightmare', in a 4-0 defeat at Sunderland in August 1980. He never played for City again.

STEWART, George (Outside-right/left)
*Apps/goals: 102/13 Born: Edinburgh, 1883
Died: Glasgow, after 1945*
Career: Wishaw White Star, Hibernian, CITY (May 1905–June 1911), Partick Thistle; retired during the First World War.
Details: An impressive, fast-raiding winger able to occupy both flanks, George Stewart was small and light with good speed. Outstanding in 1906/07, when he scored eight goals in thirty-eight appearances, including a brace in City's 3-0 Manchester derby win in December. Unfortunately, between September 1907 and December 1908, he spent a lot of time on the injured list. He returned for two decent spells in the side in 1909/10, helping City win the Second Division title, and again in 1910/11, before giving way on the right-wing to Sid Hoad. An international trialist in 1907, he won four caps for Scotland (two with City) and twice represented the Scottish League.

STEWART, Paul Andrew (Midfield/forward)
Apps/goals: 63/30 Born: Manchester, 7/10/1964
Career: Blackpool, CITY (£200,000, March 1987/June 1988), Tottenham Hotspur (£1.7 million), Liverpool (£2.3 million), Crystal Palace (loan), Wolverhampton Wanderers (loan), Burnley (loan), Sunderland (loan/signed), Stoke City (free), Workington; retired 2000; inducted into the Blackpool Hall of Fame in 2006; now lives in Poulton-le-Fylde.
Details: Attacking midfielder Paul Stewart was City's leading scorer with twenty-eight goals in four different competitions in 1987/88. At the same time, he became the first player since Brian Kidd in 1976/77 to net over twenty League goals (twenty-four in all). Teaming up well with Imre Varadi and David White and later Tony Adcock, his tally was boosted with a smart hat-trick in a 10-1 win over Huddersfield and by six separate doubles. He actually found the net against thirteen different opponents. Subsequently sold to Spurs for 'big money', he played alongside Paul Gascoigne and scored in the 1991 FA Cup final victory over Nottingham Forest. He later helped Blackpool (with whom he had his best spell: 225 games, sixty-two goals) gain promotion, Palace (1994) and Sunderland (1996) win the First Division championship and Workington win the NW Trains League title in 1999.
With ten different employers, he netted 155 goals in more than 650 senior appearances over a period of twenty years. Youth international with Blackpool, he won three full, one U21 and five 'B' caps for England.

STOBART, Barry Henry (Forward)
Apps/goals: 14/1 Born: Dodsworth near Doncaster, 6/6/1938
Career: Dodsworth County School, Wath Wanderers, Wolverhampton Wanderers, CITY (£20,000, August–November 1964), Aston Villa (£22,000), Shrewsbury Town (£10,000), Durban Spurs/South Africa, Willenhall Town (player-manager/coach; retired as a player, 1983), Dudley Town (manager); ran grocery shop in Ward Groves; then a window cleaning business in Sedgley near Wolverhampton.
Details: Barry Stobart gained an FA Cup winner's medal with Wolves in 1960, after replacing Bobby Mason at the eleventh hour. Four years later – having scored over 100 goals for the Molineux club's second team – he joined City but, after a good start, when he netted in a 2-0 win over Derby County, he lost his verve and his position, and was transferred back to the Midlands! A niggling ankle injury plagued him from 1965 onwards. As a manager he guided Willenhall to the 1981 FA Vase final.

STONES, Harold (Goalkeeper)
Apps: 12 Born: Manchester, 1868
Career: CITY (September 1892–May 1894)
Details: Reserve Harry Stones deputised for Bill Douglas in twelve League games, and at times

was left bewildered and bemused as opposing forwards fired in shots and sent in headers from all angles. In fact, he conceded thirty-two goals in eighteen hours of football, twenty-one coming in three successive defeats in the space of nine days in March 1894: 5-0 at Notts County, 10-2 at Small Heath and 6-0 at Lincoln!

Stones did not join Newton Heath in 1894. He is often confused with Herbert Henry Stone, a half-back.

STOWELL, Michael (Goalkeeper)
Apps: 15 Born: Preston, 19/4/1965
Career: Leyland Motors, Preston North End, Everton, Chester City (loan), York City (loan), City (loan, February/May 1988), Preston North End (loan), Wolverhampton Wanderers (loan), Preston North End (loan), Wolverhampton Wanderers (£250,000), Bristol City; retired June 2003.

Details: Standing 6 feet 2 inches tall, Mike Stowell possessed fine reflexes, good positional sense, and was a smart shot-stopper. Taking over from Eric Nixon, he made his City debut in a 2-1 defeat at Blackburn and was superb in League victories over Sheffield United and Ipswich, but conceded four in an FA Cup tie at Liverpool.

Understudy to Neville Southall for many years at Goodison Park, Stowell made only one appearance for Everton in five years! Later, he broke Bert Williams' all-time record for most appearances for Wolves with 448. In 1990 he hired a tractor to beat snowdrifts in the Midlands in order to report for England duty ahead of a 'B' international against Algeria.

STURRIDGE, Daniel (Forward)
Apps/goals: 32/6 Born: Birmingham 1/9/1989
Career: Aston Villa (junior), Coventry City (schoolboy), CITY (£30,000, October 2003–January 2010), Chelsea (£4.5 million), Bolton Wanderers (loan), Liverpool (£12 million).

Details: Daniel Sturridge has occupied all 'five' front-line positions and has admitted that he prefers to play on the right, which gives him the opportunity to cut inside and take shots at goal with his favoured left foot – and he's done that exceptionally well!

His development with City was rapid and after scoring a hat-trick in a reserve match, he was added to the senior squad, making his PL debut as a substitute against Reading in February 2007. Then, in 2007/08, he became the first player to score in the FA Youth Cup (final *v.* Chelsea), FA Cup (*v.* Sheffield United) and Premier League (Derby) in the same season. Voted the club's Young Player of the Season in 2009, City couldn't hold on to his talents and off he went to Abramovich's Chelsea, gaining two FA Cup, Premiership and Champions League winner's medals before switching to Anfield.

He won the first of his five full England caps as a second-half substitute in the 1-0 win over Sweden at Wembley in November 2011, being one of nine players that night who had been associated with Aston Villa. Sturridge has also represented his country on thirty-four occasions at U16–21 levels, scoring twenty-one goals, four of them in fifteen appearances for the latter. He also netted twice in five games for Team GB at the 2012 London Olympics. From a football family, Sturridge is the nephew of former strikers Simon and Dean Sturridge.

On signing Sturridge from Coventry as a fourteen-year-old, City were ordered to pay an initial fee of £30,000 with £170,000 to follow at a later date, depending on appearances made/goals scored.

SUÁREZ, Denis Fernández (Midfield)
Apps: 2 Born: Salceda de Caselas, Spain, 6/1/1994
Career: Porriño Industrial, Celta Vigo, CITY (£850,000, May 2011).

Details: City beat off interest from Barcelona, Chelsea and Manchester United to land attacking midfielder Denis Suarez for an agreed initial fee that could rise to £2.75 million depending on appearances and performances. Considered as a 'bright talent' and a possible future replacement for David Silva, Suarez played in a few friendly matches before making his senior debut as a sixty-seventh minute for Samir Nasri in a 5-2 League Cup win over Wolves in October 2011. Twelve months later he was named City's Young Player of the Year. He gained a total of nineteen caps for Spain at U17, U18, U19 and U23 levels.

SUCKLING, Perry John (Goalkeeper)
Apps: 46 Born: Leyton, London, 12/10/1965
Career: Hackney Schools, Coventry City, CITY (May 1986–January 1988), Crystal Palace, West Ham United (loan), Brentford (loan), Ernest Borel/Hong Kong, Watford, Doncaster Rovers, Wits University/South Africa, Supersport United, Dagenham & Redbridge, King's Lynn; retired 2001; Tottenham Hotspur (academy goalkeeping coach).

Details: Perry Suckling was generally a good, capable goalkeeper. An England youth international, also capped ten times at U21 level (1986–88), his career realised over 250 club appearances. City's regular number throughout the 1986/87 season, which ended in relegation to the Second Division, his career was famously damaged in 1989 when he kept goal for Crystal Palace in a 9-0 defeat by Liverpool. Suckling helped Ernest Borel complete the Hong Kong Viceroy Cup and FA Cup double in 1992.

SUGDEN, Frederick Arthur (Full-back)
Apps: 6 Born: Gorton, 1894

Career: Droylsden, CITY (June 1917–May 1920), Tranmere Rovers, Southport; retired 1926.

Details: After thirty-nine appearances during the First World War, Fred Sugden found himself reserve to Billy Henry when peacetime football recommenced in August 1919. He played in just six League games that season, debuting against the subsequent champions, WBA in early December and having last outing against Arsenal a month later.

SUGRUE, Paul Anthony (Forward)
Apps: 7 Born: Coventry, 6/11/1960

Career: Nuneaton Borough, CITY (£30,000, February 1980/July 1981), Cardiff City, Kansas City/USA, Middlesbrough, Portsmouth, Northampton Town, Newport County, Bridgend Town, Elo Kuopio/Finland, Nuneaton Borough (player-manager); Merthyr Tydfil (manager; later vice-chairman).

Details: There were rumblings around Maine Road when Malcolm Allison signed Paul Sugrue from non-League football. A smart dribbler, with a powerful right-foot shot, he had a run of four successive League games, but unfortunately he didn't make a great impression with City and was quickly dispatched to Cardiff.

SULLIVAN, Dominic (Midfield)
Apps: 1 Born: Glasgow, 1/4/1951

Career: Clyde, Aberdeen, Celtic, CITY (loan, September/October 1983), Morton, Alloa Athletic (player, then player-manager); retired May 1989; Falkirk (caretaker-manager/coach), East Stirlingshire (manager); now runs his own pub, the Railway Inn in Denny.

Details: Dom Sullivan's only first-team appearance for City was in the 0-0 draw at Torquay in a League Cup first leg encounter in October 1983. He made almost 200 appearances for Clyde, scored twelve goals in 119 games for Celtic (1979–83) and gained two U23 caps for Scotland.

SUMMERBEE, Michael George (Outside-right/forward)
Apps/goals: 452/68 Born: Cheltenham, 15/12/1942

Career: Swindon Town, CITY (£35,000, August 1965–June 1975), Burnley (£25,000), Blackpool, Stockport County (player-manager), Mossley FC; retired May 1982; owned a boutique with George Best in Manchester.

Details: A real bargain buy from Swindon by Joe Mercer, Mike Summerbee – nicknamed 'Buzzer' – arrived at Maine Road as an out-and-out right-winger, with pace, craft, crossing ability and strong shot, and he put all those assets to good use as an ever-present in his first season with City, scoring eight League goals, and making many more, as the Second Division championship was won in some style. A regular in the side, injuries

apart, for the next nine years, he gained FA Cup (1968), League Cup (1969) and European Cup Winner's Cup winner's medals (1970); added a few runner's-up prizes to his tally; played eight times for England at senior level, once for the U23s, once for the Football League, twice for the FA and for an England XI *v.* Young England in 1967.

Not a prolific scorer himself, Summerbee nevertheless bagged a 'rare' hat-trick in a 7-0 FA Cup replay win over Reading in January 1968, the same season he claimed his best goal tally for the Blues (twenty). He found the net in each of his ten seasons at Maine Road and 20,309 fans turned out to say 'thank you' for his efforts, when City beat rivals United in his testimonial match in 1975.

No doubt a very competitive footballer, always involved in the action, Summerbee made 716 League appearances during his career, 357 with City. He played in almost 250 games for Swindon and only seven players have appeared in more first-class matches for the Blues than Buzzer's total of 452. His son, Nicky (below) was a City player in the 1990s.

SUMMERBEE, Nicholas John (Right-back/winger)
Apps/goals: 156/10 Born: Altrincham, 26/8/1971

Career: Swindon Town, CITY (£1.5 million, June 1994–November 1997), Sunderland (£1 million swap deal involving Craig Russell), Bolton Wanderers, CITY (loan, August 2001), Nottingham Forest, Leicester City, Bradford City, Swindon Town (loan), Tranmere Rovers (loan), Tamworth; retired 2007; now a TV pundit and broadcaster.

Details: Signed by Brian Horton, Nicky Summerbee could double up as a right-back or winger. His forté was getting forward at every opportunity and whipping in crosses – in a style similar to that of his father. He made a fine start to his City career, scoring three goals, his first against Liverpool, in fifty-one senior appearances in his initial season. After retaining a similar role under two more managers – Alan Ball and Steve Coppell – he was pushed further forward by his fourth boss, Frank Clark, in 1996/97, netting six times, while creating scores of chances for the strikers, with Uwe Rosler the main beneficiary. His second spell with City was short and sweet.

The recipient of one 'B' and three U21 caps for England, Summerbee made 511 senior appearances during his career, helped Sunderland win the First Division title in 1999 and in 2006/07 played with ex-City defender Gerry Taggart at Tamworth.

SWANN, John Willy (Goalkeeper)
Apps: 1 Born: Broughton, 1885

Career: Northern Nomads, CITY (October 1909); did not play after the First World War.

Details: An amateur throughout his career, Willy Swann was signed on a 'standby and hope' contract and made only one League appearance in his entire career – for City in a 2-1 defeat at Stockport County in October 1909 when he deputised for Jack Lyall.

SWIFT, Frank Victor (Goalkeeper)
Apps: 375 Born: Blackpool, 26 December 1913 Died: Munich, Germany, 6 February 1958
   Career: Blackpool Schools, Blackpool Gas Works FC, Fleetwood, CITY (amateur trialist, October 1932, signed, November 1932, retired May 1949; returned to play a few games during early part of 1949/50 season); Second World War guest for Aldershot, Charlton Athletic, Fulham, Hamilton Academical, Liverpool and Reading; became a chief football reporter for the *News of the World*.
   Details: Universally popular with his natural good humour, Frank Swift's presence on the field was immense, while his formidable physique included a hand span of 11½ inches. His England teammate Raich Carter thought '...he had frying pan hands' while Stan Matthews said 'he had hands like spades, and would also occasionally head goal bound shots away. He was an excellent shot-stopper.'
   In fact, 'Swifty' was one of the first 'keepers to throw the ball out to a colleague, rather than kick it aimlessly downfield. He was a big man and a big talent, the bravest of the brave. The crowds loved his goalkeeping aerobatics, and although he was terrific with high shots and long range efforts he was, at times, caught out with quickly taken ground shots. Once, in a home League encounter against West Bromwich Albion in January 1934, he conceded seven goals, six fired low into the net from inside the penalty-area.
   Having made his debut against Derby County six days earlier, on Christmas Day 1933, and despite being beaten twelve times in his first four outings, he missed only one League game up to May 1939. An ever-present on four occasions, he had an unbeaten run of 195 consecutive League appearances between December 1933 and September 1938.
   He played in 136 Second World War games for City and continued to perform with gusto after the hostilities, retiring in May 1949, only to be asked, nicely, to make four more appearances during the first three weeks of the following season, keeping a clean sheet in his last game, a 0-0 League draw with Everton.
   Overall 'Big Frank' played in 511 matches for City, gaining FA Cup, First Division and Second Division championship winner's medals in 1934, 1937 and 1947 respectively. He played in nineteen full, ten Wartime, four Victory and four unofficial internationals for England, represented Great Britain against The Rest of Europe in 1947, played for the FA XI on four occasions and featured in an international trial (1935).

Knocked out in a 2-0 win over Scotland at Hampden Park in April 1948 (after colliding with Billy Liddell) he recovered to stun the 135,000-plus crowd with a series of terrific saves. On his return to Manchester's railway station later that evening, Swift, still wobbly, was wheeled along the platform on a porter's trolley to a waiting ambulance. An examination revealed he was 'fine' – except that he had also broken two ribs!

(SYLVINHO) Sylvio Mendes Campos Júnior (Left-back)
Apps/goals: 12/1 Born: São Paulo, Brazil, 12/4/1974
   Career: Corinthians/Brazil, Arsenal, Celta Vigo, Barcelona, CITY (free, August 2009–June 2010); retired July 2011; Cruzeiro (assistant-manager/coach).
   Details: In August 2009, just five days after beating Barcelona in a friendly at the Nou Camp, City signed the Spanish club's veteran full-back Sylvinho, who therefore returned to England to team up with his fellow countryman Robinho. Debuting against Scunthorpe in the League Cup, he had to wait until December 2009 before making his first League start *v.* Bolton, replacing the injured Wayne Bridge, and the next month scored his only goal for City in a 4-2 FA Cup win over the 'Iron' with a spectacular long range strike.
   Six months later, the club announced that his contract had expired and he would be leaving the club with Benjani Mwaruwari, Jack Redshaw, Karl Moore and Martin Petrov. Capped six times by Brazil (2000/01) Sylvinho made 490 club appearances during his career. He won five trophies with Corinthians, one with Arsenal and eight with Barcelona, collecting three La Liga and three Champions League medals.

SYME, Robert Gordon (Forward)
Apps/goals: 11/2 Born: South Queensferry, 13/12/1904 Died: Scotland, c. 1967
   Career: Dunfermline Athletic, CITY (August 1930–July 1934), Burnley, Dunfermline Athletic; retired 1939.
   Details: Twice City's top scorer in successive Central League seasons (1931–33), Bob Syme unfortunately wasn't given the change to show off his goal-technique in the first team, making only eleven appearances in four years. The first of his two goals for the seniors earned City a 1-0 win over Birmingham in September 1933, playing in the absence of Fred Tilson.

SYMONS, Christopher Jeremiah (Defender)
Apps/goals: 139/4 Born: Basingstoke, 8/3/1971
   Career: Portsmouth, CITY (£1.6 million, August 1995–July 1998), Fulham (free), Crystal Palace (£400,000; then player-caretaker-manager; retired 2005); Colchester United (caretaker-

manager), Fulham (scout, academy coach); Wales (national team coach).

Details: A virtual ever-present in his three seasons at Maine Road, during which time City slipped out of the Premiership, Kit Symons was a skilful central defender who, in his day, looked a quality player. Captain on several occasions, he was eventually replaced in the back four by Andy Morrison.

A youth international with Pompey, Symons went on to win thirty-seven full, one 'B' and two U21 caps for Wales while making 534 club appearances during his sixteen-year playing career. He helped Fulham win the Second Division in 1999 and Crystal Palace the First in 2001.

T

TAGGART, Gerry Paul (Defender)
Apps/goals: 13/1 Born: Belfast, 18/10/1970

Career: Belfast Boys, CITY (June 1987–January 1990), Barnsley (£75,000), Bolton Wanderers (£1.5 million), Leicester City (free), Stoke City (loan/signed), Tamworth Town; retired 2007; Leicester City (caretaker-manager), Oldham Athletic (caretaker-manager).

Details: A left-side defender, rugged and uncompromising, Gerry Taggart made his City debut against Portsmouth in February 1989, but eleven months later, with first-team chances rather limited, he chose to drop down a Division and joined Barnsley. Named City's Young Player of the Year in 1989, he won four schoolboy, five youth, two U23 and fifty-one full caps for Northern Ireland, helped Bolton win the First Division championship in 1997 and League Cup in 2000, and was Nicky Summerbee's teammate at Tamworth.

TAIT, David (Half-back)
Apps/goals: 4/2 Born: Glenbuck, Ayrshire, 1871

Career: Renton, CITY (May 1896/March 1897), Darwen.

Details: An attacking reserve right-half, Dave Tait scored twice in City's 3-1 League win over Burton Swifts in November 1896, having made his debut on the opening day of the season against Woolwich Arsenal (1-1). His younger brother Alex played for Tottenham, Motherwell and Preston.

TAIT, Thomas (Inside/centre-forward)
Apps/goals: 64/46 Born: Hetton-le-Hole, Durham, 20/11/1908 Died: 1976

Career: Sunderland, Hetton, Middlesbrough, Southport, CITY (£1,500, June 1928–November 1930), Bolton Wanderers, Luton Town, Bournemouth, Reading, Torquay United (Second World War guest/signed); retired 1946.

Details: After heading City's Central League scoring charts in 1928/29, Tommy Tait, a former England schoolboy international (capped *v.* Wales

and Scotland in 1923) continued his good form the following season by finishing top marksman at senior level with thirty-one goals, finding the net in six successive League games between 12 October and 16 November while forming an excellent partnership with Bobby Marshall. He was also on target in four of the last five matches. He carried on finding the net after leaving Maine Road, and was Luton's top marksman two seasons running before scoring seventy-nine goals in 144 League games for Reading. His career spanned twenty-two years, during which time he netted over 200 goals in more than 350 club appearances. A former timber worker, he enjoyed walking over the moors.

TARNAT, Michael (Full-back)
Apps/goals: 41/4 Born: Dusseldorf, Germany, 27/10/1969

Career: MSV Duisburg, Karlsruher SC, Bayern Munich, CITY (free, July 2003/May 2004), Hannover 96; retired July 2009; Bayern Munch (scout).

Details: Signed with 337 Bundesliga appearances under his belt, plus nineteen caps for Germany, Michael Tarnat became a cult hero at City within the first month following two superb Premiership goals against Blackburn Rovers and Aston Villa. Absent for a short time before Christmas, he recovered full fitness and remained as first choice left-back until the season's end when his contract expired. He won four Bundesliga titles and the Champions League with Bayern.

TAYLOR, Gareth Keith (Striker)
Apps/goals: 53/10 Born: Weston-super-Mare, 25/2/1973

Career: Southampton, Bristol Rovers, Gloucester City (loan), Weymouth (loan), Crystal Palace (£750,000), Sheffield United, CITY (£400,000, November 1998–February 2001), Port Vale (loan), Queen's Park Rangers (loan), Burnley (loan/signed), Nottingham Forest (£500,000), Crewe Alexandra (loan), Tranmere Rovers, Doncaster Rovers, Carlisle United (loan), Wrexham; retired 2012.

Details: The nine League goals, 6-foot-2-inch striker Gareth Taylor secured City a place in the Second Division play-offs at the end of his first season at Maine Road. Then, as a substitute for Lee Crooks, he helped secure promotion with victory in the final over Gillingham. The following season he assisted in a second successive promotion, although not playing a huge role, being loaned to Port Vale instead. He didn't make a Premiership appearance for City. Taylor's career yielded 137 goals in 578 club appearances. He also gained seven U21 and fifteen full caps for Wales.

TAYLOR, Henry George (Forward)
Apps/goals: 101/28 Born: Fegg Hayes, Burslem, Stoke-on-Trent, 7/8/1889 Died: Manchester, 1968
  Career: North Staffs Boys, Chell Heath, Fegg Hayes, Stoke, Huddersfield Town, Port Vale (£30), CITY (£300, June 1912, retired May 1921); served in Army during the First World War.
  Details: A beefy player with broad shoulders, Harry Taylor took over from Irvine Thornley as City's centre-forward and had a good first season at Hyde Road, scoring five goals in twenty-three appearances, two of his strikes coming in a 4-0 win at Arsenal. He netted a further eight goals in his second season and eleven in 1914/15 when he partnered Tommy Browell in attack. He managed only seven appearances after the First World War before moving back to Port Vale.

TAYLOR, Kenneth Victor (Defender)
Apps: 1 Born: Manchester, 18/6/1936
  Career: Manchester Transport FC, CITY (August 1954–July 1960), Buxton.
  Details: A reserve at Maine Road for six seasons, Ken Taylor's solitary League appearance for City was at centre-half in place of Dave Ewing in a 4-3 home win over Blackpool in March 1958.

TAYLOR, Robert Anthony (Forward)
Apps/goals: 16/5 Born: Norwich, 30/4/1971
  Career: Norwich City, Leyton Orient (loan), Birmingham City, Leyton Orient, Brentford (£100,000), Gillingham (£500,000), CITY (£1.5 million, November 1999/August 2000), Wolverhampton Wanderers (£1.55 million), Queen's Park Rangers (loan), Gillingham (loan), Grimsby Town, Scunthorpe United; retired March 2004.
  Details: Six months after playing for Gillingham in the Second Division play-off final against City, Bob Taylor joined his namesake Gareth at Maine Road and scored five goals in his first season as the Blues completed a second promotion-winning campaign. That was it as far as his career with City was concerned, although when he retired he did so with a pretty good record to his name of 143 goals in 424 club appearances.

TAYLOR, Stuart James (Goalkeeper)
Apps: 1 Born: Romford, 28/11/1980
  Career: Reading, Arsenal, Bristol Rovers (loan), Crystal Palace (loan), Peterborough United (loan), Leicester City (loan), Aston Villa, Cardiff City (loan), CITY (free, July 2009–June 2012), Reading.
  Details: Stuart Taylor decided to join City after taking advice from Brad Friedel, who had previously worked with manager Mark Hughes at Blackburn. He made his only first-team appearance in an FA Cup tie against Scunthorpe in January 2010, and

six months later signed a new two-year deal with the club, despite being officially released nine days earlier! Considered third choice behind Joe Hart and Costel Pantilimon, he left for a second time in June 2012, along with fellow 'keeper Gunnar Nielsen. The 6 feet 5 inches tall Taylor won the Premier League and FA Cup with Arsenal and gained eleven caps for England at U16–21 levels.

TELFORD, William Albert (Forward)
Apps: 1 Born: Carlisle, 5/3/1956
  Career: Tranmere Rovers, Burnley, CITY (August/September 1975), Peterborough United, Colchester United (loan); retired injured, 1976.
  Details: Bill Telford spent just thirty-two days at Maine Road, making his only appearance as a substitute for Joe Royle in a 2-0 defeat at Coventry in the third League game of the 1975/76 season.

TÉVEZ, Carlos Alberto Martinez (Striker)
Apps/goals: 147/73 Born: Ciudadela, Buenos Aires, Argentina, 5/2/1984
  Career: All Boys/Buenos Aires, Boca Juniors, Corinthians, West Ham United, Manchester United, CITY (record £25.5 million, July 2009–June 2013), Juventus (£10 million+).
  Details: After protracted negotiations, Carlos Tévez signed a five-year contract with City to become the first player to move between the two Manchester clubs since Terry Cooke in 1999. He made his PL debut as a substitute at Blackburn and scored his first goal soon afterwards against Crystal Palace in the FLC before a knee injury, suffered while playing for Argentina, sidelined him for almost three weeks. Back in business, he notched his first hat-trick for City in January 2010, in a 4-1 win over Blackburn and netted twice against his former club, United, in the first leg of the League Cup semi-final – which also featured a 'slagging match' between himself and former teammate Gary Neville. Unfortunately, Tévez couldn't repeat his scoring feat in the return leg which United won. Following a second treble (v. Wigan) he finished 2009/10 with a personal record of twenty-nine goals in forty-two games: the most by a City player in the top flight since Franny Lee's haul of thirty-three in 1971/72.
  Appointed captain at the start of his second campaign, Tévez carried on scoring, but in December 2010, despite his agent asking the club to renegotiate and improve his contract, he handed in a written transfer request, citing family reasons and a breakdown in the 'relationship with certain executives and individuals at the club'. His request was rejected, a club official describing Tévez's reasons for wanting to leave as 'ludicrous and nonsensical'. It was also revealed that Tévez would not be sold in the January transfer window and City would seek compensation for breach of

contract from his agent if he retired or refused to play. His manager, Roberto Mancini, however, was convinced that his striker would stay with City, as did his close friend Pablo Zabaleta.

Tévez eventually withdrew his transfer request, and after expressing his 'absolute commitment' to City following clear-the-air talks, flew out of the blocks (again) to reach the fifty goal mark in a just seventy-three games. Only one player has scored that number of goals faster – Derek Kevan in sixty-four games in the 1960s.

Tévez, nicknamed 'El Apache', missed the FA Cup semi-final victory over Manchester United with a hamstring injury, but returned to captain City to victory in the final against Stoke. But then, surprisingly, he looked out of form early in 2011/12, losing the captaincy to Vincent Kompany. When named as a substitute for the European game at Bayern Munich, he seemingly refused to come off the bench in the second half, although later he denied this, saying it was a misunderstanding!

His actions received widespread condemnation, Mancini claiming that he wanted Tévez 'out of Manchester City' and that he would never play for the club again. The striker was suspended for two weeks and fined heavily while an investigation was carried out; at the same time, the club's owner, Sheikh Mansour indicated that Tévez should be placed on 'garden leave' and banned from the training ground.

After a lot of debate behind closed doors, Tévez resumed training in mid-February 2012 with the backing of his fellow players, but prejudiced an easy return to the squad by giving an interview on Argentinian TV in which he said his manager had treated him like a dog, despite Mancini stating he was ready to welcome Tévez back to the fold to boost their bid for the Premier League title.

A week later Tévez made this statement, 'I wish to apologise sincerely and unreservedly to everybody I have let down and to whom my actions over the last few months have caused offence. My wish is to concentrate on playing football for Manchester City Football Club.'

Gameless for three months, Tévez was given his own fitness programme, while Mancini drew the line under his dispute with his striker, insisting that when he proved his fitness he would be considered for selection. Tévez, duly returned, fired home another treble in a 6-0 win at Norwich and went on to play his part in helping City win the Premiership title with that dramatic last-match victory over QPR. Although not a regular starter in 2012/13, he still continued to claim his fair share of goals, including another hat-trick in a 5-0 FA Cup win over Barnsley, as City made their way through to the final (beaten by Wigan).

Capped six times at both U17 and U23 levels, Tévez had scored thirteen goals in sixty-two full internationals for Argentina at May 2013. He won the Copa Liberadores with Boca Juniors in 2003, collected a gold medal and the Golden Boot award at the Athens Olympics in 2004 and was the first non-Brazilian for nearly thirty years when, in 2005, he was voted 'Best Player' in Brazil.

THATCHER, Benjamin David (Full-back)
Apps: 51 Born: Swindon, 30/11/1975

Career: Canterbury Christ Church University, FA School of Excellence/Lilleshall, Millwall, Wimbledon (£1.84 million), Tottenham Hotspur (£5 million), Leicester City (£300,000), CITY (£100,000, June 2004), Charlton Athletic (£500,000, January 2007), Ipswich Town (free); retired injured, October 2010.

Details: During his two-and-a-half years with City, Ben Thatcher, a robust, tough-tackling left-back, certainly added some steel to the defence, but unfortunately injuries and several suspensions limited his appearances. His best season with the Blues was his first (twenty-one games) when, in fact, he could have joined Fulham, after a series of burglaries unsettled his family, but the move fell through. Thatcher gained notoriety in August 2006, in a game between City and Portsmouth FC. Challenging Pedro Miguel da Silva Mendes for a loose ball, he viciously and intentionally led with his elbow, knocking Mendes into the advertising hoardings and rendering him unconscious. Mendes required oxygen at pitch side and suffered a seizure while being transferred to hospital, where he spent the night. He was discharged the next day, but remained under medical supervision. Thatcher, who apologised for his actions, was subsequently interviewed by and later severely disciplined by The Football Association and Greater Manchester Police also chose to investigate the matter. As a result, City announced that Thatcher would be banned for six matches, two of which would be suspended, and fined six weeks' wages for the challenge. This punishment was separate from the sanctions made by the FA, who suspended the left-back for eight matches, with a further fifteen game suspended ban for two years.

This was the second incident in less than three weeks whereby Thatcher's elbow had hospitalised an opponent. In early August, during a pre-season tour of China, his challenge caused a career-threatening pneumothorax to a twenty-year-old midfielder from Shanghai Shenhua. Thatcher also faced possible action from Lancashire Police over a clash with ex-Blackburn player Ralph Welch during a reserve game at Ewood Park in February 2006.

Despite all this upheaval, Thatcher made 378 club appearances and won seven full caps for Wales, having earlier played at youth and U21 levels for England.

THOMAS, Scott Lee (Winger)
Apps: 2 Born: Bury, 30/10/1974
    Career: CITY (June 1991–May 1998), Brighton & Hove Albion (loan), Northwich Victoria.
    Details: City's Young Player of the Year in 1995, Scott Thomas was able to play on both flanks but was always in reserve at Maine Road. He made substitute appearances in the last two PL games of 1994/95 against Nottingham Forest (a) and Stoke City (h). He served under manager Brian Horton at Brighton.

THOMPSON, Frank (Right-back)
Apps: 37 Born: Egerton, 16/5/1901
    Career: Atherton, CITY (February 1921–August 1927), Swindon Town, Halifax Town; retired 1930.
    Details: Understudy to Sam Cookson, stocky full-back Frank Thompson made his City debut in a fourth-round FA Cup tie against Bolton Wanderers in January 1922, following up with his League bow four days later at Middlesbrough. He had his best run in the first team in January/February 1923 and played his final game five years after his first, away at Birmingham in January 1927.

THOMPSON, George Herbert (Goalkeeper)
Apps: 2 Born: Maltby, 15/9/1926
Died: Blackburn, 7/3/2004
    Career: Chesterfield, Scunthorpe United, Preston North End, CITY (July 1956/June 1957), Carlisle United, Morecambe; retired May 1963.
    Details: Strong and competent, George Thompson kept goal for Scunthorpe in their first season of League football (1950/51) and for Preston in their 1954 FA Cup final defeat by WBA. He appeared in the first two League games of the 1956/57 season for City, conceding seven goals in a 5-1 defeat at Wolves and a 2-2 home draw with Tottenham. He had 140 League outings for Preston and 206 for Carlisle. His father and brother were both goalkeepers, while Thompson himself was also an excellent artist, well known for his caricatures of League footballers.

THOMPSON, James (Forward)
Apps: 2 Born: Chadderton, Lancs, 24/1/1889
    Career: Bathgate, Oldham Athletic, CITY (August 1920/June 1921), Stalybridge Celtic, Ashton National, Port Vale, Blackpool, Accrington Stanley, Swindon Town, Crewe Alexandra, Hurst; retired May 1929.
    Details: With the right stature and ample speed, Jimmy Thompson was a useful forward, capable of playing on both wings, but who failed to make an impression with City, appearing in just two First Division games, away to Chelsea and at home to Sheffield United during the second half of the 1920/21 season. He made only 130 League appearances for eight different clubs.

THOMPSTONE, Ian Philip (Midfield)
Apps: 1 Born: Bury, 17/1/1971
    Career: Schoolboy football, CITY (June 1987–May 1990), Oldham Athletic, Exeter City, Halifax Town, Scunthorpe United, Rochdale, Scarborough.
    Details: Nurtured through the YTS ranks, Ian Thompstone scored in his only game for City, as a substitute in a 2-1 defeat at Middlesbrough in April 1988. He made 150 League appearances after leaving Maine Road.

THORNLEY, Irvine (Centre-forward)
Apps/goals: 204/93 Born: Hayfield, Derbyshire, 23/2/1883 Died: Glossop, 24/4/1955
    Career: Glossop Villa, Glossop St James, Glossop North End, CITY (£800, April 1904–April 1912), South Shields, Hamilton Academical, Houghton FC; retired April 1922.
    Details: A powerful, lively, all-action centre-forward, difficult to contain, Irvine Thornley combined playing football with a career as a butcher. A controversial character, he was sent off at least eight times during his career, once for City *v.* Aston Villa in January 1912 and was one of the players present the first ever meeting of the Professional Footballers' Association in 1907. Soon after his transfer to City, the FA carried out an investigation into the financial activities of the club. Manager Tom Maley was interviewed and admitted that he had followed what seemed like 'standard English practice' by making additional payments to all his players. He claimed that if all First Division clubs were investigated, not four would come out 'scatheless'. As a result of their investigation, the FA suspended Maley from football for life, while seventeen players were fined and suspended until January 1907.
    Very popular with the Hyde Road supporters, he scored five hat-tricks for City and had his best season in 1905/06 with a total of twenty-one. As a reward for his service to City, Thornley was rewarded with a benefit match in 1912 when over 40,000 fans turned out, raising a then record £1,036 for the player. He helped City win the Second Division championship in 1910 and after leaving the club, netted 154 goals in 130 games in three seasons with South Shields. He gained one England cap, in a 1-1 draw with Wales in March 1907, and twice represented the Football League.

THRELFALL, Frederick (Outside-left)
Apps/goals: 74/8 Born: Preston, 7/1/1880
    Career: CITY (June 1898–June 1907), Fulham, Leicester Fosse/City; retired 1911; Cliftonville/ Ireland (trainer).
    Details: Fred Threlfall was a deft, speedy winger was one of the 'few' innocents on the Hyde Road payroll when the FA uncovered financial

irregularities (see Thornley). He had to wait until 1901/02 before having a sustained run in City's first team. The following campaign he scored five goals in twenty-six appearances.

Threlfall scored nineteen goals in 107 games for Fulham, helping the Cottagers twice win the Southern League championship, gain election to the Football League, played in two international trials (for the Professionals *v.* the Amateurs and The North *v.* The South) and was a member of the management committee of the Players' Union.

THURLOW, Alec Charles Edward (Goalkeeper)
Apps: 21 Born: Deepwade, 24/2/1922
Died: Norwich, 1956
Career: Huddersfield Town, CITY (September 1946; retired June 1950)
Details: A fine goalkeeper, Alec Thurlow made six, eight and seven appearances respectively for City in the first League seasons after the Second World War, and would certainly have taken over from Frank Swift had he not fallen ill with tuberculosis. He left the club for East Anglia to recuperate, but sadly died from the illness in 1956, aged thirty-four.

TIATTO, Daniele Amadeo (Defender/midfield)
Apps/goals: 159/4 Born: Werribee, Australia,
22/5/1973
Career: Bulleen Lions, Melbourne Knights, Salernitana/Italy, Baden/Switzerland, Stoke City (loan), CITY (£300,000, July 1998–August 2004), Leicester City, Brisbane Roar, Melbourne Knights, St Albans Saints, Werribee City.
Details: An uncompromising left-sided defender or midfielder with a 'hardman' like attitude, through fearless tackles and a generally aggressive nature, Danny Tiatto struggled to hold down a first-team place during his first season at Maine Road, partially due to indiscipline. However, 1999/2000 was more successful for the Aussie, who made thirty-five appearances while helping City gain promotion to the Premiership. But despite relegation the following term, Tiatto performed very well in a struggling team, and was won the Player of the Year award. Then, in 2001/02, he was once again a key member of the promotion winning side but on his return to the top division, found his first-team opportunities limited. A sending off against Blackburn six minutes after coming on a substitute resulted in a long exile from the first team. Injuries also restricted appearances and he made only thirteen starts in his last two years with City before transferring to Leicester.

Tiatto was the subject of a 'famous' Kevin Keegan quote, for its apparent lack of sense. 'As far as I'm concerned, Danny Tiatto doesn't exist', said Keegan. An Australian U23 international, he gained twenty-three full caps for his country.

TILSON, Samuel Frederick (Forward)
Apps/goals: 275/132 Born: Swinton, South
Yorkshire, 19/4/1903 Died: Manchester,
21/11/1972
Career: Barnsley Schools, Regent Street Congregationalists, Barnsley, CITY (£6,000, with Eric Brook, March 1928–Match 1938), Northampton Town, York City; retired during the Second World War; CITY (coach, July 1946, then assistant-manager to July 1965, later chief scout, August 1965–April 1968).
Details: Described as being 'a quick thinker with an elusive body-swerve and excellent shot', inside-left Fred Tilson, who also starred at centre-forward, was an FA Cup and League championship winner with City in 1934 and 1937 respectively. He was unfortunate with injuries – he missed the 1933 cup final – yet nevertheless averaged virtually a goal every two games for the Blues, including a club record twenty-two in the FA Cup, two of them coming in the 1934 final victory over Portsmouth. He also shares the record with Horace Barnes, for scoring most hat-tricks for City – eleven.

Capped four times by England, he scored on his debut in a 2-1 defeat by Hungary in Budapest in May 1934 and, with his pal Eric Brook as his left-wing partner, found the net in each of his next three internationals *v.* Czechoslovakia, Wales (2) and Ireland (2). Tilson also played three times for a Football League XI and was twice an international trialist. One feels that Tilson would have won more caps but for injury, and he also faced stiff competition from George Camsell, Ted Drake and 'Pongo' Waring.

He was City's trainer under manager Les McDowall, and a keen motorist and cricketer, Tilson has a road named after him in Manchester called Fred Tilson Close. He served the club for a total of thirty-two years.

TOLMIE, James (Forward)
Apps: 68/19 Born: Glasgow, 21/11/1960
Career: Auchengill Star BC, Morton, SC Lokeren/Belgium, CITY (£30,000, July 1983–May 1986), Carlisle United (loan), Markaryd IF/ Sweden, Morton; retired May 1994.
Details: Jim Tomlie was signed by Billy McNeill for City – the manager's third recruit in nine days following his move from Celtic. With two good feet, plenty of skill and a forthright approach, he appeared in forty-five games out of forty-six in his first season at Maine Road, scoring fifteen goals, second only to Derek Parlane's tally of nineteen. However, he didn't do too well over the next two campaigns, being sold following relegation in 1986. Tolmie played for a Scottish XI in 1980.

TOMPKINSON, Harold (Outside-right)
Apps: 6 Born: Manchester, 1871

Career: Longsight St John's, CITY (July 1894–May 1896).

Details: Harry Tompkinson was top scorer for City's second XI in 1895/96. However, his first-team appearances were scarce, despite having a fine League debut against Walsall Town Swifts in October 1894 when he set up two goals in a 6-1 win.

TONGE, James (Outside-right)
Apps: 5 Born: Sale, 1873
Career: CITY (October 1896–May 1900)

Details: One of many reserves to Billy Meredith, Jim Tonge's first-team appearances were few and far between, making five in four seasons, all of which ended in defeats!

TOSELAND, Ernest (Outside-right)
Apps/goals: 411/75 Born: Northampton, 17/3/1905 Died: Northampton, 19/10/1987
Career: Higham Ferrers Town, Queen's Park Rangers, Coventry City, CITY (March 1929–March 1939), Sheffield Wednesday (£1,575); Second World War guest for CITY (November 1939–November 1945), Manchester United, Rochdale and Stockport County; retired 1946.

Details: A City ever-present on three occasions, Ernie Toseland missed only nineteen League games out of a possible 368 between April 1929 and March 1938. A speedy winger – football's equivalent of Jesse Owens – his eleven goals in twenty-two games for Coventry prompted his move to Maine Road. After an initial 'breaking in' period, he became a star performer, gaining an FA Cup winner's medal in 1934 and a League championship prize three years later. He also represented the Football League *v.* the Irish League in September 1929, and was certainly unlucky not to win a full England cap. He netted ten goals in a season on three occasions when forming a terrific partnership with Bobby Marshall in 1930/31 and 1932/33 and Alec Herd in 1935/36. He spent his last season in the Cheshire League, retiring at the age of forty-one.

TOURÉ, Alioune Kissima (Striker)
Apps: 2 Born: Saint-Denis, France, 9/9/1978
Career: INF Clairefontaine, Nancy, CITY (September 2001/May 2002), Paris Saint-German, Guingamp (loan), União de Leira, Dubai Club, Olympiakos Nicosia, Paris FC.

Details: Alioune Toure's spell with City was over before it started! He suffered a deep vein thrombosis attack during a coach journey to Portsmouth a few days before coming off the subs' bench to make his debut in a League Cup tie against Blackburn. However, he was not right, and was subsequently ordered by doctors not to play for six months while receiving treatment to thin his blood. The French U19 and U21 striker eventually returned to action, having a second substitute outing against Wimbledon before departing.

Touré was a French Cup winner three times, in 1998, 1999 and 2004.

TOURÉ, Kolo Abib (Defender)
Apps/goals: 102/3 Born: Sokoura Bouake, Cote d'Ivoire, 19/3/1981.
Career: ASEC Mimosas, Arsenal, CITY (£16 million, July 2009–July 2013), Liverpool.

Details: Brother of Yaya (below) Koko Touré spent seven successful seasons with Arsenal, making 326 appearances and gaining a Premiership and two FA Cup winner's medals, before joining City, citing differences with other defenders at The Emirates as a reason for switching clubs. Named captain, he started off well alongside another new signing, Joleon Lescott, but the defensive partnership began to look insecure and following a month away in the African Cup of Nations, he returned to find that a new manager, Roberto Mancini was going to choose Vincent Kompany ahead of him.

On 3 March 2011 it was revealed that Touré had failed a drug test and had been suspended; the World Anti-Doping Agency handing him a six-month suspension from football. In 2011/12 Tourè was used as a squad player, and once again missed several games due to international duties, but his fourteen League appearances guaranteed him a Premiership winner's medal. At May 2013 he had played in 103 full internationals for his country (six goals).

TOURÉ, Gnégnéri Yaya (Midfield)
Apps/goals: 134/31 Born: Sokoura Bouake, Cote d'Ivoire, 13/5/1983
Career: ASEC Momosas, Beveren, Metalurh Donetsk, Olympiacos, AS Monaco, Barcelona, CITY (£24 million, July 2010).

Details: Powerhouse midfielder Yaya Touré has been a star performer for City over the last three years. He wrote himself into the record books in 2011 by scoring winning goals in both the FA Cup semi-final and final, versus rivals United and Stoke respectively, bagging the winner against the Potters on seventy-four minutes. He then netted six times the following season, including two in the penultimate match of the campaign at Newcastle, to help City win their first major League title in forty-four years. Strong in all aspects of midfield play, a real box-to-box, lung-bursting competitor, he is sometimes further upfield than his strikers, while seconds later, he could be back inside his own penalty-area clearing a corner or free-kick. His passing and shooting ability are for sure his keys strengths, but due to his immense physical presence, he is often referred to as a 'human train' or a 'colossus'.

He won one trophy with Mimoasas, two with Olympiacos and seven in three years with Barcelona, including two La Liga titles and the Champions League. And at May 2013, he had netted sixteen goals in seventy-eight full internationals for his country, playing several times alongside his brother Kolo in the Africa Cup of Nations. Another brother, Ibrahim, plays for FC Makasa.

TOWERS, Mark Anthony (Midfield)
Apps/goals: 165/12 Born: New Mostem, Manchester, 13/4/1952

Career: Manchester Boys, CITY (July 1967–March 1974), Sunderland (£100,000 plus Mick Horswill), Birmingham City (£140,000), Montreal Manic, Tampa Bay Rowdies, Vancouver Whitecaps, Rochdale; retired May 1986

Details: Tony Towers did exceptionally well with both City and Sunderland, but failed with Birmingham. With good ball skills, smart passing ability and a high consistency level, he put in some terrific shifts for City. A regular in the team from April 1970/May 1971, and again from December 1971–April 1973, he played alongside Colin Bell, Neil Young, Franny Lee, Rodney Marsh, Mike Summerbee and others, won the European Cup Winner's Cup in 1971 and played in the 1974 losing League Cup final *v.* Wolves.

A Second Division championship winner with Sunderland in 1976, Towers netted thirty-two goals in 324 League appearances, starred in four schoolboy, three youth, eight U23 and three full internationals for England, collecting the latter against Wales, Northern Ireland and Italy in May 1976.

TOWNLEY, William (Outside-left)
Apps: 3 Born: Blackburn, 14/12/1866
Died: Blackpool, 30/5/1950

Career: Blackburn Olympic, Blackburn Rovers, Darwen, CITY (August 1896; retired May 1897, after suffering a serious head injury); a schoolmaster by profession, was a coach/manager abroad from 1909 to 1933, being engaged by DFC Prague; Karlsruher FV, SpVgg Fürth/Austria, Bayern Munich, FC St Gallen, SV Waldhof Mannheim, SC Victoria Hamburg, Netherlands national team, Union Niederrad 07, FSV Frankfurt, Eintracht Hannover FC and Armenia Hannover.

Details: Tall and slender with a terrific shot, Bill Townley played in three drawn League games for City, against Woolwich Arsenal (1-1), Gainsborough Trinity (1-1) and Newton Heath (0-0) in September/October 1896. Earlier, he won two FA Cup winner's medals with Blackburn Rovers, making history by becoming the first player to score a hat-trick in the 1890 final 6-1 win over Sheffield Wednesday, and following up a year later with another goal when Rovers' retained the trophy by beating Notts County 3-1. Townley also

gained two England caps (1889/90) scoring twice in his second international, a 9-1 *v.* Ireland.

As a coach/manager – and a brilliant one at that – Townley won the Bundesliga title with Karlsruher (once), SpVgg Fürth (five times) and Bayern Munich (once) and also guided Armenia to the North German (South District) championship.

TRABELSI, Hatem (Right-back)
Apps/goals: 23/1 Born: Aryanah, Tunisia, 25/1/1977

Career: Sfaxien, Ajax Amsterdam, CITY (free, August 2006/May 2007), Al-Hilal Riyadh/Saudi Arabia.

Details: Hatem Trabelsi had been linked with several English clubs before choosing City. Injury and work permit problems prevented him from making his debut until a month into the season, coming on as a substitute against Reading. He scored his first goal in the 3-1 Manchester derby defeat with a left foot drive before losing his right-back place to Micah Richards and then Nedum Onuoha. Without a club for six months prior to joining Al-Hilal Riyadh, he won sixty-six caps for Tunisia between 1998 and 2006.

TRACEY, Simon Peter (Goalkeeper)
Apps: 3 Born: Woolwich, London, 9/12/1967

Career: Wimbledon, Sheffield United (£7,500), CITY (loan, October/November 1994), Norwich City (loan), Wimbledon (loan); retired March 2003; Rotherham United (goalkeeping coach), Barnsley (goalkeeping coach).

Details: One of Simon Tracey's three appearances for City came in November 1994 in a 5-0 defeat to against arch-rivals Manchester United! He played in 382 first-class matches for Sheffield United.

TRAUTMANN, Bernhardt Carl, OBE (Goalkeeper)
Apps: 545 Born: Bremen, North Germany, 22/10/1923

Career: Northwich/Cheshire & Ashton-in-Makerfield (P.O.W camps), St Helens Town, CITY (October 1949–May 1964), St Helens (briefly); Wellington Town; retired May 1965; Stockport County (administration/general manager); Preusen Munster/Germany (manager), Opel Russelheim/Germany (manager), coached in Burma, Tanzania, Liberia, Pakistan and Yemen; briefly ran a guest house in Anglesey; now living with his third wife, Marlis, in a bungalow on the coast near Valencia, Northern Spain.

Details: Bert Trautmann – the handsome Luftwaffe paratrooper who was captured by, and then escaped, from the Russians and the French resistance during the Second World War – declined repatriation to Germany to start a life as a footballer in the UK. He had a few games with St Helens prior to joining City two weeks before his twenty-sixth birthday. At the time Manchester boasted a sizeable Jewish population, and around 20,000 demonstrated against City's new acquisition. But after Dr Alexander Altmann, the communal Rabbi, appealed for the Germany player to be allowed a chance to prove his worth, insisting that an individual should not be punished for his country's sins, Trautmann stayed, became a hit with the supporters and went on to serve the club for almost fifteen years.

Taking over from the great Frank Swift, who had ironically had fought against the Germans during the War, Trautmann played in twenty-six League games in 1949/50 and missed only five matches over the next six years, being an ever-present three times. During his time at Maine Road, he made forty or more appearances in a season on ten occasions. The first German ever to play in an FA Cup final (*v.* Newcastle in 1955), he returned to Wembley for his second final twelve months later, helping City beat Birmingham 3-1, despite breaking his neck in the seventy-fifth minute. Although in pain, he remained on the pitch and at the end proudly climbed the thirty-nine steps to collect his winner's medal. Prior to that final, he was named FWA 'Footballer of the Year'.

He had produced some exceptional performances between the posts, with perhaps his best-ever game coming in the away fourth-round FA Cup tie against Southend. That afternoon, in front of 29,500 fans, he produced six terrific saves on a pitch covered in cockle shells!

Surprisingly, the usually relaxed and unassuming Trautmann was sent off at West Ham in September 1962; City collapsed and lost 6-1 and was dismissed for violent conduct playing for Wellington against Hereford in 1965. He retired in 1965, having amassed almost 600 club appearances, 545 for City. In fact, only three players have appeared in more games for Manchester City than the likeable German.

Twice a Football League representative in 1960, his testimonial match at Maine Road in April 1964 attracted a crowd of 47,901.

Trautmann, who won two iron crosses and five war medals in all (for bravery) was finally, and officially, taken as a Prisoner of War by the British Army in 1945. He initially worked on a farm, and has lived in Germany, Burma, Tanzania, Liberia, Pakistan, Yeman, England and Spain; he left his first girlfriend with a illegitimate daughter; has had three wives and three sons. The first, John, born to his first wife, Margaret Friar, the son of the Manchester City secretary, was tragically killed in a road accident soon after the 1956 FA Cup final.

He was also horrified to learn that Coronation Street actors influenced the Stockport County chairman (when he was manager at Edgeley Park); was awarded an OBE in 2004 for his tireless work

of improving Anglo-German relations... and his top wage with City was £35 a week!

TSKHADADZE, Kakhaber (Centre-back)

Apps/goals: 13/3 Born: Rustavi, Georgia, 7/9/1968

Career: Metalllung Rustavi, Dinamo Tbilisi, GIF Sundsvall, Moscow Spartak, Dinamo Moscow, Eintracht Frankfurt, Alana Vladikavkaz, CITY (£300,000, February/March 1999), Lokomotiv Tbilisi, Anzhi Makhachkala; retired 2005; Dinamo Tbilisi (manager), Standard Baku (manager), Inter Baku (manager).

Details: Sidelined with a serious knee injury in his third game of the 1998/99 season (at Fulham), 6-foot 2-inch sweeper Kakhaber Tskhadadze never played another game for City. Earlier when teaming up with fellow Georgians Murtaz Sheila and Georgi Kinkladze, he had scored a 20-yard bullet header in the League clash with Huddersfield. He won six caps for CIS (1991/92) and twenty-five for Georgia (1991/98).

TUEART, Dennis (Forward)

Apps/goals: 276/112 Born: Newcastle, 27/11/1949

Career: Newcastle Boys, Sunderland, CITY (£275,000, March 1974/February 1978), New York Cosmos/USA (£250,000), CITY (£150, January 1980/July 1983), Stoke City (free), Burnley (free), Derry City; retired 1984; became a successful businessman in corporate hospitality in Manchester; CITY (director, December 1997).

Details: Able to play on both wings, and occasionally through the middle, Dennis Tueart scored a truly memorable goal, an overhead kick from Tommy Booth's knockdown, to virtually seal City's 1976 League Cup final victory Newcastle. He also netted twice – and was sent off for a head-butt – in a 6-0 FA Cup win over Hartlepool, the previous month. By far manager Ron Saunders' best-ever signing, he top-scored for City in 1975/76 with twenty-four goals.

After a spate of niggling injuries, he left Maine Road to try his luck in the NASL, to the dismay of the supporters. He played alongside Pele and Franz Beckenbauer for the Cosmos, but returned for another three-year spell in the early eighties when once again, he produced some superb performances, although his efforts in 1982/83 failed to keep City in the top flight.

Honoured by England at U23 level, as an over-aged player *v.* Scotland in 1974, he scored in one of his three appearances for the Football League, in a 5-0 win over the Scottish League, also in 1974, and won six full caps, making his senior debut as a substitute for Kevin Keegan in a 1-0 European Championship qualifying victory over Cyprus in May 1975.

An FA Cup winner with Sunderland in 1973, Tueart also played in the 1981 final when City lost in a replay to Spurs and during a seventeen-year career, made over 500 club appearances, netting 155 goals. His goal tally for City included twenty-four penalties, the third most behind Francis Lee and Eric Brook. In 1977/78 he claimed three League hat-tricks against Aston Villa, Chelsea and Newcastle, at a time when the fans were enjoying and appreciating his polished and exciting play to the full.

TURNBULL, Alexander (Forward)
Apps/goals: 119/60 Born: Hurlford, Kilmarnock, 1884 Died: Arras, France, 3/5/1917
Career: Hurlford Thistle, CITY (July 1902–December 1906), Manchester United (until his death); First World War guest for Clapton Orient and Rochdale.
Details: 'Sandy' Turnbull, small, compact, burly Scot, was a colourful character, closely associated with the Manchester area, but it may have been a different story had he signed for Bolton in 1902, before agreeing at the eleventh hour to join City.
Described as being a 'coiled spring' of a striker, he was one of the finest headers in the game despite being only 5 feet 5 inches tall, and he could shoot with both feet. A Scottish international trialist, he helped the Blues win the Second Division title in 1903 and the FA Cup a year later before becoming one of the group of players banned by the FA over the illegal payments scandal in 1906. When his suspension was lifted, Turnbull, along with Meredith, Burgess and Bannister moved across town to join United. When the Reds won the League in 1908, he finished as top scorer with twenty-five goals, while also becoming the first player to be sent off in a Manchester derby! He collected a second League winner's medal in 1911, having in between times netted the only goal of the 1909 FA Cup final v. Bristol City. In April 1914, along with George Stacey, Turnbull was granted the United v. City League game at Old Trafford as a joint benefit, and they shared gate receipts of £1,216. Unfortunately, Turnbull's fine career ended with a life ban shortly after further betting irregularities. In 1915, he joined the Footballers' Battalion (Manchester Regiment) but sadly, two years later while on duty in France, he was killed in the Arras sector.

TURNBULL, Ronald William (Forward)
Apps/goals: 31/5 Born: Newbiggin, 18/7/1922 Died: Sunderland, 11/11/1966
Career: Jeanfields Swifts, Dundee, Sunderland (£10,000), CITY (£5,000, September 1949–January 1951), Swansea Town (£7,500), Dundee, Ashington; retired injured, 1957.
Details: After scoring sixteen goals in forty League games for Sunderland, Ron Turnbull started off superbly with City, netting in each of his first two games against Fulham and Newcastle. However, after that he bagged only two more goals in twenty-eight appearances, and one in one the following season before moving to Swansea. Turnbull died after suffering a heart attack.

TURNER, Herbert Arthur Wilmot (Forward)
Apps: 1 Born: Cheshire, 1866 Died: before 1945
Career: Chester, Stoke, CITY (January/May 1893).
Details: One of nine different 'centre-forwards' used by City in their first season of League football, Bert Turner played in the 4-1 defeat at Crewe in February 1893. He helped Stoke win the Alliance title in 1890/91.

TYLER, Herbert Ernest (Defender)
Apps: 47 Born: Eccleshall, 4/9/1889
Career: Sheffield Wednesday, CITY (May 1916–May 1921), Stalybridge Celtic, Chesterfield; retired 1936.
Details: After making almost 100 appearances for City during the First World War, Ernie Tyler played a key role in City's defence when League football resumed in 1919/20, missing only one game during that season. He slipped into the reserves after that and was subsequently transferred in the summer of 1921.

U

UTLEY, George (Half-back)
Apps: 1 Born: Elsecar, near Barnsley, 23/4/1887 Died: Blackpool, 8/1/1966.
Career: Elsecar-Wentworth FC, Sheffield Wednesday, Elsecar, Barnsley, Sheffield United (£2,000), CITY (September 1922; retired May 1923); Bristol City (trainer), Sheffield Wednesday (trainer/coach), Fulham (trainer); later assistant cricket coach and assistant groundsman at Rossall School.
Details: In February 1913, long-throw expert George Utley played left-half for England in their first-ever defeat by Ireland, 2-1 in Belfast. A battler through and through, he was one of the most competitive footballers of his era and was twice an FA Cup winner, with Barnsley in 1912 and Sheffield United in 1915. He made a total of 278 appearances in League football, 170 coming with Barnsley, but only with City v. Preston in October 1922 when deputised for Micky Hamill at centre-half.
In the early 1920s, Utley authored articles for boy's magazines including: Football by Prominent Players: 'Captaining the Cup-Winners' (*The Boys' Friend*) and 'The Complete Half-Back' (*The Boys' Realm*).

V

VAN BLERK, Jason (Full-back)
Apps: 21 Born: Sydney, Australia, 16/3/1968
Career: Sydney Colts, Blacktown City Demons, APIA Leichhardt/Belgium, Sint-Truidense VV/Belgium, APIA Leichhardt, St George FC, Go Ahead Eagles Deventer/Holland, Millwall (£300,000), CITY (free, August 1997/March 1998), West Bromwich Albion (£250,000), Stockport County, Hull City, Shrewsbury Town, Colwyn Bay, Wollongong City, Runcorn FC Halton, APIA Leichhardt; retired 2007; GHFA Spirit/Australia (manager).

Details: A tough, resilient left-back who could also play in midfield, Jason van Blerk made over 400 club appearances during his career. Making his City debut against Sunderland, he came off the subs' bench more times than he started games for the Blues (11/10). Capped twice at U20 and thirty-three times at senior level by Australia, he was sent off in his second full international *v.* Chile in 2000. His father Cliff also played for the Socceroos.

VAN BUYTEN, Daniel (Defender)
Apps: 6 Born: Chimay, Belgium, 7/2/1978
Career: JS Froidchapelle, Olympic Charleroi, UBS Auvelais, FC Somee, Charleroi, Standard Liege, Olympic Marseille, CITY (loan), Hamburger SV, Bayern Munich.

Details: Signed in a loan-exchange deal that took David Sommeil to Marseille, Daniel Van Buyten, 6 feet 5 inches tall, had an excellent touch for a huge man. He played well in his six games for City before tearing two muscles in his groin in an innocuous slip in training. Capped by Belgium once at U18 level, six times by the U21s and on sixty-nine occasions at senior level, he has won nine trophies with Bayern Munich, including three Bundesliga, two German Cups and the Champions League, and at May 2013 had made some 550 appearances for club and country.

While with City he, along with colleagues Djamel Belmadi and £4 million Mexican flop Matias Vuoso, was the victim of a theft by two bankers from the Co-operative Bank, who stole more than £350,000 from the players' accounts. The bank workers, Paul Sherwood, a cashier, and Paul Hanley, his supervisor, were jailed for thirty-two months and twelve months respectively.

VARADI, Imre (Striker)
Apps/goals: 81/31 Born: Paddington, London, 8/7/1959
Career: Central London Schools, Letchworth Garden City, FC 75 of Hitchen, Sheffield United, Everton (£80,000), Newcastle United (£125,000), Sheffield Wednesday (£150,000 plus David Mills), West Bromwich Albion (£285,000), CITY (player-exchange involving Robert Hopkins, October 1986–September 1988), Sheffield Wednesday (exchange for Carl Bradshaw), Leeds United (£50,000), Luton Town (loan), Oxford United (loan), Rotherham United, Boston United, Mansfield Town, Scunthorpe United, Matlock Town (player-manager), Guiseley (player-coach), Denaby United (player-coach); retired May 1998; Stalybridge Celtic (assistant-manager/coach), Sheffield FC (coach); worked for the PFA and as a football agent.

Details: 'Ray' Varadi was City's leading scorer with eleven goals in 1986/87, netting on his debut at Chelsea, and second behind Paul Stewart the following season. A regular marksman throughout his career and a favourite in most ports, he was fast, alert, with a good shot and netted 178 goals in a total of 502 club appearances.

VASSELL, Darius Clarke (Forward)
Apps/goals: 114/22 Born: Sutton Coldfield, 13/6/1980
Career: Romulus FC, Aston Villa, CITY (£2 million, July 2005–July 2009), Ankaragucu/Turkey, Leicester City.

Details: During his first season with City, and despite an irritating hernia problem that later required surgery, Darius Vassell scored ten goals in forty-one appearances, forming an effective partnership with Andrew Cole. He had a decent second season but struggled to find his best form in 2007/08 when, at times, he was used as a wide midfielder in manager Sven-Göran Eriksson's defensive 4-5-1 formation, yet still found time to net his fiftieth Premiership goal in City's victory in the Manchester derby. Released at the end of the season when his contract expired, Vassell gained twenty-two England caps (six goals) as an Aston Villa player. A practicing Christian, his brother Isaac played for Plymouth Argyle.

VAUGHAN, Anthony John (Defender/midfield)
Apps/goals: 72/2 Born: Manchester, 11/11/1975
Career: Ipswich Town, CITY (£1.35 million, July 1997), Cardiff City (loan), Nottingham Forest (loan/signed for £350,000), Scunthorpe United (loan), Mansfield Town (loan), Motherwell, Mansfield Town, Barnsley, Stockport County (loan), Hucknall Town; retired 2007; now works in Audi sales room, Lincoln.

Details: Manager Frank Clark made City fan Tony Vaughan's wish come true by signing him from Ipswich. Starting off well as a defender at Maine Road, he was sidelined for three months after Christmas, but returned to show commitment and flair in midfield, before reverting to the back four in 1998/99. Comfortable on the ball, Vaughan was capped by England at schoolboy and youth team levels and amassed over 300 appearances at club level.

VIEIRA, Patrick (Midfield)
Apps/goals: 36/6 Born: Dakar, Senegal, 23/6/1976
Career: FC Trappes, FC Drouais, Tours, AS Cannes, AC Milan, Arsenal, Juventus, Inter Milan, CITY (January 2010; retired July 2011; now club's Football Development Executive); appointed Goodwill Ambassador of the Food and Agriculture Organisation of the United Nations (May 2010).

Details: Signed initially by City on a six-month deal (later extended), Patrick Vieira linked up with former Arsenal colleagues Kolo Touré and Sylvinho and his former Inter Milan manager Roberto Mancini. A superb midfielder with a winner's mentality, he made his debut as a substitute in the 2-1 defeat by Hull, having his first start three days later against Bolton. He scored his first City goal in a 6-1 win over Burnley in April 2010, but had to wait nine months before bagging his second, on his fiftieth appearance, in a 4-2 win over Leicester in the FA Cup, which City won that season.

Vieira had a wonderful career. He made 750 appearances at club and international level, gained seven U21 and 107 full caps for France – the most by any player who has served with City – won seven Serie 'A' titles with three different Italian clubs, collected the Premiership winner's medals with Arsenal, was a victor in five FA Cup finals (four with the Gunners) and also helped his country lift the World Cup and the European Championship. He was also awarded the Chevalier of the Légion d'honneur in 1998.

He currently oversees aspects such as youth development, commercial partners and social responsibility programme (City in the Community) at the Etihad Stadium.

VILJOEN, Colin (Midfield)
Apps/goals: 38/1 Born: Johannesburg, South Africa, 20/6/1948
Career: Ipswich Town, CITY (August 1978– March 1980), Chelsea (£60,000); retired May 1982; became licensee of a pub near Heathrow airport.

Details: Signed by manager Tony Book, having scored fifty-four goals in 372 games for Ipswich, Colin Viljoen made twenty-five appearances for City in his first season, linking up well in midfield with Asa Hartford. His only goal followed in August 1978, in a 1-1 League Cup draw at Sheffield Wednesday. Taking British nationality in 1971, four years later Viljoen won two England caps v. Northern Ireland and Wales.

VONK, Michel Christian (Defender)
Apps/goals: 103/6 Born: Alkmaar, Holland, 28/10/1968
Career: AZ Alkmaar, SVV Dordrecht, CITY (£300,000, March 1992–December 1995), Oldham Athletic (£350,000), Sheffield United,

MVV Maastricht; retired 2001; PSV Eindhoven (coach), Sparta Rotterdam (assistant-manager/ coach, then manager).

Details: Efficient defender, 6 feet 3 inches tall, strong in the air, Michel Vonk enjoyed three successful seasons with City. Signed by manager Peter Reid, he formed a successful partnership with Keith Curle despite a few injury problems and scored four of his six goals in 1992/93 including the decider in a 2-1 FA Cup win at QPR.

Early in 1995, Vonk criticised then City manager Brian Horton in the *News of the World* that earned him a suspension and being fined two weeks wages. Subsequent City boss Alan Ball then sold him to Oldham!

W

WABARA, Reece (Defender)
Apps: 1 Born: Bromsgrove, 28/12/1991
Career: Walsall, CITY (June 2007), Ipswich Town (loan), Oldham Athletic (loan), Blackpool (loan).

Details: Reece Wabara, a central defender or left/right full back, signed from Walsall's School of Excellence, became a mainstay in City's Elite Development Squad and has committed his long-term future to the Blues by signing a three-year deal in March 2011 worth an estimated £1 million. He made his first-team debut on the last day of the 2010/11 season against Bolton, coming on as a substitute for Pablo Zabaleta. Wabara has five England U20 caps to his credit.

WAGSTAFFE, David (Outside-left)
Apps/goals: 161/8 Born: Manchester, 5/4/1943
Career: Manchester Boys, CITY (August 1958– December 1964), Wolverhampton Wanderers (£30,000), Blackburn Rovers, Blackpool, Blackburn Rovers; retired 1979; became licensee of 'Waggy's bar' (at Molineux) and later steward of the Old Wulfrunians Club, Castlecroft; now resident in Staffordshire.

Details: Dave Wagstaffe was a direct, line-hugging winger with skill and pace, and the ability to cross the ball on the run. Doing the simple things with authority, he replaced Colin Coldridge on the left flank in September 1960, was an ever-present the following season when he scored his first City goal at Sheffield Wednesday, and retained his position until April 1964. He did very well with Wolves, helping the Midland club climb out of the Second Division (1967), win the 1974 League Cup (at City's expense) and reach the UEFA Cup final. The first player to be shown a 'red' card in a Football League game when playing for Blackburn against Bolton in October 1976, 'Waggy' made a total of 564 League appearances, represented England at both schoolboy and youth team levels and played for a Football League XI.

WALKER, John (Defender)
Apps/goals: 19/1 Born: Alexandria, Dunbartonshire, 1869
Career: Vale of Leven, Grimsby Town, Gainsborough Trinity, Everton, CITY (October 1894/May 1895), Leicester Fosse; retired injured, April 1900.
Details: The versatile Jack Walker occupied four different defensive positions during his career, playing his best football at full-back. With City, he partnered Smith and Davie Robson and scored his only goal in a 7-1 home League win over Notts County in March 1895. He suffered a fractured shin playing for Leicester against Grimsby in April 1899 and never regained full fitness. Sadly, his benefit match raised only £75.

WALL, Leonard James (Forward)
Apps/goals: 41/2 Born: Shrewsbury, 1886
Career: Glossop, CITY (October 1910–November 1913), Dundee, Shrewsbury Town, Walsall; retired May 1922.
Details: The versatile Len Wall played right-half, centre-half, centre-forward and inside-left in his first season with City, scoring once, in a 2-1 defeat at Villa Park. The following term he was used as a defender, lining up alongside Tom Holford, then Bill Eadie and others.

WALLACE, Alec (Forward)
Apps/goals: 6/1 Born: Darwen, 1872
Career: Blackpool, CITY (June /October 1894), Baltimore Orioles/USA.
Details: After just half a dozen outings for City, Alec Wallace switched to the States with three Mitch Calvey, Archie Ferguson and Tommy Little. His only goal for the Blues came in a 5-2 home defeat by Grimsby.

WALLACE, William (Forward)
Apps/goals: 46/9 Born: Blaydon-on-Tyne, 1888
Career: Newburn, CITY (October 1911–May 1914), Bolton Wanderers; retired during the First World War.
Details: Taking over from Joe Dorsett on City's left wing in 1912/13, Billy Wallace was quick and skilful, but at times was quite erratic with his shooting. Nevertheless, he held his position until halfway through the following campaign. Three of his nine League goals were scored in 2-0 and 2-1 wins over West Bromwich Albion in his first season of League football.

WALMSLEY, Clifford (Goalkeeper)
Apps: 2 Born: Burnley, 25/11/1910 Died: 1983
Career: Burnley, CITY (September 1931/May 1932), Reading, Rochdale, Stalybridge Celtic; did not play after the Second World War.

Details: Reserve to Len Langford, Cliff Walmsley's two appearances for City were at Grimsby (lost) and at home to Birmingham (won) in March 1932. He later played in fifty-nine League games for Rochdale.

WALSH, Michael Thomas (Defender)
Apps: 7 Born: Blackley, 20/6/1956
Career: Bolton Wanderers, Everton (£900,000 plus Seamus McDonagh), Norwich City (loan), Burnley (loan), Fort Lauderdale/USA, CITY (October 1983–January 1984), Blackpool (£6,000), Bury, Barrow; retired 1990; Swindon Town (coach), Southport (manager).
Details: A product of the Burnden Park youth policy, Mike Walsh made 201 appearances and won the Second Division championship with Bolton and had twenty-two outings for Everton before two loan spells and a trip to the States preceded his move to Maine Road. He played only seven games for City in four months, debuting against Middlesbrough. A Republic of Ireland international, winning five caps, he later helped Blackpool gain promotion and retired with over 500 club appearances under his belt.

WALSH, Paul (Forward)
Apps/goals: 62/19 Born: Plumstead, London, 1/10/1962
Career: Blackheath Schools, South London Schools, Charlton Athletic, Luton Town (£400,000), Liverpool (£700,000), Tottenham Hotspur (£500,000), Queen's Park Rangers (loan), Portsmouth (£400,000, plus Darren Anderton), CITY (£750,000, March 1994/September 1995), Portsmouth (£500,000); retired injured, June 1996; became a players' agent, TV soccer pundit and Ambassador for FIFA.
Details: Paul Walsh, as striker partner to Uwe Rosler, had a fine first full season with City, netting fifteen goals in forty-eight outings, twelve of his efforts coming before Christmas.
Earlier, his impish, natural, predatory instincts around the penalty area earned him five England caps and four at U21 level, plus youth honours. His all-round ability was recognised by his fellow professionals who voted him as the PFA 'Young Player of the Year' in 1984.
During his career – ended by a knee injury – Walsh scored 168 goals in 633 League and Cup games for his seven clubs. He helped Liverpool complete the First Division championship and Screen Sport Super Cup double in 1986 and Spurs win the FA Cup in 1991.

WALSH, William (Half-back)
Apps/goals: 118/1 Born: Dublin, Ireland, 31/5/1921 Died: Noosa, Queensland, 11/7/2006
Career: Manchester United (amateur), CITY (May 1936–April 1951); Second World War

guest for Blackburn Rovers, Blackpool, Fulham, Manchester United, Millwall, Notts County, Oldham Athletic, Rochdale, Southampton, Sunderland, West Bromwich Albion and York City; Chelmsford City; retired 1954; CITY (scout, 1950s/60s); later emigrated to Australia.

Details: Owing to Second World War, Billy Walsh had to wait more than ten years before making his senior debut for City, although he did appear in 225 games for the Blues during the hostilities and several more as a guest for other clubs. He celebrated his first League outing, in August 1946, with his only senior goal in a 3-0 win at Leicester, and although in and out of the side through injury and loss of form during that initial post-war campaign, he did help City win the Second Division title. After that he produced some highly quality performances, missing only thirteen League games out of a possible 108 between September 1947 and March 1950. The Republic of Ireland capped him on nine occasions and five times by Northern Ireland.

WANCHOPE, Pablo Cesar Watson (Forward)
Apps/goals: 49/23 Born: Heredia, Costa Rica, 31/7/1976
Career: CS Herediano, Derby County (£600,000), West Ham United (£3.25 million), CITY (£3.65 million, August 2000–May 2004), Malaga (£500,000), Al-Gharafa, CS Herediano, Rosario Central, FC Tokyo, Chicago Fire; retired November 2007.

Details: The club's record signing, Pablo Wanchope was unable to help City survive immediate relegation back to Division One at the end of the 2000/01 season, despite scoring nine League goals. However, the following season was a mixed one for the 6-foot 4-inch Costa Rican striker. He missed several matches through injury, yet still managed twelve goals in just fifteen games and often showed his best form. After City's return to the top flight as Division One champions he played almost no part, injury again keeping him on the sidelines. And it got worse, as he was absent for the entire 2002/03 campaign. Returning to play a vital part at the end of the 2003/04 season, he netted some vital goals which helped the team avoid relegation. Remembered as an extravagant talent by City fans, his celebration of a goal at Southampton, when he grabbed a TV microphone and joyfully screamed into it, just added to his character status. He helped his country qualify for the 2002 World Cup and in all, scored forty-five goals in seventy-three full internationals.

WARD, Ashley Stuart (Forward)
Apps: 3 Born: Manchester, 24/11/1970
Career: Schoolboy football, CITY (June 1987–July 1991), Wrexham (loan), Leicester City (£80,000), Blackpool (loan), Crewe Alexandra (£80,000), Norwich City (£500,000), Derby County (£1 million), Barnsley (£1.3 million), Blackburn Rovers (£4.25 million), Bradford City (£1.5 million), Sheffield United (free); retired July 2005; became a successful property developer, renovating several luxury homes in the North West of England, including Wayne Rooney's.

Details: Developed via the YTS, Ashley Ward made just three substitute appearances for City before joining Leicester. Going from strength to strength, he moved around the country for fees amounting to more than £8.6 million, and when he retired he had scored 134 goals in 452 games at club level, without winning a single medal anywhere. One who escaped from the City nest?

WARD, Mark William (Midfield)
Apps/goals: 67/16 Born: Huyton, Liverpool, 10/10/1962
Career: Everton, Northwich Victoria, Oldham Athletic (£10,000), West Ham United (£250,000), CITY (£1 million, plus Ian Bishop, December 1989–August 1991), Everton (£1.1 million), Birmingham City (loan/signed for £500,000; then player-coach), Huddersfield Town (free), Ayr United, Wigan Athletic, Dundee, FC Valur, Altrincham; retired May 2001; Northwich Victoria (manager).

Details: Midfield dynamo Mark Ward made 565 appearances and scored sixty-four goals in a lengthy career. Released by Everton, he won England semi-professional honours with the 'Vics' and after a decent spell at Boundary Park and an excellent one with the Hammers (209 games), he spent a season-and-a-half at Maine Road, missing only two matches during that time. He helped Birmingham complete the Second Division and AWS double in 1995.

After leaving football, Ward became involved in the supplying of drugs in Liverpool. He was arrested after 4 kg (9 lb) of cocaine were found during a raid at a house in Prescot, Merseyside in May 2005. Five months later, he was jailed for eight years but was released in May 2009, having served half of his sentence in Kirkham and Walton prisons.

WARDLE, William (Outside-left)
Apps: 7 Born: Houghton-le-Spring, County Durham, 20/1/1918 Died: Yorkshire, 15/1/1989
Career: County Durham Schools, Fatfield Juniors, Houghton Colliery Welfare, Southport, CITY (£2,000, October 1937–July 1939), Grimsby Town, Blackpool, Birmingham City (£8,000), Barnsley, Skegness Town; retired June 1957.

Details: A note in a local newspaper stated 'Wardle has scintillating footwork, at which art he was unsurpassed', while another scribe said he is 'inclined to overdo the twiddly bits'. Signed as cover for Eric Brook, Bill never settled at Maine Road, and made six of his appearances in a row halfway through his first season, having a poor debut in a 4-0 defeat at Middlesbrough in October 1937 when Brook was on England duty, along with Bert Sproston and Sam Barkas. He made almost 250 club appearances after leaving City. His brother George played for Middlesbrough, Cardiff, QPR and Darlington.

WARHURST, Roy (Left-half)
Apps/goals: 41/2 Born: Sheffield, 18/9/1926
Career: Atlas & Norfolk FC, Huddersfield Town (amateur), Sheffield United; Birmingham City (£8,000), CITY (£10,000, June 1957–March 1959), Crewe Alexandra, Oldham Athletic, Banbury Spencer; retired May 1964; became a scrap metal dealer in Birmingham, while residing in Lichfield.
Details: A stocky wing-half with crunching tackle, the experienced Roy Warhurst was signed to replace the inspirational Roy Paul, having made 239 appearances for Birmingham whom he helped win the Second Division championship in 1955, but missed the following year's FA Cup final against City. During his time at Maine Road he produced some sterling displays, scoring two rare goals, in home and away games against Newcastle in April 1958. Warhurst and his former teammate Bert Trautmann are the oldest ex-City players still alive.

WARNER, John (Forward)
Apps/goals: 78/15 Born: Woolwich, London, 1898 Died: London, 1950
Career: Custom House/London, Burnley, CITY (April 1921–May 1926), Watford, Thames; retired 1934.
Details: Jack Warner had a good 1921/22 season with City, netting three goals in twenty-two appearances. A regular in the second XI the following term, he was joint-top scorer for the 'stiffs' with Tommy Browell in 1923/24, despite playing in half of the first-team fixtures. During his last two campaigns, he understudied Browell and Frank Roberts before his departure following City's relegation from Division One.

WASSALL, Darren Paul (Defender)
Apps: 17 Born: Birmingham, 27/6/1968
Career: Nottingham Forest, Hereford United, Bury (loan), Derby County (£600,000), CITY (loan, September/December 1996), Birmingham City (loan/signed for £100,000), Burton Albion; retired 2001.
Details: A Simod Cup winner with Forest in 1992, man-marker Darren Wassall made 122 appearances for Derby before his spell at Maine Road. An ever-present in City's defence, alongside Kit Symons, until damaging his Achilles tendon and

being forced onto the treatment table, he played in over 225 club games during his career.

WATERREUS, Ronald Katarina Martinus (Goalkeeper)
Apps: 2 Born: Kerkrade, Holland, 25/8/1970
Career: RKVV, Roda JC Kerkrade, PSV Eindhoven, CITY (August 2004/January 2005), Glasgow Rangers, AZ Alkmaar, New York Red Bulls.
Details: Experienced Dutch international with seven caps to his name, Ron Waterreus was signed on a short-term contract as cover for David James and played in two League Cup games before moving to Ibrox Park.

WATSON, David Vernon
Defender: apps/goals: 190/6 Born: Stapleford, Notts, 5/10/1946
Career: Stapleford Old Boys, Notts County, Rotherham United (£25,000), Sunderland (£100,000), CITY (£275,000, plus Jeff Clarke, June 1975–June 1979), Werder Bremen/Germany (£100,000), Southampton (£200,000), Stoke City (£50,000), Vancouver Whitecaps/USA (free), Derby County (free), Vancouver Whitecaps (loan), Fort Lauderdale Strikers/USA (free), Notts County (player-coach), Kettering Town; retired May 1986; later ran his own business in Nottingham.
Details: During his career, Dave Watson made well over 800 club appearances, including 660 in the Football League (sixty-five goals). He had his best spells with Sunderland (177 games) with whom he won the FA Cup in 1973 and City, gaining a League Cup winner's prize in 1976. In his early days with Notts County and Rotherham, he played centre-forward before settling down to become a commanding central defender. Strong in the tackle and in the air, he was the ideal lynchpin alongside Mike Doyle at the back. Aged twenty-nine when he joined City, yet already an England international, Watson had not tasted First Division football before making his debut for the Blues against Norwich in August 1975, but he took to the job like a duck to water and gave City excellent service for four seasons.
Watson holds the record for being the player with most England caps never to have appeared in the World Cup and was all set to go on to the 'illegal' tour to South Africa in 1983 but pulled out at the last minute. He also represented the Football League. His wife, Penny, wrote the novel *My Dear Watson*.

WATSON, Lionel Percival (Forward)
Apps: 1 Born: Southport, 1881
Career: High Park, Southport Central, CITY (July 1901/October 1902), Blackburn Rovers, West Ham United, Blackpool; retired 1911.
Details: A one-season reserve, Lionel Watson's only start for the Blues came in a 5-0 defeat at

Sheffield United in November 1901. He did much better with Blackburn: eighteen goals in fifty-five League games.

WEAH, George (Forward)
Apps/goals: 9/4 Born: Monrovia, Liberia, 1/10/1966
Career: Young Survivors, Bongrange, Mighty Barolle and Invincible Eleven (all Liberia), Tonnerre Kiarra Yaounde/Cameroon, AS Monaco, Paris St-Germaine, AC Milan, Chelsea (loan), CITY (free, August/October 2000), Olympique Marseille (free), Al-Jazeera/Indonesia; retired 2001; Liberia (national team manager); moved into politics in his home country of Liberia.

Details: The 1995 World, European and African Footballer of the Year George Weah, who won the latter award four times overall, was thirty-four when he joined City at the same time as Paulo Wanchope arrived from West Ham. After netting twice in a League Cup tie at Gillingham in September 2000, and also scoring at Anfield, he failed to make the impact manager Joe Royle had hoped for, and left within ten weeks. Standing 6 feet 1 inch tall and nicknamed the 'Lion', he won ten trophies during his varied career, including the FA Cup with Chelsea (2000), while in 1996 he scored one of the greatest goals ever seen in Italian football when he ran 100 yards, dribbled past seven opponents and placed the ball into the net for AC Milan against Verona. He also gained ninety-six caps for his country (thirty-three goals) and kept afloat the cash-stricken Liberian national team for many years.

A sporting hero in his home country, Weah is actively involved in UNICEF.

WEAVER, Nicholas James (Goalkeeper)
Apps: 207 Born: Sheffield, 2/3/1979
Career: Mansfield Town, CITY (£200,000, May 1997–August 2007), Sheffield Wednesday (loan), Charlton Athletic, Dundee United, Burnley, Sheffield Wednesday.

Details: Nicky Weaver was just nineteen when he made his City debut at the start of the 1998/99 season and his presence between the posts quickly permeated through the back four and then through the rest of the team as the drive for promotion began in earnest. A favourite of the home supporters, and coached by former Manchester united 'keeper Alex Stepney, he was outstanding throughout the campaign, kept twenty-six clean sheets (a record at the time, later bettered by Joe Hart) and produced some vital saves in the penalty shoot-out at the end of the Play-off final against Gillingham, resulting in a dancing jig round Wembley. He missed only one game in 1999/2000, before coming under pressure from Carlo Nash who eventually replaced him between the posts, as did Peter Schmeichel some

time later. But Weaver – noted for his forays upfield – returned to take his appearance tally with City past the 200-mark, having visited an orthopaedic clinic in Cleveland, USA in 2004 to have pioneering surgery on a troublesome right knee. It worked and he was still playing in 2013.

Capped ten times by England at U21 level, and also a promotion and Championship winner with City in 2000 and 2002, he was sent off after just three minutes playing for Charlton in a 2-1 League win at Plymouth in April 2008.

WEBB, Charles (Outside-right)
Apps/goals: 22/3 Born: Higham Ferrers, 4/3/1879 Died: Wellingborough, 16/1/1939
Career: Chesham Grenadiers, Higham Ferrers, Rushden, Kettering Town, Leicester Fosse, Wellingborough, Kettering Town, Southampton, Blackpool, Dundee, CITY (March 1908/June 1909), Airdrieonians; retired 1914; later manager of a bakery in Rushden, Northants.

Details: Having lost George Stewart and struggling to find a suitable replacement, City signed Charlie Webb to fill the role. He did well initially, scoring three goals (two against Preston) in his first seven outings but after a decent start to the 1908/09 season, he lost his form and his place, and eventually moved to Scotland.

WEBB, George William (Centre-forward)
Apps: 2 Born: Poplar, London, 10/2/1887 Died: Harlesden, London, 28/3/1915
Career: Shaftsbury Road School, Ilford Alliance, West Ham United, CITY (July 1912, retired October 1912); worked in the family toy manufacturing business until his death.

Details: Big, bold, centre-forward George Webb, with a hefty physique and an amateur throughout his career, made his two appearances for City in successive 1-0 League wins over Notts County and Manchester United at the start of the 1912/13 season. He also won two caps for England at senior level, scoring on his debut in a 3-0 win over Wales at Millwall in March 1911. He also played in five internationals. Webb died of tuberculocis at the age of twenty-eight.

WEBSTER, Eric (Half-back)
Apps: 1 Born: Manchester, 24/6/1931
Career: CITY (February 1952/June 1953)
Details: A one-match wonder, Eric Webster deputised at left-half for Roy Paul in a 6-0 League drubbing at Cardiff in February 1953. Phil Woosnam also made his only appearance for City in this 'best forgotten' game.

WEIR, David (Centre-half/forward)
Apps/goals: 34/13 Born: Aldershot, 7/6/1863 Died: Edinburgh, Scotland, 7/11/1933

Career: Hampton FC, Maybole FC/Glasgow, Glasgow Thistle, Halliwell, Bolton Wanderers, CITY (May 1890–February 1893), Bolton Wanderers; Maybole FC (player-coach, August 1895, retired as a player, May 1896, remained as coach and assistant-manager); Glossop (manager), Stuttgart/Germany (coach).

Details: Born the son of an officer's batman, Davie Weir was a strong attacking player who occupied the centre-half and three inside-forward positions with total commitment. He scored a hat-trick in City's first-ever competitive game, an FA Cup qualifier against Liverpool Stanley in October 1890 which resulted in a 12-0 victory. He also played, but didn't score, in the club's first Alliance game, also against Bootle in September 1891 – but did grab a goal in City's first-ever Football League game, a 7-0 win over Bootle in September 1892. Unfortunately, he was not liked by his colleagues, being described as too much of an 'individualist.' He was dropped for the 1894 FA Cup final due to his unpopularity with several Bolton players!

Capped twice by England, at centre-half against Ireland in March 1889 and inside-left *v.* Scotland a month later, he scored forty-one goals in ninety-two appearances in two spells with Bolton.

WEISS, Vladimir (Winger)
Apps: 5/1 Born: Bratislava, Czechoslovakia, 30/11/1989

Career: Inter Bratislava, CITY (June 2006–August 2012), Bolton Wanderers (loan), Glasgow Rangers (loan), Espanyol (loan), Pescara.

Details: Valdimir Weiss scored in the second leg of City's 2008 two-legged FA Youth Cup final victory over Chelsea and a month later, as a substitute, he replaced Stephen Ireland after seventy minutes to make his League debut in a 1-0 win over Bolton. He followed up with his first senior goal in a League Cup tie *v.* Arsenal in December 2009. He has played in three U19, eight U21 and twenty-seven full internationals (two goals) for Slovakia.

WESTCOTT, Dennis (Centre-forward)
Apps/goals: 72/37 Born: Wallasey, 2/7/1917 Died: Stafford, 13/7/1960

Career: Leasowe Road Brickworks FC, Everton (trial), West Ham United (trial), New Brighton, Wolverhampton Wanderers; Second World War guest for Brentford, Liverpool and Watford; Blackburn Rovers, CITY (February 1950–June 1952), Chesterfield, Stafford Rangers; retired May 1956.

Details: A big, strong, robust centre-forward, Dennis Westcott was leading scorer for City in 1950/51 with twenty-five goals and shared top spot with Johnny Hart in 1951/52 with eleven, when he also netted most goals for City's second

XI. In fact, he and his strike-partner George Smith cracked in a combined total of fifty-one goals in 1950/51.

A prolific marksman with Wolves, for whom he struck 124 goals in 144 League and Cup appearances plus another ninety-one in seventy-six Second World War games, Westcott netted four times in the Wanderers' 1939 FA Cup semi-final win over Grimsby. He missed out on a winner's medal at Wembley, although he did help the Wanderers lift the Wartime League (N) Cup. He played in four Victory internationals for England (1945/46) and represented the Football League, but a full cap eluded him. In a wonderful career, Westcott scored over 350 goals in club football alone, 211 coming in the Football League.

WESTWOOD, Eric (Half-back)
Apps: 260/5 Born: Manchester, 25/9/1917 Died: Manchester, 2001

Career: Manchester United, CITY (November 1937–June 1953); Second World War guest for Chelsea, Manchester United, Norwich City and Reading; Altrincham; retired 1955.

Details: Capped twice by England 'B' and twice a Football League representative, Eric Westwood was an amateur at Old Trafford before moving to Maine Road, making his City debut in the same day as full-back partner Bert Sproston against Tottenham Hotspur in November 1938. A steady, reliable defender, he made thirty-two senior appearances that season and, after having thirty-two outings during the Second World War period, he returned League action in 1946 and continued playing until 1953, making his last appearance for City in that year's Manchester derby. He won the 1944 Wartime Cup with Chelsea and the Second Division championship with City in 1947. As a soldier during Second World War, he was banned from riding a bicycle when off duty!

WHARTON, John Edwin (Winger)
Apps/goals: 26/2 Born: Bolton, 18/6/1920 Died: 5/5/1997

Career: Plymouth Argyle, Preston North End; Second World War guest for Carlisle United; CITY (March 1947/June 1948), Blackburn Rovers, Newport County; retired 1954.

Details: Able to play on both wings, Jack Wharton was a great crosser of the ball and provided plenty of goalscoring opportunities for the inside and centre-forwards he played with, including the City trio of Black, McMorran and Smith. His two goals earned the Blues a 2-1 League win at Nottingham Forest and a point at Blackpool. His son, Terry Wharton, played for Bolton, Wolves, Crystal Palace and Walsall in the 1960s/70s.

WHELAN, Anthony Michael (Left-back/forward)
Apps: 6 Born: Salford, 20/11/1952
Career: Manchester United, CITY (March 1973/July 1974), Rochdale, Los Angeles Skyhawks, Fort Lauderdale Strikers, Atlanta Chiefs, Philadelphia Fever (indoor), Fort Lauderdale Strikers, Witton Albion; retired 1985; CITY (coach with club's Community Programme, seasons 1987–90), Manchester United (coach, then Youth Academy director).

Details: Tony Whelan failed to make a senior appearance for United and started only three League games for City while coming on as a substitute in three more. After leaving Maine Road he played in more than 130 senior matches for Rochdale. His father, Robert, was a reserve in the early 1950s. Over the years, Whelan has gained several coaching qualifications, as well as a Bachelors degree in humanities from the Open University, and a Masters degree in sociology from Manchester Metropolitan University. He also wrote the foreword to *The First Black Footballer: Arthur Wharton 1865–1930 An Absence of Memory* (1998) and is the author of *The Birth of the Babes: Manchester United Youth Policy 1950–1957*, which explores the impact of youth development and the building of the Busby Babes side at Manchester United. In March 2008, *The Voice* included him on a list of the thirty most influential black people in English football in recognition of his work developing elite young players. Ten months later, he received an award at the House of Lords from *Kick It Out* acknowledging his inclusion in the list.

WHELAN, Glenn David (Midfield)
Apps: 1 Born: Dublin, 13/1/1984
Career: CITY (June 2000–July 2004), Bury (loan, Sheffield Wednesday (free), Stoke City (£500,000).

Details: Glenn Whelan's solitary outing for City was as a second-half substitute in the UEFA Cup match against TNS in 2003. He later made over 150 appearances for both Wednesday and Stoke, while upping his total of full caps for the Republic of Ireland to forty-two, to add to those he won at 'B' and U21 levels.

WHITE, David (Forward)
Apps/goals: 342/95 Born: Urmston, Manchester, 30/10/1967
Career: Salford Boys, CITY (April 1983–December 1993), Leeds United (£2 million, exchange involving David Rocastle), Sheffield United (loan/signed for £500,000); retired injured, May 1997.

Details: David White, a tall, strong, fast-raiding wing-forward, helped City win the FA Youth Cup in 1986 and gain promotion from Division Two in 1988. He made his Blues debut against Luton in September 1986 and was a regular in the first team for six years until his departure in 1993. Producing several superb displays and scoring some brilliant goals, he fired a hat-trick in City's record 10-1 defeat of Huddersfield in November 1987, bagged a four-timer in a 5-1 win over Aston Villa in April 1991 and netted another treble in a 5-2 victory at Oldham a year later. He was joint second top scorer with Clive Allen in 1989/90 before heading the charts on his own in seasons 1991/92 and 1992/93 with twenty-one and nineteen goals respectively. In fact, between 1990 and 1994, White and Niall Quinn were irresistible up front, notching over 100 goals between them. One of England manager Graham Taylor's follies, White was capped against Spain in September 1992. He also represented his country at Youth team level, in two 'B' team games and starred in six U21 internationals.

WHITE, Howard Kenneth (Defender)
Apps: 1 Born: Timperley, 2/3/1954
Career: Cheshire Boys, CITY (August 1970–June 1973), Bangor City.

Details: Registered at Maine Road for three seasons, Howard White was just seventeen when he made his only first-team appearance for City against Liverpool in April 1971 when manager Joe Mercer rested several players ahead of the ECWC semi-final second leg clash with Chelsea.

WHITEHEAD, James (Forward)
Apps/goals: 26/7 Born: Church, Lancs, 23/6/1870 Died: Manchester, 7/8/1929
Career: Church FC, Peel Bank FC, Accrington, Blackburn Rovers, CITY (September 1897, retired injured, July 1899).

Details: Jim Whitehead was described as being 'too lightly built for bustling tactics. He was a spruce, lively inside-right, adroit in evading weightier opponents.' Nevertheless, he had a good first season with City, scoring on his debut in a 5-0 League win over Darwen. He won two England caps as a Blackburn player, in a 6-0 win over Wales in March 1893 and in a 2-2 draw with Ireland in Belfast a year later. Injury forced him into early retirement.

WHITFIELD, Kenneth (Centre-forward)
Apps/goals: 13/3 Born: Bishop Auckland, 24/3/1930
Career: Shildon Colliery, Wolverhampton Wanderers, CITY (February 1953– July 1954), Brighton & Hove Albion, Queen's Park Rangers; retired 1961.

Details: Ken Whitfield was reserve to some quality players at Wolves and as a result switched positions from half-back to centre-forward. He made all his appearances for City as leader of the attack, scoring his first goal against his previous employers in a 3-1 win four weeks after moving from Molineux. Later switching back to centre-half, he made 175 League appearances for Brighton.

WHITLEY, James (Midfield)
Apps/goals: 46/1 Born: Ndola, Zambia, 14/4/1975

Career: CITY (June 1991–October 2001), Blackpool (loan), Norwich City (loan), Swindon Town (loan), Northampton Town (loan), Wrexham; retired June 2006.

Details: Jim Whitley was an industrious midfielder but was generally frustrated by injury. After making twenty-four appearances in 1996/97, he was joined in City's first team by his younger brother Jeff the following season and they played off and on together for two years, helping City gain promotion from the Second Division. Jim played in 155 first-class games for Wrexham and won one 'B' and three full caps for Northern Ireland.

Away from football, he is a very talented artist and an exhibition of his work was held at The City of Manchester Stadium in 2005. He is also a singer-dancer, performing as Nat King Cole and Sammy Davis junior at various theatres.

WHITLEY, Jeffrey (Midfield)
Apps/goals: 141/8 Born: Zambia, 28/1/1979

Career: CITY (June 1995–August 2003), Wrexham (loan), Notts County (loan, two spells), Sunderland, Cardiff City, Stoke City (loan), Wrexham (loan/signed), Woodley Sports, Northwich Victoria; retired May 2010; now a car salesman in Stockport.

Details: Also a keen, tough-tackling midfielder, Jeff Whitley made almost 100 more senior appearances for City than his elder brother and only he played in the 1999 play-off final at Wembley v. Gillingham. He also collected more international honours, winning two 'B', 17 U21 and twenty full caps for Northern Ireland.

Having his best season at Maine Road in 1999/2000 when he played in forty-seven out of a possible fifty-two matches, he scored four goals, three of them in home League wins over Blackburn, Portsmouth and Tranmere.

Whitley has spent time at the Sporting Chance clinic after becoming addicted to alcohol and drugs. It affected him greatly and said 'at times I would just be praying just to die'. Today he gives talks at professional football clubs about the dangers of alcohol and drug misuse.

WHITTAKER, James Harold (Outside-left)
Apps/goals: 6/1 Born: Bolton, 1880

Career: Barnsley, CITY (February 1904–May 1906), Clapton Orient, CITY (January 1907/August 1908), Clapton Orient.

Details: Reserve left-winger Jim Whittaker made all his appearances for City in his first spell at the club, scoring his only goal in a 5-1 home win over Sunderland in April 1906 when deputising for Frank Booth.

WHITTLE, Daniel (Centre-half)
Apps/goals: 31/3 Born: Sheffield, 1865

Career: Halliwell, Bolton Wanderers, CITY (July 1890–August 1894), Bolton Wanderers.

Details: Dan Whittle, rough and ready, well-built and a strong tackler, scored in City's first-ever FA Cup game – a record 12-0 win over Liverpool Stanley in October 1890. He also appeared City's first Football Alliance game v. Bootle in September 1891 and played in nine games during City's first season in Division Two (1892/93). He received a hefty fine from the club after missing the train en route to Crewe in February 1894, leaving City's ten men to earn a 1-1 draw.

WIEKENS, Gerard (Midfield)
Apps/goals: 213/10 Born: Tolhuiswyk, Holland, 25/2/1973

Career: SC Veendam/Holland, CITY (£500,000, July 1997–June 2004), SC Veendam.

Details: Six feet tall and weighing 13 stone 4lbs, Gerard Wiekens was certainly not the quickest of players but was as good as anyone in linking up his defence and attack. He produced some quality performances for City, making 172 appearances in his first four seasons that included relegation and promotion, and a Wembley victory in 1999 at the end of a season during which he scored winning goals at Wrexham and Stoke. An unsung hero at Maine Road, Wiekens was a huge favourite with the fans and never let them, or the team, down!

WILKINSON, John (Centre-half)
Apps/goals: 31/2 Born: Darlington, 1881

Career: Darlington St Augustine's, CITY (November 1906–May 1912); did not play after the First World War.

Details: A reliable reserve to Bill Eadie, Jack Wilkinson made two League appearances at centre-half in 1906/07, played and scored from inside-left against Preston in April 1908 before having his best season in terms of senior outings, with seventeen in 1908/09. It seems as if he quit football after being released by City.

WILLEY, William (Centre-forward)
Apps: 1 Born: Manchester, 1870

Career: CITY (December 1893/May 1894)

Details: Reserve Bill Willey made just one League appearance in his career, in City's 5-0 defeat at Grimsby in January 1894, being one of ten players who led the attack that season.

WILLIAMS, Alexander (Goalkeeper)
Apps: 125 Born: Moss Side, Manchester, 13/11/1961

Career: Manchester Boys, CITY (July 1978–January 1987), Queen of the South (loan), Port Vale (loan/signed for £10,000); retired September 1987; later returned to club as Community Officer); CITY (Football in the Community Officer).

Details: An England youth international and one of the first black goalkeepers to play in the Football League, Alex Williams made his City debut against WBA in 1981 and became the club's regular custodian two years later, being an ever-present in 1983/84 and 1984/85. He retired due to a back injury.

WILLIAMS, Charles Alexander (Goalkeeper)
Apps/goals: 232/1 Born: Welling, Kent, 19/11/1873 Died: Rio de Janeiro, Brazil, 1952

Career: Phoenix FC, Clarence FC, Royal Arsenal, CITY (June 1894–May 1902), Tottenham Hotspur, Norwich City, Brentford; retired 1908; Danish Olympic team (coach), Olympique Club/Lille (manager), Le Havre/Holland (coach), Rio Grande Do Sol/Brazil (trainer).

Details: Charlie Williams played in Arsenal's first-ever League game and his unorthodox style probably denied him an England cap, one game for the Football League XI being his only representative honour. He was City's first-choice goalkeeper from November 1894 until December 1901, an ever-present on three occasions, twice missing one game in a season and having unbeaten runs of eighty-nine and eighty-one League appearances. He helped City win the Second Division championship in 1898/99 and was one of the first 'keepers ever to score a League goal, doing so in April 1900 with a wind-assisted 'punt' downfield in City's 3-1 League defeat at Sunderland. He guided Denmark to the Olympic final in 1908 (beaten to the gold medal by England).

WILLIAMS, Derek (Goalkeeper)
Apps: 1 Born: Mold, North Wales, 15/6/1934

Career: Mold Alexandra, CITY (May 1951–May 1954), Mold Alexandra, Wrexham, Mold Alexandra, Oldham Athletic; retired 1957.

Details: Derek Williams, who won amateur caps for Wales, kept a clean sheet in his only League game for City – a 0-0 draw with Blackpool at Maine Road in February 1952. Deputising for Bert Trautmann, he pulled off two superb saves to deny England centre-forward Stan Mortensen.

WILLIAMS, Eric (Full-back)
Apps: 41 Born: Manchester, 10/7/1921

Career: Brindle Heath Lads' Club, CITY (March 1945–October 1951), Halifax Town; retired 1954.

Details: After ten Second World War appearances, Eric Williams was handed seven League outings in 1946/47, stepping in for both Bert Sproston and Sam Barkas. Two seasons later he partnered Westwood in fifteen games, having a fine game in the 0-0 draw with United in the Manchester derby in front of 64,502 fans at Maine Road.

WILLIAMS, Frederick (Inside/outside-left)
Apps/goals: 130/38 Born: Manchester, 1870

Career: Hanley Swifts, South Shore, CITY (November 1896–June 1902), Manchester United.

Details: Described as being 'well built, good-looking with a fine mop of hair', Fred Williams scored on his debut for City against Burton Wanderers four days after signing from South Shore. He netted five times in his first season with the Blues and thereafter contributed well, having his best spell in 1898/99 when he bagged eleven League goals, including a five-timer in the 10-0 win over Darwen and a brace in a 2-0 win over Small Heath, as City charged on towards the Second Division championship. He only made ten starts for United.

WILLIAMSON, John (Centre-forward)
Apps/goals: 62/15 Born: Manchester, 8/5/1929

Career: Manchester Transport FC, Newton Heath, CITY (August 1949–March 1956), Blackburn Rovers.

Details: Big and strong, Johnny Williamson made his League debut for City in place of Andrew Black, in a 4-1 defeat by Arsenal in April 1950. A capable reserve, he made nine appearances in his first two seasons before netting three times in fifteen games in 1951/52 and finishing joint top scorer with Johnny Spurdle the following season with a goal tally of twelve. He rounded off his career at Maine Road with sixteen more outings in two seasons.

WILLIAMSON, Samuel (Defender/midfield)
Apps: 1 Born: 15/10/1987

Career: Macclesfield Boys, Priory County, CITY (schoolboy 1997; June 2004–January 2009), Wrexham (loan/signed), Fleetwood Town.

Details: Sam Williamson initially joined City as a nine-year-old and after progressing through the Academy U18 he played in the 2006 FA Youth Cup final. A reserve over the next two years, he finally made his first-team debut in the 3-1 win over Portsmouth in April 2008, coming on as substitute for the injured Richard Dunne.

WILSON, Clive Euclid Aklana (Left-back/midfield)
Apps/goals: 126/11 Born: Greenheys, Manchester, 13/11/1961

Career: Moss Side Amateurs, CITY (April 1978-March 1987), Chester City (loan), Chelsea (£248,000), CITY (loan, March-May 1987), Queen's Park Rangers (£450,000), Tottenham Hotspur (free), Cambridge United; retired May 2000.

Details: An attacking player from left-back or midfield, Clive Wilson broke into City's first team in 1981, making his League debut in a 2-1 home

League win over Wolves. Biding his time in the second XI, he eventually bedded himself into the team in 1984/85 (thirty-three appearances) and was a regular in the side until his transfer to Chelsea. A Second Division championship winner with the Londoners in 1989 (with City runner's-up), he retired with 569 club appearances under his belt.

WILSON, Jack (Full-back)
Apps: 1 Born: Ayrshire, c. 1870
  Career: Edinburgh St Bernard's, New Brompton, Lincoln City, CITY (December 1897/May 1898), Small Heath, Swindon Town; retired 1900.
  Details: 'Jock' Wilson fell into trouble with the Lincoln management, was released and within a fortnight had joined City. At the time, one observer noted of him 'he is a powerful back who displays great judgment.' But for all that he made just one League appearance for the Blues in a 3-2 home win over Walsall in January 1898.

WILSON, William (Full-back/half-back)
Apps: 53 Born: Middlesbrough, 26/7/1898
Died: c. 1963
  Career: Hurst FC, CITY (May 1921–August 1927), Stockport County, Ashton National; retired 1932.
  Details: Billy Wilson made his League debut for City at left-half against the FA Cup holders Tottenham Hotspur in February 1922. The following season he had twelve outings at full-back before switching back to the middle line in 1923/24. He then served as a capable reserve defender until his transfer to Stockport, for whom he made 117 appearances up to 1930.

WOOD, Alfred Edward Howson (Defender)
Apps: 32 Born: Macclesfield, 25/10/1945
  Career: Schoolboy football, Macclesfield (trial), CITY (July 1961–June 1966), Shrewsbury Town (£5,000), Millwall (record £45,000), Hull City (record, £75,000), Middlesbrough, Walsall, Stafford Rangers; retired 1980; Birmingham City (promotions manager); owned a company selling sports trophies.
  Details: A City player for five years, Alf Wood was a rugged, broad-shouldered and totally committed footballer. An England youth international, he made his League debut at centre-half in place of Bill Leivers in a 1-1 draw with Nottingham Forest in April 1963, and the following season deputised for Roy Cheetham, and ray Gratrix after that before moving to Gay Meadow. Switching to centre-forward, he scored sixty-five goals in 258 League games for Shrewsbury and thirty-eight in 100 for Millwall. Wood retired in 1980, having netted over 120 goals in 534 senior games, 117 in 488 League appearances. He played at Wembley with Stafford Rangers in the FA Trophy final.

WOOD, John (Wing-half/inside-forward)
Apps/goals: 33/9 Born: West Kirby, 1880
  Career: Port Sunlight, Southern United, Derby County, CITY (June 1907–May 1909), Plymouth Argyle, Huddersfield Town, Aberdeen, retired before the First World War.
  Details: Jack Wood played with Steve Bloomer at Derby and scored seven goals in forty appearances for the Rams before spending two seasons with City. He netted seven times in twenty-seven outings in 1907/08 when he occupied the right-half and both inside-forward positions, but was basically a reserve in his second term, although he did play in an England international trial for The North *v.* The South in 1908.

WOODCOCK, Wilfred (Forward)
Apps/goals: 17/3 Born: Ashton-under-Lyne, 3/2/1892
  Career: Abbey Hey FC, Stalybridge Celtic, Manchester United, CITY (£1,000, May 1920–March 1922), Stockport County, Wigan Borough; retired 1925.
  Details: Wilf Woodcock left United for City after failing to come to an agreement regarding a benefit. A 'Red' since 1912, he topped the club's scoring charts in three of the four of the First World War seasons, finishing with an overall total of sixty-nine goals in 132 appearances. A clever little player, who lacked that bit of extra strength when opposed by powerful defenders, Woodcock toured South Africa with the FA in 1920 and played in two Commonwealth internationals. On his return he joined City, helping the team claim the runner's-up spot in Division One in his first season when he bagged two goals in wins of Bolton and Blackburn during October.

WOODROFFE, Lewis Christopher (Outside-right)
Apps/goals: 9/1 Born: Portsmouth, 29/10/1921 Died: before 2000
  Career: CITY (October 1945–June 1947), Watford; served in the Army during the Second World War.
  Details: After scoring twice in six Second World War games for City, Lewis Woodroffe made his League debut in place of Maurice Dunkley, in a 3-1 win at Millwall, setting up a goal for hat-trick hero Jim Constantine. He scored his only first-class City goal in a 2-0 home win over Luton own in April 1947.

WOOSNAM, Maxwell (Half-back)
Apps: 93/4 Born: Liverpool, 6/9/1892
Died: London, 14/7/1965
  Career: Winchester College and Trinity College/ Cambridge University, Chelsea; served with the Montgomery Yeomanry & Royal Welsh Fusiliers during First World War; Cambridge University,

also played for Corinthians (player, then club president), CITY (November 1919–October 1925), Northwich Victoria; retired May 1926; worked for ICI for thirty-one years (from 1919, becoming personnel manager); played golf and rackets; was a champion at both Real and Lawn tennis (winning the men's Wimbledon doubles title with R. Lycett in 1921, while reaching the mixed doubles final that same year); also represented Great Britain in the 1920 and 1924 Olympic Games at Lawn tennis, winning a gold and silver medals in the former in Antwerp.

Details: Dubbed the Admirable Crichton of his day, Max Woosnam – known as 'Gentleman' Max – was the son of a former Canon of Chester. Certainly one of the greatest sportsmen of his era, he was in the same class as C. B. Fry. A courageous, hard-as-nails centre-half with a solid shoulder charge, he appeared in an international trial, but only gained one cap for England, lining up against Wales at Anfield in March, 1922. Earlier in his career he played in amateur internationals for both England and Wales.

In April 1922, Woosnam suffered a serious leg injury in the final game of the season against Newcastle when he collided with a wooden fence that circled the Hyde Road pitch. As a result, he missed the whole of the 1922/23 campaign and, in fact, the injury effectively ended his career, which surprisingly realised less than 100 senior appearances, ninety-three with City! His nephew is Phil Woosnam (below).

WOOSNAM, Philip Abraham (Inside-forward)
Apps: 1 Born: Caersws, Mid Wales, 22/12/1932
Career: Montgomeryshire Schools, Wrexham, UCNW, Bangor University, Peritus FC, Bangor City, City, CITY (July 1951–July 1954), Sutton United, Middlesex Wanderers, Leyton Orient, West Ham United, Aston Villa (£27,000), Atlanta Chiefs/USA (player-coach); helped form the NASL and briefly managed the USA national team; became Commissioner of the NASL.

Details: Phil Woosnam – nephew of Matt (above) and cousin of golfer Ian – was an excellent footballer whose skills were recognised at an early age when he was chosen play for Wales at schoolboy and youth team levels. With his short-cropped hair, he was surprisingly released by City after just one League appearance, in a 6-0 walloping at Cardiff in February 1953. He later played with Bobby Moore at West Ham, appeared for a London XI v. Lausanne in the ICFC semi-final of 1957, won a total of seventeen full caps for his country, was voted Amateur Footballer of the Year in 1955, represented the Football League and helped Leyton Orient win the Third Division (S) title in 1956. He was mainly responsible for introducing Pele, Franz Beckenbauer, George Best and others to the NASL.

WRIGHT, Norman (Outside-left)
Apps/goals: 3/1 Born: Ushaw Moor, County Durham, 27/12/1908 Died: 30/1/1974
Career: Esh Winning, Grimsby Town, Crewe Alexandra, Accrington Stanley, CITY (May 1933–May 1935), Watford; did not play after the Second World War.

Details: One of many capable deputies for Eric Brook, Norman Wright scored on his City debut in a 1-1 draw with Newcastle in March 1934. He did well at Crewe and Accrington and made over 150 club appearances during his career.

WRIGHT, Thomas James (Goalkeeper)
Apps: 33 Born: Belfast, 29 August 1963
Career: Linfield, Newcastle United (£30,000), Hull City (loan), Nottingham Forest (£450,000), Reading (loan), CITY (loan/signed for £450,000, January 1997–July 2001), Wrexham (loan), Newcastle United (loan), Bolton Wanderers (loan), Ballymena United.

Details: Capped once at U21 level and on thirty-one occasions by the full Irish team, Tommy Wright helped Forest win the Division One title in 1993 and during his thirteen-year career in England, made only 184 club appearances, having his best spell with Newcastle (first time round). On loan for three months with City before signing permanently, Wright made twenty of his thirty-three outings came in the relegation season of 1997/98, with Martyn Margetson playing in the other thirty matches.

WRIGHT-PHILLIPS, Bradley Edward (Forward)
Apps/goals: 40/2 Born: Lewisham, 12/3/1985
Career: CITY (June 2001–July 2006), Southampton (£1 million), Plymouth Argyle (free), Charlton Athletic, Brentford (loan).

Details: Brother of Shaun (below) and son of father Ian Wright, the former Crystal Palace and Arsenal striker, England youth international Bradley Wright-Phillips – top scorer for City's second XI in 2003/04 – netted on his League debut at Middlesbrough in December 2004, just four minutes after coming off the bench. A substitute-supreme he made thirty-seven 'sub' appearances during his spell with the Blues. Capped five times by England at U21 level, he played in 121 first-class matches for Southampton.

WRIGHT-PHILLIPS, Shaun Cameron (Forward)
Apps/goals: 275/47 Born: Greenwich, London, 25/10/1981
Career: Hatcham College, New Cross Gate/London; Nottingham Forest, CITY (October 1998–July 2005), Chelsea (£21 million), CITY (£9 million, August 2008–August 2011), Queens Park Rangers.

Details: A real bundle of energy who prefers to play on the right side of the field, and once described as being one of 'the most exciting talents in the game', inconsistency has let Shaun Wright-Phillips down many times. However, he has persevered and by May 2013 had scored fifty-nine goals in 455 club appearances, while also winning thirty-six full and six U21 caps for England, netting six times at senior level. Released by Forest at the age of seventeen, he made his debut for City as a substitute in the second leg of a League Cup game against Burnley in August 1999, followed by his League bow two months later at Port Vale. He featured more regularly the following season before fully establishing himself in the first team under manager Kevin Keegan in 2001/02, scoring twice in forty games.

City's 'Young Player of the Year' four times in succession (2000–03 inclusive), surpassing Steve Kinsey's record of three, he became one of the main targets of racist chants from the crowd during England's 1-0 defeat by Spain in Madrid in November 2004. However, he brushed that aside with his performance in his next City game at Portsmouth, telling reporters, 'I just let the football do the talking.'

Wright-Phillips made his English National debut as a substitute against Ukraine in August 2004, scoring a fine late goal in a 3-1 win. Surprisingly, after joining Chelsea for 'big money', he missed out on a place in the 2006 World Cup squad, but after returning to City for a second spell, he was selected in place of Theo Walcott for the 2010 tournament in South Africa, and many people were shocked at his inclusion. Wright-Phillips helped City win the First Division championship (2002) and FA Cup (2011) and Chelsea lift the Premiership title (2006) and complete the FA Cup and League Cup double (2007).

WRIGHTSON, Frank Lawrence (Inside-right)
Apps/goals: 22/4 Born: Shildon, County Durham, 9/1/1906 Died: 1979
Career: Ferryhill, Darlington, CITY (March 1930–March 1932), Fulham (£2,000), Exeter City, Chester; retired during the Second World War.
Details: A transfer deadline signing following an injury to Bobby Marshall, Frank Wrightson made his debut for City twenty-four hours later, at inside-right in a 3-1 home win over Grimsby Town. Continuing to deputise for Marshall during the next two seasons, he scored his four goals against four different clubs, Aston Villa, Birmingham, Blackpool and Chelsea, all in the League, before moving to Craven Cottage. A blacksmith by trade, he netted over fifty goals for Chester.

WYNN, George Arthur (Inside-right)
Apps/goals: 128/59 Born: Treflach, Llansilin near Oswestry, 14/10/1886 Died: Abergele, Denbighshire, 28/10/1966

Career: Plant Glas, Chirk, Oswestry United, Wrexham, CITY (£250, April 1909–November 1919), Coventry City (£300), Llandudno Town, Halifax Town, Mansfield Town, Mossley; retired 1924.
Details: A former telegram boy, working for Oswestry post office, and then a carpenter on Lord Harlech's estate, George Wynn made his City debut on Christmas Day 1909 in a 2-0 defeat by Bradford Park Avenue and scored his first goal two days later against Grimsby. He ended that season with twelve goals in twenty-four games as City won the Second Division title. Maintaining his form, in each of the next three seasons he was the club's leading marksman with nine, eighteen and sixteen goals respectively. The onset of the First World War unfortunately shortened Wynn's playing career, and after making thirty appearances during the hostilities, his last senior game was against Oldham in September 1919. The following month he played in two Victory internationals for Wales v. England, having earlier won eleven caps at senior level (1909–14). He won the Welsh Cup with Oswestry in 1908 and 1909 and played briefly with Billy Meredith at Chirk.

Y

YATES, James (Outside-right/left)
Apps/goals 21/9 Born: Sheffield, 1871 Died: Southampton, 5/9/1922
Career: Burnley, CITY (November 1892–December 1893), Sheffield United, Southampton St Mary's, St Leonard's, FC Copenhagen (player-coach), Southampton, Gravesend, United, Hastings & St Leonard's; Southampton (player and scout); coached in South and North America, including Brazil; Salisbury City; retired 1909; later worked as a stevedore at Southampton docks; he committed suicide at the age of fifty-one.
Details: A dapper, clever winger, Jimmy Yates experienced every class of football in a seventeen-year career. He spent his best years with Sheffield United (1893–97) for whom he scored nine goals in 104 appearances. The recipient of two Southern League championship winner's medals with Southampton (1899 and 1901), he is the only player to sign for the Saints three times! Reserve to Bob Milarvie at City days, he made his debut in a 2-1 defeat at Lincoln in December 1892 and played his last game against Walsall Town Swifts eleven months later. He scored in five of City's last six games at the end of the first League season of 1892/93.

YOUNG, Alexander Simpson (Inside/centre-forward)
Apps/goals: 15/2 Born: Slamannan, Stirlingshire, 23/6/1880 Died: Portobello, Edinburgh, 17/9/1959

Career: Paisley St Mirren, Falkirk, Everton, Tottenham Hotspur, CITY (November 1911/May 1912), South Liverpool, Port Vale; retired and emigrated to Australia, December 1914.

Details: Alex Young scored 125 goals in 314 appearances for Everton between 1901 and 1911, gaining an FA Cup winner's medal in 1906 and winning two full caps for Scotland during his time at Goodison Park. An imposing, muscular forward, with a heart of gold, he made his debut for City in a 1-1 draw at Sunderland soon after signing, scored his first goal in his sixth game to earn a 1-0 win over Notts County and played his fifteenth and last game in a sky blue strip in a 2-1 defeat at Bolton in February 1912.

In June 1916, Young was found guilty of the manslaughter of his brother six months earlier. Evidence, produced by football officials from England, stated that during his playing career he had been subject to fits of temporary insanity, and as a result was handed a three-year prison sentence on the grounds of 'mental weakness'. He returned to his native Scotland after the Second World War.

YOUNG, James (Right-half)
Apps: 1 Born: Glasgow, 1882 Died: Glasgow, 1970
Career: Port Glasgow, CITY (October 1905–May 1907), Glasgow League football.

Details: A reserve at Hyde Road, Jimmy Young's only League game for City came in a 1-0 home defeat by Liverpool three weeks after moving south from Glasgow. He never settled in Manchester.

YOUNG, Neil James (Forward)
Apps/goals: 416/108 Born: Platt Fields, Fallowfield, Manchester, 17/2/1944
Died: 3/2/2011
Career: Manchester Boys, CITY (May 1959–January 1972), Preston North End (£48,000), Rochdale; retired injured, 1975; later ran a soccer coaching school in Wilmslow.

Details: One of City's first-ever apprentices, Neil Young came graduated through the ranks at Maine Road and made his senior debut in November 1961 against the League Cup holders Aston Villa. Twice City's top scorer, first in 1965/66 with seventeen goals and then in 1967/68 with twenty-one goals when the Second Division and then First Division titles were won, Neil Young bagged another seventeen in 1968/69, the most important coming in the FA Cup final when his twenty-third-minute belter (from Mike Summerbee's cross) beat Leicester City. A year later, he netted in City's ECWC final win over Gornik Zabrze and went on to average a goal every four games during his thirteen-year stay at Maine Road.

A star among stars, he was an elegant player, with splendid control and a stinging right foot shot, and he could pass a ball as well! He occupied every position in the forward-line for the Blues, with No. 10 (inside-left) his best, and missed very few games between 1966 and 1971. An England youth international, Young never won a single U21 or senior cap, and no-one really knows why.

YUILL, John George (Outside-right)
Apps/goals: 3/1 Born: Manchester, 1885
Died: France, 1916
Career: Northern Nomads, CITY (March 1906/June 1907), Oldham Athletic, Stockport County, CITY (January/March 1909), Chester, Port Vale (until his death).

Details: A reserve during his two spells with City, Jack Yuill made his three appearances in succession in March 1909, scoring in his second game, a 4-1 home win over Preston. He played in only one other League game in his entire career – for Stockport against Bradford City in October 1907. He was killed in action while serving with the Army.

Z

ZABALETA, Pablo Javier Girod (Full-back/midfield)
Apps/goals: 195/7 Born: Buenos Aires, Argentina, 16/1/1985
Career: Obras Sanitarias, San Lorenzo, Espanyol (£2.5 million), CITY (£6.75 million, September 2008).

Details: Pablo Zabaleta turned down a move to Juventus, saying that City's offer 'was impossible to reject.' He joined the Blues soon after winning a gold medal with Argentina at the Beijing Olympics, and a day before the club was bought by the Abu Dhabi United Group, led by the mega-rich Sheikh Mansour. Able to play right-back or in midfield, with a licence to 'get forward', he scored his first goal for City in January 2009, to earn a 1-0 Premiership win over Wigan. He made his hundredth senior appearance for the club on New Year's Day 2011, and seven months later, having gained an FA Cup winner's medal, and seen the club brush aside an approach from Italian club AS Roma, he signed a new three-year contract. A cult hero amongst the fans who to this day admire his never-say-die attitude and commitment to the club, Zabaleta struck the opening goal in City's dramatic 3-2 win over Queen's Park Rangers on the last day of the 2011/12 season which secured the club's first League title in forty-four years. He has appeared in twenty-eight U20 and nine U21 internationals for Argentina and at May 2013 had gained thirty-one full caps for his country. Due to his all-out endeavour and commitment, Zabaleta has so far been sent off four times playing for City – versus Wigan twice (including the 2013 FA Cup final), Liverpool and Arsenal. He won the Copa del Rey with Espanyol.

Late News

Two players signed by City during the summer of 2013 were internationals Fernandhino and Jesús Navas Gonzalez.

FERNANDINHO (Midfielder)
Born: Fernando Luiz Roza on 4 May 1985 in Londrina, Brazil. He played for Atletico Paranaense (2002–05) and Shakhtar Donetsk (184 apps, 312 goals) before joining City for £35 million. He has five full caps to his credit (2011–13).

NAVAS (Right-winger)
Born: in Los Palacios y Villafranca, Seville, Spain, on 21 November 1985. He started out before scoring twenty-six goals in 317 League games for Sevilla B and Sevilla, while also winning five U21 caps and netting twice in twenty-eight full internationals for his country (2009–13). City recruited Navas for £18 million.

PELLEGRINI (Manager)
Following the sacking of Roberto Mancini, City duly appointed sixty-year-old former Malaga boss Manuel Pellegrini, as the club's new manager, secured on a four-year contract.

Wartime Football

Several guest players assisted City during the two wartime periods. These were engaged from major Football League clubs, from intermediate and local non-League teams and also late inclusions to make up the eleven-man team. Although listed here as being guests, some players were on trial with City during the hostilities, others were local amateurs and a handful were engaged on a non-contract basis, and were signed as full-time professionals for the 1919/20 season.

NB: *All guest players are indicated thus **

FIRST WORLD WAR (1915–19)

Listed here are the personal records of players who featured for City during the Lancashire League competition and Subsidiary tournaments (Southern section) during the Great War.

Player	Apps/goals	Goals
A. J. Allen	4	
A. S. Armstrong*	4	
H. Barnes	73	73
E. E. Blackwell*	2	
W. Bottomley	32	
J. Brennan	94	4
H. Brierley*		11
J. Broad*	1	
T. Broad*	46	2
T. Browell	33	18
A. E. Brown*		2
A. Capper*	1	5
J. E. Cartwright	60	9
T. Catlow*	4	
J. Clegg*	2	
J. E. Connor*		1
J. Cope*	6	1
P. Corcoran*		1
G. L. Crowther*	1	
J. Cruse*	4	2
C. Cunningham*	8	2
A. Davies*	18	1
J. A. H. Dorsett	7	3
B. Duffy*	1	
C. Elliott*	2	
A. Fairclough	6	8
P. Fairclough	102	13
R. Fielding*		1
E. Fletcher	133	3
P. Gartland	32	
R. Geddes*	1	
H. Goddard*	3	3
A. J. Goodchild	130	
E. T. Hanney		3
R. Hargreaves*	2	
J. Henderson		33
W. A. Henry	25	
S. J. Hoad	3	1
G. Hoare*	1	1
F. J. Howard	7	4
J. T. Howarth*	4	
G. A. Howe*		1
E. Hughes	65	2
A. James*	1	
A. Johnson*		1
T. C. F. Johnson	5	4
F. Jones*	1	
W. L. Jones	37	6
R. Kelly*	1	
J. Kenyon*	4	3
P. Kite*	1	
F. Knowles	1	
M. Lee*	1	
T. E. Lewis*	1	
E. F. Lievesley	11	8
R. Lingard*	3	
E. Lloyd*	1	
W. Lomas	45	23
F. McIlvenney*	2	1
W. McRay*	1	
R. Malone*	1	
J. Mann*	2	1
W. H. Meredith	107	7
T. Miller*	4	
H. Moses*	11	4
W. Murphy	23	2
J. Nelson*	6	2
H. Newton*	5	1
W. A. A. Newton	14	1
E. Ollerenshaw	3	
J. E. Osmond*	2	
F. Parker	24	
C. Petrie*	1	

Player	Apps	Goals
J. Roberts*	1	
S. Royle	7	4
S. Scott	10	
S. Sharp	2	
J. Skeldon*	1	
A. Smith*	6	
A. W. Smith*	7	2
E. Smith*	8	
S. Spruce*	2	
F. A. Sugden		39
J. D. Tavo*	2	1
H. G. Taylor	32	14

Player	Apps	Goals
J. Thompson	21	7
L. Thorpe*	2	2
E. F. Tompkins*	2	
T. Tomlinson*	1	
H. E. Tyler	94	7
C. R. Voysey*	2	
H. Waldon*	2	1
W. Watson*	17	4
W. Woodcock*	2	1
R. T. Woodhouse*	1	
J. Wray*	8	1
G. A. Wynn	30	9

SECOND WORLD WAR (1939–46)

Here are the records for the players who appeared for City in the Western Regional League, North Regional League, Football League (N), Football Regional League War Cup, Football League Jubilee Fund (1939) and the three void Football League matches of August/September 1939, but not in the 1945/46 FA Cup competition.

Players	Apps/goals:	Goals
J. Bacuzzi*	1	
M. Baillee	1	
H. V. Baker*	1	1
E. Barber	3	
C. E. Barclay	18	3
L. Bardsley	21	2
S. Barkas	75	3
A. Beattie*	2	
L. Beaumont*	1	
A. Bellis*	1	
S. Bentham*	1	
W. Blackshaw	8	2
J. Boothway	76	57
W. Bootle	32	6
L. Boulter*	1	
J. Bray	180	11
J. Breedon*	2	
E. F. G. Brook	7	3
H. Brookes*	1	1
A. R. G. Brown*	15	6
E. Brown	7	
T. Burdett*	1	
R. J. Burke*	4	3
M. P. Butler*		1
L. Butt	1	
J. Campbell*		1
T. A. Capel	1	
L. Cardwell	48	
J. J. Carey	4	1
W. J. Carey	9	
D. F. Carter*		1
L. Cassidy	1	
F. G. Chappel		7
S. Charlesworth*	29	
K. M. Chisholm*	1	
G. V. Clark	180	

Players	Apps/goals:	Goals
H. Clark	8	1
J. Constantine	34	25
F. J. A. Cox*	13	2
J. Crompton	1	
R. A. Cunliffe	1	
J. Currier*	113	84
D. Daniels	3	
D. W. Davenport	2	
J. Davenport*	3	
R. W. Dellow*	13	5
J. Devlin*	1	
P. Dickie*	1	
L. Dodd	3	
P. D. Doherty	92	62
M. E. F. Dunkley	63	16
E. Eastwood		163
R. Eastwood*	2	
A. T. Emptage	34	5
J. F. Fagan	10	
B. R. V. Fenton*	11	7
E. Gemmill	2	1
W. G. Goddard	1	
E. I. Goodall*	2	
W. Grant	13	
B. A. C. Hall*		2
A. J. Hanson*	1	
J. P. Hart	4	1
J. A. Heale	44	33
G. R. Henry*		1
A. Herd	93	60
J. Hilton	1	
R. Hodgson	5	
W. J. J. Hogan	5	1
J. G. Hope	1	
H. Iddon*	1	
L. Jackson	20	
C. W. Jones*	8	3

J. T. Jones*	2		H. J. Pritchard	48	9
L. J. Jones*	2		J. D. J. Reid	1	2
A. J. Keeling		1	J. J. Robinson		60
F. Kenny	1		P. Robinson	32	2
F. A. B. King*	51	20	A. W. Roxburgh*	5	
W. J. D. Kinghorn*	1		J. J. Rudd	14	3
T. W. Kirton	7		K. Rudman*		1
R. Laing	1		G. Scales	21	
F. Leech	3	2	W. E. Sellers		1
J. E. Linaker	6		G. B. Smith	90	45
C. J. McCormack*	1		L. G. F. Smith*	1	
L. G. McDowall*	117	8	B. Sproston	77	5
J. M. McIntosh*	1		D. Stuart	30	7
J. McMillan	8		F. V. Swift	136	
H. McShane*	23	2	J. Taylor	34	3
A. Malam*	14	9	A. Thomson*	1	
R. C. Meiklem	1		J. Thomson*		1
J. Milsom	2	2	W. F. Thorpe*	3	
B. Moore*	3		F. S. Tilson*	1	1
A. Mulraney*	6	3	E. Toseland*		2
W. Murray*	4		H. Turner*	11	
G. Mutch*	4	1	G. Vose*	1	
R. Neilsen	25		C. E. Walker*	33	
E. Nuttall	1		S. Walker	3	
H. O'Donnell*	1	1	W. Walsh*	229	8
J. Ollerenshaw	1		A. Watt	1	
F. L. Owen	9	6	D. Welsh*	1	2
J. Parlane	4	1	E. Westwood	32	1
J. Paton*	3	2	A. Wild	16	2
T. J. Paton	1		E. Williams		10
S. Pearson	6	2	J. Williams*		1
W. G. Pearson*	14	6	W. M. J. Williamson*	62	39
J. Percival	37	3	F. Wilson*	1	
D. W. Pimbley	2		L. C. Woodroffe	6	2
B. Poole*	1		J. Worrell	2	
W. Porter*	2		H. Worsley	2	1
I. V. Powell*		1	T. B. Wright	3	1

The Managers

Here are details of the men who have managed City since the club's first-ever competitive game – an FA Cup qualifying match – in October 1890.

Manager	Time in office	Record			
Name	From/To	P	W	D	L
Lawrence Furniss+	August 1889 – May 1893	26	10	4	12
Joshua Parlby+	August 1893 – May 1895	59	22	5	32
Sam Omerod	August 1895 – July 1902	240	111	50	79
Tom Maley	July 1902 – July 1906	150	89	22	39
Harry Newbold	July 1906 – July 1912	245	93	61	91
Committee	July 1912 – September 1912	2	2	0	0
Ernest Mangnall+	September 1912 – June 1924	350	151	117	82
David Ashworth	July 1924 – November 1925	59	20	13	26
Albert Alexandra°	November 1925 – April 1926	31	13	8	10
Peter Hodge	April 1926 – March 1932	261	122	59	80
Wilf Wild#	March 1932 – December 1946	352	158	71	123
Sam Cowan	December 1946 – June 1947	30	20	6	4
Wilf Wild	August 1947 – November 1947	16	5	5	6
Jock Thomson	November 1947 – February 1950	115	35	35	45
Les McDowall	June 1950 – May 1963	592	220	127	245
Gorge Poyser	July 1963 – April 1965	89	38	17	34
Committee	April 1965 – May 1965	5	1	3	1
Joe Mercer, OBE**	July 1965 – October 1971	340	149	94	97
Malcolm Allison	October 1971 – March 1973	78	32	21	25
Johnny Hart	March 1973 – October 1973	22	11	5	6
Tony Book*	October 1973 – November 1973	7	2	3	2
Ron Saunders	November 1973 – April 1974	29	10	9	10
Tony Book	April 1974 – July 1979	269	114	75	80
Malcolm Allison	July 1979 – October 1980	60	15	20	25
Tony Book*	October 1980	1	0	0	1
John Bond	October 1980 – February 1983	123	51	32	40
John Benson	February 1983 – June 1983	17	3	2	13
Billy McNeill, MBE	June 1983 – September 1986	156	63	42	51
Jimmy Frizzell**	September 1986 – May 1987	42	10	12	20
Mel Machin	May 1987 – November 1989	130	59	27	44
Tony Book*	November 1989 – December 1989	3	0	0	3
Howard Kendall	December 1989 – November 1990	38	13	18	7
Peter Reid	November 1990 – August 1993	136	59	31	46
Tony Book*	August 1993	1	0	1	0
Brian Horton	August 1993 – May 1995	96	29	33	34
Alan Ball, MBE	June 1995 – August 1996	49	13	14	22
Asa Hartford*	August 1996 – October 1996	8	3	0	5
Steve Coppell	October 1996 – November 1996	6	2	1	3
Phil Neal*	November 1996 – December 1996	10	2	1	7
Frank Clark	December 1996 – February 1998	59	20	17	22
Joe Royle	February 1998 – May 2001	171	74	46	51
Kevin Keegan, OBE	May 2001 – March 2005	176	77	39	60
Stuart Pearce	March 2005 – May 2007	96	34	19	43
Sven-Göran Eriksson	July 2007 – June 2008	45	19	11	15
Mark Hughes	June 2008 – December 2009	77	36	15	26
Roberto Mancini	December 2009 – May 2013	191	113	38	40
Brian Kidd*	May 2013 – July 2013	2	1	0	1
Manuel Pellegrini	July 2013 to date				

+ Secretary-manager
° Worked with a committee
Continued as secretary until 1950
* Caretaker-manager
** Continued as general manager

Bibliography

While compiling *Manchester City Player by Player*, I have referred to several publications including many hardback football books, club and supporters' handbooks, soccer annuals, hundreds of home and away programmes featuring the club, various football magazines (from 1925 onwards) and an assortment of nationwide newspapers.

In respect of ascertaining information regarding players' statistics, personal details (i.e. birth dates and deaths) there are some conflicting references, certainly relating to the older players (pre-First World War), and therefore I have made a judgment as to what is likely to be correct when several possibilities have been forthcoming.

Clayton, D., *Man City Miscellany* (History Press, 2011)
Clayton, D., *Manchester City One This Day* (Pitch Publishing, 2011)
Davies, G. M. and I. Garland, *Welsh International Soccer Players* (Wrexham: Bridge Books, 1991)
Farror, M. and D. Lamming, *A Century of English International Football, 1872–1972* (London: Robert Hale & Co., 1972)
FA Yearbook (1951–2000, published annually) (London, The Football Association)
Gibbs, N., *England: The Football Facts* (Exeter: Facet Books, 1988)
Gibson, A. and W. Pickard, *Association Football And The Men Who Made It* (4 vols) (London, Caxton Publishing Company, 1906)
Goble, R. and A. Ward, *Manchester City – A Complete Record* (Breedon Books Sport, 1993)
Goldsworthy, M., *The Encyclopaedia of Association Football* (London: Robert Hale & Co., 1969)
Goldsworthy, M., *We Are The Champions* (London: Pelham Books, 1972)
Horsnell, B. and D. Lamming, *Forgotten Caps* (Harefield, Middlesex: Yore Publications, 1995)
Hugman, B. J. (ed) *PFA Footballers' Factfile 1996–97 to 2000–01* (Hertfordshire: Queen Anne Press, 1996–201)1
Hugman, B. J. (ed.) *PFA Footballers' Factfile 2001–02* (Basildon: AFS, 2001)
Hugman, B. J. (ed.) *PFA Footballers' Factfile, 2002–03 to 2005–06* (Hertfordshire: Queen Anne, Press, 2002–06)
Hugman, B. J. (ed.) *PFA Premier and Football League Players' Records: 1946–1998* (Hertfordshire: Queen Anne Press, 1998)
Johnson, F., *Football Who's Who* (London: Associated Sporting Press, 1935)
Joyce, M., *Football League Players' Records: 1888–1939* (Nottingham: Tony Brown/Soccer Data, 2002)
Lamming, D., *Who's Who of Scottish Internationalists: 1872–1982* (Basildon: AFS, 1982–83)
Penney, I., *The Maine Road Encyclopedia* (Mainstream Publishing: 1995)
Penney, I., *The Essential History of Manchester City* (Headline: 2000)
Pringler, A. and M. Fissler, *Where Are They Now?* (London: Two Heads Publishing, 1996)
Rollin, J., *Soccer At War: 1939–45* (London: Willow Books Collins, 1985)
Spiller, R. (ed.), *AFS Football Who's Who*: 1902–03, 1903–04, 1907–08, 1909–10 (Basildon: AFS, 1990)
Whitney, S. *The Ultimate Book of Non-League Players*: 2002–03 (Newcastle: Baltic Publications Ltd., 2003)
Williams, T., (ed) *Football League Directory: 1992–1995* (London: *Daily Mail*, 1992–95)

Other Publications
Manchester City official programmes: 1925–2012
Manchester City FC handbooks, reviews, magazines, supporters guides, 1954–2012
AFS Bulletins (various)
Rothmans Yearbooks (1970–2013), vols 1–43 (various editors)
Charles Buchan Football Monthly: 1951–69
Sports Argus Football Annuals: 1949–68
Goal Magazine: 1966–78
Soccer Star Magazine: 1963–67
Shoot Magazine: 1990–2004

I have also referred to several other national and local newspapers, various club histories, Complete Records and Who's Who books, autobiographies and biographies of players and managers, scores of general football books and magazines and hundreds of assorted match-day programmes.

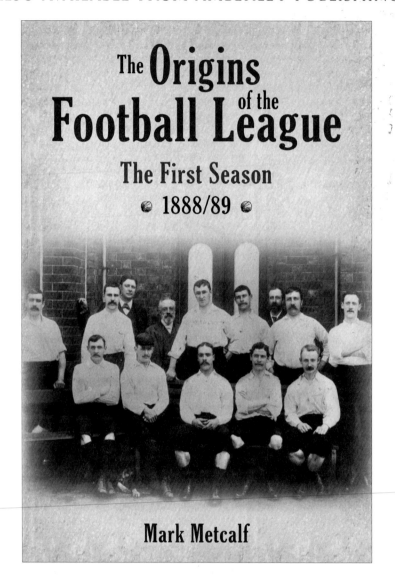

The **Origins** of the
Football League

The First Season
● 1888/89 ●

Mark Metcalf

The Origins of the Football League

Mark Metcalf

Who scored the first-ever goal in the history of the Football League?
For the first time, the history of the Football League's first season is
told in great depth, with reports on every match and profiles of all
those who played.

978 1 4456 1881 4

224 pages, 32 illustrations

Available from all good bookshops or order direct
from our website www.amberleybooks.com